Wit and Whiggery:
The Rev. Sydney Smith (1771-1845)

Howard Mackey

Copyright © 1979 by

University Press of America, Inc.™

4710 Auth Place, S.E., Washington D.C. 20023

All rights reserved

Printed in the United States of America

ISBN: 0-8191-0756-5

Library of Congress Catalog Card Number: 79-64194

Preface

After completing a research project several years ago it was suggested that I might be interested in doing something on the Rev. Sydney Smith. I had previously read a number of his reviews, and I was familiar with many of his best known quips. I originally began with an eye to writing on his American attitudes, but as I read background material I became aware of the limitations of secondary works on him, and I resolved to write a full-scale biography. My decision was taken not because the previous biographies were written in error, but because many of them were either uncritical or directed only to one aspect of his life. My work does not really refute any of the previous studies, but in refuting bits and pieces of them, and by adding hitherto overlooked details and interpretations I hope that it will present a truer and more complete picture. My purpose has been neither to elevate nor defame a man whose reputation is long since made, but to try to evaluate him without political, social, or temporal prejudice. I have tried to be objective in judging him, and the sources on him, and if I have not always succeeded in being objective my failings are human rather than intentional. Rationally I stand close to Sydney Smith and the liberal Whigs of his period, but emotionally I prefer the Tories. As an American I can feign indifference to either camp.

I am most grateful for the help and advice of Professor R. G. Cowherd of Lehigh University. His energy and example have served me well, and I am confident that he will continue to inspire thought and writing by his penetrating analyses. Mr. A.S. Bell of the National Library of Scotland, who is in the process of preparing the definitive edition of Sydney Smith's letters, was of incalculable service to me in providing leads to unpublished letters and papers. Mr. Cyril Ramsay Jones of the Home Office proved to be a fortuitous but fortunate friend whose interest and assistance was constantly encouraging. Professor John Lukacs of Chestnut Hill College read several of my chapters, and I appreciate his criticism and encouragement, as well as a delightful academic relationship. I also wish to thank the American Philosophical Society for an invaluable travel grant, and Lamar University and the late President Richard W. Setzer for a developmental leave in 1969. I owe a great deal to the Vicar of Flaxton Parish, York; Mr. A.R.B. Fuller of the Library, St. Paul's Cathedral; Mr. Neville

i

Webb of the Borthwick Institute, York University; and to the staff at Bristol Cathedral. I am also very grateful to Mrs. Beverley Sevier, Mrs. Judith Freeman, and Mrs. Judith Fulton for their tireless and unrewarded efforts in proofreading and typing.

I am also deeply appreciative of the cooperation of the following libraries and collections: The British Museum; the Public Record Office; the Fondren Library, Rice University; The Widener Library, Harvard University; The Archives of the Thomas Coram Foundation; The County Record Office, Hertfordshire; The County Record Office; Staffordshire; The Wedgwood Museum, Barlaston; The Greater London Record Office; the Western Reserve Historical Society; The General Library, University of California; The Hampshire Record Office; The National Library of Scotland; The John Rylands Library; The Royal Institution of Cornwall; The Public Library, Taunton; Edinburgh University; Trinity College Library, Cambridge University; the Miriam Lutcher Stark Library, University of Texas; the Bodleian Library, Oxford University; University College Library, University of London; The Somerset Record Office; The Henry E. Huntington Library and Art Gallery; The National Library of Wales; The Archives of the Metropolitan Water Board; The Library, Castle Howard; The Osborne Collection, and the Beinecke Collection, Yale University; The Derby Public Library: The Victorian and Albert Museum; The Library, Lambeth Palace; The Royal Archives; The Library of the Athenaeum Club.

Table of Contents

	PREFACE	i
I.	Introduction	1
II.	Netheravon and the Establishment of Connections, 1794-1798	20
III.	The Edinburgh Emancipation, 1798-1803	41
IV.	Political Economy and the Founding of the Edinburgh Review	70
V.	London. 1803-1807	104
VI.	1807-1809	150
VII.	The New Beginning in Yorkshire: The Beneficed Clergyman, 1809-1829	192
VIII.	Politics and Intellectual Activities at Foston, 1809-1828	222
IX.	The Achievement of Reform, and Clerical Success, 1828-1832	263
X.	Canon to the Right	300
XI.	London. 1831-1845. The Last Years	342
XII.	The Wit in Retrospect	391
	BIBLIOGRAPHY	414
	INDEX	425

CHAPTER I

It is customary in any biographical study of an outstanding Englishman to search accounts of preceding generations, preferably as far bask as Boadicea, for some genealogical clue which would explain his genius or prominence. But the assumption that only heredity can account for wit, charm or excellence has been so thoroughly exploded that no apologies need to be made for Sydney Smith's parvenu origins. Sydney himself later poked gentle fun at the snobbery of the pedigreed, asserting that "the Smiths never had any arms and have invariably sealed their letters with their thumbs,"[1] and that his grandfather had disappeared about the time of the assizes, so they never asked questions.[2] He adopted the motto Faber meae fortunae, or "Smith of my own fortune," and later he was to assert that neither he nor his brother Bobus were aristocratic enough to suffer from the gout,[3] despite which, nonetheless, both did. His grandfather, a woolen merchant, had moved from Devon to Eastcheap and had amassed a respectable fortune in the witney trade. He died leaving three sons and two daughters, the eldest of whom was Sydney's father, Robert Smith.

It is with Robert Smith that Lady Saba Holland,* Sydney's eldest daughter, demonstrated her penchant for genealogical adulation, or in this case, denigration; for she wrote a good deal of feminine nonsense about the eccentric old man, most of which was faithfully copied by Sydney's later biographers. In her memoir of Sydney, she describes Robert Smith as penny-pinching, acrimonious, unbalanced, totally unpredictable, and possessed of no business sense whatsoever. Some of these charges are certainly true, but an examination of Saba Holland's mother's memoir (Catherine Amelia Smith) reveals that in her reminiscences as Sydney's widow she was torn between depicting Robert Smith as an illustrious father, a man of great charm and ability, or painting him in the darkest hues as an unpaternal parent to whom Sydney, in his climb to fame and fortune, owed less than nothing.[4] With regard to Robert Smith's business ability,

---

*Saba Smith (1802-1866) married Dr. Henry Holland (1788-1873), a court and society physician who was later Sir Henry Holland, in 1834. He was not related to Henry and Elizabeth Fox, Lord and Lady Holland.

Saba Holland asserted that he spent his life traveling restlessly, and that he diminished his fortune "...by buying, altering, spoiling, and then selling about nineteen places in England....."[5] In fact, he did travel to America twice, and he left on his second trip immediately after the conclusion of his marriage ceremony to Maria Olier and apparently before its consummation, leaving his new bride with her mother until his return. Robert did indeed buy and sell several estates, but when he died he still possessed a very substantial fortune, ten thousand pounds of which he left to Sydney.[6] Saba Holland was a very materialistic woman living in a materialistic age, more materialistic indeed than the present age cares to admit; and what really disturbed her about her grandfather's wealth was that he began his career with a large fortune and ended his life with about the same amount in an age of enormous economic expansion when many fortunes, wisely or unscrulously managed, were multiplied during a lifetime.

It is obvious from these contradictions that Saba Holland's opinion of her grandfather Robert Smith cannot be taken very seriously. Other sources, however, add more to a still incomplete picture of the old gentleman of whom it can positively be said that he was a gentleman, a Whig (as were most gentlemen of his era), an Anglican, and that he was a man of considerable ability and extensive connections. Even Saba Holland implies that Sydney's ability was probably derived from his father.[7] Robert Smith sent his four sons through public school, and two of them through the university in an age when birth and influence counted far more than ability; and, he helped to secure extremely lucrative appointments for three of them. The fact that he did little for Sydney embittered Saba Holland more than it did Sydney, for Sydney may have understood that his father had his own reasons for his seeming inaction where Sydney was concerned.

Of Robert Smith's wife, Maria Olier, little needs to be said except that she was apparently a woman of beauty, high character, charm and culture. Of Huguenot extraction, she was married under the bizarre circumstances mentioned earlier. She gave birth to Robert Smith's five children, and probably had most of the responsibility for raising them. It is also probably that she was an epileptic, and it is certain that she suffered later in life from a nervous disorder of some description of which she ultimately died.[8] She was a good mother to her children, all of whom appear to have been gifted, and she probably encouraged them in the voracious appetites they exhibited for reading and argumentation.

Sydney, the second of five children, was born on June 3, 1771 at Woodford, Essex. His elder brother, Robert Percy Smith better known as "Bobus," had been born a year earlier and was to become widely acclaimed for his skill in Latin. The other brothers, Cecil and Courtenay, were born in 1772 and 1773 and were both talented students. After finishing their educations, the other three Smith brother secured appointments in India through their father's influence with John Roberts, a director and later chairman of the East India Company. Bobus and Courtenay were able to amass great fortunes in India, but Cecil, who started as clerk in India and finally became Accountant-General of Madras, appears to have been the black sheep of the family. Frequently deep in debt, even when in public school, his marriage was so unfortunate that it ended in divorce in an age when divorce was possible only by an act of Parliament. Further, more, he was accused of financial wrong doing as Accountant-General, and of mutiny. Cleared of the charges against him because his father's connections, but still under a cloud, he died almost penniless at the Cape of Good Hope in 1814 while returning to England on leave.

Of the two surviving brothers, Bobus remained one of Sydney's closest friends for the rest of their lives, dying only a week after Sydney. During Sydney's trying times in Yorkshire, Bobus was to lend Sydney money and to assist in paying for the expenses of his eldest son's education. Courtenay, on the other hand, returned to England with a vast fortune and became a recluse. When he died in 1843, his wealth was divided between Sydney, Bobus, and Cecil's son. Thus, among the four brothers, all of whom demonstrated considerable ability, none was to win the fame and reputation of Sydney, not even Bobus who was considered to be a Latin poet of great stature, in addition to his success in law.

Sydney probably received the rudiments of an education at home, and when he was six years old, he was sent to a school in Southhampton. Robert Smith sent Bobus to Eton, but Sydney and Courtenay went to Winchester, all attending on scholarships. Sydney's years at Winchester were among the unhappiest of his life, even though he excelled in Classical studies and rose to become the head of the school. He loathed sports and was not good at any of them, and he despised the living conditions at Winchester. Years later when his reputation was established, he was asked by a lady if he had not been a remarkable boy, and he replied, "Yes, Madam, I was a remarkably fat boy."[9]

Many of his ideas on education appear to have begun to take shape as the result of his experience at Winchester, and he maintained those opinions, once formulated, for the rest of his life. Generally, he was favorable towards education, but believed that more practical subjects should be taught in addition to the Classics, and he opposed the tyranny and physical hardships encountered in the public schools. In 1820, despite his misgivings, he sent his eldest son, Douglas, to Westminster School, later reporting to a friend that Douglas left for school with a heavy heart and that he, Sydney, expected him to encounter "...an intense system of tyranny, of which the English are very fond, and think it fits a boy for the world, but the world, bad as it is, has nothing half so bad."[10] Sydney did however, believe that children, at least those of the upper classes, should be sent off to school, and he observed in 1815 to Lord Holland "...that the health of delicate children very often improves in proportion as they are removed from the perilous kindness of home.[11]

Upon leaving Winchester, Sydney traveled to Mont Villiers in Normandy where he spent six months perfecting his command of French. This was in 1789, and the eighteen-year-old schoolboy entered a France in which the great Revolution had begun, but before that upheaval had reached its radical phase. According to Saba Holland, he joined the local Jacobin club, becoming "Le Citoyen Smit, Membre Affilie au Club des Jacobins de Mont Villers" for reasons of personal safety. Since there were no Jacobin Clubs in existence in 1789, Sydney probably joined the local literary society in Mont Villiers, which later became a Jacobin Club, and it seems more probable that Sydney, with the built-in Whiggish inclinations of his family, saw the Revolution as a re-enactment of the Glorious Revolution of 1688, and he may have felt he could enter into this enterprise with some enthusiasm.

Osbert Burdett, one of Sydney's biographers, asserted in 1934 that Sydney's six-month visit to France made him an "ardent liberal," but no evidence exists to confirm or deny Burdett's theory.[12] The absence of positive evidence makes one opinion about as valuable as another, but it might be suggested as an alternate explanation that since Sydney was a member of a Whiggish mercantile family, he already possessed the rudiments of liberalism, especially towards royal absolutism, and his visit to France only reinforced that liberalism. It appears to be true that none of the Smiths ever supported the Tory reaction to the Revolution in the 1790's or later, and Sydney, in his later writings and sermons, was a voice of moderations towards France, the Revolution, and even Napoleon - at least by comparison with the reactionary elements.

Upon his return to England, he entered New College, Oxford to which he was admitted on February 5, 1789. Once again he excelled in his studies, and at the end of his second year he was given a fellowship worth about $100 per year. Though a sizeable amount for that age, it was not adequate to support a student in high style. Saba Holland claimed that from that time forward, he received no further financial assistance from his father, but recently discovered letters to his father prove that Robert Smith continued to contribute to his son's education for several years.[13]

The elder Smith was probably short of cash because of his continual speculation in land, and because of the expenses occasioned by Bobus, who had taken his degree at King's College, Cambridge. He received the degree of Master of Arts in 1797, and was called to the bar the same year. During the preceding period, Bobus had received from his father, apparently in addition to the cost of his education, an allowance of $250 per year, which seems to have been a good deal more that Robert Smith allowed Sydney.[14]

One result of his father's penuriousness towards Sydney was that he was financially unable to engage fully in the social life of Oxford University which consisted chiefly of port-drinking and making future business, social and political connections - activities generally considered to be at least as important as the Classical training offered. This financial disadvantage, galling as it was at the time, may actually have been a blessing in disguise. For, in being deprived of a gentlemanly social life, Sydney appears to have read widely instead, and to have dabbled in anatomy and medicine. He would have liked to study for the bar, but his father was apparently unwilling, and was perhaps unable to make the kind of financial sacrifices for his second son that he had made for his firstborn. Then, too, Sydney may have been unwilling to burden his father with continuing educational expenses.

Sydney's natural inclinations were for the law, but his father only gave him a choice between entering the hierarchy of the Church or becoming a college tutor. A third alternative, a promising position in the China trade, had been elicited by his father from the East India Company, but at the last moment it failed to materialize,[16] so he chose priesthood in the Church of England. To assert that he had a "call" to the priesthood would be absurd, and such motivation was not expected of clergymen in the eighteenth century. Saba Holland says that he entered the Church "from duty" to his father,[17] which is quite possible; but the Church also offered a respectable profession to a gentleman and it was an enterprise in which a gentleman might advance both in dignity and wealth, in addition to its spiritual opportunities. Although Sydney had probably been a practising Anglican prior to his decision to enter the priesthood, he had shown none of the zeal for religion that is commonly associated with more modern clergymen.

The Church of England in the eighteenth century is a difficult institution for non-Anglicans to understand. The Church conceived its proper role in the world to be as much a civilizing mission as one of converting the heathen or of saving souls. Candidates for the ministry were required to be gentlemen and to have a university degree, but their theological training was meager, if they had any at all. Thus Sydney's lack of a "call" was not at all unusual, and was probably less objectionable to his fellow clergymen than a surfeit of zeal. The Church of England was the Established Church, instituted and supported by law, and it performed a large number of essentially civil functions. In many small villages the parson alone was literate, and he performed the functions of magistrate, physician, overseer of the poor, and registrar of births, deaths, and marriages. It can be seen from these roles that education and social stature were as important, if not more important, than religious ardor.

In Sydney's first appointment, as curate of

Netheravon, he was the only person having a rank which even approached that of the landlord.[18] Advancement in the Church, or even to the initial living, was decided mainly on the basis of family connections and politics, with ability taking a poor third, and piety a still poorer fourth place. "Ability" in the Church might be demonstrated by publications, not necessarily on relibious subject, which brought the author to the attention of the royal family, local patrons, or important politicians; but it was manifested more commonly by outstanding preaching in a polished, learned, and rational manner. The Evangelical movement was beginning within the Church, but the 1790's were still a period of "rational religion," which Sydney Smith vigorously endorsed. Later, much later in his life, he was to say to a friend that whenever he saw a clergyman of his age, he saw a bad clergyman.[19] His statement was fair neither to himself, nor to many other fine Anglican clergyman who, like Sydney himself, were capable and conscientious priests, even if they did lack a passionate faith or at least the public execution of the same. The word "enthusiasm" was much used in the eighteenth and early nineteenth centuries, and its use at that time is widely misunderstood in the 20th century. If one substitutes the word "fanaticism" for "enthusiam", the meaning becomes clear. Later, when Sydney claimed the "the Bible contained no enthusiasm," he didn't mean that one should not believe and perhaps believe fervently, but rather that one should, in the Anglican tradition, express his emotions with a proper decorum rather than to act ecstatically, crudely, or intolerantly. If the Anglican clergy lacked an outward warmth of religious expression, they generally compensated for it by an equal lack of bigotry.

Sydney, in entering the Church under the conditions he did, was not typical of all Anglican Clergyman, but neither was he atypical. He was personally a believing Christian, and his belief in Christianity was very important to him. He was sincerely an Anglican, believing that the Church of England was the True Church and the best of such institutions for worshipping God, for preaching His word on earth, and for achieving personal salvation. In his own words: "The Church of England is the wisest and most enlightened sect of Christians. I think so, or I would not belong to it another hour ..."[20] He was no bigot, however, and his faith in his own church did not prevent him from being tolerant of other sorts and conditions of Christians. Throughout his life he endorsed the precept of "rational religion," which meant, among other things, the broadest toleration of non-Anglican dissent.

Sydney Smith probably did enter the Church from a sense of duty towards his father, and from a lack of suitable alternatives. He was ambitious for advancement and recognition in the Church, and for the ease, comfort and dignity which the higher salaries would bring. He was, like most Englishmen of his age, quite materialistic, a fact that he never denied. If in his sermons he could admonish the rich to be "God's almoner, and to purchase eternal life...and to live to higher purposes than others live...,"[21] he could then say privately but unashamedly that for "...every guinea I have gained I have been the happier."[22] To complement his ambition he wisely added his principle that "...in this world, the salary or reward is always in the inverse ratio of the duties performed."[23] From the time he entered the Church he looked upon his future as a gamble, or a lottery. Many gentlemen entered the Church, but there were few rich livings and still fewer sees. A clergyman could hope to win one of these grand prizes in the Church, but the odds were against him. Nonetheless, Sydney favored the "lottery" system in that it brought gentlemen into the priesthood, and their wealth into the Church, for a gentleman could hardly be expected to live off the proceeds of the smaller livings; and many, if not most, clerical gentlemen possessed independent means.

In the unpublished draft of her memoir, Saba Holland seemingly could not decide whether to deplore her father's entry into the Church on the grounds that it held him back in the world, or to apologize for his having been a clergyman.[24] In fact, there was no need for her to espouse either viewpoint. Sydney Smith did very well in his clerical career in the long run, advancing further than most of his contempories, and he was a good clergyman, religious if not pious, and conscientious if not fervid. Whether he might have made a still greater name for himself in law, politics, or literature outside the church remains problematical. Saba Holland's difficulty lay in her own social position, and in the fact that she felt compelled to justify her father's attitudes and actions, which were esentially those of the eighteenth century, in terms of 1855, a year when the Church had been reformed by the Evangelical movement and the Oxford movement. These innovations in religion were new and repugnant to gentlemen of Sydney's era, and it should be remembered that he, too, had been at Oxford, but quite a different Oxford from that of John Henry Newman.

It has been said of the Oxford of the 1790's that the gentlemen-students never did anything but drink and pray,[25] and the latter in moderation. Lectures were given on a variety of subjects, but there is no evidence that Sydney ever studied theology or religion at Oxford. He knew little or nothing about theology when he left Oxford, and he never troubled to learn much. His attitudes were thoroughly practical, and were chiefly concerned with admonitions to his parishoners to do good and to lead good lives. In living by the precepts of Christianity, he believed, men would be happier in this life, and in the life to come.[26] Andre Chevrillon was probably correct when he wrote that Syndey "vegetated" at Oxford, where he encountered no new ideas.[27] Yet the end result of his training at Winchester and Oxford was good, despite his denunciation of both institutions. Sydney ended his education with a writing style that was so flowing and easy that only rarely did he revise his pages. He was also a rapid and retentive reader with a lively curiosity and catholic interests, and he retained his interest in Classical studies to the end of his life.

Sydney received his Bachelor of Arts degree from New College on 10 October, 1792, and his degree of Master of Arts four years later. He continued to hold his fellowship, even after he left Oxford, until 1800, when his marriage violated its terms. As at Winchester, he was not happy at Oxford, but he found the income from his fellowship very useful, Osbert Burdett attributes his unhappiness to the fact that he was not popular, and that he was poor and liberal.[28] His lack of popularity may have stemmed from his weight and his abhorrence of sports, but even so he probably was more liberal than most of his fellow students. He was most likely poorer than most Oxford students, but to refer to Sydney Smith as having lived in poverty is as erroneous as it is ridiculous. His widow, writing after his death, said that "...from poverty he was constrained to forego on the great advantages of College, namely the early intimacies there formed with his contemporaries, which in after life, are so often productive of good." Written in ink, her manuscript was read and annotated by another hand in pencil, and the second hand scrawled a large "Q" above "<u>poverty</u>." Mrs. Smith, in some apparent indignation at this questioning of her opinion, wrote on the back of the preceding page: "Why not <u>poverty</u>, for poverty it was. CAS", --?29

In fact, it was not poverty, nor was Sydney Smith ever a poor man. "Poor" to eighteenth and early nineteenth-century England meant that a man depended upon a wage or salary, or conversely, that he did not have an independent income. Sydney Smith was the son of a gentlemen who did possess an independent income, and he can in no way be compared to a poor person of the laboring classes. No poor person attended either Winchester or Oxford, and the §100 fellowship that Sydney's widow and daughter described as a pittance was several times greater than the annual income of many working class families. These ladies were reflecting their own affluence, social attitudes, and the rampant materialism of the age in their evaluation. Since Sydney was not as rich as Lord Holland or Sir Robert Peel, they adjudged him to be "poor", when he actually had a modest income. For those ladies to have compared his income with that of a laborer was unthinkable. Sydney was never poor in the sense that he worked for wages, for his fellowship at Oxford was granted to him as a gentleman, and it was not given for the performance of any task. He continued to collect it for years after he left the university because it was his privilege to do so. Later in life he was given various livings in Church, and they became his property, essentially to dispose of as he saw fit. Certain duties and requirements were stipulated, but these were neither very onerous nor very stringently enforced, their fulfillment being more generally left to the honor and conscience of the man involved.

One of Sydney's complaints about Oxford had been that although his fellowship permitted him to complete his degrees, it did not allow him to live in circumstances as comfortable as he would have desired. His father was a strange man where money matters were concerned, and Sydney chose to live less than elegantly, and to make meticulous accounts of his spending, in order to avert quarrels with his father. It has been said earlier that Robert Smith refused to finance Sydney's legal training, but in actuality the father seems to have strongly discouraged his son from studying law by making him choose either a subsidy to see him through his study for the bar, or a sizeable legacy at his father's death. If Sydney chose the former, it would mean forfeiture of his inheritance. According to his widow, Sydney chose the Church and the expectancy, perhaps from a sense of duty to his father, or perhaps simply to avoid friction with him.[30]

The origins of the quarrel between Sydney and his father, which all of his biographers have dwelt on to a greater or lesser degree, began at least as early as 1789, and may have stemmed from the question of Sydney's future, but it is indisputable that the quarrel came to be very real, and it lasted for many years. Its beginnings were obsured by the sentimental gushings of Catherine A. Smith, but recently discovered letters offer a better and more satisfactory description. She asserted that the quarrel had begun over her dowry at the time of her marriage to Sydney in 1800. According to her, Sydney prearranged to put the bulk of the §8000 she brought to the marriage in trust for her alone in order to prevent his father from pressuring him into lending it to him for land speculation.[31] She further maintained that she did not believe that Robert Smith could be really that bad, until as a new bride, the young couple visited her parents-in-law and he burst out: "... your Father should have been first thought of: What right had you, where you had it in your power to benefit me, to indulge in such silly, romantic notions of securing to her her property? Could it be any where safer than in the hands of your Father?"[32] Such was Catherine Smith's recollection of the origin of the dispute, and it was reiterated essentially by Saba Holland and other biographers, but two things should be recalled about Catherine Smith. First, she was writing nearly half a century after the events; and second, she was less than an intellectual giant, so much so that Sydney had to soothe her at the theatre by assuring her that the happenings on the stage were only play acting. In addition, the whole passage has an understandably feminine ring to it, as if it might be exactly what Catherine Smith wanted it to be. Finally the use of the word "romantic" is troublesome. In common usage by 1855, it seems unlikely that the erratic but tough-minded Robert would have used it in this context in 1800. By way of summation, Catherine's passage must be taken to be little other than a flight of embellished imagination, reinforced with imperfect remembrance and little solid fact, especially in the light of presently available documents. She undoubtedly faced a problem in writing her memoir, and she attempted to resolve it in the best way she could. She relied on her memory, which was faulty, and on her imagination, which was fanciful. Nevertheless, a confrontation of bride and father-in-law probably did take place, and it was probably unpleasant for her.33 The disposition of her fortune was very likely one of the issues in the confrontation, but the whole picture of the disagreement and eventual estrangement of Sydney Smith and his father was much more involved that this argument over her property.

There is, however, some substantiation for Catherine's account, which appears in a further passage in her manuscript. She says that some months later, after Sydney's mother had died, his father wrote to him saying:

> So long as poor Jona lived (the name he always gave Mrs. Smith) I have borne patiently with you because I knew that if I had a quarrel'd with you it would have broken her heart; -but now that she is gone, I never <u>will</u> see you more; for I never will <u>forgive</u> and never shall forget your Wife's fortune, as to put it out of your power to assist your <u>Father</u>.34

This passage would seem to be fairly definitive, but no other trace of this letter exists, and further, it has the ring of what Catherine Smith might have believed strongly enough, but what may also have been little more than a flight of fancy, especially in the italicized sections. Since both this excerpt and the earlier passage have the semblance of truth about them, and since any further evidence seems to be lacking, previous biographers have accepted these stories without question. Nonetheless, the letters in the Huntington Library prove beyond any doubt that either these accounts were maliciously fabricated, at least in part; or at best, they were based on poorly remembered facts.

Few of Sydney Smith's letters from the 1790's have survived, and of those that do exist, still fewer were written to his father; but even these few indicate several serious discrepancies in Catherine Smith's memoir. On 26 June, 1796, Sydney wrote to his father explaining his previous requests for money to cover his expenses in making repairs to his chambers and in taking over his curacy at Netheravon. He reminds Robert Smith that he had "...agreed to allow me §122.122 per An. My mother by yr desire kept the copy of the particulars. -This was exclusive of a horse - I recd from you last 40. -which leaves 18 for the horse...," which had cost an additional §24/2/5. He had paid §1/3/6 in fees for his ordination, which brought his year's expenses to §127/7/11, of which he had received §12/10 from his curacy, §40/12/10 from his father, and he had yet to receive §50 from his fellowship, all of which added up to an income of §103/2/10 (which he incorrectly totalled as §102/10). He asked his father for an additional §25 to pay off his debts.[35]

From this section of the letter, it can be seen that Robert Smith, despite both Catherine Smith's and Saba Holland's vigorous denials, had continued to extend financial assistance to Sydney at Oxford, albeit with some reluctance, and that he had done so in a regularized manner. It would also appear that the fellowship paid no more than §50 annually, but this figure may represent a semi-annual payment, and it is even possible that Sydney concealed the exact amount of his income from his father. It is interesting, also, to find that, far from cutting Sydney off without a further shilling when he was granted his fellowship, Robert Smith had continued to subsidize the young curate for at least two years after he had taken his degree.

Sydney's letter of 26 June, 1796, is a very long letter for him, and it goes on to say that-

> "...I hope my dr Fr you will not look upon it in a bad light, if I apply to you to make good to me these small sums. -but really they are serious sums to me, & in spite of all my economy-& the assistance you are so good as to afford me-I am sometimes without a shilling in my picket."[36]

Here again is unquestionable evidence that Robert Smith did continue his financial support, even if his contributions did not enable Sydney to live on a princely scale; and even more importantly, that serious disagreements between Sydney and his father, probably over money matters, were present in 1796, four years earlier than the date given by Catherine Smith.

In another letter, written two weeks later, he says:

> My Dearest Fr. -I thank you most sincerely for your Lr as I look upon it to be a proof of returning affection. I am extremely sorry that any misunderstanding ever [subsisted?] between us..& certainly think myself to have been more in the wrong, than I suspected I was some time ago....Against one part of yr Lr my dear Father-I must enter my protest-your memory in this instance fails you. -I never did directly or indirectly make use of the expressions you impute to me, to this assertion, I must adhere. You are under a great mistake if you suppose that I do not love my Father & reverence his talents, it is utterly unprofitable to convince any man against his will. I can only solemnly assert it to be the truth.[37]

Here is a very firm corroboration of a misunderstanding which has obviously lasted over an extended period of time, the fault for which Sydney accepts. But, reading between the lines, he does so in the spirit of reconciliation which will reappear in his later letters, and it is obvious that he considers his father's role in the quarrel to have been unreasonable, and possibly even irrational.

By November 1797, despite the olive branch held out by Sydney, the quarrel deepened still further and he wrote: "Once again my dear Father give me leave to express a hope, that you will soften your resolution, & permit me to stay a longer time with you & the faimily-than you limited me to at my departure."[38] He said that he wanted his father to reconsider his decree requiring Sydney's separation from the family, for it might mean a complete rupture of relations. He said further, that he had already acknowledged his fault, and he reminded his father that he would be gone to Scotland for at least two or three years, and that during that time Robert Smith might die and Sydney's mother most probably would die, and that separation from his mother under such circumstance would be a more severe punishment for Sydney than his father intended.

On 25 November, 1797, another letter was written which offers still more information on the dispute. From this letter it is clear that Sydney had not shown "the fair and rational obedience which a Son owes to his

Father," or so, at least, he confesses. In an effort to placate his irate parent, he admits once again that he had thought he was right in the controversy, but that he had realized his error.[39] Robert Smith probably held it against Sydney that he alone of the four sons persisted in following his own inclinations rather than parental directions. Bobus was studying law with Robert Smith's blessing, and Courtenay and Cecil had gone to India to make their fortunes. Only Sydney acted indepently, which was an outrageous act to *pater familias*. Sydney added, somewhat surprisingly:

> "I hope the conversation upon suicide which passed between us, has produced no other unpleasant sensation in your mind than the want of respect to you, of which I am sorry to say, you have the right to accuse me.[40]

From these letters the quarrel can be understood to have centered around Robert Smith's petulant accusations of unfilial condect on the part of Sydney, and it is fairly obvious that those accusations were both ill-founded and based on Sydney's financial needs. That Robert Smith was a difficult individual cannot be denied, and that this irritability was not confined to Sydney alone is borne out in a later letter from Sydney to his father, in which he refers to the elder Smith's accusation of "deceit" on the part of Sydney's brother, Cecil.[41] This would indicate that charges of general irascibility, oversensitivity and suspicion could properly be attributed to Robert Smith's personality, and no doubt he was plagued with these emotions, but he seems to have harbored a special animosity towards Sydney, perhaps because Sydney was, like himself, a very strong-minded person.

In one respect, Catherine Smith's account of the quarrel was entirely correct, and that was that Sydney did indeed place his wife's dowry in trust for her, and saw to it that it was invested in the funds. This was both a good and a secure investment, and Catherine was probably right also in that he did so in order to keep the money out of his father's hands.[42]

In another letter, which unfortunately is not dated although it was obviously written shortly after the marriage of Catherine Amelia Pybus to Sydney on 2 July, 1800, this aspect of the quarrel surfaces lucidly. In the letter, Sydney replies to accusations made by his father in an earlier letter, or possibly during a visit by the young couple to Sydney's parents. Robert Smith felt that he had not been adequately consulted concerning the marriage and the financial settlement, the latter of which Sydney states to have been his own and done against the wishes of his wife and mother-in-law. Robert Smith was a contentious person, and Sydney pointed this fact out to him while, at the same time, maintaining that he, in turn, had been very patient with his father.[43]

Shortly after this time, in 1801, Sydney's mother suffered what has been described as a fatal epileptic seizure. Sydney wrote his father a consoling letter, but their quarrel had previously heated up to the point that he felt compelled, even in a letter of sympathy, to reply to calumnies charged by his father. He retorted to his father's previous letter (which quite possibly was the one in which he informed Sydney of his mother's death) wherein his father had called him

> "...Rascal Villain Fool -Scoundrel-Pedant-etc-etc... as well as your animadversions upon my wife I do now as I have often done before very sincerely forgive. -any condemnation of my conduct by you founded upon fact-and expressed with moderation and dignity--I should very seriously regret. -but after an escperience of 15 years this very energetic language-produces no other effect upon me than to make me regret the unhappy state of mind which must have given birth to it-[44]

It is interesting to observe that Sydney says the quarrel dates back fifteen years, and that he suggests that his father may be deranged. He also offers his forgiveness to the abrasive old man, which is probably the most infuriating thing that can be done to a person with imaginary injuries who wants to argue. In the same letter he advises his father not to listen to idle gossip, and to remember that he is a man of the world, while Sydney is a man who lives among books, all of which made an understanding between them more difficult.

By 1801 Sydney was thoroughly tired of the contest, but Robert Smith went on writing his venomous notes. In reply Sydney simply said that his father could not be persuaded by facts, arguments, or even by total submission, and that it was hopeless to try. He told Robert Smith that his unhappiness could not be improved unless he redisposed his mind, and he added annoyingly: "I forgive you most sincerely for the numberless & most injurious invectives...."[45]

As late as 28 March, 1803, Robert Smith's peevishness continued, but Sydney's patience had worn thin, and his obvious exasperation was indicative of his desire to end the quarrel with a complete estrangement. His father's letters had made the usual list of accusations, not only against Sydney, but also against Catherine, and Sydney defended her hotly. Robert Smith must have realized that the protracted dispute was not going his way, and he had offered to use his interest to help Sydney obtain preferment in the Church, but Sydney curtly refused his offer. Although Sydney was in Edinburgh, he was about to leave for London and he refused to offer any explanation of his motives to his father.[46]

The complete rupture of relations between Sydney and his father occurred sometime during this period and possibly as a result of the letter just cited, but Sydney Smith was not a heartless man. He broke with his father not because he wanted to, and not because he had no feelings of affection for him, but only because his repeated efforts at reconciliation invariably resulted only in a familiar recitation of the catalog of ills, or of old and groundless allegations. Moreover, all attempts to soothe the old man or make him be reasonable had been equally unsuccessful. Contrary to Catherine's "Letter," quoted earlier,[47] it was Sydney, probably greatly to his father's consternation, who effected the breach. Robert Smith evidently thrived on contention with Sydney, and he was apparently eager to continue indefinitely in the same vein; but Sydney, filled with disgust and weak from emotional exhaustion, had reached the point where he was no longer willing to play his father's game. In March or April of 1803, Robert Smith offered to receive Sydney's children, but Sydney refused to permit it, hoping at the same time that his refusal would not be too great an affront to his father.[48]

Sydney wrote once again to his father on 15 April, 1803, saying:

"I hope you will not for a moment imagine at the sight of a letter from me-that it

> is my intention to plague you with ap-
> lications for reconciliation. - & to
> prevent you from living at peace your-
> self because you will not live at peace
> with me."49

He said further that he had no hope for a reconciliation, although he had hoped that Bobus and his wife
might help in such a project, and he added that he wrote
them not from "<u>indifference</u>" but from "<u>despair</u>". Robert Smith had conjured up new complaints against him
which he brusquely rejected, asking his father to look
back and "...see if any one of your sons has ever behaved more honorably upon the subject of money...." He
concluded his letter with a plea to his father not to
groundlessly accuse him of dishonesty or immorality in
public, for his reputation was his fortune, and his father was endangering it.50

By this time, Sydney was exhausted with the quarrel and resigned to the estrangement. Robert Smith
wanted a reconciliation, but he wanted to argue about
the terms of a reconciliation, and Sydney wanted an end
to argument. In an undated letter, he wrote to his father: "Unless I am certain we meet to put an end to
the most groundless and esctraordinary [sic] differences
that I believe ever escisted- I beg to leave to decline
meeting at all-"51 On those terms, however, if his father accepted them, he would meet with him anywhere at
all.

Despite the fact that Sydney regarded the split as
complete and final, Robert Smith continued to write and
to demand that his son perform various tasks for him in
London. The handling of Cecil's divorce was the most
important of these tasks, and Robert Smith insisted that
he conduct the intricate negotiations, and then criticized his efforts. Sydney refused at this time to meet
with his father unless he came to him and took his hand52
at which he again chose to take umbrage. This last letter, written on 25 March, 1805, seems to have brought
an end to the quarrel. By this time, Sydney had made
it clear that he would no longer continue to squabble
to no purpose, and that his father could do so by himself if he chose. In April, 1805, Sydney was able to
write to Francis Jeffrey:

> I am at last reconciled for my father.
> He was very ill, **very** much out of spirits,

> and tired to death with the quarrel the moment he discovered I ceased to care a half-penny about it. I made him a slight apology-just sufficient to save his pride, and have as in duty bound exposed myself for these next 7 or 8 years to all the tyranny, trouble and folly with which I have no manner of doubt at the same age I shall harrass my children.[53]

Surprisingly enough his fears proved to be groundless, and having brought about the rapprochement Sydney and his father lived amicably until Robert Smith's death at the age of eighty-seven. In 1821 Sydney wrote: "My father is one of the few people I have ever seen improved by age. He is become careless, indulgent and anacreontic."[54] Upon his death he left Sydney a large legacy which he made still larger shortly before his death, but he left the bulk of his estate to his grandson Cecil, who was the child of his favorite son, Cecil.

The wrangling between Sydney and his father had thus begun as early as 1796, and probably a good deal earlier, and it had continued on to 1805. While a knowledge of it is of no great value historically, it does raise questions as to the reliability of the works of both Catherine Smith and Saba Holland, and of all who have used their work uncritically. It further reveals Sydney Smith as a man of reason, justice and moderation; and his father as a man less well-endowed with those virtues. Their useless haggling went on and on for years, but the quarrel between him and his father, while obviously of the greatest importance to the old man, was only a minor occupation to the younger Smith. During these same years Sydney had entered into one of the most creative periods of his life.

CHAPTER II

Netheravon and the Establishment of Connections, 1794-1798.

In the unpublished memoir of her husband, Catherine Smith had deplored his "poverty" at New College, and his consequent exclusion from the active social life that might have enabled him to establish friendly relations with those young men of quality who were destined to occupy England's most influential offices. But here she is contradicted by Saba Holland's manuscript which asserts that Sydney met at least one promising young man at Oxford-- Michael Hicks-Beach, who later appointed Sydney curate at Netheravon.[1] Yet, Osbert Burdett seems to assume that Sydney had been appointed to that curacy through more distant channels of the Church, and that he came to Hicks-Beach's attention only after his appointment.[2] On the whole, Lady Holland's account of the appointment is the most convincing since Hicks-Beach was the major landowner of the area, and although Sydney was named by the absentee Vicar of Netheravon to be his curate, Halpern credits Hick-Beach with being Sydney's patron and with securing the position for him.[3] The Netheravon curacy was no plum for any aspiring cleric, for it only offered a salary of less than $50 a year, and it was in a poverty-stricken village tucked away in an enclosed and forgotten corner of the Salisbury Plain. But it was a start.

Sydney went to Netheravon as a curate in 1794. He had taken his Bachelor of Arts degree from New College in 1792, but he stayed on at Oxford until 1794, possibly until he reached the requisite age of twenty-three, when he was ordained to the deaconate of the Church. It is certain that he entered the deaconate, but records regarding that event are no longer in existence. Presumably he was ordained at Salisbury Cathedral by the Bishop of Sarum, but this is inconclusive as a gap exists in the records of Salisbury Cathedral from 1791 to 1796. Thus, it is possible that he was ordained elsewhere by Letter Dimissory. His ordination to the priesthood took place at Christ Church Cathedral, Oxford, on May, 1796, the same year he was granted his Master of Arts degree.[4]

Though Sydney had now become a priest, he had also become an object of pity: an unbeneficed clergyman. A number of good "livings," which is to say an appointment as rector of a parish, were generally held in the hands

20

of lay patrons, bishops, or Cathedral chapters, and the fashionable or profitable "livings" were doled out to members of the family, friends, those who were politically favored, or occasionally to clergymen of great and proven ability. Livings were granted for the life of the nominee, and having been once granted they gave to the gentleman appointed that "independence" coveted by all, for barring the most outrageous transgressions of human or divine law, they were irremovable. The income of the parish, which consisted chiefly of tithes, the income from glebe-land, and fees and offerings of various kinds became the incumbent's property during his lifetime. He could, for example, move to Italy if he found the climate in England unpleasant, and although he was under some obligation to provide for the spiritual needs of the parish, not all absentees did so. Some absentee rectors simply pocketed the income and forgot about their responsibilities, which was undoubtedly their right even if it was a violation of the spirit of that right; others put in an appearance seasonally or occasionally, while still others pocketed the bulk of the income and paid a pittance to a curate to serve in their stead.[5] Curates, who were miserably remunerated for the most part, thus performed a large part of the work of the Church while receiving only a very, very small part of its income. The Vicar of Netheravon "lived" in the parsonage but he spent all of his time in Salisbury, forcing Sydney not only to perform all of the spiritual work connected with the parish church and that of the neighbouring village of Fittleton, but also to find housing elsewhere. Sydney obligingly lodged in two rooms of a nearby farmhouse.[6]

Curates were not appointed permanently and they could be removed at will by their benefactors. Many clergymen served as curates as a sort of apprenticeship for the priesthood in the first few years of their service to the Church, going on to more desirable livings after their ordination. Many others, however, unblessed by fortune, family connections or outstanding ability, continued to eke out a precarious existence as curates for the rest of their lives. Thus Sydney's beginnings as a curate of Netheravon were as humble as those of any Anglican clergyman could have been. When his biographers in copying Lady Holland's plaintive lamentations asserted that he had no friends, they meant simply that he had no friends or connections who could, or would, appoint him to a remunerative living at that time.

Perhaps Netheravon was a strange place for a man

destined for fame, to begin his clerical career, but it could hardly have been as bad as Lady Saba Holland described when she wrote: "Sydney Smith, a curate in the midst of Salisbury Plain!"[7] Actually Netheravon was a poor, miserable and permanently depressed village, but it was near Stonehenge and not far from Salisbury. Sydney himself described it as "a pretty feature in a plain (Salisbury) face."[8] His major complaint was that it was not a fashionable living in the London whose society he loved and longed for, for he was a pre-romantic who found little charm in the country. He had said he would stay no longer than two years, yet he stayed nearly four years in all despite the boredom with which his correspondence is peppered:

> I am just returned from allying the splendid Pyck to the antient house of the Maskelynes. I thought when I turned my eyes on the enchanting couple that I was marrying a Baboon to a Sow. However it went off very well, they were very thankful; he was all love and she was all modesty. Nothing can equal the profound, the unmeasurable, the awful dulness of this place, in which I lye dead and buried, in hope of a joyful resurrection in the year 1796...[9]

On 11 January, 1796, he wrote to Mrs. Hicks-Beach, "I quit this place in March -- I have heard of no successor; a Gentleman Curate called to Day to survey place, and premises, and galloped away in 2 minutes with ev'ry mark of astonishment, and antipathy."[10] Although he wrote deprecatingly of Netheravon he did get his start there, both in his clerical profession and in the realization of valuable associations with influential people. With regard to his work in the Church at Netheravon, he later published several volumes of sermons, some of which undoubtedly date from this period. Also he was active in establishing the first parish Sunday school, and founded a school of industry. Since Sunday schools have so greatly altered their character since the time of Sydney Smith, it is necessary to point out that they originated in eighteenth-century England, and that their intention was to teach Bible reading. Conducted by the Church of England and also by various dissenting bodies, the Sunday schools provided the means by which children, who were often working children of working class parents, might learn to read and also learn the basics of writing and arithmetic at little or no expense to their families. Despite the poverty and ignorance of Netheravon the children came eagerly to the Sunday school, enabling Sydney to make the following report to Mrs. Hicks-Beach:

> In our conversation about the poor of N. you agreed with me that some of the boys and girls might possibly be prevented from attending church, or the Sunday School from want of proper clothing, and you were so good as to add, that you would endeavor in some degree to remove this impediment, if it were found to exist. On Sunday last there were 3 or 4 children with their feet upon the cold stones without any shoes, and one came a perfect <u>Sans culottes</u>- or at least only with <u>some</u> grinning remnants of that useful garment, just sufficient to shew that he was so clad from necessity, and not from any ingenious theory he had taken up against such a useful invention. If the Sunday School had begun, I should have imagined that the poor boy thought it his duty to come ready for whipping, as a fowl is sent from the poulterers, trussed and ready for roasting. In whatsoever manner and to whatsoever extent you may chuse to alleviate this species of misery, be so good as to remember that I am on the spot, and shall be happy to carry your benevolent intentions into execution....[11]

The above letter was probably written in the winter of 1794-95, and although the school had still not opened by April, 1795, Sydney was working out the details of its operations with Hicks-Bench. It was decided that due to a shortage of rooms and funds to pay two teachers, the separation of the sexes would be precluded. In this same letter Sydney asked that Hicks-Beach send him sixty spellers, twenty <u>Books of Common Prayer</u>, twenty <u>New Testaments</u> and a hundred of Hannah More's moralistic little books.[12] By May the school had opened its doors and Sydney was satisfied with the early results. The children were so eager to learn that they voluntarily met with the master two or three nights a week in addition to their Sunday lessons.[13] By January, 1796, Sydney reported excellent progress among the students, some of whom were ready to read the Book of Common Prayer.14

Whether the Sunday School and a school of industry for poor girls which he also set up, was primarily Sydney's idea, or whether he was carrying out the desires of Mrs. Hicks-Beach, cannot easily be determined. Since Sunday Schools were beneath his later dignity, at least in the opinion of his widow and his daughter, they said little about his role in them. Osbert Burdett, however, points out that during this period Sunday Schools were being established in all well-administered parishes, and by implication he gives Sydney most of the credit.15 On the other hand, certain passages in Sydney's letters regarding Sunday Schools make it appear that the project was originated by Mrs. Hicks-Beach, and that Sydney was merely carrying out her instructions. These letters hint at an almost fawning eagerness on his part to ingratiate himself with that eminent family. Reid suggests a third alternative, namely that Sydney and the Hicks-Beaches, who were concerned landlords and a ranking family, worked out the conception of the Sunday School jointly and that Sydney put it into operation with their approval and financial support.16 It might even be suggested that the idea was his, but lacking both the authority and the means to get such a project started, he persuaded his patrons of its merit and secured their support. No documentary evidence that would prove this last suggestion has come to light, but it is well-evidenced that Sydney was a proponent of education generally, and specifically of the education of the poor. Furthermore, he defended the education of the lower classes at a time when many members of his class opposed it on principle.17

Sunday schools were intended chiefly for the poor, and Sydney Smith was later to be described as a champion of the poor. In many respects he was exactly that, but his political philosophy needs to be closely examined. He was a Whig, which is to say that he opposed an absolute monarchy politically, and a society dominated by the royal family. He stood for aristocratic political and social principles which he believed should be interpreted broadly enough to include all members of the "responsible" classes which meant chiefly the aristocracy and the upper middle classes. If the term "public" is defined in its Whiggish eighteenth-century connotative meaning as those people who counted, and "populace" is likewise defined as the rest of the population, then Sydney Smith might have paraphrased President

Abraham Lincoln's later oft-quoted description of the ideal government as being "of the public, by the public, and for the populace." Sydney believed that the populace could not and should not be entrusted with political power, but that if Whig aristocrats were permitted to exercise that power they would instinctively use it in the best interests of the general population. Sydney was a believer in the revolutionary settlement of 1688, and he believed that the well-being of the state depended on Whig aristocrats like those who had overthrown James II, and whose descendants continued to defend the liberties of freeborn Englishmen from royal encroachment. He felt these aristocrats alone were qualified to govern the state. He saw English society accurately, as a stratified society with enough individual freedom for gifted or lucky individuals to rise socially without undue hindrance. Never a democrat, Sydney believed along with most of the gentlemen of his age that democracy meant mobocracy, and he had no patience with political or social equality.

To Sydney Smith, the Whig, the purpose of society and government was not democracy, but rather the creation of ornaments of society like Lord Grey or Lord Holland--wealthy, urbane aristocrats who embraced liberal principles and who, as humans, least resembled the beasts. In 1810 Sydney wrote, "And why do you not scout more that pernicious cant that all men are equal? As politicians they do not differ, as Locke thinks they do; but they differ enough to make you and all worthy men sincerely wish for the elevation of one, and the rejection of the other."[18] In 1822, for example, he rejoiced at a marriage in the Whiggish Russell family, "For," he opined, "the manufacture of Russells is a public and important concern."[19]

Whig political philosophy was eminently practical, divorced from metaphysics and religion, and without difficult abstractions. Individual freedom was upheld not because that principle was indisputable, but because its results were adjudged to be good, tangible and material. Many Whigs espoused the cause of the abolition of the civil disabilities of the Roman Catholics decades before their emancipation was accomplished because they saw a relationship between Catholic legal inferiority and the cost of living.

A definition of the Whig party of Sydney Smith's day is difficult, and the usual political terminology does not suffice. To say that the Whigs were liberal and the Tories conservative falls far short of the truth, for there was considerable variation within both parties, and both were led by essentially conservative aristocrats. Perhaps it would be more accurate to describe the Whigs as the party of change and the Tories as the party of continuity, but even that definition should be made cautiously so as to prevent any assumption that "change"meant sweeping or precipitate change, or that "continuity" implied no change at all. In reality, Tories frequently looked with favor upon social reforms which their Whiggish opponents abhorred. Even the time-honored formula that the Whigs represented the mercantile-inductrial middle classes and the Tories the landed aristocracy must not be accepted without question, for the great Whig families were all major landowners, like the Russells or Cavandishes. Moreover, many leading Tories such as Sir Ro-ert Peel, the cotton king, were industrialists or merchants.

Of course, it should be remembered that neither the Whig nor the Tory party was highly organized or tightly disciplined, and a good deal of difference of opinion existed within each party. Each was united by the desire of its members for a share of the power in the state and for the dignities and salaries of office. But even their cupidity can be easily exaggerated, as Sir Lewis Namier points out so convincingly.[20] Very briefly, the Whigs stood for the liberty of the squirearchy and all that that liberty entailed. It meant civil liberties for the independent and enlightened gentlemen, resistance to arbitrary monarchical government that might threaten those liberties through parliamentary supremacy over the crown, the exercise of relatively unrestricted local political power by the squirearchy, and the subordination of the Church to Parliament nationally and to the aristocrats locally. Explicit in the whole Whig viewpoint was their insistence on legality, propriety, and the maintenance of existing precedents and privileges, unless their continued affirmation endangered the existing constitution.

In many respects the Tory position was as pragmatic as that of the Whigs, but they differed from the Whigs in that they placed the claims of crown and church above those of the squirearchy. As aristocratic as the Whigs, and probably more so, they believed that their well-being and that of the country was better protected by a powerful monarch than by a less dependable Parliament.

On specific issues such as that of Catholic emancipation, Tories voted against relieving Catholic disabilities not because they hated Catholics more than the Whigs did, or because they opposed religious toleration, but rather because they either genuinely believed that disburdening the Catholics would threaten that cherished institution, the Church; or in the case of the Tory leaders to whom Catholic emancipation was a pawn in the game of power politics, because they believed that change in that respect might lead to an undermining of the party and its policies. Similarly they opposed the reform of avowedly bad and archaic laws from fear that their reform might bring more extensive reform that would endanger the constitution and the social order. Panic-stricken by events across the channel during the Revolution, Tory resistance hardened into a suspicion that the mildest reform proposal was revolution or, at the very least, could only result in revolution and the destruction of the "Matchless Constitution" and all that the possessing classes held dear. They came to believe that any concession to the popular outcry for reform would only open the floodgates of wholesale and ill-considered change, and their defense of traditional institutions was so persuasive that many of the more conservative Whigs either joined them or supported their policies.

From the standpoint of the exaltation of conservatism and the denunciation of liberalism as subversion, the period of the age of French Revolution in Great Britain may be fairly compared with that of the "McCarthy Era" in the United States. In actual fact, the moderate Whigs who were denounced as "Jacobins" had a program that amounted to little more than a little education for the lower classes, some concessions to the dissenters, and some minor electoral reforms in the House of Commons.[21] Sydney Smith, who favored this minor political reform in the early part of the century, later supported the Great Reform Bill of 1832, but with reluctance and only then because he believed that the failure of timely minor reform earlier necessitated the major reform of 1832.[22]

More important than their proposed policies of reform was the role of the Whigs as the loyal opposition, a role that was theirs for an unanticipated length of time as the result of continuing Tory majorities in the House of Commons. The Whigs wanted both the power and the spoils of office, and they hoped to win the double prize by opposing Tory rule and by exposing Tory corruption and incompetence. Sydney has been upheld as a paragon of principle by his biographers; he has been portrayed as a confirmed Whig who stood by his principles at the expense of promotion within the Church and social ostracism, and as one who did so in a totally disinterested way, without hope of reward of recognition. "...Thank God," Lady Saba Holland quotes him as saying, "I never acted from the hope of preferment, but from the love of justice and truth which was bursting within me. When I began to express my opinions on Church politics, what hope could any but a madman have of gaining preferment by such a line of conduct?"[23]

His assertion is true in the sense that he did unwaveringly endorse Whig principles, and it is even more true in that he was poorly rewarded during the first two-thirds of his clerical career; but an examination of surviving letters and documents proves that Sydney Smith was no more disinterested than the average gentlemen. He maintained a gentle but constant pressure on Lord Holland to secure better livings for him, and on 9 March, 1820, he said: "I leave myself implicitly to your kindness to me and to your feelings of propriety for yourself. My second object is to grow richer, my first to do what is right and proper upon all occasions -"[24] It would be unfair and probably inaccurate to deny his statement, especially since he did not switch his allegiance, but it is grossly erroneous to claim that he pursued his first objective without regard for the second, as has often been stated. In 1808, having accepted a living in Yorkshire in which he could survive in comfort if not opulence, he wrote to Lady Elizabeth Holland,* "My lot is now cast and my heritage fixed - most probably. But you may chuse to make me a Bishop, in which case I shall return...with great shouting and glory. If you do make me a Bishop I think I shall never do you discredit ..."[25]

Sydney Smith supported the Whig party because he believed in its principles, and he did so at a time the Whigs were out of power; but he endorsed the Whig position in the full expectation of being rewarded with promotion in the Church. The fact that his rewards were

*Lady Elizabeth Holland (1770-1845), formerly Elizabeth Webster, married Henry V. Fox, 3rd Baron Holland in 1797. Renowned as the hostess of Holland House, she was not related to Dr. Holland or Lady Saba Holland.

not impressive until late in his life apparently points to his placing of principle above self-interest, but in actuality it meant that his friends were not in office. He supported the Whigs who were out of office in the 1790's, but he did so in the expectation that they would regain a parliamentary majority in the immediate future, and that when they did they would reward the faithful. British history in the eighteenth century certainly indicated that probability, and he could hardly have known that the Tory ascendancy would last, with only brief interruptions, until 1830.

During most of the period from 1796 when he was ordained to the priesthood, until 1830 when the Whigs returned to office, Sydney was a gentleman-in-waiting for the honors and dignities of the Church. He was forced by circumstances to go his own way and make his own fortune, and his biographers have bewailed the fact that lesser men advanced beyond him in the Church, and that his adherence to principle held him back. These lesser men, Lady Saba Holland soberly stated, were promoted over him because of their connections and their unprincipled political opinions; but she also claims that Sydney Smith, when he did later advance in the Church, did so solely on the basis of the long-overdue recognition of his ability.[26] She is to be commended for her loyalty to her father's memory, but as an historical judgement her opinion is worthless. Sydney did indeed receive overdue recognition in the Church, but he received it on exactly the same basis as his Tory competitors: political connections and a political reward. An aura of self-sacrifice, amounting almost to martyrdom, was painted around his career in the Church, but the hard realities of his situation are that he was a Whig clergyman for almost fifty years, nearly forty of which were dominated by Tory politics and Tory-controlled advancement in the Church.

To Sydney Smith the failure of the Whigs was a source of disappointment which merged into bitterness, and it led him to adopt postures and to make statements that do little credit to his memory. He could be a partisan politician with a vengeance, and his partisanship occasionally beclouded his judgement. In 1806 following the death of Pitt, he said:

> The change in administration (tho' I am not ordinarily a great politician) has made me extremely happy both because I

> believe the War will not be protracted
> longer than honor and safety require,
> and because the Law and the Church will
> be refreshed by the elevation of men
> of Whig principles under which appela-
> tion I find as I see more of the World
> all the truly honest and able men (who
> are of any party at all) ranging them-
> selves. I cannot describe to you how
> disgusted I am by the set of canting
> rascals who have crept into all kinds
> of power during the profligate resign
> of Mr. Pitt, who patronized hypocrisy,
> folly, fraud and anything else which
> contributed to his power-- peace to his
> ashes and from them, but whatever feel-
> ings and proprieties it violates I must
> say he was one of the most luminous elo-
> quent blunderers with which any people
> was ever afflicted. For 15 years I have
> found my income dwindling away under
> his eloquence, and regularly in every
> session of Parliament he has charmed
> every classical feeling and stript me
> of every guinea I possest. At the
> close of every brilliant display an ex-
> pedition failed or a Kingdom fell, and
> by the time that his Style had gained
> the summit of perfection Europe was de-
> graded to the lowest abyss of Misery.
> God send us a stammerer, a tongueless
> man, let Moses come for this heaven-
> born Aaron was failed.[27]

Such was his opinion of Pitt and he was not alone in his condemnation. However, later historical opinion was not quite as partisan, and the younger Pitt has generally been classified as one of England's great Prime Ministers.

Sydney's prejudice was expressed not only against Pitt but also against Tories in general. He assumed that their policies and principles were wrong and misguided, and that all Tories were corrupt and incompetent. In 1809 he expressed the violence of his opinion in a letter to Lord Grey which said:

> I cannot help looking upon it as a most
> melancholy proof of the miserable state

> of this country when men of integrity
> and ability are employed. If it was
> possible to have gone on without them,
> I am sure they would never have been
> thought of.[28]

His concern for his country was real, but the logic of his thought leaves a good deal to be desired. Tories were to be denounced for employing incompetents and placement, and they were to be railed at even if they replaced them with better men.

Sydney also occasionally expressed himself in verse or rhyme, and although it is fortunate that his reputation does not rest on his poetry, he used that vehicle to attack the Tories about 1812:

> If Silly School Boy Jokes & Doggrel Rhymes
> Can save the falling state and mend the Times
> If threats and [pertness?], petulance and pride
> Can freeborn nations rule, and Senates grinde
> If he who mouths his timid words like Pitt
> Inherits all his mighty Masters wit-
> Come forward C--n--g seise the reins of State
> & pun and jest away impending fate.
> The Sage old Woman shall correct thy youth
> Much honor'd Castlereagh shall teach the truth
> & thou shalt Catch from the romatic Rose
> that patriot fire which in his bosom glows
> Learn from his Spotless life a Scorn for fees,
> and Jobs, and parings of the public Cheese.
> Then when the Christian Perceval has hung
> A Bag of his own venom on thy Tongue
> Taught thee with movements of his gospel face
> to bleed and torture the Milesian race
> Then in unbounded mischief shalt thou rule
> Nor want while [Sturges?] lies a flattering fool
> Then shall our antient freedom day by day
> Escisting circumstances melt away
> Then shalt thou Squander as in times of old
> In just & necessary wars our gold
> heap on thy race the fruits of others Toil
> & cram each Low born cousin with the Spoil
> While they who banished for vain pretence
> Grenvilles deep knowledge, Howicks manly sense
> & from them turgid nonsense sought defense
> In bitterness shall curse the evil hour
> Which placed them in a Shallow Jesters power.[29]

It is interesting that, in this unpublished poem, he issues a blanket condemnation of the Tories and an equally sweeping endorsement of the Whigs like Granville and Howick.

Smith's censure of the Tories, who were the government during his time, was occasionally so unrestrained as to ring of obvious unpatriotism, if not downright disloyalty. He compared the abilities of the Tory ministers with those of Napoleon, and 1805 he said in a letter that Napoleon's victories in Germany did not surprise him: "...I allowed Bonaparte 28 days to knock both the armies clunes super kaput (as the vulgar have it), to conclude a peace, make a speech of the Senate, and illuminate Paris; he is as rapid and as terrible as the lightning of God...", to which he added in another clause, "...would he were as transient."[30] In an earlier letter to his father he had cautioned against any peace negotiations with Napoleon without safeguards.[31]

Sydney was utterly loyal to England, but his scorn for Tory conduct of the war led him to sneer at the British war effort, which has induced some people in the twentieth century to characterize him as a pacifist, but he was not that either. He scoffed at the patriotic slogans of the Tories, such as the "just and necessary wars" mentioned in his preceding poem. He did stand against was per se, as a tenet of liberalism, but he recognized the fact that British interests were at stake in the Napoleonic Wars. In 1827 during the British intervention in the War for Greek Independence, he voiced his opinion that there "is no such thing as a 'just war' or, at least, as a wise war...."[32] He doubted the ability of Wellington, possibly England's greatest military leader ever, because of his politics, but he rejoiced in the final victory and in the British gains that came from it even if he deplored the prestige that accrued to the Tories from it. He was a patriot but he disliked the term, and his political opinions and his terminology obscured his true feelings.

Samuel Johnson had defined patriotism as "the last refuge of the scoundrel" in the eighteenth century, and Sydney essentially endorsed that definition; but he tended to equate patriotism with Jacobinism, with which he may have sympathized in the early phase of the French Revolution but from which he parted company when it turned radical.[33] "In the young," he said, "patriotism if often little else than an universal suspicion and abuse

abuse of all government."34 In his sermon "On the Love
of our Country" he said that "The Life of our country
has...been so often made a pretext for bad ambition,
and so often given birth to crude and ignorant violence,
that many good men entertain no great relish for that
virtue....", to which he added that "...there is, and
there ever will be, a Christian patriotism, a great system of duries which man owes to the sum of human beings
with whom he lives: to deny it is folly; to neglect it
is a crime."35 It is obvious from this passage that
what he rejected was selfishly motivated of misguided
"super-patriotism," and that by "Christian patriotism"
he intimated responsible citizenship and respect for
national institutions and laws.

By way of refutation of those who might choose to
regard Sydney Smith as a pacifist, particularly in the
light of twentieth-century clerical opposition to war,
stands his sermon "On Invasion," preached before a body
of volunteer officers in 1804, England's darkest hour.
He employed pulpit language when preaching, and quite
another form of English in conversation and writing,
but even so his sermon "On Invasion" is still stirring.
He said that England must fight, and must win, and although God was on her side, "...Heaven has made with us
no convenant, that there should be joy, and peace here,
and wailing, and lamentation in the world besides..."36
He reminded his military congregation that liberty is
priceless, that the value of life without liberty was
greatly diminished, and that seeing one's life and property at the disposal of others in the event of a French
invasion and victory, would be unendurable. "...remember... the cry of Maccabeus," he said, "that it is better
to die in battle than to behold the calamities of young
people, and your sanctuary."37 And addressing himself
to the aristocratic qualities of the officers he questioned whether they, who had been "...Born to higher and better things, would...lead a life of manual labor? Would
you cultivate the earth you had once possessed, and if
you could put up with such a life, could you endure it
for others, whom you live more than yourselves?"38

"Has not England," he asked, "good laws? And is
she not free and blessed with pure religion, cultivated
manners, wealth, power and renown?" But for his "Anglican reserve," he said, he "would answer with great
shouts."39 He regarded the war as a Christian war
against ungodliness, and he denounced the French for
placing their faith in their arms rather than in God.

He further assured his listeners that God would always be present on the battlefield to hear the prayers of distant kinfolk and to receive Christian souls. Sydney stated quite accurately that Great Britain was engaged in the greatest war the world had yet seen, and that the British were fighting not merely for Great Britian, but for the future of freedom in the world. Defeat and the loss of liberty would make a desert of the earth and would make life not worth living; but he believed that a combination of Divine Providence and British courage would produce ultimate victory. "I have a boundless courage in the English character," he said, and further:

> I believe that they have more real religion, more probity, more knowledge, and more genuine worth, than exists in the whole world besides; they are the guardians of pure Christianity; and from this prostituted nation of merchants (as they are in derision called), I believe more heroes will spring up in the hour of danger, than all the military nations of antient, and modern Europe have ever produced. Into the hands of God, then, and his ever merciful Son, we cast ourselves, and wait in humble patience the result: First we ask for victory, but if that cannot be, we have only one other prayer-- we implore for death.[40]

Thus Sydney was unquestionably a patriot, even if he objected to the title, yet his attitude towards the royal family was not entirely what might have been expected from a patriotic Englishman. On the occasion of the Duke of York's expedition to Walcheren in 1799, he predicted defeat, to which he added: "I know perfectly well the issue of that royal idiot's going to Holland-many gallant gentlemen of England will be slaughter'd and leave their weeping Tailors behind them..."[41]... Church and King," he said in 1804, "in moderation are very good things, but we have too much of both." In 1826, he closed a letter with "God save the King from your sincere friend Sydney Smith." Part of both of these statements is obviously wit, and most of the rest is Whiggish reserve vis a vis the crown; but Sydney had little love for either George III or George IV (both of whom supported Tory governments during much of Sydney's life). As his fortunes advanced in the Church, his affection for the monarchy was to increase in a similar ratio, so that he was to express little antipathy for William IV, and none at all for Victoria. In his younger and more liberal days, however, he missed no opportunity to snipe at the monarchy. In 1804 in a letter to Caroline Fox, sister of Lord Holland, regarding George III's insanity, he wrote:

> It is generally believed that our excellent monarch is insane, and rumored that he set off full Gallop immediately on his arrival at Windsor pursued by Dr. Simmonds, 5 other physicians, and the Apothecary in waiting, Gold Stick, all the Canons, several dogs, Dr. Langford, and a great number of his liege subjects too obscure for the records of history.[43]

Sydney was delighted with the Mary Anne Clarke scandal in 1809, in which the Duke of York's mistress was exposed as the go-between in the corrupt sale of commissions and decorations; for, as a partisan politican, he saw the possibility of embarrassing the monarchy and toppling the Tory ministry. He saw the real or potential popularity of the royal family as a major threat to English liberty and he believed that the popularity of the current sovereigns could be reduced without endangering the institution of monarchy.[44]

In November, 1810, Sydney commented on the madness of the King again, and he added that he would not be sorry if death ended the King's misery, for Sydney believed that the survival of the Whigs depended on his death. By December, 1810, Sydney's impatience with the persistence of life in the old Kind had increased to the point that he asserted that if he "were in Parliament for a Borough of my own, with a clear fortune of 10,000 pr Annum I would bring in a short bill for deposing George the third."[45] As late as 1826 he was still concerned about "the horrible atrocities perpetrated under even mild Monarchies....;"[46] and even in 1839 he could write that "Charles the first was properly beheaded. The only objection to such acts is their frequency but resorted to at rare intervals they are of great value to mankind...."[47]

Such sentiments are surprising, perhaps, in an Anglican clergyman, but the relative unpopularity of the Hanoverians and Sydney's political partisanship should be recalled. Conversely, in his social philosophy, he was more orthodox, and if he ministered to the lower classes as in his Sunday school program at Netheravon, he did so in the constant awareness of class distinction. There was never any doubt in his mind about the humanity of the lower classes who made up the vast bulk of his rural parishes, and he had real concern for their moral and spiritual interests, but he was never fully persuaded that their spiritual equality, which he proclaimed in his sermons, compensated for their social inferiority.[48] Practically speaking, the parish priest who scrupulously carried out his spiritual responsibilities, and who ministered to the poor and needy, was doing exactly what he was intended to do, and Sydney and many other parish priests did carry out those duties fairly conscientiously; but such activities did not pave the path to recognition and advancement in the Church. The Netheravon parish registers have not yet come to light, if they still exist, but those of Foston-le-Clay, Sydney's next rural parish, indicate that he ministered almost exclusively to the working classes. An examination of the Foston registers shows, for example, that almost the only fashionable marriage performed during his tenure of nearly twenty years was that of his own daughter in 1828.[49] The other matches were almost invariably between laborers and spinsters. In a very real sense, that of administering the sacraments and conducting worship services, the gentlemen of the Anglican priesthood served the common people. The average Anglican clergyman no doubt aspired to a genteel living where he could rub shoulders with the best of English society, and where his services were likely to be noticed and suitably rewarded; but his more probable fate was a living like Netheravon or Foston, where he could look forward to years of service amongst the laboring classes.

Of Sydney Smith it has been said that: "Under the wit and repartee was a very real concern for the poor and the weak and the oppressed."[50] Like many other statements about him, this one needs to be examined, and his attitude towards the poor must be understood in terms of the social attitudes of his day. He certainly did have a concern for the poor, but that concern was expressed not through a desire to end their poverty, but rather by way of moral elevation and through the relief of their immediate needs. Sydney Smith accepted the social thinking of his age, which was chiefly upper class thought, and which assumed that God had created different classes of people. He assumed that the poor were poor because they had been born that way, and that they were inclined by heredity towards profligacy, ignorance, laziness, drunkenness, etc. His purpose as a priest was to minister to their spiritual well-being, to encourage them to be industrious, thrifty, and obedient to authority, and to discourage "vice," which meant idleness, sexual immorality, drunkenness, and insolence towards their social superiors. Many Smith sermons were obviously directed at the lower classes, and they invariably admonished the laboring class to embrace those virtues and to avoid the vices. "What does it cost, "asked Sydney, "to doff your hat when a gentleman approaches? Gentlemen will notice the civility or incivility, and they could reward courteousness and punish impertinence." In his "Advice to Parishioners" he added:

> When first I came to this parish, Squire Tempest wanted a postillion. John Barton was a good, civil fellow; and in thinking over the names of the village, the Squire thought of Barton, remembered his constant civility, sent for one of his sons, made him postillion, then coachman, then bailiff, and he now holds a farm under the Squire of §500 per annum. Such things are constantly happening.[51]

Within the context of condescension for natural inferiors from above, and respect if not obsequiousness from below, Sydney liked the lower classes, got along well with them, and was concerned about their best interests. A spirit of camaraderie existed between him and those of the working classes with whom he was brought into contact, and he was kind to them, giving them clothes, books, food, and medicines, in addition to moralistic advice. The village children called him "Parson Doctor," and he could be counted upon to have sugar plums or pennies for fruit tarts in his pocket for them. Lady Saba Holland reported that he presented a penny to one urchin, advising him to buy a tart that should "be large and full of juice, Johnny, so that it may run down both corners of the mouth."[52] Mrs. Jane Marcet is quoted as having noticed during a visit that Sydney spent half an hour a day with a laborer who was dying of tuberculosis, splitting his time equally between preparing the poor man spiritually for the next world, and in making his last days in this one as comfortable as possible.[53] Lady

Holland said that he visited an epileptic cottage regularly, despite a strong aversion to that malady as a result of his mother's affliction with it during his youth; and he is reputed to have left an elegant gathering to minister to a feeble newborn child, returning to announce that he had baptized it and had given it a dose of castor oil, thus preparing the child for either world.[54] These may be relatively isolated instances of his concern for common people, but they are not the only such examples mentioned in the various biographies of Sydney Smith, and since most biographers are more interested in associating their subject with famous and powerful men rather than the poor and humble, it may be hypothesized that he certainly had many such contacts with the poor.

Sydney's attitude towards the lower classes generally extended to servants, of whom he said: "People complain of their servants: I never had a bad one; but then I study their comforts ..."[55] The result was good and faithful service and a mutual bond of confidence, it being said that Sydney never lost a servant except by death or marriage, but no trace of egalitarianism was to be found in the relationship. He believed that there must always be social distinctions, "...and it is most devoutly to be wished, that the good sense and firmness of this country may ever preserve them..."[56] He gave his servants security and kind treatment, and he expected obedience and respect from them. He believed in treating them well, but not in spoiling them. On one occasion, Lady Holland reported that he asked "Bunch", a village girl whom he had trained to perform a variety of tasks, including that of butler, whether she preferred roast duck to boiled chicken, and Bunch, "--who had probably never tasted the one or the other in her life," replied, "'Roast duck, please, Sir'," and disappeared.[57] Either Lady Holland was not well informed regarding the surreptitious diet of servants, or Sydney saw to it that his servants' victuals were not above their station.

"If you desire the common people to treat you as a gentleman," he said, "you must conduct yourself as a gentleman should do to them"[58] He annually entertained the local farmers, a class often caricatured comically, and dutifully saw to it that they became properly tipsy, and that they remained suitably respectful.[59] On the other hand, he could be relatively indifferent to the comforts of his farm laborers when his own interests were at stake. In 1821 he mentioned that he saved his grain crop by "injecting great quantities of fermented liquors into the workmen, and making them work all night."[60] In 1829, when he moved to Combe Florey, in Somersetshire, he was delighted by the beauty of Southern England and the presence of more numerous social equals, but he stated, without further comment: "The people are starving, --in the last stage of poverty and depression."[61]

But if Sydney Smith was generally kind and considerate towards the industrious and courteous laboring poor, it can be suggested that he predictably exhibited less sympathy for the more unsavory elements of that class. In 1795 he dispassionately reported that "Mr. Dyke is gone his annual journey with his Cargo of pale females,"[65] which presumably referred to pregnant paupers being removed from the parish to prevent their progeny from becoming a local responsibility. He may also have an aversion to baptizing illegitimate children, for of nine illegitimate baptisms in Combe Florey between 1829 and 1845, he baptized only one. However it is possible that this apparent disapprobation resulted from ill-health, old age, or his absence in London.[63] If he had only condemnation for the less well-behaved of the lower classes, however, his attitude was thoroughly typical of his age, and he did demonstrate a concern for the deserving poor, which, if not as "indefatigable" as his widow asserted, was very real. He conducted Bible classes in his parishes, and he encouraged his wife to direct classes in singing and bonnet-making.[64] He also subdivided several acres of his glebe at Foston and rented them at minimal rents to the poor, which may have improved their physical well-being substantially.[65] It should be pointed out that his social attitudes applied not only to the lowest classes, but also to the middling classes as well. In 1829 he wrote to a friend that his neighbour had died leaving his estate and §4000 a year to a linendraper with eight grown sons, "all brought up to low professions, and they are all coming to live here. What can this be but a visitation of Providence for my Whig Principles? This is indeed a severe dose of the People."[66]

Since Sydney Smith believed that social distinctions were divinely ordained, and since the Church implicitly accepted the existing social order, it is not easy to clearly separate his social philosophy from his religious beliefs. His attitudes, social and religious, were not unusual for his time and he was a man of his age, but his abilities were irrepressible, and they were sufficient for him not only to achieve a growing success in life, but also through that success to rise above his age.

CHAPTER III

The Edinburgh Emancipation, 1798-1803

Sydney's tenure at Netheravon has lasted about four years, and although he had complained of his humdrum existence in the village, his time had not been entirely wasted. He had written sermons, conducted worship services, ministered to his parishoners, and continued his reading. More important perhaps than those activities, he had made important connections with the Hicks-Beach family, which were to be of inestimable value to him in the future. It has been stated already that advancement in the Church depended as much or more on who one was, and whom one knew, than on what one's abilities were and how one used them. Michael Hicks-Beach was a man who counted in the social order, and whose acquaintance opened doors to social acceptance and political or clerical promotion. He had been born Michael Hicks, a person of some importance and he had married the daughter of William Beach, adding her name to his own upon the extinction of the male line in her family. William Beach had purchased a considerable estate at Netheravon, and the Beaches already owned large holdings in the adjoining parish of Fittleton, all of which passed into the hands of Michael Hicks-Beach. He also possessed extensive estates elsewhere, including Williamstrip Park, Gloucestershire, and London properties; and he sat as a Member of Parliament for Cirencester. He was wealthy and influential, and he probably did have a hand in Sydney's original appointment to Netheravon where he played an active role in parish affairs. But even if he did not participate in Sydney's appointment, he certainly was a man of enough influence to have prevented his nomination to that curacy, or to have had him removed.

Michael Hicks-Beach, in short, was the kind of person whose acquaintance and influence was important to a young and ambitious clergyman, and Sydney carefully cultivated his relationship with him and his family. Sydney's pursuit of a close social tie with the Hicks-Beaches at Netheravon was made easier by the fact that he was alone was of a class nearly equivalent to theirs, and also he occupied a position from which he could expedite their wishes in the parish. A relationship between a person of wealth, power, and social station, like that of Hicks-Beach, and one less well-endowed with those gifts, like Sydney Smith, immediately suggests obsequiousness and sycophancy; yet it appears that Sydney trod a narrow path between a sturdy independence of mind and a servile truckling to his social superiors, but with a decided lean to the former. He treated his betters with respect, and he obviously tried to establish and further social contacts with them. He attempted to ingratiate himself with them on most occasions but without stooping beneath the dignity of one gentleman dealing with another. He admired and respected wealth, rank and power, but his admiration did not extend to toadying to the great and mighty, and if they expected servility from him they were more often than not, disappointed. Very likely his independence of spirit made a better and more lasting impression on them than an imitation of Uriah Heep would have. He was condescending to the lower classes, but he did not reserve his occasionally sharp tongue and his contumely expressly for them. A story is recorded of a baronet who came to Sydney complaining. Sydney inquired of him, "What is the matter? ...are any of our institutions in danger?" The baronet replied, "No, but I have just been with Brougham...but, upon my word, he treated me as if I were a fool."

"Never Mind," said Sydney, "he thought you knew it."[1]

Sydney also engaged in a bout of repartee with the Prince of Wales, later Prince Regent and George IV, in which Sydney clearly took second place, but not by intent. The encounter took place on 30 July, 1807, at Holland House, and various accounts of it have been written in various places. In essence what took place was that Sydney was holding forth, addressing the whole company rather than the Prince alone, as was his custom. "The wickedest man who ever lived," he said, "was the Regent, the Duke of Orleans, and he was a Prince." The Prince of Wales quickly retorted: "The wichedest man who ever lived was Cardinal Dubois, the Regent's prime minister, and he was a priest."[2]

These are extraordinary examples since Sydney was generally more respectful of his betters in Church, State and Society, but even so he was frequently thought to be bumptious. Lady Saba Holland mentioned an account of his arrival in Yorkshire and his attendance at a large dinner party which included the Archbishop. During the dinner party Sydney dominated the conversation and charmed the company, somewhat to the consternation of the Archbiship, who did not expect such a performance from a new clergyman in an inferior position.[3] Sydney knew that his future might well be marked for good or for ill by powerful individuals, and he treated them considerately, even humbly, but without abandoning his self-respect. He carried out the parochial policies of the Hicks-Beaches in Netheravon, making himself as agreeable to them as possible. There is no evidence that he ever disagreed with their policies, or did anything for them that seemed personally repugnant to him. His rewards were close relations with the family during their visits to Netheravon, invitations to visit them at Williamstrip, and privileges in enjoying some of the Netheravon properties during their absence.

Sydney's wit and scholarship made a lasting impression on Michael Hicks-Beach, who asked him to inquire into the advisability of sending his son to a German university. Sydney complied, and no doubt pleased his patron by his ready sources of information, and Hicks-Beach asked him to accompany young Michael as his tutor-advisor, and at a substantial salary. The university finally settled on was Weimar, which impressed Sydney as being sufficiently enlightened and pro-British. Sydney's continental plans for his pupil extended to the hiring of a tutor in German; but alarums and excursions resulting from Napoleon's inconsiderate campaigns, forced a last-minute cancellation of the plans for study in Germany. Sydney offered to withdraw from the agreement, but Hicks-Beach agreed to consider the substitution of the University of Edinburgh, where his son might prepare himself for admission to Oxford. Even at that late date, April, 1797, Sydney reported to his father (who did have a genuine obsession for money) that "nothing was said of Salary, nor can be I suppose with propriety till our plan is definitely arranged."[4] In November, he told his father that he preferred to introduce the subject of salary "by Letter, for I am sure I shall not do it well in conversation,"[5] and on 31 December, 1797, he wrote: "Nothing but the greatest shyness in the world has prevented Mr. Beach from settling with me upon the Subject of Salary."[6] An undated, but obviously later note contained the details of the agreement, which were that Sydney was to be paid $1000 for a two-year period, plus expenses.[7]

Sydney's relations with the Hicks-Beaches transcended the usual tutor-parent relationship, they remained friends and associates, even if Hicks-Beach played the role of primus inter pares. As Sydney had said to his father:

> I do not consider my connescion with
> Mr. Beach, in the light of a common
> connescion between Parent, & tutor.
> -Long before they had any views of this
> kind I escperienced from Mr. & Mrs. B.
> the greatest hospitality, kindness, &
> regard, which I never can, or will for-
> get- I cannot from my situation in life
> wave all consideration of Salary...[8]

When the details were agreed upon, Sydney and young Michael set out for Edinburgh, beginning their trip by a Grand Tour of Britain, the usual Grand Tour of the Continent being impossible as a result of Napoleon's campaigns.

Before his departure on this lesser Grand Tour, however, Sydney's attention was drawn in another direction, which proved ultimately to be of great importance to him. Also in 1797, December he traveled to Bowood, Lord Lansdowne's great country estate, where he performed the marriage ceremony for his brother Bobus and Miss Caroline Vernon. By this marriage Bobus allied himself, and Sydney indirectly with the Vernon family and through his wife's two half-sisters, to the Fox and Petty families. Henry Vassall Fox, the third Baron Holland, was one of the richer and more influential men in England, the possessor of Holland House, and politically a Whig. William Petty, better known as Lord Shelburne before he bacame first Marquis of Lansdowne, was also a Whig who had made Lansdowne House a political center of the first magnitude. Both Lord Holland and Lord Lansdowne were related by blood, marriage, or political interest to virtually every important Whig in the nation. Such a company might have intimidated a lesser man who was a mere unbeneficed clergyman, but Sydney appears to have made a good impression on these great people, which, if of no immediate benefit to him, did serve him well in the long run. If the idea of switching party allegiance had ever crossed his mind, and it does not appear that it ever did, his connections with these great Whig aristocrats and the almost infinite possibilities presented by that relationship, made such a political transfer most improbable for him.

Returning from that etheral society of potential patrons to the more mundane company of the Hicks-Beaches, Sydney and the young Michael Hicks-Beach set forth on their trip to Edinburgh. They travelled in easy stages, for they were pressed neither for time nor money; and Sydney, who loathed riding horses, found the alternate solution of poor coaches and bad roads quite vexing. They took about six weeks to complete the trip, and in the process Sydney saw most of the obligatory sights, and made most of the usual comments on them. On the subject of summer homes at the Lakes, he asked, in a letter to Mrs. Hicks-Beach:

> Is it necessary to sit upon boards painfully hard, and put your feet upon malthouse floors because you retire to a beautiful lake for 2 or 3 of the hot months of the year?- There is surely some medium between mind, and marble, and huccaback, and brocade.

And on the subject of Skiddaw he wrote:

> Off we set, Michael, the guide and myself at one in the morning to gain the summit of Skiddaw. I who find it rather difficult to stick upon my horse on the plainest roads, did not find that facility increased by the darkness of the morning, or the precipitous paths we had to ascend. I made no manner of doubt, but that I should fall down into the town of Keswick the next morning and be picked up by the Town Beadle dead in a gutter. Moreover I was moved a little for my reputation for as I had a bottle of brandy in my pocket, placed there by the special exhortations of the guide and Landlord, the Keswick Coroner and jury would infallibly have brought me in "<u>a Parson as died of drinking</u>" ...a more <u>woe-begone piteous face than Michael</u> put on you never say; no Taylor tried, cast, and condemned for filching small parcels of Cloth, ever looked so unhappy.[9]

Once arrived in Edinburgh Sydney took lodgings at 38 South Hanover Street where he and Michael stayed for a year, moving at the end of that time to another house just around the corner at 19 Queen Street. There Sydney remained until he returned with his new bride in the fall of 1800 when he rented a small house at 46 George Street. Michael proved to be an adequate, neither inspired nor inspiring, student; and Sydney became more of a companion than a tutor to him. He made regular and surprisingly modern reports on his progress to his parents, noting that his complexion was improving (Sydney believed as a result of sea bathing) and also that he was unenthusiastic about his studies but generally good-natured, and that he spent too much time dressing and primping. Michael became sulky when taxed with that accusation, but Sydney laughed him out of his sullenness. He concluded that Michael liked horses and dogs better than books, but that he was willing to make at least the minimal effort towards learning.[10] Little more need be said regarding Michael Hicks-Beach, who went on to Christ Church, Oxford. His place with Sydney was taken by his brother William, and Sydney also acquired another pupil in the person of Alexander Gordon, an illegitimate sone of Lord Aberdeen.[11] From all appearances, his pupils made enough progress to satisfy their parents, and although none of them ever gained great renown they seem to have retained an affection for their tutor and their experiences in Edinburgh.

Scotland is a beautiful country, and Edinburgh is one of her finest cities. Sydney Smith came to love both even though, as a <u>Sassenach</u>, he felt constrained to poke fun at Scots customs, language, and thought ever after. He was particularly taken with the beauty, the society, and the intellect of Edinburgh, because he came to that city after four years in a rural retreat. A remarkably gifted intellectual community resided in Edinburgh, centering around the University which was undoubtedly superior at that time in every respect, to both Oxford and Cambridge. Whereas students at Oxford and Cambridge plodded lethargically through the stultifying program of Classical studies, sports, and social gatherings, Edinburgh students were stimulated by the ideas of political economy, the French Revolution and Scottish metaphysics. These were subjects that attracted the more liberal elements like Sydney Smith to Scotland, and which horrified the timid and hidebound traditionalists. It is amusing to see that as late as 1845 the writer of Sydney's obituary in the London <u>Times</u> attacked his memory on the basis of his association with the University of Edinburgh which was, at least in his opinion, an indirect casting of aspersions on the quality and Englishness of the great English Universities.[12]

Sydney entered into the spirit of the university enthusiastically, and into the politics of the city as well. As early as 31 May, 1798, he reported that "There has been some little Fracas here in the Corporation-The Subject of Contention seems to be who should serve Mr. Dundas with the most implicit obedience. -he is omnipotent in this place."[13] Sydney had a particularly violent aversion to the power of Henry Dundas, later Lord Melville, mainly because of the peculiar political system under which the Scots, in exchange for numerous civil and military offices, always supported the government. Their political conformity, which was intended to further Scottish interests by providing extensive employment throughout the Empire, was not complemented by conformity to English customs or English thought.

Edinburgh was an intellectual capital of the English-speaking world, and in those years, probably one that was equalled only by London. The university was organized along continental rather than English lines, and it was developing a tradition of creative thought which was exemplified by men like Dugald Stewart and Thomas Brown in philosophy, and John Playfair in mathematics. The liberal reputation of the university attracted the sons of Whig aristocrats from England who were repelled by the royalist-clerical aspects of Oxford and Cambridge. These men chose to send their sons first, to Edinburgh for a few years for its educational and intellectual benefits, and then to Oxford or Cambridge for their social advantages. Prior to the French Revolution they had sent their sons either on the Grand Tour or to a continental university, but when Napoleon's activities closed the continent to them, they thought of Edinburgh.

Sydney was quite taken with the intellectualism of Edinburgh, and he noted in December, 1797: "There is a professor here a Dugald Stewart who beats every speaker I ever heard in manner & acting;"[14] but later Sydney expressed grave doubts about the values of the abstractions of Scottish philosophy. Scots philosophers, he said, "...reason upon man as they would reason upon X, they pursue Truth, without caring if it be useful truth. They are more fond of disputing on mind and matter than on anything which can have reference to the real world...."[15] He believed that the Edinburgh philosophy had infected the entire nation, and for that reason it was safe to make love to Scots ladies, for...

> ...love, tho' a very acute disorder in Andalusia, puts on a very Chronic shape in these high northern latitudes; for

> first the lover must prove <u>metapheez-
> ically</u> that she ought to yield; and
> then in the fifth or 6th year of court-
> ship, or rather argument, if the sum-
> mer is tolerably warm, and oatmeal
> plenty, the fair one yields.[16]

In 1808 his impatience with the pure intellect of the philosophers was expressed in a letter to Lady Caroline Holland in which he said:

> I take the liberty to send you two brace
> of grouse, curious, because killed by a
> Scotch metaphysician; in other and bet-
> ter language they are mere ideas, shot by
> other ideas, out of a pure intellectual
> notion called a gun.... The modification
> of matter called Grouse which accompanies
> this note is not in the common apprehen-
> sion of Edinburgh considered to be depen-
> dent upon a first cause, but to have ex-
> isted from All Eternity.[17]

Nonetheless, Sydney attended Dugald Stewart's lectures, and both Stewart and his student and successor Thomas Brown became close friends of Sydney. Although he was fascinated by their thought and undoubtedly influenced by it in some ways, he did not adopt it as his own.

Church-going Scots intellectuals had been appalled at the skeptical implications of the philosophy of David Hume which carried many of the lines of thought of Newton and Locke to their logical conclusions. They inclined towards the "common sense" philosophy of Thomas Reid, another Scot, who accepted historically proven intuitive knowledge as truth. Reid's thought was a refutation to Hume's insistence that no knowledge exists apart from perception, and also to Bishop Berkeley's claim that ideas alone have reality. Reid's common sense philosophy meant that thinking men could still accept traditional Christianity as being historically verified, while subjecting the material world to a different kind of scrutiny.[18]

In his later lectures,[19] Sydney Smith indicated clearly that he had some understanding of Locke, Hume, Reid, and Dugald Stewart, but metaphysics was not his forte; and if he inclined towards any philosophical system it was that of William Paley, a contemporary, who was also Archdeacon of Carlisle. Sydney's thought, life, and writing bear so many traces of Paley's influence that one is tempted to assume that his remark from Netheravon to the effect that he was going to use his exile as an opportunity to read theology,[20] meant that he would read Paley, who was at that time in vogue. Like Sydney, Paley was a clergyman and a rationalist who wrote well and with the greatest clarity. He followed Locke in dividing his concept of law into three parts: the law of honour, the law of the land, and divine law. The law of honor, he felt, was not adequate to insure a proper regard for the general welfare; the law of the land was not always extensive enough to cover obvious transgression that did not violate its letter; so that divine law, as expressed through Scripture, was the only sufficient law. From this reasoning he derived his definition: "Virtue is the doing good to mankind, in obedience to the will of God, and for the sake of everlasting happiness."[21] Such a statement might almost sum up Sydney's purpose in life, and it is safe to assume that that formula had some bearing on it.

Paley, as a clergyman like Sydney, was compelled to prove the truth of revelation, which he did by the time-honored "argument from design" in the universe, and on the basis of which he could assume the existence of God. His evidences of God were entirely external; and his philosophy which largely ignored the theological content of religion was enthusiastically seconded by the life and writings of Sydney Smith. God to both of them was the great watchmaker of the eithteenth century who had performed miracles only rarely and then long before Sydney's time. But miracles were unnecessary, other than as evidences of the divinity of Christ or the power of God, for the very good reason that the watchmaker's instrument ran smoothly enough without them. "...the age of miracles," Sydney said in one of his sermons, "is no more, and the necessity for their occurrence removed by the diffusion and security of the Gospel...."[22] Like Sydney Smith, Paley had little interest in metaphysics.

Despite his philosophical background being largely shaped by Paley, and his impatience with Scottish metaphysical abstractions, Sydney admired Edinburgh intellect so much that he said that the academic community there never saw a fool or a common person.[23] Alert to the avant garde principles of free enterprise, he was keenly aware of the role of the Scots in the formulation of the doctrines of laissez-faire capitalism.[24] Edinburgh,

49

intellectually, was truly an emancipation for the eager young cleric who sought out Scots learning for his pupil and himself with the avidity of a convert.

One branch of learning in which the Scots clearly surpassed their condescending Sassenach neighbours, and in which it is asserted that Sydney had already shown some interest while at Oxford, was medicine. In 1799 he said: "I attend the hospitals where I learn the elements of a puke & the rudiments of purging the viscera rustica will pay for this when I am settled in my parish...."[25] In a charity sermon preached for the purpose of raising funds for the Scotch Lying-in Hospital, he lauded that institution not only for its service of Christian love and charity, but also as one of the classrooms for the Edinburgh medical school whose graduates were known and respected throughout the world.[26] Sydney did acquire some medical training in Edinburgh which later was to be of great benefit to him and to his parishioners. He also performed a double service in that he recommended John Allen, who was a poor but talented medical man of Edinburgh, to Lord Holland to be his family physician. Allen made such an excellent impression that he was retained by the Hollands, with whom he remained for the rest of his life on terms which virtually made him a member of the family.[27] Sydney thus ingratiated himself with the powerful Hollands, and planted one of his friends in their affluent midst. Likewise, the Hollands were pleased to have a good physician who was also good company, and who came to double as a Whig strategist.

Just as Scotland provided a fine physician, so she also produced some excellent tutors, whom Sydney recommended to his friends. He wrote to Lady Grey, saying, "A Scotchman full of knowledge, quiet, humble assiduous civil, and virtuous you will easily get; and I will send you such a one per coach...."[28] Nonetheless he could not contain his wit when it came to Scots tutors, and in 1809, in a letter to Lady Holland, he wrote:

> You are aware that it is customary to fumigate Scotch Tutors. They are excellent men but require this little preliminary Caution. They are apt also to break the Church Windows, get behind an hedge and fling Stones at the clergyman of the parish, and betray other little Symptoms of irreligion; but these you must not mind.

> Send me word if he has any trick of this
> kind. I have droves of them, and know
> how to manage them.[29]

Despite his admiration for Scots learning he is also reputed to have said that "Greek was a witch, and, as such, could not cross running water, nor ever get beyond the Tweed."[30] And if the Scots produced scholars and learned lawyers, they also produced bores and pedants, which tedium they attempted to pass off as wisdom. Lady Holland recalled an account of one of Edinburgh's most notorious bores whose avocation was the North Pole, and having trapped Francis Jeffrey, later editor of the Edinburgh Review, in a narrow lane, the bore was shocked when Jeffery damned the North Pole and fled. "Oh, my dear fellow," replied Sydney to his outraged complaint, "never mind; no one minds what Jeffrey says, you know; he is a privileged person; he respects nothing....Why, you will scarcely believe it, but it is not more than a week ago that I heard him speak disrespectfully of the equator!"[31] Sydney also believed verbosity to be a general failing of the Scots, who, he asserted, "...can never condense, they always begin a few days before the flood, and come gradually down to the reign of George the Third forgetful of nothing but the shortness of human life and the volatility of human attention."[32]

Sydney enjoyed nothing more than poking fun at Scottish rationalism. He wrote to John Allen in 1814 alleging that if he were in a terrible storm at sea and in immediate danger of foundering, and if the sailors held up the image of a saint and the storm abated, "...you would be more sorry for the encouragement of superstition than rejoiced for the preservation of your life, --and so would every other man born, and bred in Edinburgh.... I should not care a farthing if the storm had generated a thousand new, and revived as many old Saints."[33] He wrote again to Allen in 1841 telling him cheerfully that "I never see you without thinking of the thousands of years you will be boiling in seas of burning Liquid, calling in vain upon the clergy to pull you our, [The Rev.] John Vane and [The Rev. John] Image delighting in your torments."[34] And in a letter to Lady Grey in 1839, Sydney described a fire at Lord Lilford's in which "Lady Holland woke up Allen, who upon hearing the crackling of the flames, and smelling the smoke and seeing Lady Hd conceived he had slipt off in the night to a very serious place at an high temperature--; he attempted to recollect a prayer, but entirely failed...."[35] In his recommendation of Allen to Lord Holland he said that Allen had been raised "in this monastery of infidels,"[36] despite which he was later to say: "...the reduction of his legs is a pure and unmixed good; they are enormous, --they are clerical! He has the creed of a philosopher and the legs of a clergyman; I never saw such legs, --at least belonging to a layman."[37]

Sydney believed that Scottish women, at least women of the working classes, had larger feet, which were usually bare, and thicker legs than their English counterparts. "When I lived there," he said, "very few maids had shoes and stockings, but plodded about the house with feet as big as family Bibles, and legs as large as portmanteaus."[38] But of the Scots generally he also said: "...they are larger in body than the English, and the women in my opinion (I say it to my shame) handsomer than English women...."[39] Scotland, "for a literary man," he believed, "...is the most eligible situation in the Islands. It unites good libraries, liberally manag'd, learned men without any other System than that of pursuing truth, --very good general society--large healthy virgins, with mild pleasing countenances, & white swelling breasts...."[40] On other Scottish female characteristics he paid tribute to those of the Duchess of Atholl, whose horses taking flight "...she flung herself out of the chaise--& escaped injury by lighting upon her bum a part upon which she might certainly descend from much greater heights, with equal impunity."[41]

The pretended fertility of Scottish women, which is readily explained by the chilliness of the climate, was well known, and Sydney predictably commented on that subject:

> The despair is universal at Lord Melville's not making a part of the administration. As long as he is in office the Scotch may beget younger sons with the most perfect impunity. He sends them by loads to the East Indias, and all over the world--a most important bounty to this country where every lady has 12 or 13 Children; and as evil communication corrupts good manners ladies who have long resided here may catch this unfortunate fecundity.[42]

On the other hand, he hoped for some of that formidable fecundity in the marriage of his friend John Archibald

Murray, an eminent Scottish lawyer who was also one of the Edinburgh reviewers, to Mary Rigby in 1826. Miss Rigby had a fortune of §60,000 and was accomplished in Greek, mathematics, and music, and a meeting of the two was arranged by Sydney's wife.

> Ten days finished the matter; indeed she has no time to lose since she is 39. I never saw two longer fatter lovers, for she is as big as Murray. They looked enormous as they were making love in the plantations. She is so fond of Murray that she pretends to love porridge, cold weather and metaphysics. Seriously speaking it is a very good marriage, and acting under the direction of medical men, with perseverance and the use of stimulating diet there may be an heir to the house of Henderland.[43]

Sydney's enthusiasm for Scotland and things Scottish was not dimmed by the lack of public sanitation, which was shocking to him even though similar facilities in England were undoubtedly not optimal. Writing to Hicks-Beach in 1798, he said:

> No smells were ever equal to Scotch smells. It is the School of Physic; walk the streets, and you would imagine that every Medical man had been administering Cathartics to every man woman and child in the Town. Yet the place is uncommonly beautiful, and I am in a constant balance between admiration and trepidation--
>
> Taste guides my Eye, where e'ver new beauties spread
> While prudence whispers, 'look before you tread'.[44]

Writing to a friend later in the same year, he said that Edinburgh seemed to have "...a total want of all foecal propriety and excremental delicacy.-- They seem to vye with one another here in the work of concoction, to glory in the work of the lower bowels and to revel in the Alvine discharge...."[45]

The age of Sydney Smith was not a great age of cleanliness, but he saw, or thought he saw, greater filth in Scotland than in England. He is credited with saying that Lord Palmerston's style of oratory was like a person washing his hands: "...the Scotch members don't know what he is doing."[46] "When an human creature is lean, lousy, and Logical we know him to be a Scotchman..."[47] wrote Sydney to Lord Holland in 1812; and, he was equally critical of Scots table manners during the Turbot season:

> I never witness'd any thing equal to the voracity with which this Savory monster of the deep is devour'd... a serious silence prevails at table--the passage of the voice is entirely shup up--people are hermetically choak'd--no sooner is the mouthful reduc'd to atoms of Turbot--than another than has been resting impatiently against the Lips & panting for maceration is admitted dripping with liquid Lobster .... the Eyes stare--the Garments are loosen'd--the Labor is intense....[48]

Making fun of Scotsmen is a grand sport, and no nationality enters into it with greater zest than the Scots themselves, so Sydney's generally kindhearted jibes should not be taken as having offensive intent. Much to the contrary, no nationality was exempt from his exuberant wit as he hurled witticisms indiscriminately at Americans, Irishmen, Frenchmen, Russians, Germans, and Chinese. But, if anything, he reserved his sharpest arrows for his own countrymen, and he never deviated from his genuine affections for the nation of thistle and heather. In 1803 he wrote to Francis Jeffrey who had suceeded him as the editor of the Edinburgh Review, and said:

> I left Edinburgh with great heaviness of heart. I knew that I was leaving & was ignorant to what I was going - my good fortune will be very great if I should ever again fall into the society of so many liberal, correct, and instructed men....[49]

He wrote again to Jeffrey in 1819, to reminisce:

> When shall I see Scotland again? Never shall I forget the happy days I passed there amidst odious smells, barbarous sounds, bad suppers, excellent hearts,

and most enlightened, and cultivated understandings.[50]

Sydney Smith had come of age in England, but it is Scotland which can claim credit for having provided him with both the means and the stimulation necessary for his continued intellectual growth. He continued tutoring, and he maintained and extended his connections with the Edinburgh _literati_, and presumably went on with his dabbling in medicine. As tutor to Michael Hicks-Beach, and later to his brother William, he found himself in comfortable financial circumstances. He wrote to a friend in October, 1799, that he had not decided whether or not to go on tutoring, but he added quickly that the money would probably incline him towards continuation.[51] A few months later he informed Mrs. Hicks-Beach that he had an income of §600 per year, and that he felt secure enough to marry. His income at this time seems to have been made up of §500 a year from Hicks-Beach, plus §100 from his fellowship at New College which he would be forced to relinquish when he married. In June, 1800, he wrote to Hicks-Beach, saying:

> I have to thank you my dr Sr for the note of hand you gave me for §500. I will make no apology for speaking to you on that Subject, because I am a poor man and I must look to my provision. It is a matter of indifference to me whether this money remains in yr hands or in the funds; I shall think it equally safe in one, or the other -- if you keep it, I hope you will have no objection to pay me 4 pr Ct for it, which at the present price of Funds 63 or thereabouts is surely reasonable....If you do not like to be troubled with a concern of this nature, I will thank you to order the money to be paid to Messrs Drummond Bankers Charing Cross, who will place it in the funds for me.[52]

Here is an assertion by Sydney that he was a "poor man," but by that description he obviously meant that he did not possess a substantial estate, either in land or in other property, and that he depended upon his salary. It is illuminating that, despite his claims of poverty, and his impending marriage, he asks Hicks-Beach to hold his salary and to pay him interest on it.

Marriage for an English gentleman, lay or clerical, was not to be entered into unadvisedly or lightly, but reverently, discreetly, advisedly, and soberly; which meant not only that he should consider his future bride's wealth and social status vis a vis his own, but also the feelings of his family, the possibilities of political or clerical advantage and disadvantage, his own emotional feelings toward her, and even hers toward him. Sydney's intended was Catherine Amelia Pybus, who was the daughter of a London banking family, an heiress to a modest fortune, and a friend of Sydney's sister. He had decided to marry her earlier, certainly as early as 1798, for in that year he announced his engagement to his father and asked his permission to marry. His courtship, which was as far as can be known, his only love affair, was not carried out unadvisedly or lightly, and he told his father that he knew "but one woman who unites fortune, understanding & good disposition in a degree that makes an alliance desirable with her...." He added," ...at the proper time of asking it, nobody means to marry -- at the usual time of asking it nobody means to follow advice, unless it agrees with his previous determination." Obviously not engaged in light courting and having already had his differences with his father, Sydney was determined on the match.[53] Catherine Pybus was enthusiastic about Sydney as was her widowed mother, but Catherine's brother considered an unbeneficed and Whiggish clergyman to be beneath his sister's station in life. Also, from the tone of Sydney's letter to his father, one can infer that that cantankerous old man did not approve. Although Sydney had asked his father for a financial settlement to enable him to marry in 1798, it is fairly obvious that he expected no money from him, but rather at the very best, a grudging acquiescence. "you have done enough for me," he said, and "I am more obliged to you for the education you have given me than if you had put me in a way to get rich." He admitted to his father that he would not do as well as his Bobus had in marrying, but "...when I look upon my pretensions I really think I have done as well as I had fair reason to expect -- & when I look to my heart--I am quite content."[54]

In her memoir of her husband, Catherine Smith asserts that Robert Smith's reply to Sydney's request for a financial settlement was "not one penny,"[55] and although her testimony is open to question, it does appear that Sydney received no further financial assistance from his father. Nonetheless, especially since he probably did not expect parental aid, he continued his plans to marry; and it is interesting to note that he observed Thomas Robert Malthus's injunction not to marry until one was able to support a family. He did not do so because he was a Malthusian (although he was), but because he was a gentleman who was concerned about his future and that of his family. The error of Malthus, if it was an error, was that he, too, was an English gentleman and therefore thought like a gentleman. But, being what he was, he assumed that his attitudes were universally true, and that his admonition against marriage without adequate provision, while universally desirable, was equally universally inapplicable. Thus, even in England it could reasonably apply only to the privileged classes. In September, 1799, Sydney informed a friend that he was intending to marry, and the following month, apparently in reply to an incredulous answer to his previous letter, Sydney said, "How can you my good friend misname the sober communications of a priest, the ravings of a Bacchanal?"[56] In another letter he told his father that he was preparing to marry, but that the arrangements were being held up by the lawyers who were handling the details of Catherine Pybus' estate. In the meantime, he said, "I am very happy - preaching - & Studying & teaching without a moments interval of time __"[57]

Sydney left Scotland in the spring of 1800, and he and Catherine Amelia Pybus were united in the holy sacrament of matrimony on 2 July, 1800, in the parish church at Cheam. Oddly enough both Catherine Smith and Lady Saba Holland gloss over the actual wedding, so it may be assumed that it was less than a gala affair, and it was probably boycotted by both Sydney's father and Catherine's brother. A visit by the newlywed couple to Sydney's father seems to have resulted in a debacle, and a tour with the Hicks-Beaches brought on a quarrel and a near-estrangement of Sydney and the elder Hicks-Beach. The full details of the misunderstanding involved a slight, real or imagined, of Catherine by Mrs. Hicks-Beach, who, Catherine claimed, invariably took the best and most comfortable accomodations for herself. Perhaps Mrs. Hicks-Beach showed condescension towards her, or perhaps she only thought she had, but her feathers were ruffled, and Sydney seconded her indignation.[58] The ever contentious Robert Smith wrote to Sydney as late as three years after the fact to accuse Catherine of having caused the breach, by then long since healed, by her "pride and folly"; but Sydney defended her warmly, saying the reverse was true.[59] Partial explanations and partial apologies assuaged the situation, and Hicks-Beach continued as Sydney's patron for another three years. This incident is interesting also in that it shows with some clarity the fact that while Sydney courted the favor of the great and the rich, he was neither a sycophant nor a toady. Faced with a choice of supporting his bride in a complaint that may well have been wholly imaginary or challenging his benefactor, upon whom he was almost totally dependent, he appears to have chosen the latter course without hesitation.

Saba Holland recounts a story that Sydney, shortly after his wedding, rushed into a room where his new bride was seated, threw six small and badly worn silver teaspoons into her lap, and said, "...there Kate, you lucky girl, I give you all my fortune!"[60] His wit took many forms, but perhaps most characteristically it had an elfin and spontaneous quality about it, and his earliest biographers, those who knew him, insist that this spontaneity was typical of him. He burst forth with it constantly, not only at fashionable dinners, but also with his children, friends, servants and tradesmen.

In actual fact, of course Sydney was not poor. He had at least §500 banked with Hicks-Beach, who presented him with an additional §750 as a wedding gift. It is interesting to note that in reading over his letters from 1794 he speaks only rarely of being poor; and that it was in his later years that he recalled this phase of his life as having been lived in poverty. But rich or poor, and he was certainly neither, his marriage was an unqualified success. Catherine Amelia proved to be an excellent spouse and mother; and if she was not his intellectual equal, she made up for it by her charm and sociability. Sydney's definition of marriage as "a pair of shears, so joined that they cannot be separated; often moving in opposite directions, yet always punishing anyone who comes between them,"[61] could well apply to his own marriage.

Sydney married in 1800 and returned to Scotland to take up his tutoring and his studies once again. He had been preaching before his marriage at Charlotte Chapel in Edinburgh, and he continued to do so after his return. Since the Scottish Episcopalians were not required to keep records, and either they kept none, or more likely they kept only the minimal records necessary for the functioning of the chapel, and they made little effort to preserve those. Therefore, almost no record of his activities at Charlotte Chapel, apart from his own letters and his published sermons, have survived. His letters, however, sketchy as they are, do indicate that he underwent a religious crisis at Edinburgh. He was not attracted by the Church of Scotland, which he regarded as tedious, even though he admired the interest in religion and the regular church attendance of the Scots. It would be incorrect to call what happened to him a conversion, for it had little to do with his faith in God, but it appears that he felt compelled to reassess his situation in life and to decide whether or not to continue in the Church. He enjoyed the life he was leading in Edinburgh, but apart from his occasional preaching at Charlotte Chapel, he was acting essentially as a layman in his tutoring and his own study. His failure to advance quickly in the Church undoubtedly discouraged him, and he was jealous of men he considered to be less talented than himself who, because of better connections and more acceptable politics, had moved ahead of him. He had some prospects for preferment in the Church, but they appeared, in 1798, to be very distant and dim; and he seems to have considered some other vocation, such as tutoring, on a more permanent basis. He was favorably impressed with the religiosity of the Scots as compared to that of the English, but the Church of Scotland, he said years later, baffled him.

> It is in vain that I study the subject of the Scotch Church. ...I know it has something to do with oatmeal, but beyond that I am in utter darkness.[62]

Of the piety of Scots he had no doubt, as he observed in a letter to Mrs. Hicks-Beach in 1798:

> In England I maintain that (except amongst Ladies in the middle class of life) there is no religion at all. The Chergy of England have no more influence over the people at large than the Cheesemongers of England have. In Scotland the Clergy are extremely active in the discharge of their functions, and are from the hold they have on the minds of the people a very important body of men.[63]

Sydney respected the Scots clergy, and he noticed that

common people in Scotland were more often critics than pupils of the clergy. His comments on English religion, coming as they did from a minister of the Established Church, seem to have upset Mrs. Hicks-Beach, for he wrote s second letter to her about five weeks later in which he said:

> You may depend upon it my dr Madam that observations upon the Clergy are just. Religion (I am sorry to say) is much like Heraldry, an antiquated concern; a few people attend to the one and the other, but the world laughs at them for engaging in such a superannuated pursuit. In 50 years more the whole art of going to church--how the Squire's Lady put on her best hat and cloak, and how the Squire bowed to the parson after church and how the parson dined with the Squire, and all these ceremonies of worship will be in the hands of the antiquarians....[64]

His disillusionment with the Church of England seemed to be complete, but it is appropriate to note that although he says "Religion (I am sorry to say)...is antiquated," it can be argued that his only regret was that if the Church was foundering, his hopes of ease, comfort, and dignity in a rich living would go down with it. Still, ample evidence exists that he was a convinced Christian and a believing Anglican in addition to being a professional priest.

The issue of whether or not Sydney Smith was a sincere Christian has been befogged since his time by charges that his later political and literary activities were unbecoming to a clergyman. For the most part, these charges were made by sectarians whom he had reviled in his reviews and by pompus critics who took offense at such quips as "What a pity it is that in England we have no amusements but vice and religion,"[65] or, "Don't you know, as the French say, there are three sexes--men, women, and clergymen?"[66] It is possible that Sydney, despairing of success in the Church, came to see the Church of England, as did his biographer Andre Chevrillon as being an empty form of a church whose heart no longer beat; an immobile, dead religion of a society which no longer knew anxiety, effort, or aspiration; a society which had divided England among itself and believed that since it was in the best of all possible worlds, there was no reason to dream of another world.[67] And such was, in many ways, the Anglican Church at its worst. Yet even at its worst a hearbeat could be heard and the clergy still could prick the conscience of society; and, there were some, Sydney Smith among them, who could dream of heaven. John R. H. Moorman in his work, A History of the Church in England, said flatly that Sydney was a "publicist rather than a Churchman; he had been ordained of necessity rather than choice and always regretted that it had been his lot. He disliked parish life and kept away from his flock as much as he reasonably could."[68] He is correct, of course, in that Sydney was ordained as a second choice, and that he probably disliked parish life; but he did not dislike parish life per se so much as he preferred London and Society, and he did participate in parochial activities with some enthusiasm. His status as a gentlemen-priest was no doubt a detriment to the establishment of the kind of parochial life that is expected of a twentieth-century clergyman, but even in this respect he was typical of his age. As for being a publicist rather than a churchman, he was ahead of his time in realizing the power of the press to embarrass Authority and to bring about overdue change. The reforms he sought were needed, and certainly it cannot be said that his desire to further religious toleration and to extend justice was un-Christian. Many considered that clergymen should not meddle in political or social questions, but then, as now, the line separating the purely religious sphere from the political or social one could not always be easily drawn. Moorman is also correct in that Sydney is remembered for his work as a publicist rather than his career as a priest, but; then again, what priest is remembered for having served a parish well? Of the eleven thousand clergymen in England during his time, what memorial apart from a stained glass window or a dusty tablet remains of the majority of those who dedicated their lives to their parishes? Clergymen of that description no doubt endeared themselves to their parishioners, but recognition came more commonly through literary achievements, familial bonds, or through preaching before important congregations. The fact that Edmund Cartwright was an inventor did not make him a bad priest, nor did Gregor Mendel's work in genetics make him a bad monk. Sydney Smith's work as a publicist set him apart from much of his contemporary clergy, but it did not prevent him from being a churchman. Moorman is fully correct in his assessment of Sydney Smith only if by his statement he means that Sydney chose the avenue of political publication as his path to preferment. In 1798, discouraged by his prospects in the Church, Sydney seems to have considered abandoning all hope of a clerical career, and to have contemplated other possibilities. He was ambitious and materialistic, and what persuaded him to continue his pursuit of a career in the Church is not clear, but in that year he wrote to his father, saying: "I am almost confident that if I do not distinguish myself in this line I shall never distinguish myself at all--."[69] From this time forward it does not appear that he ever wavered from that resolution to remain a clergyman. He already had a patron in the person of Hicks-Beach, and he had friends who might well assist him, especially if the fortunes of the Whig party changed for the better. In the meantime he continued to tutor and to preach at Charlotte Chapel.

Sydney's career as a preacher is difficult to deal with for a number of reasons. It has been mentioned that he employed pulpit language when preaching, which meant chiefly that he used the customary and expected vocabulary of contemporary preachers; and he did so in direct violation of his own warning to preachers to avoid platitudes and trite phrases such as "Putting off the old man--and putting on the new man." He also published various editions of his sermons, and although some are clearly identified as having been preached at a certain time and place, many others are not. He objected to the cold and laconic style of preaching which was so common in the Anglican Church, and he used as an example the priest who clings to the cushion, eyes "riveted upon his book, who speaks of the ecstasies of joy and fear with a voice and face which indicate neither.... Why call in the aid of paralysis to piety?"[70] He suggested that many priests resembled "holy lumps of ice," despite which he conducted himself with the utmost dignity when in the pulpit. He did not practice all he preached, and especially of what he preached about preaching.

Sydney was, however, a good and popular preacher, and if he was never able to bring himself to abandon the traditionally aloof demeanour of the Anglican clergy in the pulpit, and if he left his renowned wit outside the chancel rail, he did win recognition as a preacher. Few records of his success in Edinburgh remain, but Francis Horner wrote in a letter dated 1801:

We went afterwards to hear Sydney Smith

>preach, who delivered a most admirable sermon on the true religion of practical justice and benevolence, as distinguished from ceremonial devotion, from fanaticism, and from theology. It was forcibly distinguished by that liberality of sentiment, and that boldness of eloquency, which do so much credit to Smith's talents. I may add that the popularity of his style does equal honor to the audience to whom it is addressed ....[71]

He published some of his sermons in 1801, which might indicate a very high degree of popularity, but in a letter to his father in the previous year he had indicated that only one hundred copies were to be printed.[72] Nevertheless, the sale of that many volumes to a limited reading public, and one in which the readers of sermons were probably still more limited, was not insignificant.

The nature of his association with Whig-liberals and even anticlerical forces, led his critics to denounce him as a theist, an atheist, a philosopher, or a freethinker. Meanwhile, his liberal and intellectual friends, slightly baffled by the presence of a genuine clergyman in their ranks, tried to explain away his association with the Church. Sydney himself never tired of ridiculing himself as a clergyman, at least to his liberal friends, and he engaged in constant self-denigration with regard to his preaching. In 1799 he had said in a note to his father, "I continue to preach now & then & see the faithful yawning at my feet--."[73] He is credited with having said, "There is not the least use in preaching to anyone, unless you catch them ill;" and also with regard to a dull preacher who apparently believed that sin was to be taken from men as Eve was taken from Adam "by casting them in a deep sleep,"[74] he made equally pointed remarks. This multiplicity of opinions on his sermons has deepened the confusion, and a twentieth-century reader of Sydney Smith sermons may be disappointed to find them not atypical of old-fashioned sermons, and quite devoid of humor. His sermons must, of course, be read in the context of the period in which they were preached, and it must be remembered that while Sydney was distressingly conformist by twentieth-century standards his preaching style deviated enough from the norm of his era that he was regarded as a most unusual pulpit personality. One of his best known sermons in Bristol

Cathedral, that on Catholic Emancipation, reads innocuously enough to a secular and ecumenical reader of the present, but when it was first preached on Guy Fawkes day near the height of the controversy, it so offended the members of the Corporation that they reputedly absented themselves from the Cathedral for a matter of years.[75] Similarly, his sermons do not cause either great soul-searching or profound reflection in the late 20th Century, but they were different enough to attract the admiration of men like Horner and Dugald Stewart.[76]

It is generally conceded that Sydney Smith knew little or nothing about theology, and he invariably skirted around that shortcoming by preaching sermons that were "practical and useful."[77] He justified this practice by defining the role of the priest in preaching as one of instructing a heterogeneous flock in basic Christian principles. Most of them, he knew, were neither interested in the abstract niceties of theology, nor were they intellectually equipped to deal with them had they been so inclined. He once said of the clergy:

> [They] are allowed about twenty-six hours every year for the instruction of their fellow-creatures; and I cannot help thinking this short time had better be employed on practical subjects, in explaining and enforcing that conduct which the spirit of Christianity requires, and which mere worldly happiness commonly coincides to recommend .... God forbid it should be necessary to be a scholar, or a critic, in order to be a Christian. To the multitude, whether elegant or vulgar, the result only of erudition, employed for the defense of Christianity, can be of any consequence: with the erudition itself they can be of any consequence: with the erudition itself they cannot meddle, and must be fatigued if they are doomed to hear it.[78]

His contention that a theological disputation before a mixed audience of rich and poor, literate and illiterate, is of dubious value is irrefutable, even if he personally was not qualified to engage in such a monologue. In the preface of the 1846 edition of his sermons the following passage, written by an editor rather than by Sydney, reasserts much the same purpose:

> The author...has...<u>studiously</u> confined himself to the plain and simple truth of our holy religion, avoiding <u>purposely</u> all difficult and disputed points, and endeavouring only to install into the hearts of men, that beautiful and heavenly simplicity of the Gospel, which would lead to a Christian life while they here remain, and open to them, through the Almighty Creator, an humble hope that their exertions, however imperfect, through the infirmities of human nature, may yet be "pleasing and acceptable" in his sight.[79]

Sydney's sermons might seem prosaic and even dull to a present-day congregation but their reception at the time they were originally given, and the later popularity of Sydney as a preacher, says a great deal about the preaching of his contemporaries. As he said, preaching had come to be synonymous with a boring address, and that meaning is still employed in the popular vernacular. Despite its defects the Church of England had preserved the tradition of the short sermon, an undoubted boon and blessing to Christian belief, and Sydney believed that though long sermons were desirable from the standpoint of instruction, in actual practice it was impossible to hold a congregation's attention for an extended period of time. "Piety," he said, "stretched beyond a certain point, is the parent of impiety."[80] If read aloud, his sermons require from twenty to thirty minutes to deliver, but that experiment is not fully valid, for it is known that he added "materially" to some of his sermons when preaching, and he may well have deleted sections from others.[81] It is highly probable, in fact, that his printed sermons differ substantially from those he presented to his various congregations. His practice was to draw up a very rough draft of a sermon, deliver it, and then to draw up a second and very careful draft for publication.[82] It is possible, of course, that he may have used some of his published sermons in later services, preaching directly from the printed text.

Sydney published his first volume of sermons in Edinburgh in 1801, and despite the limited number printed it was a successful publication which helped to establish his reputation as a preacher and writer. His sermons reveal him as a theist, but a convinced Christian as well. Although he has often been called a sceptic, his sermons demonstrate a genuine horror of scepticism which he believed was a danger to young men who were ashamed to acknowledge their religious beliefs. Wanting recognition, they were tempted to parade heterodox opinions which led them to become deists, from which point he believed they questioned Divine Providence and ended as complete sceptics. He believed that it would have been better for such a person to have died in youth.[83] He was deeply disturbed by the apparent descent of scepticism from the metaphysicians to the lower orders "who have no beautiful, and classical theory of morals to substitute in its place, but who, if they are not Christians, must be wild beasts...."[84]

Sydney was slightly upset by the Scottish non-observance of Holy Week in 1799, mentioning in a letter to Mrs. Hicks-Beach that the shops were open, the churches closed, and that there was not even the odor of hot-cross buns in the bake shops. He pretended to be shocked at the spectacle of the theatre being open during that week, yet he sent Michael to see the play, and he would have gone himself had the supporting actors been more proficient.[85] He saw to it that Michael took Communion for the first time, and he reported to Mrs. Hicks-Beach that her son had behaved "with the most perfect propriety" in receiving the sacrament.[86] Like many other Anglicans of the period, Sydney appears to have taken and administered Holy Communion only seasonally, or at most by the "rite of St. Primus" on the first Sunday of each month. The practice of offering and receiving the Holy Eucharist rarely rather than regularly was of long standing, and it probably predated the Reformation. Sydney took the sacramental view of Holy Communion, and of the seven sacraments, Hesketh Peason quotes him as saying that he "could name a certain minister of the Gospel who does not, in the bottom of his heart, much differ" from the Roman Catholic position.[87] With regard to ritual Sydney claimed that:

> No reflecting man can ever wish to adulterate manly piety...with mummery and parade. But we are strange, very strange creatures, and it is better perhaps not to place too much confidence in our own reason alone. If anything, there is, perhaps, too

little pomp and ceremony in our worship, instead of too much. We quarrelled with the Roman Catholic Church, in a great hurry and a great passion, and furious with spleen; clothed ourselves with sackcloth, because she was habited in brocade; rushing, like children, from one extreme to another, and blind to all mediums between complication and barrenness, formality and neglect. I am very glad to find we are calling in more the aid of music to our service.... Of what value it may be asked, are auditors who come there from such motives? But our first business seems to be, to bring them there from any motive not undignified and ridiculous, and then to keep them there from a good one: those who came for pleasure may remain for prayer.[88]

It might be presumed from this passage that Sydney was a High Churchman or even what was later to be called an Anglo-Catholic, but an analysis of this paragraph, and of his writings more generally, reveals that his was the broad Anglican position. He approved of more ritual and ceremony than was generally employed in many churches, but excessive pomp becomes "mummery and parade." Also, he felt that the intemperate use of reason in religion could lead to results that were totally unanticipated. He seems to have approved of the more extensive use of vestments, but he himself like the later Rev. Edward Bouverie Pusey, a leading figure in the Oxford movement, never wore them, and he does not appear to have altered the sober ceremonial of his youth in his own services.[89] He approved of the use of music in the services, but his approval was restrained and balanced by emphasis on "rational religion." His Whig political opinions were liberal enough to outrage conservatives of his era, but were not radical enough to satisfy liberals of the twentieth century and so he occupies the middle position in doctrine and ritual. He professed his belief in traditional Anglican practices and convictions, but he was tolerant of rather wide variations in form.

Despite professions such as these, his clerical garb, and his obviously clerical profession, Sydney was not infrequently described as an atheist or a heretic. John Gibson Lockhart said, "I fancy the whole set of the

Edinburgh Reviewers were really most thoroughly infidels, and S. Smith at the top of them in that respect as in all others."[90] In reflecting on Lockhart's charge it should be recalled that in that age of intense political controversy, charges such as that of "infidel" were commonly hurled at those with whom one differed politically, and that they signified little more than that. Similarly, reviewers wrote reviews of literary works not so much on the basis of the works themselves, but rather on the grounds of the author's political or social viewpoints. It was this approach that led Francis Jeffrey to write his famous opening line: "This will never do," in his review of Wordsworth's Excursion.[91] It also led to hostile criticism of Sydney's published sermons in the pages of the Tory Quarterly Review. It has been argued that Jeffrey saw himself as the guardian of good taste and literary quality, and therefore his reviews and his policy were more than political nattering at opponents, but certainly the reviewers generally, including Sydney Smith, were more political than literary critics. And, Sydney, who never concealed his politics, or his partisanship, especially in conversation, which in the limited Society of Great Britain travelled very quickly, made a particularly vulnerable target to charges of infidelity. He is reported to have so irked a country squire in a conversation that the latter said: "If I had a son who was an idiot, by Jove, I'd make him a parson." "Very probably...," replied Sydney, "but I see your father was of a different mind."[92]

Sydney poked fun almost constantly at his profession, and even more at his own role in it, and the sanctimonious could not help being outraged. To Mrs. Jane Marcet, who complained of insomnia, he recommended two volumes of his sermons, which he described as a "perfect soporific.... I recommended them once to Blanco White, and before the third page he was fast."[93] To Hicks-Beach in 1800 he characterized his sermons as "lethargies."[94] From passages such as these it might be assumed that he did not take his role in the Church seriously, and many people made that assumption, but a total evaluation of Sydney and his work indicates that such was not the case. Jokes are often told and repeated about Roman Catholicism, and it has been said that the most amusing of them are told by Irishmen, who are able to make light of their faith precisely because they are devout believers in it. Sydney was not devout, and few of his contemporaries were, but he did enjoy his faith and he took constant pleasure in nonsense and innocent merriment.

That he included religion and the Church in his nonsense should be taken not as evidence of his infidelity, but rather as grounds for assuming that he had a secure faith.

CHAPTER IV

Political Economy and the Founding of the Edinburgh Review

One of the interests of the intellectual group in Edinburgh with which Sydney came into contact was that of the new "science" of political economy, or economics in Twentieth century parlance. Edinburgh was the nursery, if not the birthplace, of political economy, and Edinburgh gave birth to the new system of non-interference economics. Virtually every thinker of that city, and certainly every "liberal", came to endorse the principles of political economy. To be a liberal meant being a rationalist and the economists were nothing if not rational. Economic doctrine provided an intellectual justification for cold-blooded economic and social policies under which those policies could be pursued without abandoning pretensions of Christianity and humanitarianism. Sydney basically accepted the teachings of political economy in toto, even if he tempered them slightly with his innate Whig paternalism, and few examples of his violation of sound economic principles can be found in his writings. On at least one occasion he did become exasperated with the abstractions of the "science" which he called a "school of metaphysics,"[1] but he did not forego its principles; and if he did so it was because he allowed his nationalism to override his concern for consistency in economic policy. Thirty years later he was to satirize the preoccupation of the country gentleman with the defense of the Corn Laws in one of his more successful poetic sallies:

> EPITAPH WRITTEN IN ANTICIPATION OF THE FATE
> OF A SOMERSETSHIRE COUNTRY GENTLEMAN IN 1845
>
>   Here Esdaille lies; he lost his life
>   from struggles in a civil strife
>   And left his widow all forlorn
>   Whilst reasoning on the price of corn
>   'Tis thus that human projects fail,
>   for life is but a "sliding scale."[3]

The new economics also influenced Sydney's attitudes toward the poor who, he believed, were suffering from the effects of their own improvidence. In a letter to Mrs. Hicks-Beach in 1798 he observed that there were far more beggars in Scotland than in England, but is is clear from his letter that he believed that the wages of the poor were adequate for their own support if properly expended. Like many gentlemen of the period, he suspected that the poor squandered their wages on liquor and expensive foods, such as "fine wheaten bread" when they should have been more frugally consuming borth.[4] He was able later, to comment on the intense poverty and suffering of rural laborers with perfect equanimity because of his knowledge of the Rev. Thomas Robert Malthus and his law of population.[5] In agreement with Malthus, Sydney came to believe that Britain was already overpopulated and that the burgeoning population threatened to destroy the established social and political order. "I have much the same feelings as Malthus," he said, "Man wants so much here below -- and it is so difficult to supply these wants that it is almost better not to be born than to be born poor...."[6] He described William Godwin, Malthus' old antagonist, as being almost insane in his refusal to accept the law of population. In one of his sermons he said: "...it is not so much an object, that there should be many people, as that those who are should exist in the greatest attainable comfort and be exposed to the least possible degree of peril and disturbance."[7] In her sermon "Upon the Best Mode of Charity" he exhorted his affluent congregation to give to the poor in the spirit of charity, and not to rely on the poor law to care for the poor. "...The law," he observed in a most thoroughly Malthusian manner, "must hold out a scanty and precarious relief, or it would encourage more misery than it relieved...the law degrades whom it relieves...."[8]

Just as Sydney could believe in the Church of England and still make fun of that institution, he likewise endorsed Malthus and Malthusianism while making jocular comments about both. In 1835, on hearing of Malthus' death, he wrote:

> Poor Malthus! everybody regrets him;
> --in science and in conduct equally a
> philosopher, one of the most practically wise men I ever met, shamefully
> mistaken and unjustly calumniated, and
> receiving no mark of favour from a Liberal Government, who ought to have interested themselves in the fortunes of
> such a virtuous martyr to truth.[9]

Sydney liked Malthus and they met and visited on numerous occasions as well as corresponding with each other over a period of years. Nevertheless, Sydney could write to Lady Holland:

> I told Vernon [Robert Vernon Smith his nephew] if he would persevere he would have a little girl at last. I might have said if he did not take care he would have 20 little girls. What is there to prevent him from having a family sufficent to exasperate the placid Malthus?[10] Philosopher Malthus came here last week. I got an agreeable party for him of unmarried people. There was only one Lady who had had a Child, and for her I apologized, saying nothing of a recent misfortune; but he is a very goodnatured man, and if there are no appearances of approaching fertility is civil to every lady.[11]

In 1833 Sydney wrote that "The Hibberts [Mr. and Mrs. Nathaniel Hibbert, his daughter and son-in-law] are with us -- Mrs. Hibbert confined to her Sofa a close prisoner. I was forced to decline seeing Malthus who came this Way. I am convinced her last accident was entirely owing to his Visit." And on the subject of that same pregnancy he commented that "Mrs. Hibbert is not allowed to walk up any Hills -- her complaint is that which Dr. Malthus considers as so injurious to the Commonwealth."[12]

In spite of his attitudes toward the poor, and his acceptance of Malthusian interpretations on population, Sydney could still preach eloquently, even sentimentally, in a sermon entitled "For the Scotch Lying-in Hospital." Published in his collection of sermons in 1809, it might have been preached in Edinburgh; but regardless of the time and place, he showed great concern for poor mothers.

> ...how awful the spectacle of a mother driven by hunger and despair, to the destruction of her child; To see a gentle creature hurled from the bosom to which it turns--grasped by the hands that should have toiled for it,--mangled, by her who should have washed it with her tears and warmed it with her breath, and fed it with her milk. You may enjoy a spectable far different from this; you

may see the tranquil mother on the bed
of charity, and the peaceful child slum-
bering in her arms; you may see her
watching the trembling of every limb,
and listening to the tide of the breath,
and gazing through the dimness of tears,
on the body of her child. The man who
robs, and murders, for his bread, would
give charity to this woman; good christians, have mercy upon her, and death
shall not snatch away your children;
they shall live and prosper; mankind
will love them! God defend them! ...
When you see a humble workman toiling
from sun to sun, and still unable to
rise above the necessities of the present hour! will you not save to such
an useful, honest being, the anguish of
returning to a sick house; the sight of
agonies which he cannot relieve, and of
wants to which he cannot administer?
give me a little of your abundance, and
I will lift off this weight from his
heart; listen to me when I kneel before
you for humble wretched creatures; help
me with some Christian offering, and I
will give meat to the tender mother, and
a pillow for her head, and a garment for
the little child, and she shall bless God
in the fullness of her heart....if you
remember how women lighten the sorrows
of life; if you are the disciple of the
Saviour Jesus, to whom they kindly ministered, forsake them not this once, and
God shall save you in the hour of death,
and the day of deep distress.[13]

Sydney was also enough of a rural gentlemen to believe that the poor and their problems could be better
handled in the country, or in small towns where they
could be controlled "by those whose favour it is in their
interest to cultivate, and by whose resentment it would
be their misfortune to provoke." In a great city like
London he believed the poor could absent themselves from
Church and squander their wages in "riotous intoxication"
in perfect anonymity, but in the village they had the
squire and the parson to reprove them.[14] His attitude in
this respect was that of the Whig paternalist rather than
the laissez-faire economist, but he assumed that the

country gentlemen could, by admonition, make the working poor both, more content with their lot, and less expensive to society.

Although he was well known for his sympathy for the Irish, his compassion did not extend to the violation of laissez-faire principles when it came to improving the lot of that poverty-stricken people. He warned Malthus against undue criticism of the "middlemen" in Ireland, those who stood between the often foreign and absentee landlord and the starving and exploited Irish peasant, of whom he said:

> You may just as well inveigh against Woolen Drapers who step in between the makers of cloth and the wearers of breeches. Equally absurd is the clamor against landlords for high rents. It is not a question of feeling...nor am I bound as a landowner to sacrifice any part of my income.... I let out land, and I will get the utmost farthing for it....[15]

Sydney Smith was a practitioner, one might even say a victim, of that over-simplified liberal-economic thought which held that most existing evils resulted from bad laws, and that once those laws were repealed or amended the evils would instantly disappear. In a general way, and as a result of his inclination toward laissez-faire economic thought, he believed that much of the injustice then present resulted from regulations which thwarted the free operation of natural law in economic processes. He consistently opposed governmental interference in that area. He opposed the Old Poor Law, for example, on the grounds that by relieving poverty indiscriminately it encouraged population growth and interfered with the natural laws that ordered population control. He was alert to the most trivial threat, or potential threat, to his economic freedom as revealed in a letter he wrote in 1819:

> I hope you have studied Lord Carlisle's pamphlet upon colouring and wrapping up poisons. What are we to do for our boot-tops which are cleaned by oxalic acid if we may not purchase oxalic acid but when coloured by rosepink? Are we to walk about with rose-pink boots? Did any

> Government ever yet prescribe a colour
> for boots, and if a colour, such a colour?[16]

Similarly, he sympathized with the plight of the factory children, or said he did, but his view of factory legislation was that of the doctrinarie economist who believed that factory conditions were regulated by the free play of economic forces, and that the government should not interfere in that "natural" process. He wrote, "...it does seem to be very absurd to hinder a Woman of 30 from working as long as she pleases but mankind are getting mad with humanity and Samaritanism."[17] The fact that most thirty year-old women had no choice as to the hours they worked in the factories had undoubtedly crossed his mind, but he felt that governmental action to help them gain a shorter working day would deprive both them and their employers of economic freedom. Shortly afterwards he again wrote, "The protection of Children is perhaps right but every thing beyond is mere mischief and folly."[18] By "mischief" he meant damage to the interests of the manufacturers, and by "folly" the foolishness of trying to interfere with the free operation of natural law. As a member of the Political Economy Club he prided himself on staying abreast of contemporary economic thought.

With one group of devotees of advanced economic thought, the Benthamites, Sydney did not agree, for the Philosophical Radicals were both too philosophical and too radical for his tastes. He admired some of Bentham's thought, but he deplored much of his writing; and even if he could say of Benthamism in 1810 that it "existed before time and space and goes on by immutable rules," his daughter could quote him as saying:

> Yes, he is of the Utilitarian school. That man is so hard you might drive a broad-wheeled waggon over him, and it would produce no impression; if you were to bore holes in him with a gimlet, I am convinced sawdust would come out of him. That school treat mankind as if they were mere machines; the feelings or affections never enter into their calculations. If everything is to be sacrificed to utility, why do you bury your grandmother at all? Why don't you cut her into small pieces at once, and

make potable soup of her?[19]

The hardness and basic inhumanity of the Utilitarian doctrine repelled Sydney, as did their advanced notions on social improvement. They proposed to revolutionize society by the application of various Benthamite formulae, but Sydney was essentially satisfied with British society as it was. He had expressed his doubts on the economic validity of the Old Poor Law, but as a minister of the gospel he could not question the social value of charity. In his sermon, "Upon the Best Mode of Charity," he advised every wealthy person to take on a poor family and to contribute time, money, and intelligence to it. It was not enough, he felt, to merely relieve the poor with money, but rather they should be visited regularly and encouraged in the ways of virtue. He believed that it was important not only to do good, but to do it in the best manner possible; and he cautioned his hearers not to expect too much either by way of results or by way of gratitude. In his opinion charity needed to be selective to fulfill its purpose, but if handled correctly it could result in "happy cottages, and smiling villages" in which the rich were given a taste of doing good, and the poor a veneration for rank.[20] It might be assumed from these exhortations that Sydney Smith practiced extensive personal charity, but such does not seem to be the case. Lady Holland records a few instances of his assistance to needy individuals,[21] and there probably were others, but by and large his life is much more the story of the accumulation of wealth than its distribution. In his defense it should be recalled that throughout much of his life his income was little more than sufficient to enable him to support himself with dignity, and that he was often preaching to congregations of much greater affluence than himself. Even on a subject as sacred to the age as charity, which not even Malthus could denounce, Sydney was still able to make his wisecracks. In 1817 he said, "I am going to preach a charity sermon next Sunday. I desire to make three or four hundred factory-owning weavers cry, which is impossible since the late rise in cottons."[22] Of charity more generally he said that "you find people ready enough to do the Samaritan, without the oil and twopence."[23] And he also asserted that universal benevolence was a natural instinct of the human mind:

> When A sees B in grievous distress, his conscience always urges him to entreat C to help him.[24]

With his universal interests and his social and political proclivities it was only natural for Sydney to seek out the company of like-minded men in Edinburgh, and such he had found soon after his arrival. His interests in Michael Hicks-Beach's education led him to the University of Edinburgh, and there he joined the Academy of Physics which was a more philosophical than a scientific group. He also joined the Speculative Society which, although founded for purposes of encouraging literature and good public speaking, had become an island of Whiggish free expression in a moribund sea of Tory conformity. Scotsmen like Dugald Stewart, Francis Horner, Francis Jeffery, and Henry Brougham belonged to both groups, and with Sydney Smith they attended the stimulating meetings of the societies. It was from this latter group that the Edinburgh Review was to spring, and although some doubt has previously been expressed as to Sydney's role in the founding of the review, none remains any longer. John Clive, in his Scotch Reviewers: The "Edinburgh Review" 1802-1815, carefully analyzed the conflicting accounts of its founding and he concluded that the conflicts could be resolved. Sydney's account of the founding written in 1839 had claimed credit for originating the idea and for having been the first editor, but his dating was vague and there were discrepancies in his recollections such as his describing the original meeting place as Jeffery's lodgings on the "eighth or ninth story" of a three-floored house. His recollections of who was present and of others who were involved was also confused, but Clive resolved these discrepancies by hypothesizing two meetings, each of them as having been later described by the participants as the original meeting.[25] Since the publication of Scotch Reviewers, Mr. A. S. Bell of the National Library of Scotland has discovered a letter dated 13 January, 1802, in the Wedgwood Museum which was written by Sydney Smith to James Mackintosh. This letter proves the Clive hypothesis beyond any doubt:

> Dear Mcintosh.-
>
> Allen, Thomson, Horner Murray - Jeffry - Hamilton & myself intend to undertake a review. -- The 2 first confine themselves to chemical- & medical subjects. - Hamilton is strong in oriental languages - & has already review'd a good deal in the Asiatic register. Jeffry is an extremely clever little man who

will write de onmi Scribili - Brown
will assist - I mean if possible to
persuade Maltby to give us some classical articles, and we shall have aid
from many other literary men, more
obscure than they deserve to be - It
is our intention to comprehend foreign
as well as domestic publications --
to put out a 5s volume every quarter
day -- selecting the works of some
merit -- & passing over all the refuse
of the press. -- The rocks & shoals to
be avoided are religion, politics, excessive severity, & irritable Scotchmen
-- If nothing else -- the common sense
of every mans concern will of course
teach him the necessity of the utmost
decency upon the first two points --
in the 3d point I do not think we shall
offend over much--& in the last the
danger of a broken head will made us
wise--

You will do me & my associates a very
great favor if you will point out to us
what bookseller in London is most likely to be active in pushing forward the
publication. --we wish to derive no
pecuniary Emolument from it for the
first year. --& have chosen Constable
for our Edinburgh bookseller. --What do
you think of the form of the publication? & of the probability of Sale --
we wish to weigh the matter well -- &
if your literary experience can suggest
any thing for the improvement of the
plan. -- we shall be extremely thankful to you for your counsel.--

...If any of the members of the King
of Clubs have a mind to barbicue a poet
or two or strangle a metaphysician to
do any other act of cruelty to the dull
men of the Earth we are in hopes they
will make our journal the receptacle of
their exploits -- we shall make it a
point of honor neither to mutilate contributions, or to reveal the names of
contributors.

> ...Whatever good may result from the scheme, or whatever evil it will at least have the effect of imparting some degree of animation to this metaphysical monastery.--
>
> We do not intend to publish our first Vol before Midsummer--& our plan is that the price after the manner of some foreign journals should vary from 5s to 7s according to the quantity of manner....
>
> We shall certainly have Dugald Stewart, Parr & Rennel in the first Number--& I hope you will give us an opportunity of including another celebrated name.--[26]

It is interesting to note that Brougham, who was later to claim some share in the formation of the review, is not mentioned at all, and that many of the later policies of the review had been formulated as early as January, 1802. With this letter, Clive's complete analysis and the original evidence, all doubts are banished and it can be said with assurance that Sydney originated the idea of the review as well as serving unoffically as its first editor. His tutoring and his occasional preaching doubtless left him with time on his hands, and thus his active mind most likely conceived the review in the mood of a youthful escapade. This conception took place in late 1801, or perhaps even early 1802, although Sydney's letter to Mackintosh reveals that a good deal of thought and planning had been accomplished by 13 January, 1802. Sydney undoubtedly "edited" the first number of the review, and the third, with a great deal of assistance from Francis Jeffrey. It was also Sydney who made the financial arrangements with Archibald Constable, but Francis Jeffrey became the Edinburgh Review's first editor in the formal sense of bearing that title.[27] It has been suggested that in origin the review began as a boyish prank, for of the original founding group Sydney was nearly the eldest at thirty-one, while Horner was only twenty-four and Brougham only twenty-three. But both Brougham and Horner had already been admitted to the Scottish bar, and thirty-one was no longer youthful to Sydney who was ordained, married, and a father, even if he was the most fun-loving of the group. His letter to Mackintosh has the ring of seriousness about it, and it would not appear that he was thinking of the undertaking in terms of a frolic. He did characteristically suggest as a motto for the review *Tenui musam meditamur avena* (We cultivate literature upon a little oatmeal), but it was rejected as being distressingly accurate; and Publius Syrus' more sober *Judex damnature cum noces absolvitur* was adopted.[28]

The purposes of the Edinburgh Review were stated in an "Advertisement" in the first number, and they coincided rather closely with the purposes Sydney had mentioned in his letter to Mackintosh several months earlier. The journal would not attempt to review every book published, but only those that seemed to be of particular importance or value. Publication was to be quarterly rather than monthly in order to give the reviewers time to reflect on their reviews, and in order to assess public opinion. Reviews were not to be continued from one number to the next, but the advertisement warned that they would in some cases be of much greater length than that to which the public was accustomed.[29] The anonymity of the reviewers was to be jealously guarded and, according to Constable, "Smith was by far the most timid of the confederacy, and believed that unless our *incognito* were strictly maintained we could not go on a day. This was his object for making us hold our dark divans at Willison's office to which he insisted on our repairing singly and by back approaches, or by different lanes."[30] Another policy of importance was the independence of the reviewers from the control of booksellers who had converted earlier reviews into vehicles for the sale of their works. Archibald Constable, who agreed to publish the review, also agreed not to interfere in the critical opinions of the reviewers, which gave them an almost unprecedented freedom of expression.

The appearance of the first number of the *Edinburgh Review* on 10 October, 1802, created a literary and intellectual sensation that spread quickly from Edinburgh to London. Appearing in the buff and blue colors of Charles James Fox, it was Whiggish from the beginning; because, having been conceived by Sydney Smith it could hardly have been otherwise. Yet, it was not to become openly "political" for several years. Most of the reviewers were Whigs and liberals who were generally inclined to fear arbitrary royal power more than the threat of popular violence. Their reviews excited strong antipathy and exaggerated charges, often from aggrieved authors, but in reality the reviewers were respecters of freedom and responsible authority. If they did advocate reform, what they really had in mind was moderate reform that could avert the creation of a revolutionary situation.[31] Originally Constable printed seven hundred and fifty copies of the first number which, in itself, was fairly ambitious. But the sensation brought about by its appearance was such that it sold out almost immediately and was followed by a complete sellout of the second edition, so that within a year Constable's investment had been rewarded by the sale of 2150 copies in Edinburgh alone. The sale and the excitement exceeded the expectations of the most optimistic of the reviewers, "even Smith himself," as Brougham later said; and it was indeed a remarkable success in a nation that probably numbered no more than one hundred thousand in its reading public.[32] By 1814 the circulation was to increase to 13,000 despite the price of six shillings which put the journal beyond the means of humbler readers.[33]

The success of the Edinburgh Review may be attributed to various factors such as the freshness of the writing of the young and untrammelled reviewers, their courage in asserting modern opinions, their sheer ability and the innovation of a publication which was not subservient to the establishment. Its writers were ultimately numerous, but the quality of its early reviews guaranteed the continuing success of the whole endeavour. Sydney's contribution to this success was by no means minor. Between 1802 and 1827 he wrote a considerable number of reviews and, according to the Wellesley Index, Sydney, Brougham and Jeffrey together wrote fully one-half of the work up to 1824. In his collected works in 1839 Sydney claimed the authorship of sixty-four reviews,[34] one of which, entitled Observations on the Historical Work of the Right Honourable Charles James Fox by George Rose, is unquestionably the work of Francis Jeffrey.[35] It is a devastating review, but it does not seem likely that Sydney knowingly claimed Jeffrey's article. In all probability either he claimed it erroneously or a clerk at Longman's merely misinterpreted his frequently illegible handwriting, especially since he did write the review of Philopatris Varvicensis' Characters of the Lake Charles James Fox in the same issue. His daughter, Lady Holland, listed seventy-six of his reviews,[36] all of which were his work except for Rose's Observations which she too listed as having been written by her father. The Wellesley Index lists a total of ninety reviews, describing the authorship of five of these as questionable, one as probable, and one claimed.

It may be assumed from this latter source that Sydney wrote at least eighty-three reviews over a twenty-five year period, and quite possibly as many as ninety or more.

However, the number of Sydney's articles in the Edinburgh Review is not the criterion of his contribution to it. His wit shines through most of his writings, and although he was not the only witty reviewer, his reviews were generally entertaining as well as informative or destructive. A typical Sydney Smith article was characteristic of his own personal contradictions in being written with a seriousness of purpose and a lightness of style that bordered on impudence. His seriousness was real enough but it did not approach that of Francis Horner who, when ordered by a physician to stay abed and to read amusing books, was found propped up scanning the pages of The India Traders Complete Guide.[38] Sydney was later to remind Horner that "Edinburgh is a very grave place, and that you live with philosophers -- who are very intolerant of nonsense. I write for the London, not for the Scotch market, and perhaps more people read my nonsense than your sense."[39] Sydney never troubled to deny his frivolity or limitations, and in 1819 he was to defend his reviews, while confessing that he was "...a very ignorant, frivolous, half-inch person; but such as I am, I am sure I have done your Review good, and contributed to bring it into notice." Still later he would admit that one of his articles was "light and scanty," but he reminded Jeffrey that "lightness and flimsiness are my line of reviewing."[41]

Sydney manifested his style of reviewing in the first number of the Edinburgh Review in which he wrote seven of the twenty-nine reviews published. His first review, that of Samuel Parr's Spital Sermon appears as the second article, and it fetchingly begins:

> Whoever has had the good fortune to see Dr. Parr's wig, must have observed that while it trespasses a little on the orthodox magnitude of perukes in the interior parts, it scorns even Episcopal limits behind, and swells out into boundless convexity of frizz....After the manner of his wig, the Doctor has constructed his sermon, giving us a discourse of no common length and subjoining an immeasurable mass of notes which

> appear to concern every learned thing,
> every learned man, and almost every
> unlearned man since the beginning of
> the world.[42]

From that beginning he proceeded to commend sections of Parr's attack on the English philosophe William Godwin's teachings on the subject of universal benevolence, and to reprove him for his pedantry and labored literary style which Sydney parodied as "...profundity without obsurity, perspicacity without prolixity - ornament without glare - terseness without barrenness - penetration without subtlety - comprehensiveness without digression - and a great number of other things without a great number of other things." He claimed that Parr's writing was so contrived and so elaborate that

> Every expression seems to be the result
> of artifice and intention; and as to the
> worthy dedicatees, the Lord Mayor and
> Aldermen, unless the sermon be done into
> English by a person of honour, they may
> perhaps be flattered by the Doctor's po-
> liteness, but they can never be much edi-
> fied by his meaning.... In some of his
> combinations of words, the Doctor is sin-
> gularly unhappy. We have the din of super-
> ficial cavillers, the prancing of giddy
> ostentation, fluttering vanity, hissing
> scorn, dank clod, &c. &c. &c.[43]

He concluded his review with a not entirely objective observation:

> How painful to reflect, that a truly de-
> vout and attentive minister, a strenuous
> defender of the church-establishment, and
> by far the most learned man of his day,
> should be permitted to languish on a lit-
> tle paltry curacy in Warwickshire![44]

He appended a footnote to this to the effect that Dr. Parr had since been rewarded with a valuable living.

The maligned Dr. Parr also figured in Sydney's second artice, for it was a review of William Godwin's Reply to Parr. A very short review, it began by applauding and quoting certain sections of Godwin's reply which Sydney considered better than Parr's criticism, but it ended by condemning Godwin for his refusal to accept the Malthusian law of population, and for his endorsement of abortion and infanticide as solutions for overpopulation.

> In gratitude for these noble remedies [said Sydney] of social disorder, may we take the liberty of suggesting to Mr. Godwin the infinite importance of shaving and blistering the crown of his head, of keeping the prima via open, and of strictly pursuing an antiphlogistic regimen. By these means, we have sometimes seen the understandings of great philosophers wonderfully and rapidly improved.[45]

Sydney's first article had been a review of a sermon, and his third, fifth and seventh articles were sermon reviews also. In this he was unique, as no other reviewer dealt with published sermons. As "editor", he undoubtedly chose the sermons he reviewed, and despite his anonymity, it may be assumed that readers of the Edinburgh Review recognized his reviews as having been written by a clergyman. His review of Thomas Rennel's sermons opened by deploring the lack of eloquence in contemporary sermons, a theme he had adverted to in the preface to his own earlier volume of sermons. He attributed the relative inarticulateness of the English clergy to the nature of their appointments by men who gave a living to a priest, and yet who had no real interest in his ability to preach. Yet, these same men would never have dreamed of furthering the career of a tonguetied lawyer or a stammering Member of Parliament. Sydney felt that the English over-reacted to French elegance and savoir faire with "patriotic solidity, and loyal awkwardness." In response to criticism of pulpit tedium, he pointed out the following incongruity:

> It is argued...that a clergyman is to recommend himself, not by his eloquence, but by the purity of his life and the soundness of his doctrine; an objection good enough, if any connexion could be pointed out between eloquence, heresy, and disssipation: But, if it be possible for a man to live well, preach well, and teach well, at the same time; such objections, resting only upon a supposed incompatability of these good qualities, are duller than the dullness they defend.[46]

Similarly he argued that although it was claimed that many clergymen preached badly and tediously in a conscious effort to avoid "novelty" in an already overtilled field, that "...that might be a very good reason for preaching commonplace sermons, but is a very bad one for publishing them."

Sydney did praise one of Rennel's sermons and it was predictably a practical sermon on the evils of gambling, but he took Rennel to task for preaching too frequently and too violently on the excesses of the French Revolution. Upon those "enormities" he said there could be but one opinion, and there was no place for it in the pulpit. He implied that preachers like Rennel who spoke on that subject did so only in hope of political notice and reward, and he warned against treating sophisticated thinkers like Voltaire and Rousseau with contempt based only on ignorance. William Godwin, according to Sydney, was at one time treated with ignorant contempt, and his prestige as a thinker grew and grew until he was soundly refuted by Malthus. Rennel, Sydney felt, expressed only disdain for influential thought he could not comprehend while retreating into an undue veneration of the classical past.

In this passage Sydney exhibited two elements that he was to employ frequently in future writing -- a denunciation of the romantic longing for the past, and a propensity to turn an opponent's own words against him in such a way as to produce ridicule. For example, when Rennel claimed that the people of his era were living in "an _evil age_ - an _adulterous age_ - _an ignorant age_ - an _apostate age_ - and a _foppish age_, it caused Sydney to write in response:

> Of the propriety of the last epithet, our readers may perhaps be more convinced by calling to mind a class of fops not usually designed by that epithet -- men cloathed in profound black, with large canes and strange amorphous hats -- of big speech, and imperative presence -- talkers about Plato -- great affectors of senility -- despisers of women, and all the graces of life -- fierce foes to common sense -- abusive of the living, and approving no one who has not been dead for at least a century. Such fops, as vain and as shallow as their fraternity in Bond

>   -street, differ from them only as
>   Gorgonius differed from Rufillus.[47]

Similarly, when Rennel engaged in gratuitous self-pity on behalf of the clergy generally with the expression "afflications to be borne", Sydney professed ignorance of what afflictions he referred to, until he recalled the more than 1,850 legal actions in the previous eighteen months against non-residency of the clergy. Finally, he described Rennel's warnings against the dangers of Roman Catholicism as laughable, and he insinuated that Rennel hoped for preferment as a result of his silly attacks on the Catholics whose emancipation might be retarded but could not be stopped.

Langford's <u>Sermons</u> which was the subject of Sydney's fifth review in the first number of the <u>Edinburgh Review</u>, he dismissed in half a page. He began:

> An accident, which happened to the gentleman engaged in reviewing this Sermon, proves in the most striking manner the importance of this charity for restoring to life persons in whom the vital power is suspended. He was discovered, with Dr. Langford's discourse lying open before him, in a state of the most profound sleep; from which he could not, by any means, be awakened for a great length of time. By attending, however, to the rules prescribed by the Humane Society, flinging in the smoke of tobacco, applying hot flannels, and carefully removing the discourse itself to a great distance, the critic was restored to his disconsolate brothers....
>
> This...will suffice for the style of the sermon. The charity itself is above all praise.[48]

Nares' sermons required a little more attention, but Sydney disposed of them in a neat two-and-a half page essay which combined the logic of ascertaining divine intervention and a brief discourse on the principle of supply and demand. He used Nares' own words to show that he denied God's direct interference in the form of positive miracles, and then asserted that God used wind or rain to punish sin. Nares also both tried to lay the blame for high grain prices on avaricious farmers and called for government controls on grain sales, all of which stimulated Sydney to demonstrate his skill in political economy. He said of Nares' reasoning:

> ...pardonable enough in those who argue from the belly rather than the brains; but in a well-fed and well-educated clergyman, who has never been disturbed by hunger, from the free exercise of cultivated talents, it merits the severest reprehension. The farmer has it not in his power to raise the price of corn; he never has fixed, and never can fix it. He is unquestionably justified in receiving any price he can obtain; for it happens, very beautifully, that the effort of his effort to better his fortune, is as beneficial to the public, as if their motive had not been selfish. The poor are not to be supported, in time of famine, by abatement of price on the part of the farmer, but by the subscription of residentiary canons, archdeacons and all men rich in public or private property; and to these subscriptions, the farmer should contribute according to the amount of his fortune. To insist that he should take a less price, when he can obtain a greater, is to insist upon laying on that order of men the whole burden of supporting the poor; a convenient system enough, in the eyes of a rich ecclesiastic; and objectionable only, because it is impracticable, pernicious, and unjust....
>
> The question of the corn trade, has divided society into two parts--those who have any talents for reasoning, and those who have not....
>
> The most benevolent, the most christian, and the most profitable conduct the farmer can pursue is to sell his commodities for the highest price he can possibly obtain.... We wish....the Reverend Mr. Nares to attend, in future, to practical, rather

> than theoretical, questions about provisions. He may be a very hospitable archdeacon; but nothing short of a <u>positive miracle</u> can make him an acute reasoner.[49]

The last two articles Sydney contributed to the first number of the <u>Edinburgh Review</u> were reviews of foolish books, and he obviously enjoyed dissecting their faults. Richard Philips' <u>Public Characters of 1801-1802</u> he dismissed deftly in a review of less than a whole page, which he introduced by saying:

> The design of this book appeared to us so extremely reprehensible, and so capable, even in the hands of a blockhead, of giving pain to families and individuals, that we considered it as a fair object for literary police.... Upon the perusal of the book, however, we were entirely disarmed. It appears to be written by some very innocent scribbler, who feels himself under the necessity of dining, and who preserves, throughout the whole of the work, that degree of good humour, which the terror of indictment by our Lord the King is so well calculated to inspire. It is of some importance, too, that grownup country gentlemen should be habituated to read printed books; and such may read a story-book about their living friends, who would read nothing else.[50]

John Bowles' <u>Reflections at the Conclusion of the War</u>, to the contrary, was still fairer game since it was equally foolish, contradictory, and steeped in Tory political prejudice; and Sydney modestly attempted not merely to efface any positive effect the book might have had, but to destroy the author as well.

> If this peace be, as Mr. Bowles asserts, the death warrant of the liberty and power of Great Britain, we will venture to assert that it is also the death warrant of Mr. Bowle's literary reputation; and that the people of this island, if they verify his predictions, and cease to read his books, whatever they may lose in political greatness, will evince no small

> improvement in critical acumen. There
> is a political, as well as a bodily
> hypochondriasis....
>
> The pamphlet is written in the genuine
> spirit of the Windham and Burke school;
> though Mr. Bowles cannot be called a
> servile copyist of either of these gen-
> tlemen, as he has rejected the logic of
> the one and the eloquence of the other,
> and imitated them only in their head-
> strong violence, and exaggerated abuse.

He pointed out Bowles' contradictions in an analysis which showed that he asserted the aggressive power of Napoleon on one page, and his fatal weakness on the next; the necessity of Britain fighting to restore French lib- erties, along with the conclusion that those liberties were so well established that Napoleon could not suppress them; and finally the fact that France was suffering be- cause of her execution of Louis XVI, coupled with the simultaneous claim that her troubles were divine retri- bution for her intervention in the American Revolution. Bowles also pretended to see a real danger to King and country in Whig dinners, and especially in the "alarming practice of singing after dinner." Turning his thought around on him, Sydney commented:

> If Parliament, or Catarrh, do not save us,
> Dignum and Sedgewick will quaver away the
> King, shake down the House of Lords, and
> warble us into all the horrors of republi-
> can government. When, in addition to these
> dangers, we reflect, also, upon those with
> which our national happiness is menaced,
> by the present thinness of ladies petticoats
> (p. 78), temerity may hope our salvation,
> but how can reason promise it?[52]

Bowles ended his book with a solemn vow to dedicate his life to the service of the crown, to which Sydney rejoin- ed that if Bowles were really sincere he would take that vow as a "virtual promise that he will write no more."

Sydney's seven reviews made up nearly a quarter of those published in the first number, but, since some were so brief, only about a tenth of the text. Four had been devoted to sermons, and although they were generally des- tructive he had made his points on good preaching, practical sermons, and responsible clergymen. The other three reviews had dealt with economic and political questions, and Sydney had emerged as a champion of laissez-faire economics and liberal politics, and as a voice of moderation in the midst of the anti-French hysteria. His writing was clear, witty, and compelling, and it reflected his active and energetic mind. His first seven reviews were all adverse reviews, as were most of the articles in the first number, but those he reviewed deserved what they received; and if Sydney occasionally did an author a disservice he was neither the first nor the last to do so.

His last year in Edinburgh marked his most productive period as a reviewer, for in the first four numbers of the journal, he wrote no fewer than twenty-one reviews, plus two more which were printed in October, 1803, immediately after he left. He was to publish an additional two reviews in the number that appeared in January, 1804, but from that time forward he became a frequent, rather than a major, contributor. He published no more reviews until October, 1806, and although he was to write, in all, about sixty-five more between 1806 and 1827, in no instance did he ever again write more than three in any one number. His witty reviews enriched the early volumes of the Edinburgh Review, but his role, great as it was, should not be overestimated. Some of his biographers imply that he carried the major burden of the review, but an analysis of the known authors who contributed to it shows that both Brougham and Jeffrey wrote about three times as many reviews as Sydney.[53] Still, the original idea for the review had been his, and he had been instrumental in bringing together the original founders. Furthermore, his contributions had not been slight; and, as he was to say later, his reviews "did good" for the journal.

In the second number of the Edinburgh Review Sydney certainly wrote two articles, and possibly four. Of the possible latter two, Sonnini's Travels in Greece and Turkey may well be his although it bears few signs, if any of his wit; and, neither the book nor the review of it are worthy of any great attention. The second "possible" review, Mme. Necker's Reflexions sur le Divorce is longer, and it contains lines of a Smithian bent, such as "... every person will be ready to acknowledge that filial respect and duty must be the greatest consolation of old age. But it is not so easily discovered that Glaciers derive any advantage from violets growing in their neighborhood."

It also condemns the overuse of trite classical examples and allusions, which is not unlike Sydney, but all in all it is not a review of great importance either.

Sydney's review of Lewis' Alfonso is quite a different story. Not a long piece, it is one of only five or six essays of real literary criticism among his reviews. M. G. Lewis was not a great writer, nor was Alfonso a great play, but it had at least more claim to being literature than the pamphlets Sydney had reviewed in the first number. He obviously enjoyed writing an overdone synopsis of its overdone plot, which concludes with the villain dying "in the usual dramatic style, repeating twenty-two hexameter verses." Insofar as Sydney was a literary critic, he expected art to mirror life and to entertain. He found the plot and characters of Alfonso too contrived to do justice to the former, and that the violence and imperfections of the play were too frequent to produce the latter; but he did commend the beauty of the language in some passages of the play.[56]

Sydney's review of Neckar's Last Views was as different from his review of Lewis as it could possibly be. Far and way his longest, most ambitious, most reflective, and most laudatory review up to that date, he found much in it to comment on and a great deal to agree with. He was in accord with Neckar in attempting to determine national greatness not from the size of a state, or a list of its military victories, but rather by such factors as the wisdom and justice of the administration of its laws, its political stability, and its credit. Throughout the article Sydney implied the superiority of the British system over that of the revolutionary French, and he did so chiefly on the grounds that liberty and order were firmly established in Britain, whereas France, who was still building her constitution, would be forced to undergo the "rashness" and "imperfect view" of legislators who had to create a whole new system. He predicted a century of disorder for France "before rational liberty becomes feeling and habit, as well as law," and during that century, he believed that while Britons enjoyed liberty, the French would groan under the yoke of unsurpers and military despotism.

He admired the objectivity with which Neckar viewed the topic on which he wrote, but Sydney deplored the fact that Neckar had never lived under a free system, and this resulted in his difficulty in distinguishing between a revolutionary uprising in France, and an English mob.

> "...the tranquility of an arbitrary government is rarely disturbed, but from the most serious provocations, not to be expiated by an ordinary vengeance. The excesses of a free people are less important, because their resentments are less furious; and they can commit a great deal of apparent disorder, with very little real mischief. An English mob, which, to a foreigner might convey the belief of an impending massacre, is often contented by the demolition of a few windows."[56]

Similarly, Sydney felt that the English experience would have guided Neckar away from setting up both property qualifications and a minimum age of twenty-five for legislators. Lest Sydney be thought democratic, he said that he believed that there should be a certain number of legislators "representing interests very distinct from those of the people."

Given the choice of the republican form of government or hereditary monarchy, Sydney unhesitatingly chose the latter, for he believed republics would work well only in small states, and possibly in the United States, whose twenty-year experience with republicanism was too short to be judged. He also felt that America, in being sparsely populated, free of an "idle discontented populace," and possessed of abundant food and land, could not really be compared with the European states. Neckar suggested the possibility of various governmental reforms for a restored French monarchy, some of which Sydney approved of vigorously. A peerage which included some peers appointed for life only, he maintained, could bring able men into an upper house without saddling the nation with their untalented offspring, who might through poverty become tools of the crown. Sydney also approved of removing the Bishops from the upper house; but he believed that, if that were done, the Church should be given some form of representation in the lower house. Above all he upheld the genius and stability of the British Constitution: "A nation grown free in a single day," he said, "is a child born with the limbs and the vigour of a man who would take a drawn sword for his rattle and set the house in a blaze, that he might chuckle over the splendour." Always the Whig, Sydney felt compelled to add that:

> "...long experience enables us to conjecture the real motives by which men are actuated; to separate the vehemence of party spirit from the language of principle and truth; and to discover whom we can trust, and whom we cannot. The want of all this, and of much more than this, must retard for a very long period the practical enjoyment of liberty in France, and present very serious obstacles to her prosperity; obstacles little dreamed of by men who seem to measure the happiness and future grandeur of France by degrees of longitude and latitude, and who believe she might acquire liberty, with as much facility as she could acquire Switzerland or Naples.[57]

The one who was not to be trusted was Pitt, of whom Neckar observed to Sydney's delight, that he had confidently predicted France's fall with the decline in her credit and the value of her paper money, only to find French power at a peak when the <u>assignats</u> had lost all value. Despite his partisanship, it is a relief to find that Sydney could praise a book, and he concluded his review by saying:

> "...we cannot help entertaining a high respect for its venerable author, and feeling a fervent wish, that the last views of every public man may proceed from a heart as upright, and be directed to objects as good.[58]

The second number of the <u>Edinburgh Review</u>, in which the Neckar review had been printed, had appeared in January, 1802 as scheduled; and probably as early as that Sydney had decided to leave Scotland and settle in London. A letter to Mrs. Hicks-Beach in that month gratefully declined the offer of another year's tutoring.

> I have one child, and I expect another: it is absolutely my duty that I should make some exertion for their future support. The salary you give is liberal; I live here in ease and abundance; but a situation in this country leads to nothing. I have to begin the world, at the end of three years, at the very same

point where I set out from; it would be the same at the end of ten. I should return to London, my friends and connections mouldered away, my relations gone and dispersed; and myself about to begin to do at the age of forty, what I ought to have begun to do at the age of twenty-five.[59]

Another letter to his father confirmed what his father already knew: that Sydney would move to London in that year,[60] and by the end of April he had decided to leave for London around the end of September.[61] Saba Holland says that her mother had a great deal to do with the decision to quit Edinburgh for London,[62] and it seems likely that she preferred English society and saw the professional advantages for Sydney in England, but no confirmation of her role can be found in his letters. Mrs. Sydney, as she came to be called by most of their friends, had given birth to a daughter in 1802, and she was expecting a second child in the spring of 1803. Sydney had been delighted with his first child and had named her Saba, which he borrowed from the 72nd Psalm, in order that she might have a unique name. His second child, a son, was born in the spring, and was named Noel. He was a sickly and delicate child, and although he survived the move to London, his strength did not improve and he died in London the following December. The birth of this second child and Mrs. Sydney's recovery were the things which delayed the move to London; but once they were accomplished Sydney, having firmly decided to continue his pursuit of a career in the Church, left Edinburgh with some sadness but with high hopes for his future.

Sydney's aspirations for the coming years were based to a large extent on the success he had experienced with the Edinburgh Review, the circulation of which had risen to 2300 by April of 1803, with another thousand copies projected. Sydney has often been described as being poor and friendless in London, but in actual fact he returned to old friends and connections, and he told Jeffrey that when he joined the other members of the Edinburgh circle in London, "The London Committee will now be tolerably strong."[63] During the summer of 1803, he had urged Archibald Constable to continue the review, which was of benefit to the public and a source of profit to Constable. He had also asked him to pay §200 a year to the editor, and ten guineas a sheet (which averaged out to sixteen printed pages) to the contributors.[64] His advice was

94

followed, and Constable's substantial pay scale enticed gentlemen to write, or to keep writing, and insured the quality of the review for decades to come.

Sydney himself wrote extensively for the review in 1803, publishing six reviews in the April number, four in July, and two more in the October publication. His omnicompetence is impressive in that, of twelve reviews, three may be categorized as church or religion-oriented, two were largely military, five were chiefly concerned with travel, one was literary, and the last dealt with humor. He was remarkable, but not unique, in his willingness to write on disparate topics, some of which he knew nothing about whatsoever. He had never travelled beyond Normandy or Scotland, yet he did not hesitate to write learnedly about Greece, Turkey, Australia, and Russia; and he knew nothing of military science, but that did not prevent him from criticizing military campaigns. The anonymity of the Edinburgh Review no doubt contributed to his disposition to write in largely unknown fields, but he was reinforced in his self-confidence by the faith of the English in the gentleman who trained in public school and the university, was capable of facing any problem; and in the security of his belief that, in his mental framework of liberal rationalism, all questions could be comprehended and coped with. As a consequence, he approached a review on travel in Russia, of which he knew nothing, with the same confidence that he felt in dissecting a sermon on which he presumably might claim some expertise. Not all of his reviews are of equal importance, and it is apparent that he gave far less consideration to some than to others; but since he used his reviews as a vehicle for the expression of his opinions on topics frequently far removed from the subjects of the books, it is perhaps important to at least mention most of his reviews.

A history of the penal colony in New South Wales does not seem to be too promising a subject for a literary review, but in Sydney's hands it became two treatises, one on the non-application of the modern principles of political economy, and the second on erroneous ideas in penology. He endorsed the benefits British civilization brought to the Australian wilderness, and he rejected the romantic ideal of the noble savage in favor of a Machiavellian view of seeing man as he is, rather than idealistically. His concept of criminal punishment was curiously physically and dogmatic in that he expressed a constant concern for danger of the encouragement of crime through improved prison conditions, or through transportation to the colonies. He affected a belief that prison reform made houses of detention more attractive to the lower classes than honest labor, and he believed that transportation and ultimate freedom in a country like Australia was nothing short of an inducement to a crime wave. He said that an accused person hearing a judge say "not guilty" could justifiably feel that he had been deprived of a golden opportunity. He felt also that transportation was too expensive to the state, and he disapproved of the role of government in establishing a colony and in building it up by means of forced labor. He suggested that the end result would be to "spend another hundred millions of money....to humble ourselves before a fresh set of Washingtons and Franklins...."

His strictures on frugality in government reflected his opinions on political economy, and he objected strenuously to the unenlightened economic policies of the colony. The colonial governors of New South Wales, not having been instructed in modern economic thought, had indulged in efforts to fix wages and prices, and to regulate the sale and consumption of alcoholic beverages. All of these things, in Sydney's opinion, should be left to the free and unhampered operations of natural law. If future governors could avoid such errors, and if they would apply liberal policies, Sydney predicted a bright future for Australia.[65]

Sydney's review of J. Fievee's account of his travels in England gave him a better opportunity to express himself with his expected wit. He began by saying:

> Of all the species of travels, that which has moral observation for its object is the most liable to error, and has the greatest difficulties to overcome, before it can arrive at excellence. Stones, and roots, and leaves, are subjects which may exercise the understanding without arousing the passions. A mineralogical traveller will hardly fall foul upon the granite and the felt spar of other countries than his own; a botanist will not conceal its non-descripts; and an agricultural tourist will faithfully detail the average crop per acre: but the traveller who observes on the manners, habits, and institutions of other countries, must have emancipated

> his mind from the extensive and powerful dominion of association, must have extinguished the agreeable and deceitful feelings of national vanity, and cultivated that patient humility which builds general inferences only upon the repetition of individual facts....Books of travels are now published in such vast abundance, that it may not be useless, perhaps, to state a few of the reasons why their value so commonly happens to be in the inverse ratio of their number.[66]

He attacked travel books of that description because they were ill-conceived, founded on superficial observation, and based on a system of observation rather than a system that resulted from observation. Few reviewers have ever scorched an author more thoroughly than Sydney when he said:

> ...we are wasting our time in giving a theory of the faults of travellers, when we have such ample means of exemplifying them all from the publication now before us, in which Mr. Jacob Fievee, with the most surprising talents for doing wrong, has contrived to condense and agglomerate every species of absurdity that has hitherto been made known, and even to launch out occasionally into new regions of nonsense, with a boldness which fairly entitles him to the merit of originality in folly, and discovery in impertinence. We consider Mr. Fievee's book as extremely valuable in one point of view. It affords a sort of limit or mind-mark, beyond which we conceive it to be impossible in future that pertness and petulance should pass. It is well to be acquainted with the boundaries of our nature on both sides; and to Mr. Fievee we are indebted for this valuable approach to _pessimism_. The height of knowledge no man has yet scanned; but we have now pretty well fathomed the gulph of ignorance.[67]

Such were his opinions of Fievee's work on travel in Britain, but a book on travel in Ceylon elicited a more objective appraisal. He lauded British expansion into the Indian subcontinent, expressing some liberal doubts at the same time about the more general wisdom of imperialism. He demonstrated that he had decided opinions on natural characteristics, describing a Ceylonese Dutchman as:

> ...a coarse, grotesque species of animal, whose native apathy and phlegm is animated only by the insolence of a colonial tyrant: His principal amusement appears to consist in smoking; but his pipe, according to Mr. Percival's account, is so seldom out of his mouth, that his smoking appears to be almost as much a necessary function of animal life as his breathing. His day is eked out with gin, ceremonious visits, and prodigious quantities of gross food dripping with oil and butter; his mind, just able to reach from one meal to another, is incapable of farther exertion; and, after panting and deglutition of a long protracted dinner, reposes on the sweet expectation that, in a few hours, the carnivorous toil will be renewed. He lives only to digest; and, while the organs of gluttony perform their office, he has not a wish beyond....[68]

His description of the Portuguese and Malayans of Ceylon was equally unflattering, and that of the King of Kandy was almost totally fanciful. The Ceylonese pearl fisheries caught his fancy, and he reported on them in some detail, saying that in the case of divers who were suspected of having stolen and swallowed pearls, "the police apothecaries are instantly sent for; a brisk cathartic is immediately dispatched after the truant pearl, with the strictest orders to apprehend it, in whatever corner of the viscera it may be found lurking."

Sydney was undoubtedly fascinated by travel books, which he read avidly, but his fascination did not extend to visiting exotic and un-English climates, of which he had the gravest doubts, or to approving of alien forms of life:

> The list of Ceylonese smakes is hideous; and we become reconciled to the crude

and cloudy land in which we live, from
reflecting, that the indiscriminate
activity of the sun generates what is
loathsome, as well as what is lovely;
that the asp reposes under the rose;
and the scorpion crawls under the fra-
gant flower, and the luscious fruit.

The usual stories are repeated here, of
the immense size and voracious appetite
of a certain species of serpent. The
best history of this kind we ever remember to have read, was of a serpent
killed near one of our settlement in the
East Indies; in whose body they found
the chaplain of the garrison, all in
black, the Rev. Mr.   , (somebody or
other, whose name we have forgotten),
and who, after having been missing for
about a week, was discovered in this
very inconvient situation.[69]

Denmark was closer to England that Ceylon, and a book on Denmark brought out opinions that were chiefly liberal and economic in nature, and which were simultaneously an encouragement to liberal reform in Britain, and an apology of her peculiar institutions. Sydney summarily rejected the author's argument that the release of accused prisoners on bail was unjust because the poor could not avail themselves of that privilege. He could not envisage any other system that would guarantee the appearance of poor prisoners for trial. Capital punishment in Denmark, he claimed, had been executed with such a flourish that hanging had served as an incentive to murder, and reforms had to be effectuated to make public executions "dull, as well as deadly, before it ceased to be an object of popular ambition." He felt that Danish commercial policies had been established on "very liberal and enlightened principles," which enabled the Danes to profit at British expense during wartime. Similarly Sydney applauded Danish religious toleration of both Calvinists and Quakers, the latter of whom he said were:

> ...characterized by the same neatness,
> order, industry, and abusrdity, as their
> brethren in this country; taking the ut-
> most care of the stick and destitute, and
> thoroughly persuaded that, by these good
> deeds, aided by long pockets and slouched

hats, they are acting up to the true
spirit of the Gospel.[70]

His approval of books on travel was somewhat less discriminating than on other topics, and he gave a general commendation of a book of Russian travels, even though he observed that the author apparently believed that the Russian climate could be moderated by lighting more fires in that country.[71] Still another book on travel in Turkey excited Sydney to a defense of Napoleon against charges of atrocities committed at Jaffa against both captured Turkish soldiers and his own sick and wounded troops who, it was alleged, he had ordered to be poisoned. His defense of Bonaparte was lucid and well reasoned out, and he raised very valid questions about the nature of the evidence which was being used against him; and if history has proven Sydney to be wrong on this point, he was wrong because he refused to be stampeded into accepting as fact what might well have been a spurious allegation. Despite his disagreement with the author on that point, he gave the book a commendable review, and he recommended it to his readers as "an excellent lounging book, full of pleasant details."[72] In still another article on the Egyptian campaign, this one combining four books in one review, Sydney again commented on the alleged atrocities at jaffa: "We are no very violent partizans for the morality of the First Consul," he said, "but we love justice, and respect the old English proverb so much, that we would give even the devil his due, and by no means say all ill of him which we could not prove." His opinion of British military leaders and their tactics was generally unfavorable, and he believed that the wonder was not that they had been able to win in a less than "masterly manner," but that they had won it all. The victory in Egypt he attributed to the energy of the government, the character of the English, and the courage of the soldiers. His admiration of Napoleon and the French did not extend as far as might be imagined, and he concluded his review on a patriotic note:

> Europe is the light of the world, and
> the ark of knowledge: upon the welfare
> of Europe, hangs the destiny of the
> most remote and savage people. Europe
> to be great and happy must be free; and
> to be free, she must ever strive against
> the usurpations of faithless ambition,

with the same unquenchable courage which
this little island has always displayed
in the perils of nations, and which she
will never lose, but in the extinction
of that manly race in whose hearts it
lives.[73]

Sydney echoed his English nationalism in the first paragraph of his review of Mme. de Stael's <u>Delphine</u>:

This dismal trash, which has nearly dis-
located the jaws of every critic among
us with gaping, has so alarmed Bonaparte
that he has seized the whole impression,
sent Madame de Stael out of Paris, and,
for aught we know, sleeps in a nightcap
of steel, and dagger proof blankets. To
us it appears rather an attack against
the Ten Commandments, than the government of Bonaparte, and calculated not so
much to enforce the rights of the Bour-
bons, as the benefits of adultery, murder, and a great number of other vices,
which have been somehow or other strangely neglected in this country, and too
much so (according to the apparent opinion of Madame de Stael) even in France.[74]

He considered the book to be poor and weak, both in conception and execution, and the characters and incidents as vulgar. Mme. de Stael, he said, was so lacking in literary artifice that no surprises were possible in her work; "Leonce is robbed and half murdered; the apothecary of the place is certain he will not live; we were absolutely certain that he would live, and could predict to the hour the time of his recovery." <u>Delphine</u> and Leonce had between them "eight very bad <u>typhus</u> fevers... besides <u>haemoptoe</u>, <u>hemmorrhage</u>, <u>deliquium animi</u>, <u>singultus</u>, <u>hysteria</u>, and <u>foeminei ululatus</u>, or "screams innumerable," which is admittedly a great deal, even in six volumes. Sydney also accused the translator of being an inexperienced Caledonian who translated Mme. de Stael from French into Scottish English. He deplored the language of the novel, and he resented the tacit and explicit immorality of Delphine, which was, he said, the old morality of Farquhar and Congreve which did not admit that the seventh commandment was ever intended for the protection of husbands who were incapable of witty repartee.[75]

101

Sydney published two other articles bearing on morality, but is is obvious that he did not think highly of either book, and also that he did not invest a great deal of thought or effort in either one.[76] He did, however, give his full attention to a third review which, while not quite as moralistic as that on Delphine, was of greater direct interest to him. The question of the residence or non-residence of the clergy was a vexing one, for non-residence often meant the dereliction of clerical duty, the acquisition of livings for purely mercenary reasons, and the growth of cynicism and irreligion in clergy and laity alike; and enforced residence could mean both an end to the established system in the Church, and genuine hardship on the clergy in some instances. Sydney favored the idea of residence of the clergy, but he wanted to leave enough loopholes in the law to preserve some degree of necessary pluralism. He disagreed vigorously with the proposal that the power to order residence should be placed in the hands of Bishops, whom he distrusted instinctively. His conclusion was that what was desirable was a system that would bring about more extensive residence by the clergy in their livings, but without interfering with their right to live outside a particular parsonage, to perform other legitimate functions (such as teaching), or to absent themselves five months a year from their parishes. These reforms, he believed, would punish those clergymen "who regard church preferment merely as a source of revenue, not as an obligation to the discharge of important duties." He said that his chief concern was to propose terms that were "attainable" rather than those that were the most desirable theoretically. He suggested, for example, that residence of the clergy should not be required in livings valued at less than §80 per year; and that if it was, it could not be enforced.[77]

His article on the residence of the clergy was written very seriously, and little humor appears in it, but a later review on Irish "bulls" was amusing, if not very elevating. A "bull", a now archaic word referring to a joke centered around a grotesque blunder in language, was then a more popular form of humor. An example would be that quoted by Sydney of a man seated in a hotel lobby writing a letter, and observing in the letter that an Irishman was hanging over his shoulder reading every line he wrote; upon which the Irishman burst out saying, "You lie!" Not an elevated form of humor, the review of "this rambling, scrambling book" did give Sydney an opportunity to defend the Irish and to express his definition of wit. Wit to Sydney Smith was largely a matter of surprise; making a connection between the congruous and the incongruous, or demonstrating that what was apparently congrous was not.[78] He was a teller of jokes rather than a truly witty conversationalist, and no one enjoyed his jokes more, or laughed louder at them, than Sydney himself. Other wits of the age prepared and polished their lines carefully, and it may be assumed that Sydney did too, to some extent; but a great deal of his humor was spontaneous and was intended for his own amusement, or for that of his children or the servants, rather than to impress social figures. His form of wit had already amused and charmed many people, and he carried it basically unchanged to London and to his future in the Church and in the world.

CHAPTER V

(London: 1803-1807)

After his success in Edinburgh, Sydney's transfer to London was very logical. He moved from the Gaelic periphery of Great Britain to its economic, social, and intellectual center; and from a stronghold of Presbyterianism back to the hub of the Church of England, where an able and ambitious clergyman could most readily be noticed. Sydney's daughter and his widow, in their respective memoirs of Sydney, both mentioned that Sydney came to London alone, poor, friendless, and without prospects; which would make it appear either that he was a very daring young man indeed, or that he was one who was none too intelligent. Catherine Smith said: "It was a fearful & nervous thing to find himself <u>alone & friendless in this vast metropolis</u>";[1] and Saba, Lady Holland, added that he was alone and poor, "without family or friends to support him'.[2] Andre Chevrillon followed their lead, and asserted that when Sydney arrived in London he was regarded as a revolutionary, a Jacobin, an atheist, and that "all doors were closed to him."[3]

Had these assertions been true, it would be difficult to imagine why Sydney left the relative prosperity of his tutoring in Edinburgh, as well as the security of his circle of friends. He did prefer England to Scotland, and a more southerly climate to that of the extreme North; but he had no pronounced antipathy for Scotland, which he left with very real regrets. Although Mrs. Sydney and Saba were completely sincere in their belief of his poor status at the time of his arrival in London, they contradicted themselves in succeeding sentences. Mrs. Sydney added to her comment that Sydney liked the Russell Square area of London because of his brother's friends in the legal profession - friends like Scarlett, Romilly, Mackintosh, "& several other young lawyers". Saba's observations are similarly offset by her succeeding paragraphs. Sydney's move back to England was, in fact, a carefully planned migration from a situation of limited opportunities to one of immeasurable prospects, especially in regard to the Church.

Upon his arrival in London, Sydney moved into 77 Upper Guildford Street, the home of Col. Gerard Noel, a friend from Edinburgh, who permitted him the use of his house until Sydney could locate more permanent quarters.

Col. Noel was also responsible for introducing him to the New River Company. Sydney's brother had served on its board of directors, and his father was apparently a stockholder in the company.[4] There is no question but that Sydney moved to London with the prospect of a position on the board of the New River Water Company. The surviving records of the New River Company, now located in the archives of the Metropolitan Water Board, are sketchy, but they add some details to the story of Sydney's early years in London.

The New River Company was a venerable commercial undertaking which dated from 1605, and which had completed an artificial watercourse from Hertfordshire to London, a distance of about forty miles, as early as 1613. The enterprise required the building of two hundred and fifteen bridges, some tunnelling, and the construction of two lead-lined wooden aqueducts of six hundred and sixty feet and four hundred and sixty-two feet.[5] An ambitious project, the plan was put into operation largely through the initiative of Sir Hugh Myddleton, "citizen and goldsmith", who saw it to its completion. Although successfully completed, the watercourse produced little profit for the first thirty years. Shares in the New River Company originally sold for §500, and the profits, low or non-existant in the early years, began to grow until they amounted to §33/2/8 in 1640, §145/1/8 in 1680, §201/16/6 in 1700, and §431/5/8 by 1794. Profits, as well as the value of the shares, continued to increase until by 1899, a share in the New River Company sold for §120,000.[6] The substantial profits attracted competition, but as late as 1848-1849, the New River Company was the largest of the London water companies, and the 15,500,000 gallons it supplied daily amounted to twice that of its nearest rival.[7]

Catherine Smith says in her memoir that a friendship had blossomed in Edinburgh between her husband and Mrs. Noel and her two sons; and that Col. Noel not only lent Sydney his house on Upper Guildford Street, but also appointed him to watch over his interests in the New River Company.[8] Thus, by Catherine Smith's own assertion, Sydney did not go to Longon "alone & friendless". He had friends, in the city, and definite prospects. As early as 29 October, 1803, he had accepted an invitation to be elected to the Board of Directors of the New River Company to replace his brother. Shortly thereafter, Sydney purchased a deed of trust from Col. Noel for one share of stock in the company, and this enabled him to sit on the Board for ten shillings and "every year one peppercorn at the feast of Saint Michael the Archangel (if lawfully demanded)...."[9] Later he was duly elected to the Board and appointed auditor of the books for which he was paid $50 a year.[10] Col. Noel may have paid Sydney for representing him, and there were probably other means of profiting from the position. Catherine Smith typically depreciated the salary in later years in her efforts to prove that Sydney was poor, but she recollected that he received about $70 annually from his position How much more he took in cannot be known today, but since he gave up a $500 salary in Edinburgh, it can be assumed to have been considerably more than either his official salary of $50 or the $70 mentioned by Mrs. Smith. In 1807, he mentioned in a letter to Francis Jeffrey that he had doubled his income,[11] presumably meaning his income while in Edinburgh, and although he had other sources of money by that time, some considerable share of the increases may have been from his connections with the New River Company. He appears to have performed his tasks for the company efficiently and conscientiously, as no complaints can be found in the records against him. He was to remain auditor of the company until he removed to Yorkshire; and the last references to him in the books of the New River Company record a final payment of $25 for the previous biennial audit on 2 March, 1809, along with his letter of resignation dated 4 May, 1809.[12] Sydney's brother Bobus returned from India in 1811 and took up his seat on the board once more and he was to become its chief legal counsel in the ensuing years.

Sydney moved to more permanent quarters at 8 Doughty Street later in 1803. The dating of many of his letters of this period is uncertain, but it appears that he had arrived in London in late August, and that he located on Doughty Street probably by early October, where he remained until 1806. Doughty Street is the Russell Square area and it was there that Sydney was able to contact the young lawyers he had met in Edinburgh, or whom he knew through his brother, and the "London Committee" of the Edinburgh Review. In September, he wrote to Jeffrey, saying that he had not seen much of Francis Horner who, he said, "...lives very high up in Gordon-Court, and thinks a good deal about mankind....[13]" Horner was one of the most brilliant of Sydney's Edinburgh friends. He was an outstanding lawyer who had been called to the Scots bar in 1800, and to the English bar in 1807, as well as one of the original founders of the Edinburgh Review. A

Member of Parliament for about ten years after 1806, he established an enviable record defending liberal causes, and a fine reputation as a speaker. His friends thought of him as an outstandingly able man in many fields, and as one whose dour Scots countenance gave the impression of an intimidating seriousness of purpose - so much so, that Sydney claimed he had the Ten Commandments written on his face, and Sir Walter Scott added:

> I cannot...admire your Horner; he always reminds me of Obadiah's bull, who, whough he certainly never did produce a calf, nevertheless went about his business with so much gravity, that he commanded the respect of the whole parish.[14]

Horner was, nonetheless, a handsome man who was very attractive to the opposite sex, and Sydney, when asked to recommend a governess for a friend's children in Bombay, asked Jeffrey to interview a lady in Edinburgh. Regarding Horner, he added:

> Pray let Horner see her if you think there is any probability she will do; but let him see her under the influence of yr presence, or he will impregnate her. There is a fecundity in his very look; his smiles are seminal.[15]

Sydney was frequently in the company of Horner and other bright young men of the legal profession, but his greatest social triumph, and the one of the greatest significance for his future, came as a result of his being introduced to Holland House again. Most of his biographers assumed that he had not previously visited the great house, but an examination of the <u>Dinner Books</u> of Holland House shows that he had been there as early as 16 June, 1797, and that he visited again in 1800, 1801, and probably in the spring of 1803.[16] In a letter written to his father in 1796, which may imply some connection between Lord Holland and the elder Smith, Sydney had deplored the scandalous events which culminated with Lady Webster leaving her husband for Lord Holland.[17] Although she divorced her husband and married Lord Holland, the couple's actions were so unusual in that age that Lady Holland was never received at court. In revenge, she established a rival Whig court at Holland House. To some extent being a Whig came to mean accepting her socially, and accomodating her imperious nature. Russell commented that Lord Holland was "always recruiting for the Liberal army, and an Edinburgh reviewer was a recruit worth capturing".[18] He was not aware, though, that Sydney was already acquainted with the Hollands when he came to live in London and that Lord Holland had probably recruited Sydney at an earlier date, which leads to the assumption that Sydney came to London in the expectation of a continuing entree to Holland House. He was an ideal recruit for Lord Holland because his liberalism was of the orthodox eighteenth century Whig type - enough to embarrass the Tory administration without unduly upsetting the Whig magnates like himself. Sydney's connections with the Hollands became closer after his arrival in London, and he was to maintain and expand them throughout his life. He was, as his biographers have said, a useful addition to the Holland circle, for he was a liberal and right-thinking man who, as an Edinburgh reviewer, could help influence public opinion through his writing. In addition, he was an asset to any dinner or social gathering as his wit and common sense invariably contributed to the evening. "With Henry Luttrell and Samuel Rogers, he formed a memorable Holland House trio of minor literati - and of the three, Smith was the most rewarding companion."[19] David Cecil described him at Holland House as the "most humane of the Clergymen, crackling away like a genial bonfire of jokes and good sense and uproarious laughter...."[20] His geniality extended even to Lady Holland, with whom he established a modus vivendi that ripened into mutual respect and lasting friendship. That he deferred to her cannot be doubted, but he was never obsequious. For example, an incident was recorded in which Lady Holland reportedly ordered him, in her usual commanding tone: "Sydney, ring the bell". to which he replied, "Oh yes! and shall I sweep the room?"[21]

This retort is typical of Sydney's relations with the very rich and very powerful members of society. They demanded a degree of deference which he was willing to accord; but beyond that tacit acknowledgement of their superiority, he met them on a basis of equality. In ordinary social situations, he spoke to them as a gentleman conversing with gentlemen, or as one of two gentlemen discussing a mutually advantageous quid pro quo. Lord and Lady Holland offered him excellent dinners in some of the best company of England, and the promise of future preference in the Church. He offered them, in return, witty and entertaining conversation, a talented and influential publicist's pen and a voice for liberal reform in the Church. If he could hope for their influence on his behalf in obtaining preferment in the Church, they could expect that his voice in the Edinburgh Review and his influence in the Church would be exercised on behalf of their party. Being gentlemen, neither Sydney nor Lord Holland ever expressed themselves quite so baldly, but both clearly understood the other's position, and both were able to make an agreement of this kind without sacrificing any of their principles.

Another of the Edinburgh reviewers with whom Sydney associated in London and encountered frequently at Holland House, was Henry Peter Brougham, later Lord Chancellor and First Baron Brougham and Vaux, whose relations with Sydney, and with nearly everyone else, were always problematical. The most ambitious and ultimately the most successful of the reviewers, he was also the most prolific writer among the original group. Jeffery came to depend on his reviews to keep the journal going, for Brougham could be relied upon to meet Jeffrey's deadlines and to write learnedly, if superficially, on any subject whatsoever. Brougham was, however, in Sydney's eyes, and in those of many of the leading Whigs, a decidedly erratic person, both personally and politically. Sensitive and suspicious to a fault, he was under the impression, and not without some justification, that Sydney was trying to undermine his influence in the review.[22] In 1808, Sydney was to bear out his mistrust by writing:

> Our friend Brougham has been bolting out of the course again in the Edinburgh Review. It is extremely difficult to keep him right. He should always remain between 2 tame elephants. Abercrombie and Wishaw, who might beat him with their tusks, when he behaved in an unwhiglike manner.[23]

Brougham's difficulty was that he refused to accept the eighteenth century concept that the Whigs were a club of aristocratic cousins as the final form of the party, but the other hand, he was not a political extremist. His political innovation, in the mildest form, was his mother's refusal to accept the scandalous Lady Holland socially; and in its most extreme form, he questioned the value of the landed aristocracy and this allied him with the radicals. Sydney liked Brougham, and at a later date he was to write congratulating him for a major courtroom triumph:

> There is nothing makes me so angry as
> to see a man enjoying a reputation he
> does not deserve or more happy to see
> a man like yourself taking his proper
> station in Society- and appearing to
> all the World as he has long appeared
> to his friends.[24]

He could also write to Brougham to say that one of his reviews was "long and vigorous like the penis of a jackass",[25] but his comment was intended as a compliment.

In addition to reviewers like Brougham and Horner, the elite Whig society of Holland House, and the legal fraternity at Russell Square, Sydney also frequented the home of his aunt, Miss Olier, probably Mary Olier, in Portman Square. His mother's sister, she was apparently a person of quality and substance who conducted a finishing school of sorts for young heiresses, admitting four annually and charging $1000 a year.[26] She doted on her nephew, and this is almost certainly the "Aunt Mary" mentioned in Lady Holland's memoir who was to leave Sydney a substantial legacy.[27] From all of these sources of society, it may be seen that Sydney was anything but "alone & friendless" in London, and that he found the city delightful. He developed a love for London that was to remain with him for the rest of his life, and never failed to compare the countryside or other cities unfavorably with it. Perhaps his best known comment on London is that on the "Parallelogram":

> I believe the parallelogram between Ox-
> form-Street Picadilly, Regent-street,
> and Hyde Park, encloses more intelli-
> gence and human ability, to say nothing
> of wealth and beauty, than the world has
> ever collected in such a space before.[28]

Sydney's life in London was generally happy, although the death of his son Noel in December, 1803, cast gloom over the family for a period of time. In 1805, a second son, Douglas, who was to be Sydney's favorite child, was born. Although he too was none too strong, the child survived and gave promise of future ability. In 1807, Mrs. Sydney gave birth to a second daughter, Emily, who, like elder sister Saba was to be healthy and long-lived. Immediately after the death of Noel, Sydney wrote to Jeffrey in Edinburgh to say that his wife, Mrs. Sydney, as he and his friends often called her, was slowly recovering from the loss of her first-born son, and that "Children are horribly insecure; the life of a parent is the life of a gambler."[29] But his spirits could not long be kept down, and just before the birth of Douglas he wrote, again to Jeffrey, to say:

> I am sure you will be glad to hear of Mrs. S. first. I have been expecting that she would be brought to bed every night for the last eight days, but to the amazement of the obstetric world she is still as pregnant as the Trojan Horse.[30]

With the exception of the death of Noel, and the crisis of an occasional childhood disease, the Smiths fared well. Although they were not as rich as the Hollands, their marriage was a great success and they had income enough to live comfortably and in dignity.[31] The "poverty" that his widow and his daughter were later to expound on so copiously was not poverty at all, but rather Sydney's inability to live as affluently as he would have chosen. It is recorded that he went to dinner parties on foot, and that he joked with the servants while removing his overshoes;[32] and that he took his wife to fashionable dinners in an inelegant hackney cab, which made them the butt of sarcastic sneers and superior grins. The London society of his day was frequently ill-mannered, and many were eager to flaunt their wealth and jeer at those who had a lesser income, The jeers of the uncouth were a gnawing source of annoyance to Sydney, not so much because he envied the grinning fops and sneering fools, but because he felt that they humiliated Mrs. Sydney.[33]

His life with Mrs. Sydney was almost idyllic, even though they were quite different in many respects. What Mrs. Sydney lacked in intellect, which was a great deal, she made up in charm and grace; and although Sydney numbered many women among his closest friends, no hint of scandal attaches to any of those friendships. All of his friends liked her, and she assisted Sydney by giving suppers where he was undoubtedly the presiding figure. Invitations to her suppers, which were often attended by twenty to thirty people, came to be much desired in London.[34] She did not always accompany Sydney when he was dining out, but with or without her, he was to become one of the "diners-out" in greatest demand in society, or at least Whig society, for the next four decades. His ready wit and noisy laughter were a pleasant relief from ordinary English stuffiness and decorum, and his capacity to amuse and entertain saved many a dinner party from disaster. Some guests at these parties were so grave and sober that they thought he was insane, and it occasionally required a good deal of effort to tediously explain to them that he was joking, and then to explain his jokes. On English manners he wrote:

> ...manners are often too much neglected; they are most important to men, no less than to women. I believe the English are the most disagreeable people under the sun; not so much because Mr. John Bull disdains to talk, as that the respected individual has nothing to say, and because he totally neglects manners. Look at a French carter; he takes off his hat to his neighbour carter, and inquires after "la sante de Madame", with a bow that would not have disgraced Sir Charles Grandison; and I have often met a French soubrette with a far better manner than an English duchess. Life is too short to get over a bad manner; besides, manners are the shadows of virtue.[35]

But if he could be critical of English manners, he could also give credit where it was due, and in 1806, he commended a Miss Markham, who, although he:

> ...splashed her with gravy from head to foot; and though I saw three distinct brown rills of animal juice trickling down her cheek, she had the complaisance to swear that not a drop had reached her. Such circumstances are the triumphs of civilized life.[36]

He could also write to Richard Heber, a contemporary clergyman, in 1804 to complain that Heber '...helped me very badly to Asparagus on toast - and only 3 heads of the vegetable. I don't suppose you meant any thing by it - but it had an unfriendly appearance."[37] At another dinner, he found himself next to a lady who firmly believed that it was always high tide at London Bridge at twelve o'clock, and who asked him to confirm her opinion. He replied with the utmost gravity and propriety; "It used not to be so, I believe, formerly, but perhaps the Lord Mayor and Aldermen have altered it lately".[38]

Sydney's ability to talk led him from relative obscurity to eventual fame; and although his renown as a conversationalist and a wit was founded in Edinburgh, it was in London that he was put to the acid test, and not found wanting.

At this point in his career, around the end of 1803 and the beginning of 1804, a confusion in dating appears which is not fully soluble by means of reference to the Church records or existing letters. Sydney talked his way into preaching a few random sermons at various London churches, but without experiencing the desired effect of being appointed to a remunerative living. In the process, though, he came to the attention of Sir Thomas Bernard, one of the great philanthropists of the age, who, although he was in the evangelical camp of the Church, saw such an attractive preaching talent in Sydney that he recommended him as an alternate evening preacher in the chapel of the Foundling Hospital.

The Foundling Hospital was an old and prestigious foundation even in Sydney's time, having been founded in 1739 by Thomas Coram, a philanthropic sea captain who had been shocked at the sight of exposed and dead children on London streets. With the help of genteel ladies, the Hospital performed its humanitarian work well. It provided a refuge for illegitimate or orphaned children throughout the eighteenth and nineteenth centuries, and still exists today under the name of the Thomas Coram Foundation. The foundlings brought to its doors were so tragically numerous, that some had on occasion to be turned away and a regular system of admissions established. Once admitted to the hospital, the foundlings received adequate food, minimal medical attention, spiritual training, and were apprenticed as early as possible in order to make space for more foundlings. The care they received was probably the best the foundation could offer, and although a serious effort was made to apprentice the children well, and to check on them in ensuing years, life for the foundlings in the hospital was a grim struggle at best, because of 14,934 received only 4,400 survived to be apprenticed.[39] Appalling as those figures are, they were probably not too much higher than the general infant mortality rate among the lower classes. Similarly, the Dublin Foundling Hospital, in much the same period, recorded 12,641 children admitted, of whom at least 9,804 died, and only 145 were known to be living.[40]

In the early nineteenth century, Sir Thomas Bernard was treasurer of the Foundling Hospital, and one of the most important figures on its General Committee, and he assisted Sydney in obtaining a preachership in its chapel. Necessity makes strange bedfellows indeed, and it is almost mystifying to find Bernard, one of the most outstanding evangelical humanitarians of the period, assisting Sydney, who came to be known as one of the most eminent exponents of rational religion and liberal ideas, to obtain such a position. The explanation is that Bernard correctly assessed Sydney as the kind of preacher who would be popular at the Foundling Chapel, and knew that Sydney needed the money and the prestige that were attached to the preachership. The Foundling Chapel, oddly enough, had become a popular and fashionable church for the elite of the area, and its popularity and income depended upon the quality of its preacher.

According to Saba Holland, Sir Thomas Bernard was so struck by Sydney's "sense and originality" that he recommended him for a preachership, and it was given to him; but the facts are a little more complicated. A popular London preacher was at least as much a performer as he was a pastor, and as early as 13 June, 1804, Sydney had been asked to preach a baptismal service at the chapel of the Foundling Hospital on the following Sunday evening.[40] This was the kind of opportunity Sydney sought in London, and he was more than able to comply, especially since he lived within walking distance of the Chapel. He sent a note which was entered in the minutes for 20 January, 1804, saying that he was flattered by their resquest, and that he would preach with "great pleasure". The minutes for the same day recorded the thanks of the General Committee for his "Excellent Discourse".[42]

In reality, his first sermon at the Foundling Hospital was little less than an audition before a discerning congregation, and critical General Committee; and he appears to have passed the test with honors. He had no further connections with the General Committee until 16 January, 1805, when he was asked to preach a morning sermon on 10 February in place of a Rev. Mr. Hutton.[43] He replied on 19 January, accepting the invitation and apologizing for not having answered sooner. The reason for his tardiness, he said, was that he had been unable until that time "to arrange the business of my own chapel."[44] In this instance, Sydney was in luck, for he gave the sermon on 10 February, and the following day the Rev. Mr.

Archer Thompson, an alternate evening preacher at the Foundling Chapel, died. With Sydney's sermon still fresh in their minds, the General Committee met on 13 February and agreed to meet in one week's time to recommend a successor to Mr. Thompson.[45] At their meeting on 20 February, the General Committee unanimously recommended Sydney for the position.[46] On 27 February, testimonials of his moral and clerical character were presented to the Committee, along with evidence of his ordination to Priest's Orders, and the following recommendation:

> We recommend the Rev. Sydney Smith, A.M. as one of the Evening Preachers of this charity in the room of the Rev. Archer Thompson, deceased, he being in our opinion a proper person for the situation.[47]

It is interesting that although Sir Thomas Bernard was quite probably his patron, the recommendation was not signed by him, but by Thomas Everett and John Hunter, both of whom were members of the General Committee. Although their action does not appear in the minutes, the General Committee apparently confirmed Sydney at that time, for on 3 April, 1805, the secretary recorded a letter from Sydney, thanking the General Committee for his confirmation.[48]

Sydney was undoubtedly a good preacher, and he demonstrated his ability in the chapel at the Foundling Hospital. On 8 May, 1805, the General Committee presented their thanks to him for a sermon which was evidently one of two charity sermons which had brought in §180.[49] The chapel was an important source of revenue for the Foundling Hospital, and Sydney's preaching seems at least to have maintained and possibly to have augmented that income. Pew rents were two guineas a sitting, and the weekly collections ranged from §20 to §60, with substantial additional sums collected for charitable or patriotic causes. A thanksgiving offering for the victory at Trafalgar, collected on 11 December, 1805, brought in §293/11 for the Patriotic Fund;[50] and on April, 1806, two charity sermons raised a total of §243.[51] It can be seen that the chapel at the Foundling Hospital, in addition to serving as a center for spiritual instruction for the foundlings, and a chapel of ease for the elite of the area, was a significant source of revenue for the foundation. At the poorest, the chapel must have grossed at least §1000, but more likely the total was nearer §3000 or §4000. Since there were several preachers at the chapel, it is difficult to assess Sydney's role in this continuing financial success, but he undoubtedly contributed to it.

Disappointingly, no records of the chapel itself survive, or if they do, they cannot be located by ordinary research methods; so nothing can be learned about when Sydney preached in the Foundling Chapel, or how many people attended his services. He was an alternate evening preacher, and his biographers and others claim that he was outstandingly successful.[52] Since no evidence to the contrary exists, it may be assumed that they were correct. Certainly the General Committee of the Foundling Hospital was satisfied with his performance, even though few additional references to him appear in their minutes. On 12 June, 1805, he asked permission to absent himself for four weeks, and in July of 1805 through 1808, he made the same request for five week vacations. In each instance, the General Committee readily agreed.[53] He also exhibited a general interest in the problems of preaching in chapels, and as early as 10 April, 1805, he joined with two other preachers to ask for the erection of a sounding board to facilitate their preaching. The committee rejected the request on the grounds that it was not necessary, and that it would obstruct the view of the children.[54] Their rejection of the petition was not a reflection of their opinion of Sydney's ability, for in March, 1808, the General Committee instructed:

> "...the Secretary write to the Rev. Sydney Smith, and request he will interest himself with the Board of the New River Company for a supply of water for the First and second stories of the Hospital.[55]

In his position as auditor of the New River Company, Sydney accomplished that task without difficulty. He resigned from his preachership at the Foundling Hospital on 23 October, 1808, in order to move to Yorkshire. His resignation was accepted by the General Committee on 9 November, 1808, and Sydney ended his connection with the Foundling Hospital.[56]

Of no great importance, but in order to prevent a future "expose" of Sydney Smith as the putative father of an illegitimate child in the foundling Hospital, it should be mentioned that there was a foundling in the hospital during Sydney's time who was named "Sidney" or "Sydney" Smith. When admitted to the hospital, he had been assigned the number 18, 452, and only two references to him appear in the minutes of the General Committee, both in 1807. John McGowan, a bootmaker of number 314 the Strand, had requested that the foundling be apprenticed to him and the foundation was willing to comply if a medical examination showed that the child was strong enough. A medical examination evidently demonstrated that he was, and the boy was duly apprenticed on 28 October, 1807.[57] He was then probably about nine years old, for baptismal records of the Foundling Hospital reveal that he had been baptised on 10 June, 1798.[58] It is possible that this child was Sydney's natural son, but the likelihood is so slim as to make it improbable Sydney had been in London in 1797, and he could have engaged in an illicit union which could have resulted in the child, which the mother could have named for him; but the probability is still slimmer since illegitimate children took their mother's name, which would have required that the foolish virgin also be named Smith. It seems likely too, that if Sydney had had illegitimate children, he would have acknowledged them and made some provision for them. He was not known for his amorous escapades, and to attribute this child to him is saying no more than that he was the father of any illegitimate child born in London who was named Smith. No references to such a child exist anywhere in Sydney's letters, or in his will, and the name "Smith" in the records of the Foundling Hospital is scarcely a sound basis for such a charge.

Sydney's success in the chapel of the Foundling Hospital may well have been his first triumph in the metropolis, but his reputation in Edinburgh had preceded him, and his letter of 19 January, 1805, had said that he already had a chapel to attend to. He refers to the chapel without naming it, so it may have been a temporary situation; but he was probably referring to Berkeley Chapel, on John Street, Berkeley Square, or he may even have meant Fitzroy Chapel, on Maple Street, Fitzroy Square, for he was alternate morning preacher at both chapels. Usable records on Sydney Smith from either chapel are sorely lacking, although some may exist in private hands. Some records of Fitzroy Chapel from 1786 to 1793, and a register from 1815 to 1827, are to be found in the Greater London Record Office but, since Sydney did not serve Fitzroy Chapel during any of those years, they are of no value in a study of Sydney Smith. Also, no public records at all appear to have survived from Berkeley Chapel. Ecclesiastical records generally suffered great destruction during World War II, and Fitzroy Chapel, which had become the church of St. Saviour's in 1863, and had been attached to the church of St. John the Evangelist in 1913, was totally destroyed by a bomb in 1945.[59] Berkeley Chapel was demolished a "good many years" before 1921.[60] To complicate matters still more, both chapels were proprietary chapels, operating under license. Built by wealthy individuals, and intended as much, probably, for the convenience of a locality as for profit, their primary function was to offer Sunday morning worship services, and the proprietor was under no legal compulsion to keep records. The proprietor, a Mr. Bowerbank in the case of Berkeley Chapel, merely hired a preacher or preachers, took up collections, rented out pews, paid the preachers, maintained the chapel, and pocketed the remainder of the income.

This lack of records makes Sydney's activities in Berkeley and Fitzroy chapels rather uncertain, but some information about the chapels may be gleaned from other sources. In a letter dated by Nowell Smith "about October, 1806",[61] Sydney mentioned that he had been at Berkeley Chapel for "nearly two years", which would place his appointment some time in the autumn of 1804; but Nowell Smith fairly obviously misdated the letter, for another letter, in the Wedgwood Museum, dealing with the same subject is dated December, 1805.[62] Both letters were written at about the same time, so this would mean that Sydney must have been appointed to a morning preachership in the winter of 1803-1804. If such is the case, he must have been appointed to Berkeley Chapel a year and a half before his appointment to the Foundling Hospital; so his first London accomplishments probably took place there rather than at the Foundling Chapel. Records are still more scanty on Fitzroy Chapel, but it would appear that he secured an appointment to that chapel in 1805.[63]

To say that Sydney was a successful preacher in London would be an understatement. It would be better to describe him as a sensation. Church-going was more nearly universal during that period, and preaching performances were judged with a form of criticism unually reserved for politicians or eminent actors in the twentieth century. Times, and the public attitude towards preaching, changed rapidly, and as early as 1845, the writer of Sydney's obituary in the Gentleman's Magazine expressed astonishment at Sydney's role in the world of religion and entertainment:

> One of the publications of that period describes him as having been "engaged" to preach at those places of resort; just as one might speak of a theatrical "star" being "engaged" to perform at Covent-garden or Drury-lane. Doubtless the Rev. Sydney Smith was, in his own way, a star of the first magnitude; and too happy were the proprietors of whatever trading chapel had the good fortune to place in their pulpit a man whose sermons were pointed and elaborate without the appearance of art; natural, without the affectation of ease; and spirited, without any flagrant breach of "the ecclesiastical proprieties."[64]

Reginald Colby, writing in 1966, could describe Sydney as:

> The greatest of all preachers, the Rev. Sydney Smith ...made his reputation in Mayfair. He was engaged as Morning preacher at the Berkeley Chapel.... Sydney Smith the Smith of Smiths-thundered at his congregations and did not spare their feelings. Crowds flocked to hear him; at the same time he was lecturing on moral philosophy at the Royal Institution...and preaching the evening sermon at Fitzroy Chapel.[65]

It is too much to say that Sydney Smith was the greatest of all preachers, or even that he was the greatest preacher of his period, but he was clearly an outstanding preacher. Saba Holland says that Berkeley Chapel had previously been almost deserted, so much so that Mr. Bowerbank was trying to dispose of it, but within a few weeks after her father began to preach there, it was filled to overflowing.[66] Originally hired for two years, he was to remain until his departure for Yorkshire in 1809. A farewell sermon, written in 1809, but not published until 1846, expresses what may have been his sentiments on leaving Berkeley Chapel:

> I have not long to express my sentiments in this place ....there remains to me

only the painful task of bidding adieu
to this congregation. I am exceedingly
grateful for the attention with which
I have always been heard, and I can
safely and conscientiously say that I
never got into this pulpit but with a
sincere desire of doing good, and with
a perfect indifference to every consequence I might incur in my attempt to
do it. I have not so much desired to
please, as to be really and permanently
useful; to promote those sound morals,
and that rational religion, which I
most firmly believe to be the only pass-
ports to present happiness and future
salvation.[67]

Of Fitzroy Chapel, much less can be learned. It was a plain brick chapel on the north side of Maple Street at the corner of Whitfield Street. Built by the Rev. Anthony Bromley on lease from Lord Southampton, it had been opened in 1788, and Sydney was there from 1805 to 1808.[68] It had a distinguished congregation in the early nineteenth century, which included the painters Benjamin West, B. R. Haydon, Sir David Wilkie, and Sir Charles Eastlake, all of whom, Sydney is reputed to have said, "had sat at Gamaliel's feet, and that it was he who had made them what they were."[69] Another farewell sermon of 1809 exists which may have been delivered at Fitzroy Chapel, and in which Sydney said:

I have always endeavoured to do my duty
like an honest man, always remembering
that I was not here to please, but to
bear witness boldly to the truth. It
is very possible I may have pushed this
feeling too far; if I have, I beg you
to forget it...the meaning has always
been good.[70]

Opinions varied concerning Sydney's preaching, and Reid was to write that while he was a very popular preacher, he was never a great one, certainly never a theologian; and that his sermons were nothing more than sanctified common sense, delivered with vigor and freshness.[71] Far more liberal than most of his competitors, he was also more outspoken in the pulpit than most of them. His daughter described his "...grand form and powerful countenance, noble and melodious voice. In reading the Lessons and Psalms he read so as almost to make a commentary on every word, and the meaning came out so rich and deep.[72] His obituary in the *Times* is rather surprising in that although it was generally hostile, it commended the sparkle and competence of his preaching, and asserted that because of those qualities "...there was no lack of self-elected judges to dispute his orthodoxy, or of blunderers to criticize his style."[73]

Despite his critics, Sydney's preaching style was a success in London, and by 1805, he had proven himself in Berkeley Chapel, Fitzroy Chapel, and the Chapel of the Foundling Hospital. His future looked much brighter. Although his income was improving, the salaries of his various positions are still uncertain. His widow said that she believed his preachership at Berkeley paid §90 a year,[74] but that she was not at all certain. This amount would seem to have been a reasonable salary, although he might have demanded more in later years. Saba Holland said about his employment at the Foundling Hospital:

> About this time he made the acquaintance of Sir Thomas Bernard, who was so much struck with his sense and originality that he recommended him to the preachership of the Foundling Hospital, at §50 per annum, which employment, small as was the remuneration, was gladly accepted. Slight as this service was, and probably suggested more for the benefit of the Hospital than for that of my father, I must still feel grateful to one who thus held out a helping hand to a clever and friendless young man struggling with the difficulties of the world and eager to perform the duties of his profession....[75]

Reid, obviously quoting Saba, also listed his salary at the Foundling Chapel as §50, but Chevrillon, without quoting a source, says his salary there was §250. Although that sum might seem high for an alternate evening preacher, it should be remembered that by the time Sydney was appointed to that position he had an established reputation both as a preacher and a lecturer. His salary at Fitzroy Chapel cannot be known with any certainty, but since Fitzroy Chapel was frequented by elite society, the salary must have been attractive and may have been substantial. It is difficult to total up dubious and unknown figures, but it would appear that by 1805, Sydney was earning at least §200 per year from his preaching, and more likely closer to §400. In addition, he was receiving §50 a year from the New River Company, possibly a good bit more, and he was also in receipt of §100 a year from his brother Bobus in India.[77]

Sydney's reputation as a reviewer, and his growing prestige as a popular preacher, enabled him to acquire some additional wealth and a good deal of fame from his lectures at the Royal Institution. Founded only in 1799, the Royal Institution had already drawn a good deal of public attention through the lectures of Sir Humphrey Davy, but Sydney's lectures were to create a positive furor that was of great benefit in furthering the Institution's program of popularizing science. Sir Thomas Bernard had recommended Sydney to the Royal Institution as a lecturer in moral philosophy, and he began his lectures in November, 1804. It may seem surprising that his lectures on moral philosophy should have occasioned such a stir, and especially since everyone, Sydney included, agreed that he knew nothing whatsoever of philosophy. The reverse of the coin, though, was that he was an accomplished preacher, and his lectures differed from his preaching style only in the humor he employed and in the sources he quoted (In fact, they were often the same.) Actually, however, Sidney did know some philosophy, for as a gentlemen and a university graduate, he was expected to be conversant on all topics, and he had attended lectures on philosophy in Edinburgh and read at least a limited amount of philosophy. Of Sydney's projected lectures, Francis Horner, writing to a friend in Edinburgh in 1804, said:

> I suppose you know that Smith begins to lecture on Moral philosophy next Saturday...You would be amused to hear the account he gives of his own qualifications for the task, and his mode of manufacturing philosophy; he will do the thing very cleverly...and he is sufficiently aware of all the forbearances to be observed. Profound lectures on metaphysics would be unsuitable to the place; he may do some good, if he makes the subject amusing. He will...make the real blue-stockings a little more disagreeable than ever, and sensible women a little

more sensible.[78]

A week later, Horner wrote to another friend to say:

> Our friend Sydney gave his first lecture on Saturday; I was not there, but all the accounts I have collected from different sorts of people agree in its favour, and that it took extremely well.[79]

Despite, or perhaps because of, his unorthodox methods of preparing and delivering his talks in moral philosophy, Sydney's lectures became one of the sensations of the year, and the lecture hall was always crammed with elegant listeners. From six to eight hundred fashionable ladies and gentlemen crowded into the hall, and the lobbies around it, and seats were not to be procured at any price. Before each lecture, the crush of arriving carriages was such that Albemarle Street and Grafton Street were jammed. His salary was modest, §50 and two passes for life to the Royal Institution, which does not seem like a great deal for twenty lectures. Sydney himself deprecated his efforts as a philosopher by describing his lectures as "the most successfull swindle of the season",[80] and in April of 1805, near the close of the first series, he wrote to Jeffrey to say:

> My lectures are just now at such an absurd pitch of celebrity, that I must lose a good deal of reputation before the judgment of the public settles into a just equilibrium respecting them. I am most heartily ashamed of my own fame, because I am conscious I do not deserve it, and that the moment men of sense are provoked by the clamour to look into my claims, it will be at an end.[81]

Sydney's disparagement of his own work notwithstanding, the fact of his success at the Royal Institution indicates that his course of lectures possessed qualities of some worth. He brought philosophy down out of the clouds for many of his auditors; and if he remained more a preacher than a philosopher, he preached on philosophy in a robust style with an optimistic theology as he compared the thought of Greece and England. In contrast to the usual practice of most of the scholars of his age, Sydney richly approved of progress, reason, and the modern improvements of the nineteenth century. He, therefore, never hesitated to assert the superiority of Bacon over Aristotle, England over ancient Greece, and the present over the past. His lecture style was lucid and brief for he did not so much develop his ideas as state matters of fact which he and his audience could grasp as being intuitively true. He was an original thinker in philosophy only in the sense that he contined to uphold the traditions of observation and experimentation which were derived from Newton and Locke.[82]

If what Sydney described can be called a system of thought, it was characteristically British in seeing "things as they were" rather than through the eyes of a system artificially imposed on a body of data. He had an innate distrust of metaphysics, and if philosophy or logic contradicted habitual conceptions, he assumed that the philosophy had to be in error. His view of life was theological and practical, and he believed that the object of life was to live it sanely and with purpose in society. His views were theological in the sense that he acknowledged the practical value of religion and the Church, for which reason he regarded an atheist as a social outcast who threatened both society and happiness.[83] Lecture XIX is the key to an understanding of his purpose in the lectures, and it is probably the key to an understanding of their success as well. Sydney was not so much addressing himself to ethics, which purpose he had earlier denied, as he was offering moral instruction on the principles of liberalism and common sense. It might even be said that he was offering an explication of the intellectual mystique of the enlightened English aristocrat, along with a general admonition to his audiences to become aware and not to accept hackneyed platitudes.[84] If his lectures are read with this concept in mind, their popularity becomes clear, and a picture of Sydney emerges in which he stands not as a great philosopher, but as an inspired teacher.

The lectures were so successful that Sydney was engaged to give a second series, for which he was paid $120, and a third series, presumably at the same price. As a result of this acquisition of wealth, he was able to move from his modest quarters on Doughty Street to a more comfortable and imposing home at 18 Orchard Street, Portman Square, which he furnished. Although he may have considered continuing his lectures, or giving them again under different auspices,[85] he scoffed at them in less exuberant moments, and refused to consider publication. He later burned some of them but the surviving manuscripts were published by his widow. When asked about them in 1843, he said that:

> My lectures are gone to the dogs, and are utterly forgotten. I know nothing of moral philosophy, but I was thoroughly aware that I wanted §200 to furnish my house. The success, however, was prodigious....[86]

The lectures certainly were neither literary nor philosophical masterpieces, yet they were successful because Sydney carefully gauged the capacity of his well-bred audience and said competently not so much what they wanted to hear as what they could understand. His lectures were not on philosophy in the academic sense, but they were philosophy in the literal sense of love of wisdom. They were calculated to stimulate thought on a moderately elevated level in a group of people who devoted little of their time and effort to thinking of any description. Given Sydney's opportunity, a philosopher of the period would probably have either bored his hearers with a skillful demonstration of his contributions to knowledge, beginning with positions at best dimly understood by the audience; or he would have exhausted them with a recital of the developments of the various philosophical systems. Sydney did neither. He began by warning the assemblage that he intended to be dull, boring, at best uninteresting, and then proceeded to refute himself by holding his audience in the palm of his hand throughout the series. His wit brightened the lectures, and he could say:

> I promised, in the beginning of these lectures, to be very dull and unamusing; and I am of opinion that I have hitherto acted up to the spirit of my contract; but if there should perchance exist in any man's mind the slightest suspicion of my good faith, I think this day's lecture will entirely remove that suspicion, and that I shall turn out to be a man of unsullied veracity![87]

In one of his early lectures, he asserted the value of moral philosophy in a way that not only defined his purpose, but also explained a great deal of his own world view.

> If it is useful to our talents, and virtues, to turn the mind inwardly upon itself, and to observe attentively the facts relative to our possions and faculties, this is the value and this the object, of Moral Philosophy. It teaches, for the conduct of the understanding, a variety of delicate rules which can result only from such sort of meditation; and it gradually subjects the most impetuous feelings to patient examination and wise control; it inures the youthful mind to intellectual difficulty, and to enterprise in thinking; and makes it as keen as an eagle, and as unwearied as the wing of an angel.... With sensation alone, we might have possessed the earth, as it is possessed by the lowest order of beings; but we have talents which bend <u>all</u> the laws of nature to our service.... All these things Moral Philosophy observes, and, observing, adores the Being from whence they proceed.[88]

He spoke admiringly of Socrates and Plato, but Aristotle, by comparison with Bacon, fared rather badly:

> To Lord Bacon we are indebted for an almost daily extension of our knowledge of the laws of nature in the outward world; and the same modest and cautious spirit of inquiry extended to Moral Philosophy, will probably at last give us clear, intelligible ideas of our spiritual nature. Each succeeding year is an additional confirmation to us that we are traveling in the true path of knowledge; and as it brings in fresh tributes of science for the increases of human happiness, it extorts from us fresh tributes of praise to the guide and father of true philosophy. To the understanding of Aristotle, equally vast, perhaps, and equally original, we are indebted for fifteen hundred years of quibbling and ignorance; in which the earth fell under the tyranny of words,

> and philosophers quarreled with one another like drunken men in dark rooms who hate peace without knowing why, or seeing how to take aim. Professors were multiplied without the world becoming wiser; and volumes of Aristotelian philosophy were written which, if piled one upon another, would have equalled the Tower of Babel in height, and far exceeded it in confusion. Such are the obligations we owe to the mighty Stagirite; for that he was of a very mighty understanding, the broad circumference and the deep root of his philosophy most lamentably evince.[89]

Sydney's abhorrence of metaphysics appeared early in the lectures, and he never deviated from it, even though he made it clear from time to time that he had some passing acquaintance with metaphysics. Regarding the popular view of philosophy, he said:

> A great deal of unpopularity has been incurred by this science from the extravagances and absurdities of those who have been engaged in it. When the mass of mankind hear that all thought is explained by vibrations and vibrantiuncles of the brain, --that there is no such thing as a material world, -- that what mankind consider as their arms and legs, are not arms and legs, but _ideas_ accompanied with the notion of _outness_, --that we have not only no bodies, but no minds; -- that we are nothing, in short, but currents of reflection and sensation; all this, I admit, is well calculated to approximate, in the public mind, the ideas of lunacy and intellectual philosophy.[90]

Sydney expounded further on Bacon, as well as Locke, Hartley, and Priestley; and of his friend Dugald Stewart, he could not resist saying that:

> He is the _first_ writer who ever carried a feeling _heart_ and a creative fancy into the depth of these abstract sciences, without rendering them a mess of

>declamatory confusion. He has not rendered his metaphysice dry and disgusting, like Reid; he has not involved them in lofty obscurity, like Plato; nor has he poisoned them with impiety, like Hume. Above all, he has that invaluable talent of inspiring the young with the love of knowledge, the love of virtue, and that feeling of modest independence which has ever been the ornament of his conduct. I have been his pupil, and have received kindnesses at his hands ...I know of no reason why he is not ranked among the first writers of the English language, except that he is still alive; and my most earnest and hearty wish is, that *that* cause of his depreciation may operate for many, many years to come![91]

Throughout his lectures Sydney constantly exhibited a chauvinistic admiration for British thinkers, as well as a tendency to downgrade foreigners. Thus he was able to say:

> Descartes has perished, Leibnitz is fading away; but Bacon, and Locke, and Newton remain, as the Danube and the Alps remain;-the learned examine them, and the ignorant, who forget lesser streams and humbler hills, remember them as the glories and prominences of the world. And let us never, in thinking of perpetuity and duration, confine that notion for the physical works of nature, and forget the eternity of fame! God has shown his power in the stars and the firmament, in the aged hills and in the perpetual streams; but he has shown it as much, in the minds of the greatest of human beings! Homer and Vergil and Milton, and Locke and Bacon and Newton, are as great as the hills and the streams; and will endure till heaven and earth shall pass away, and the whole fabric of nature is shaken into dissolution and eternal ashes.[92]

Of Kant, to the contrary, he said:

> This superb list is terminated by Professor Kant, the explanation of whose philosophy I really can not attempt: first, from some very faint doubts whether it is explicable; next, from a pretty strong conviction that this good company would not be much pleased to sit for another half hour and hear me commenting on his twelve categories; his distinctions between empirical, rational, and transcendental philosophy; his absolute unity, absolute totality, and absolute causation; his four reflective conceptions, his objective noumenal reality, his subjective elements, and his pure cognition. I am very far from saying that these terms are without their share of relish and allurement; I must only decline, myself, the interpretation of them, and refer those whose curiosity they may excite, to the exposition of Villiers and Degerando, in their lately-published history of philosophy.[93]

Just as his sermons were practical and untheological, so his lectures were practical and unmetaphysical. Sydney reminded his listeners that genius was more frequently the result of application and hard work that it was of inspiration, and that this contention was borne out in the lives of Burke, Gibbon, Cicero, Milton, Pascal, etc.[94] He tried to persuade an audience whose interest were chiefly material and social of the value of learning and knowledge.

By this time in his life, Sydney's wit was well known, and his lecture on wit and humor must have been received with the greatest interest. The lecture, though, of no particular orginality, was well thought out, and demonstrated that while he was a spontaneous wit, he had given a good deal of thought to the subject. He defined a pun as "the wit of words", and gave the example of a schoolboy who pronounced "patriarch" as "partridge", thus giving a friend the opportunity to observe that he was making game of the patriarchs.[95] He felt that the essential ingredient of wit was surprise: that of making an unanticipated association. As an example, he mentioned an unhappily married French gentleman who had spent his evenings with a congenial mistress for a matter of years. His wife dies, and when a sympathetic friend asked him why he did not marry the mistress, he replied that if he did, he would not know where to spend his evenings.[96] He defined other forms of wit as:

> Buffoonery is voluntary incongruity ....to counterfeit some peculiarity incongruous enough to excite laughter ....Buffoone-y is general in its imitations; mimicry is particular.... Parody is the adaptation of the same thoughts to other subjects. Burlesque is that species of parody, or adaptation of thoughts to other subjects, which is intended to make the original ridiculous....bulls admit apparent relations that are not real.[97]

In his conclusion, he defined a witty man as a kind of dramatic performer who could not survive without applause.

> "A witty man...can no more exist without applause than he can without air; if his audience be small, or if they are inattentive, or if a new wit defrauds him of any portion of his admiration- it is all over with him....The applauses... are so essential to him that he must obtain them at the expense of decency, friendship, and good feeling...."[98]

> Sydney certainly did not intend these lines to be self-descriptive, but even though his wit rarely violated decency and never terminated friendship, they do present a very accurate picture of him.

Sydney's judgements and advice to those attending his lectures, were eminently down-to-earth, homely admonitions. His concepts of beauty, for example, was relative for he said that one man might believe the ornate sign post on a public house to be more beautiful than a masterpiece, and that he would be right; but only insofar as his own taste was concerned, Sydney also believed that more objective aesthetic standards could be established, not by "...universal suffrage, but by requiring that a man shall have forty shillings a year in common sense, and have paid the usual taxes of labor, attention, observation, and so on."[99] He urged his audiences to read widely and intensively, as well as regularly and admonished them to be good listeners rather than contradictors.[100]

Sydney's lectures were not exactly religious, but they gave him additional recognition of the kind that made it possible for him to hope for further advancement in the Church. When appointed alternate evening preacher at the Foundling Hospital, he had already made a name at the Royal Institution, and his reputation as a preacher was established. His preaching and lecturing did not occupy him fully, and he turned his hopes and attention to a dissenting chapel on York Street, St. James's Square. Privately owned, it was leased to a sect known as the Christians of the New Jerusalem; but the lease was near expiration, and Sydney hoped to lease the chapel and preach in it. The only requirement, apart from the financing, which Sydney evidently intended to do himself, was to secure the permission of the rector of the parish in which the chapel was located - in this case, the Rev. Gerrard Andrewes, St. James's, Picadilly. The dating of this event has been obsured by Sydney's biographers, who date it only in the vaguest terms; by Sydney himself who apparently failed to date some of his letters; and by Nowell Smith, who cautiously and probably incorrectly dated the first of his letters to Andrewes "Before October 1806".[101] In that letter, however, Sydney said that in applying to Andrewes he realized that he would also have to apply to the patron of the living, but that he believed it proper to apply to the clergyman first. Two letters from Sydney in the Wedgwood Museum pertain to the chapel, Josiah Wedgwood appearing to be its patron; and the first of these letters, dated 6 July, 1805, asked for the refusal of the lease when it expired.[102] Unless Sydney was not being fully honest with Andrewes, his letter to Wedgwood would indicate that he had written to Andrewes still earlier. None of the other letters in Nowell Smith's edition narrow down the date any closer that "Winter 1806-7",[103] which date is apparently in error by at least a year.

Sydney based his request to Andrewes on the ground that there was not enough room in the places of worship of the Established Church in the heavily populated St. James's parish, and that he could provide another Church of England chapel, which Andrewes would prefer more than

the present dissenting congregation. He also appealed
to Andrewes to aid a young and struggling clergyman,
and referred to himself as a curate. In the light of
the twentieth century, Andrewes' response was amazing
for he refused Sydney the permission he needed on the
grounds that his predecessors had established a policy
of not permitting Anglican services in the chapel, and
he did not want to impose any obligations on his successors. Sydney's rejoinder, a plea that he be permitted to preach only during Andrewe's life, was courteously but firmly refused.[104] Why the Rector of St.
James's took such a position is puzzling, even if one
tries to view the situation without present mindedness.
It is quite possible that his fear of establishing a
precedent was really his reason. Sydney's widow, who
apparently knew Andrews later in life, wrote:

> Dr. Andrew's patron Bishop Porteus was
> the Parent of the New Evangelical School,
> fast spreading thro his powerful influence into importance. Dr. Andrews did
> not dare exercise any of the good feelings of his nature, by letting an enlightened & liberal minded young man
> into his Parish, lest it should be displeasing to his narrow Minded Bishop.[105]

Having written those words, however, she crossed out the
entire passage in her memoir, and then she or someone
else crossed it out again in red ink. She saw Bishop
Porteus as the villain of the scene; but she wrote over
forty years after the event, and both her memory and her
interpretations are not reliable. An alternative explanation of Andrewes' action is that he refused Sydney
permission to hold Anglican services in his parish simply because it was his right and privilege to do so. He
stood to gain nothing by giving Sydney leave to preach,
and he might conceivably have lost some of his parishioners to him, even though Andrewes has been described
as an able and amiable man. It was, nevertheless,
Andrewes' right to deal with Sydney's application as he
saw fit. For these reasons, or perhaps more simply because it was less trouble to deny the request than to
approve it, Andrewes satisfied his own pleasure in the
matter.

    This anomaly of a country which advocated religious
freedom but also had a Established Church; a country in
which any sectarian was free to open a place of worship,

but where voluntary Anglican chapels could operate only at the whim of the rector of the parish, did not escape Sydney's attention. In an article in the <u>Edinburgh Review</u> in January, 1808, he wrote:

> ...as the law now stands, any man who dissents from the established church may open a place of worship where he pleases. No orthodox clergyman can do so, without the consent of the parson of the parish, -who always refuses because he does not chuse to have his monopoly disturbed; and refuses, in parishes where there are not accomodations for one half of the persons who wish to frequent the Church of England, and in instances where he knows that the chapels from which he excludes the established worship, will be immediately occupied by sectaries.[106]

When he spoke of the injustice of permitting dissenters a freedom which was denied to Anglicans, Sydney probably had the Christians of the New Jerusalem in mind; but his review was on the Methodists, against whom he was particularly prejudiced. His antipathy for Methodists is all the more remarkable because he was renowned for his enlightened views on religious toleration, and, though he was keenly aware of the Catholic origins of Anglican practices, he was certainly not in favor of high church ritual. His hostility to Methodism was caused first of all by their deviation from sober and accepted Anglican procedures, and secondly by their divergence from Sydney's dearly-held tenets of "rational religion". In all fairness to both Sydney and the Methodists, it should be said that his anti-Methodist position was regrettably without discrimination and that he used the term "Methodist" to mean any religious fanatic, specifically the "Arminian and Calvinistic methodists, and ...the evangelical clergymen of the church of England." To which he added: "We shall use the general term of Methodism, to designate these

> three classes of fanatics, not troubling ourselves to point out the finer shades, and nicer discriminations of lunacy, but treating them all as in one general conspiracy against common sense, and rational orthodox christianity.[107]

Most of the Methodists of his age were still communicants of the Church of England, and the Church evangelicals were moderate and responsible people; but Sydney lumped all evangelicals together and used "Methodist" as a term of opprobrium. While upholding their right to differ and dissent, he looked upon them in much the same way a respectable twentieth century clergyman looks upon the most irresponsible street-corner evangelist. Eight years later, he was to say about the Methodists in his own parish:

> I endeavour in vain to give them more cheerful ideas of religion; to teach them that God is not a jealous, childish, merciless tyrant; that he is best served by a regular tenour of good actions, -not by bad singing, ill-composed prayers, and eternal apprehensions. But the luxury of false religion is, to be unhappy.[108]

He regarded them not as hypocrites, but as "enthusiasts", who, in trying to be friends of religion, and by believing themselves the sole recipients of present revelation, made themselves unwittingly the enemies of true religion. He reiterated his conviction that they conspired against reason, and the results were:

> ...fatuity, folly, idiotism....This is the spectacle at which they should tremble who believe that religious feelings do not require the control of reason, and the aid of sound instruction.[109]

He believed further that Methodism removed all "the sweetness and comfort out of religion, and made earth an hell, God a tyrant, and man a wretch."[110]

Sydney's reviews on the Methodists are among his wittiest and most biting. In them he invariably contrasted the "manly, rational, and serious" character of the Church of Scotland and the Church of England with the wild emotions of the "Methodists". His method in 1808 was delightfully unfair, for he copiously quoted the emotional absurdities of various evangelical publications, and the quotations, ridiculous enough in themselves, took on added inanity when reprinted in the pages of the Edinburgh Review:

> **Interference respecting Swearing, -a bee the instrument.** A young man is stung by a bee, upon which he buffets the bees with his hat, uttering at the same time the most dreadful oaths and imprecations. In the midst of his fury, one of these little combatants stung him upon the tip of the unruly member (his tongue), which was then employed in blaspheming his Maker. Thus can the Lord engage one of the meanest of his creatures in reproving the bold transgressor who dares to take his name in vain.
>
> **The Reverend Mr. Mead's sorrow for his sins.** This wrought him up to temporary desperation; his inexpressible grief poured itself forth in groans: "O that I had never sinned against God! I live a hell here upon earth, and there is a hell for me in eternity!" One Lord's day, very early in the morning, he was awake by a tempest of thunder and lightning; and imagining it to be the end of the world, his agony was great, supposing the great day of divine wrath had come, and he was unprepared; but happy to find it not so.[111]

Sydney did not totally deny Special Providence or divine interference, although, like most of his contemporary practitioners of rational religion he believed that the age of miracles was past. He felt that most incidents in ordinary life were explainable by reference to natural law and that it was nothing short of blasphemy for the ignorant to claim every insignificant event to be miraculous, or to denounce anyone, lay or clerical, who disagreed, as an atheist. The examples he chose were unfair in that they were extreme, and did not reflect the beliefs of all the "Methodists". Nevertheless, his remarks did tend to make all Methodists look ridiculous and witless.

Despite his essential toleration, and his previous denunciation of "No Popery" slogans, Sydney was definitely on the offensive against the Methodists, and was trying to raise the cry of the "Church in danger". He feared Methodist interference from within the Church more than he did Roman Catholic threats from without, and it

was for that reason that he listed the respectable
Church evangelicals along with the less well-bred. He
felt that the evangelicals were a genuine danger to the
Church because of their active proselyting spirit. This,
accompanied by the reality of a concerted, systematic,
well-planned, and well-financed infiltration of the
clergy, posed a real and present threat. And even if he
had not thought of them as a menace to the Church, he
believed that their ideas were grossly erroneous and
their life-style an abomination. The Methodists, he
said:

> ...hate pleasure and amusements; no
> theatre, no cards, no dancing, no
> punchinello, no dancing dogs, no blind
> fiddlers; -all the amusements of the
> rich and of the poor must disappear,
> wherever these gloomy people get a
> footing. It is not the abuse of pleas-
> ure which they attack, but the inters-
> persion of pleasure, however much it
> is guarded by good sense and modera-
> tion; -it is not only wicked to hear
> the licentious plays of Congreve, but
> wicked to hear Henry the Vth, or the
> school for scandal; it is not only dis-
> sipated to run about to all the par-
> ties in London and Edinburgh, -but danc-
> ing is not fit for a being who is pre-
> paring himself for eternity. Ennui,
> wretchedness, melancholy, groans and
> sighs are the offerings which these un-
> happy men make to a Deity, who has
> covered the earth with gay colours, and
> scented it with rich perfumes; and shown
> us, by the plan and order of his works,
> that he had given to man something bet-
> ter than a bare existence, and scattered
> over his creation a thousand superfluous
> joys, which are totally unnecessary to
> the mere support of life.
>
> ...The Methodists lay very little
> stress upon practical righteousness.
> They do not say to their people, do not
> be deceitful; do not be idle; get rid
> of your bad passions; or at least (if
> they do say these things) they say them
> very seldom.....
>
> ...The Methodists are always desirous of

> making men more religious, than it is possible, from the constitution of human nature, to make them....there is not a mad-house in England, where a considerable part of the patients have not been driven to insanity by the extravagence of these people. We cannot enter such places without seeing a number of honest artizans, covered with blankets, and calling themselves angels, and apostles, who, if they had remained contented with the instruction of men of learning and education, would still have been sound masters of their own trade, sober christians, and useful members of society.[112]

Sydney never changed his opinion of the "Methodists", and in April, 1809, he returned to the attack in a review of a pamphlet by John Styles which attacked his earlier article on the Methodists. He obviously relished writing this review, and he began by saying:

> In routing out a nest of consecrated cobblers, and in bringing to light such a perilous heap of trash as we were obliged to work through, in our articles upon the Methodists and Missionaries, we are generally conceived to have rendered an useful service to the cause of rational religion. Every one, however, at all acquainted with the true character of Methodism, must have known the extent of the abuse and misrepresentation to which we exposed ourselves in such a service. All this obloquy, however, we were very willing to encounter, from our growing conviction of the necessity of exposing and correcting the growing evil of fanaticism. In spite of all misrepresentation, we have ever been, and ever shall be, the sincere friends of sober and rational Christianity. We are quite ready, if any fair opportunity occur, to defend it, to the best of our ability, from the tiger-spring of infidelity; and we are quite determined, if we can prevent such an evil, that it shall not be eaten up by the nasty and numerous vermin of Methodism. For this purpose, we shall

proceed to make a few short remarks upon the sacred and silly gentlemen before us....

These very imprudent people have one ruling canon, which pervades every thing they say and do. <u>Whoever is unfriendly to Methodism, is an infidel and an atheist</u>. This reasonable and amiable maxim, repeated in every form of dulness, and varied in every attitude of malignity, is the sum and substance of Mr. Styles's pamphlet. Whoever wishes to rescue religion from the hands of didactic artisans, -whoever prefers a respectable clergyman for his teacher, to a delerious mechanic; -whoever wishes to keep the intervals between churches and lunatic asylums as wide as possible, -all such men, in the estimation of Mr. Styles, are nothing better than open or concealed enemies of Christianity....

We are a good deal amused, indeed, with the extreme disrelish which Mr. John Styles exhibits to the humour and pleasantry with which he admits the Methodists to have been attacked; but Mr. John Styles should remember, that it is not the practice with destroyers of vermin to allow the little victims a <u>veto</u> upon the weapons used against them. If this were otherwise, we should have one set of vermin banishing small-tooth combs; another protesting against mouse-traps; a third prohibiting the finger and thumb; a fourth exclaiming against the intolerable infamy of using soap and water. It is impossible, however, to listen to such pleas. They must all be caught, killed, and cracked, in the manners, and by the instruments which are found most efficacious to their destruction; and the more they cry out, the greater plainly is the skill used against them. We are convinced a little laughter will do them more harm than all the arguments in the world.[113]

Sydney denied opposing the poor, asserting that to the contrary he opposed only "the writing poor, the publishing

138

poor, -the limited arrogance which mistakes its own trumpery sect for the world...we have attacked them...for want of modesty, want of sense, and want of true religion....", all of which Styles defended. In response to Sydney's earlier charges of blasphemy in Methodist claims of miracles and special interference in trivial instances, Styles had replied that "with Providence nothing is great, or nothing little", at which Sydney scoffed that "the creation of a worm or a whale, a Newton or a Styles, are equally easy to Omnipotence. But are they, in their results equally important to us?"[114] Sydney also quoted Styles' accusation that he was a student of Hume, Voltaire, and Kotzebue, and that he approved of the theatre, dancing, and seduction; to which Sydney replied:

> These are the blessings which the common people have to expect from their Methodistical instructors. They are pilfered of all their money, -shut out from all their dances, and country wakes, -and are then sent pennyless into the field, to gaze on the clouds, and smell the dandelions![115]

As a rational Christian who was materialistic and fun-loving, and who loathed the countryside, Sydney could not have constructed a more venomous sentence.

Styles' claim that the Established Church was indolent was admitted by Sydney to an extent, but he meant that its clergy were sane and responsible. "The fair way", he said, to compare Anglican and Methodist clergymen, was

> to estimate what the exertions of the lacrymal and suspirious clergy would be, if they stepped into the endowments of their conpetitors. The moment they ceased to be paid by the groan, -the instant that Easter offerings no longer depended upon jumping and convulsions, -Mr. Styles may assure himself, that the character of his darling preachers would become quiet, and their minds reasonable.

The world does not hate piety, said Sydney, what it hates is "the lust of power, when it is veiled under the garb of piety; -they hate canting and hypocrisy....."[116]

Styles also attacked another of Sydney's reviews, on Indian Missions, and once again Sydney was able to use his victim's own words to ridicule him.

> Having concluded his defense of Methodism, this fanatical writer opens upon us his Missionary battery, firing away with the most incessant fury, and calling names, all the time, as loud as lungs accustomed to the eloquence of the tub usually vociferate. In speaking of the cruelties which their religion entails upon the Hindoos, Mr. Styles is peculiarly severe upon us for not being more shocked at their piercing their limbs with kimes. This is rather an unfair mode of alarming his readers with the idea of some unknown instrument. He represents himself as having paid considerable attention to the manners and customs of the Hindoos; and, therefore, the peculiar stress he lays upon this instrument, is naturally calculated to produce, in the minds of the humane, a great degree of mysterious terror. A drawing of the kime was imperiously called for; and the want of it is a subtle evasion, for which Mr. Styles is fairly accountable. As he has been silent on this subject, it is for us to explain the plan and nature of this terrible and unknown piece of mechanism. A kime, then, is neither more nor less than a false print in the Edenburgh Review for a knife; and from this blunder of the printer has Mr. Styles manufactured this Daedalean instrument of torture, called a kime! We were at first nearly persuaded by his arguments against kimes; -we knew frightened; -we stated to ourselves the horror of not sending missionaries to a nation which used kimes: -we were struck with the nice and accurate information of the Tabernacle upon this important subject: -But we looked in the errata, and Mr. Styles to be always Mr. Styles, -always cut off from every hope of mercy, and remaining for ever himself.[117]

In essence Sydney continued the line he had taken in his review: that fanatical missionaries caused revolts in India and threatened the whole British position there by their excesses, without creating any real hope for widespread conversion. He pointed out the sectarian differences between the various missionaries, their hatrad of the Anglican Church, and he sneered at the suggestion that sectarian missionaries could convert Hindus, who could be made over into Anglicans. Always a practical man, Sydney was more concerned about the safety and well-being of his brothers and numerous friends in India than he was about visionary projects to evangelize the sub-continent. He did endorse missionary activity generally, provided it was carried on in a sober and responsible manner, and he was certainly at least as well informed about the prospects of the conversion of India as were his adversaries. He exhibited real concern for Indian converts, who, having lost caste by converting, frequently slid back into Hinduism, where they found themselves outcasts. In response to the "low malignity" of Styles, Sydney concluded his review by saying:

> ...we are, as we always have been, sincere friends to the conversion of the Hindoos. We admit the Hindoo religion to be full of follies, and full of enormities; -we think conversion a great duty; and should think it, if it could be effected, a great blessing: but our opinion of the Missionaries and of their employer is such, that we most firmly believe, in less than twenty years, for the conversion of a few degraded wretches, who would be neither Methodists nor Hindoos, they would infallibly produce the massacre of every European in India; the loss of our settlements; and consequently the chance of that slow, solid, and temperate introduction of Christianity, which the superiority of the European character may ultimately effect in the Eastern world. The Board of Controul (All Atheists, and disciples of Voltaire, of course) are so entirely of our way of thinking, that the most peremtory orders have been issued to send all the missionaries home upon the slightest appearance of disturbance. Those who have sons and brothers in India may now sleep in peace. Upon the transmission of

this order, Mr. Styles is said to have destroyed himself with a *kime*.[118]

Sydney's suspicion of the evangelical impulse had also been reflected in January, 1809 in his review of a work on the Society for the Suppression of Vice- an organization which, he agreed, was capable of doing a great deal of good if properly handled, but which could be, in the hands of fanatics, a menace to society and social peace. He accused the Society of attempting to suppress the pleasures of the poor, who were powerless to defend themselves, while ignoring the very real vices of the rich. He was dubious of the value of what he called organized informers for although he believed that a few informers in a country like England, which had almost no police protection, could be an aid to law and order; he feared that a large, organized, and subsidized body of informers or snoops "would either create an insurrection, or totally destroy the confidence and cheerfulness of private life."[119] He suspected further that the society might be used by individuals to conceal private vices and crimes under a smokescreen of accusations directed toward others. He approved of the suppression of cruelty to animals, and pointed out a list of such cruelties:

> Running an iron hook in the intestines of an animal; presenting this first animal to another as his food; and then pulling this second creature up, and suspending him by the barb in his stomach.
> Riding a horse till he drops, in order to see an innocent animal torn to pieces by dogs.
> Keeping a poor animal upright for many weeks, to communicate a peculiar hardness to his flesh.
> Making deep incisions into the flesh of another animal, while living, in order to make the muscles more firm.
> Immersing another animal, while living in hot water.
> Now we do fairly admit, that such abominable cruelties as these are worthy of the interference of the law: and, that the Society should have punished them, cannot be matter of surprise to any feeling mind. --But stop, gentle reader! these cruelties are the cruelties of the Suppressing Committee, not of the poor.

>   You must not think of punishing these.[120]

The cruelties were, of course, angling, hunting, the making of brawn, the crimping of cod and the boiling of lobsters; all of which were restricted to the well-to-do, and none of which had excited the indignation of the society. Sydney was touching an exposed nerve, as he well knew, for all of the evangelical societies concerned themselves with reforming or "bettering" the poor, while ingratiating themselves with, or at least not offending, the ruling classes. The justification of the societies was apparently hypocritical but actually pragmatic, for without the support of the rich and powerful the Evangelicals could not hope to reform the manners of the country at large. It was this qualitative distinction between the prohibited pleasures of the poor, and the ignored vices of the rich that gave Sydney his opportunity to play the gadfly, and to challenge an organization which he distrusted because of its "methodist" affiliations. He concluded his review by adding:

> In the present instance, our object has been, to suppress the arrogance of suppressers, -to keep them within due bounds, -to show them, that to do good requires a little more talent and reflection than they are aware of, -and, above all, to impress upon them, that true zeal for virtue knows no distinction between the rich and the poor; and that the cowardly and mean can never be the true friends of morality, and the promoters of human happiness. If they attend to these rough doctrines, they will ever find in the writers of this Journal their warmest admirers, and their most sincere advocates and friends.[121]

Sydney's distrust of the Evangelicals was endless, and it extended to his review of Hannah More's <u>Coelebs in Search of a Wife</u>, published in the <u>Edinburgh Review</u> in April, 1809. An eminent Anglican evangelical and philanthropist, she was also the first woman to achieve widespread success with her writing, and she possessed a near-prophetic reputation for her moralistic publications. Sydney, nonetheless, opened his review by saying:

> This book is written, or supposed to be

> written, (for we would speak timidly of
> the mysteries of superior beings), by
> the celebrated Mrs. Hannah More! We
> shall probably give great offence by
> such indiscretion; but still we must be
> excused to treating it as a book merely
> human, -an uninspired production, the
> result of mortality left to itself, and
> depending upon its own limited resources.
> In taking up the subject in this point
> of view, we solemnly disclaim the slight-
> est intention of indulging in any inde-
> corous levity, or of wounding the reli-
> gious feelings of a large class of very
> respectable persons. It is the only
> method in which we can possible make
> this work a proper object of criticism.
> We have the strongest possible doubts
> of the attributes usually ascribed to
> this authoress; and we think it more
> simple and manly to say so at once, than
> to admit nominally superlunary claims,
> which, in the progress of our remarks,
> we should virtually deny.[122]

After an almost insulting résumé of the trite plot and lugubrious morality of the book, he expressed his distress at Mrs. More's apparent inability to make qualitative distinctions regarding sin; for while he too deplored dissipation in life, he felt that she was being too hard on the "ordinary amusements of mankind". Sydney objected to immorality in the theatre, but Hannah More opposed "the word <u>Playhouse</u>, which seems so closely connected in the minds of these people, with sin and Satan, that it stands in their vocabulary for every species of abomination." And her other prohibitions were:

> No cards--because cards are employed in
> gaming; no assemblies--because many dis-
> sipated persons pass their lives in as-
> semblies. Carry this but a little fur-
> ther, and we must say, -no wine, because
> of drunkenness; no meat, becuase of glut-
> tony; no use, that there may be no abuse!
> ....These little abstinences are the cock-
> ades by which the party are known, -the
> rallying points for the evangelical fac-
> tion. So natural is the love of power,
> that it sometimes becomes the influencing

> motive with the sincere advocates of
> that blessed religion, whose very
> characteristic excellence is the humi-
> lity which it inculcates.[123]

Similarly, Mrs. More's objections to revealing gowns led her to admonish even the most promiscuous young ladies to cover themselves fully in order to make their persons more alluring, which led Syndey to suggest that if such were the case, then the most virtuous women should go about in the nude. He saw in the book the mournful results of over-religiosity in humans who were not made for that kind of over-emphasis; and he ended his review by recommending the book to women and children, with the warning that husbands and fathers should see that they understood the piety and christianity in it, while rejecting the "trash and folly of Methodism".[124]

Sydney opposed "Methodism" because it opposed "rational religion", but he also believed that it endangered the Established Church, of which he was an ordained priest, as well as a rising and ambitious one. His successes in Edinburgh and London have already been outlined, and when, in 1806, Pitt died, a coalition cabinet came into office, which meant that some of the long-suffering Whigs were to be rewarded. Sydney had spoken resignedly of his lack of prospects in the Church in 1804, and had described his future as hopeless as late as 1805.[125] In 1806, however, the Whigs obtained at least some of the fruits of political success, and since Sydney's name stood high on the list the Lord Chancellor, Thomas Erskine, acting under pressure from the Hollands, gave him the living at Foston-le-Clay in Yorkshire.[126] His biographers have often disparged Foston because it was outside London and southern England, and because it was not a genteel parish. Even with these shortcomings though, it had an income of §500 a year, plus privileges that could be converted into cash; and, Sydney became a beneficed clergyman, by the aquisition of that living. A great deal of nonsense has been written about Sydney's opposition to giving preferment in the Church on the basis of connections rather than ability, but his objections were based on his inability to utilize Tory connections; and his appointment to Foston was based on his services to the Whigs rather than on his proven ability in the Church. He is reported to have approached Lord Erskine to thank him for the living, to which Erskine replied: "Oh, don't thank me, Mr. Smith. I gave you the living because Lady Holland insisted on my doing so; and if she had desired me to give it to the devil, he must have had it."[127]

It is also interesting, in the light of what has been written about Sydney's attitude towards pluralism and absenteeism in the Church, especially with regard to Tories, that he immediately set out to establish himself as a pluralist and permanent absentee from Foston. On the basis of his preachership at the Foundling Hospital, he requested and was granted the right of non-residence by the Archbishop. Russell, in his biography of Sydney Smith, mentioned that he was "curiously irritated" by Spencer Perceval's Clergy Residence Act of 1806, but there seems to be no reason why it should be "curious" that Sydney desired to reside in London, holding his lucrative preacherships and still collecting his salary from Yorkshire. Traditionally, except for Perceval's Act, it was his privilege to do so, and he entered into that hitherto-denied privilege with the greatest zest. Also, one of his earliest acts was to double the rent of the farmer of his glebe land.[128] Perceval's Act, however, hung over his head, and he knew that he would ultimately be forced either to reside at Foston or to resign the living. One other alternative existed though-- that of exchanging it for a living of equal value in a more congenial location. He tried for several years to effect such a trade, but without success.

Sydney was already a pluralist in the sense that he was officially the rector of Foston while he held three preacherships in London, but his ambition led him to hope for still more positions. In June, 1808, he asked to be appointed chaplain to Lord Holland,[129] apparently as a further justification of his absenteeism, and suggested to Lady Holland that any new living he might be awarded should be "under value".[130] In the same year he also asked Lord Grey to appoint him as his chaplain,[131] with the same purpose in view, but evidently he was never appointed chaplain by either man.

Perhaps as a result of his failure to achieve these appointments, the new Archbishop of York, the Rt. Rev. Dr. Vernon Harcourt, ordered Sydney to either reside on his living at Foston or to resign it. With great reluctance he resolved to leave the attractions of London rather than forego the security and prestige of his benefice in Yorkshire. His course was determined by 24 October, 1808, and he resolved to leave for Foston in March of the folliwing year.[132]

In October, 1808, the Edinburgh Review published his review of a work bearing on a proposed bill to regulate the salaries of curates.133 In essence the bill would have required that rectors of all parishes valued at more than §500 a year pay their curates one-fifth of the income, and that the power of enforcement be vested in the bishops. Intended for the improvement of the Church and for the benefit of poor curates, the bill and its discussion elicited a reaction from Sydney which, though not entirely inconsistent with his previous principles, was remarkable in its violence of sentiment--especially so since the bill had already been rejected. He was avowedly a defender of the Church and its amelioration, and had previously sneered at absentee Tory clergymen; yet when this bill appeared, he attacked with an intensity approaching blind rage. His reasons for doing so are fairly obvious. The bill attacked established privilege, which, as a dedicated Whig, he defended. If passed, the bill would have cost him §100 a year for his curate at Foston, or that share of §100 above what had already been paid to him. It might seem derogatory to accuse Sydney Smith of acting in a selfish manner for writing annonymously in the pages of the Edinburgh Review, but he was, after all, a mortal who could be and was interested in his own private concerns as well as high-flung liberal principles, and the proposed legislation touched him very directly.

Sydney opened his diatribe against Perceval's bill by saying:

> The poverty of curates has long been a favourite theme with novellists, sentimental tourists, and elegaic poets. But, notwithstanding the known accuracy of this class of philosophers, we cannot help suspecting that there is a good deal of misconception in the popular estimate of the amount of the evil.134

Sympathy for the poverty of curates, he said, was often misplaced, for many of them were independently wealthy young gentlemen who were serving their apprenticeship in the Church and who were relatively indifferent as to their salaries; while most of the permanent curates were from "a very humble rank in society" and were not accustomed to high salaries. He did not mention his "lottery" system in this review, but he clearly had it in mind when

he opposed equalizing salaries throughout the Church.
If one wished to upgrade salaries, he said, the only real
alternative was to raise an additional "million or two
for the church". Instead Perceval proposed to penalize
only one class of rectors: those with incomes over §500.
He also objected strenuously to the projected increase
in the power of the bishops over their clergy, for he
distrusted all bishops, and believed that they were
under the direct control of the Crown. To Sydney, a free
England meant a Church with powerless bishops.135

   Sydney complained that the bill proposed to rob some
rectors to reward curates, but that the incomes of the
wealthiest clergymen, the bishops, were to be left untouched, as were those of the lay proprietors, because
of their political power. He added that an enforced increase of this nature in the salaries of curates would
cause them to lose their traditional frugality, and that
it would poison the good relations between rector and
curate. As a means of raising the salaries of curates,
he proposed that bishops should introduce competition
among curates by not permitting a curate to occupy a
living worth over §500 unless he had a master of arts
degree.

>   The object is, to fix a good clergyman
>   in a parish. The law will not trust the
>   non-resident rector to fix both the price
>   and the person; but fixes the price, and
>   then leaves him the choice of the person.
>   Our plan is, to fix upon the description
>   of person, and then to leave the price
>   to find its level; for the good price by
>   no means implies a good person, but the
>   good person will be sure to get a good
>   price.136

He claimed that the average non-resident clergyman was
deeply concerned about securing a curate to fulfill his
parochial duties, and that he was equally concerned
about the quality of his curate. Sydney believed that
forced disclosure of the true value of a living was an
unwarranted intrusion into the "private circumstances"
of the individual rector, which illustrates his belief,
and that of his age, that an office in Church or state,
once bestowed, became the inviolable private property
of its possessor. He denied that he was putting the
case on the basis of purchase and sale, but added:

> Is it possible to prevent a curate from pledging himself to his rector, that he will accept only half the legal salary, if he is so fortunate as to be preferred among a host of rivals, who are willing to engage on the same terms? You may make these contracts illegal: What then? Men laugh at such prohibitions; and they always become a dead letter. In nine instances out of ten, the contract would be honourably adhered to; and then, what is the use of Mr. Perceval's law? Where the contract was not adhered to, whom would the law benefit? - A man utterly devoid of every particle of honour and good faith. And this is the new species of curate, who is to reflect dignity and importance upon his poorer brethren?.... Did any ecclesiastical law, before this, ever depend for its success upon the mutual treachery of men who ought to be examples to their fellowcreatures of every thing that is just and upright? [137]

Finally, to poison the well, Sydney asserted that the origin of the bill was "the Tabernacle", and that its purpose was to sow the seeds of "discord and treachery" in the Church.

CHAPTER VI

London (1807-1809)

Sydney's hostility towards the "Methodists" has been explained and he might be considered something of an Anglican bigot. His actions in other respects, though, exonerate him from that charge. He was prejudiced against that faction to be sure, but his distaste for them was based on a rational analysis of their beliefs, thoughts, and actions, and although he feared the influence they might exert on the English Church and the English people he did not wish to limit their religious liberty in any respect. Superficially it might appear that his Anglican bigotry led him to oppose all high-minded non-Anglicans out of religious prejudice, but such was not the case. His test of dissenting or deviating sects, factions, or churches was to determine whether or not they conformed in some general way to "rational religion", and whether or not they endangered the Established Church.

In the first decade of the nineteenth century the Church of England was an ubiquitous institution whose influence extended far beyond the physical limits of its chapels, churches, and cathedrals. Among its other activities it numbered education, and the Church exercised a strong, if not preponderant influence on the schooling of the English. In that decade, and for many decades to come, education was so inextricably intertwined with religion that any controversy on education automatically became a religious discussion. Never was this more true than in the case of the Lancaster-Bell dispute. There was a strong demand for extended educational opportunities in many quarters of Great Britian, and although some reactionary elements opposed the education of the lower classes, it is probably not too much to say that public opinion generally supported the idea of more education for more people. The problems of expanding the educational system, however, appeared to be almost insuperable, for a lack of money, teachers, buildings, and materials existed; and if everyone was agreed that religion should be taught in the schools, a national system of schools that taught Anglican doctrine was as repugnant to the numerous and influential dissenters, as was any system that did not do so to the still more numerous Anglicans. The problem of expense had been partially solved by Andrew Bell, an Anglican educator who devised the monitorial system in Madras; and by Joseph Lancaster, a convert to the Society of Friends, who put a system similar to that of Bell into operation in Southwark. Under it a teacher taught rudimentary information to a class of older and more gifted students, each of whom then drilled a group of younger pupils in what they had learned. In this way, one teacher could handle a vast number of students, theoretically up to a thousand, and the expense per pupil was greatly reduced. The expense was reduced still further by the practice of writing in sand or on slates rather than on paper. In a very unseemly controversy between Bell and Lancaster, both claimed to have originated the system, which incidentally had been widely discussed in France years before, and each stood up for the superiority of his particular variation of it. Bell's system was somewhat more dogmatic in its methods than was Lancaster's, and it was definitely Anglican in its religious teaching; while Lancaster's method was christian, but non-denominational in its intent. In essence the controversy centered around the merits of Bell's Anglican teachings in his schools, while those of Lancaster, which were most emphatically non-Quaker teachings, and non-denominational, were regarded by many Anglicans as being hostile to the Church of England because they were non-Anglican.

Sydney entered into this debate in July, 1806, and if he had been expected to play the role of the Anglican bigot, in view of his earlier articles on the Methodists, his actions were certainly surprising. He reviewed a work by Mrs. Sarah Trimmer·which was highly critical of Lancaster's schools, and quickly took the side of the Lancastrian system:

> This is a book written by a lady who has gained considerable reputation at the corner of St. Paul's Church-yard; who flames in the van of Mr. Newberry's shop; and is, upon the whole, dearer to mothers and aunts than any other author who pours the milk of science in the mouths of babes and sucklings. Tired, at last, of scribbling for children, and getting ripe in ambition, she has now written a book for grown up people, and selected for her antagonist as stiff a controversialist as the whole field of dispute could well have supplied. Her opponent is Mr. Lancaster, a Quaker, who has lately given to the world new and striking lights upon

>   the subject of education, and come forward to the notice of his country by spreading order, knowledge, and innocence among the lowest of mankind.
>
>   Mr. Lancaster, she says, wants method in his book; and therefore her answer to him is without any arrangement. The same excuse must suffice for the desultory observations we shall make upon this lady's publication.
>
>   The first sensation of disgust we experienced at Mrs. Trimmer's book, was from the patronizing and protecting air with which she speaks of some small part of Mr. Lancaster's plan.[1]

Sydney, who already believed in the pressing need for more widespread education, observed that Mrs. Trimmer had noticed the great national concern for education, but he pointed out the English failure to implement that pretended concern. "...when you ask," he said, "where are the schools, rods, pedagogues, primmers, histories of Jack the Giant-killer, and all the usual apparatus of education, the only thing she can produce is <u>the act of uniformity and common prayer</u>."[2]

In response to Mrs. Trimmer's charges that certain of Lancaster's methods were unchristian, Sydney replied:

>   She begins with being cruel, and ends with being silly. Her first observation is calculated to raise the <u>posse comitatus</u> against Mr. Lancaster, to get him stoned for impiety; and then, when he produces the most forcible example of the effect of opinion to encourage religious precept, she says, such a method of preventing swearing is too rude for the gospel. True, modest, unobtrusive religion--charitable, forgiving, indulgent Christianity, is the greatest ornament and the greatest blessing that can dwell in the mind of man. But if there is one character more base, more infamous, and more shocking than another, it is him who, for the sake of some paltry distinction in the world, is ever ready to accuse conspicuous persons of irreligion- to turn common informer for the church - and to convert the most

> beautiful feelings of the human heart to the destruction of the good and great, by fixing upon talents, the indelible stigma of irreligion.[3]

Mrs. Trimmer had also objected to Lancaster's system of promotion and dignities on the grounds that students thus honored and dignified would aspire to the places of England's hereditary aristocracy. To this obviously overdrawn anxiety Sydney replied:

> We think these extracts will sufficiently satisfy every reader of common sense, of the merits of this publication. For our part, when we saw these ragged and interesting little nobles, shining in their tin stars, we only thought it probable that the spirit of emulation would make them better ushers, tradesmen, and mechanics. We did, in truth, imagine we had observed, in some of their faces, a bold project for procuring better breeches for keeping out the blasts of heaven, which howled through their garments in every direction, and aspiring, hereafter, to greater strength of seam, and more perfect continuity of cloth; but for the safety of the titled orders, we had no fear; nor did we once dream that the black rod which whipt these dirty little dukes, would one day be borne before them as the emblem of legislative dignity, and a sign of noble blood.[4]

Sydney might be accused of religious intolerance, and indeed he was intolerant of the "Methodists", as he defined them; but he was quite prepared to defend Lancaster, the Quaker, against the Anglican attacks of Mrs. Trimmer. He favored education, and he equated her irrational approach and her lack of common sense in attempting to refute Lancaster with "Methodism", even if he did not make that accusation in his review. Regarding toleration, not only of Quakers, but also of Mrs. Trimmer, he concluded his review by saying:

> Mr. Lancaster is, as we have before observed, a Quaker. As a Quaker, he says, I cannot teach your creeds; but I pledge

myself (and If I deceive you, desert me, and give me up) to confine myself to those points of Christianity in which all Christians agree. To which Mrs. Trimmer replies, that, in the first place, he cannot do this; and, in the next place, if he did do it, it would not be enough. But why, we would ask, cannot Mr. Lancaster effect his first object? The practical and the feeling parts of religion, are much more likely to attract the attention, and provoke the questions of children, than its speculative doctrines. A child is not very likely to put any questions at all to a catechizing master, and still less likely to lead him into subtle and profound disquisition. It appears to us not only practicable, but very easy, to confine the religious instruction of the poor, in the first years of life, to those general feelings and principles which are suitable to the established church, and to every sect; afterwards, the discriminating tenets of each subdivision of Christians may be fixed upon this general basis. To say that this is not enough, that a child should be made an Antisocinian, or an Antipelagian, in his tenderest years, may be very just; but what prevents you from making him so? Mr. Lancaster, purposely and intentionally to allay all jealousy, leaves him in a state as well adapted for one creed as another. Begin; make your pupil a firm advocate for the peculiar doctrines of the English church; dig round about him, on every side, a trench that shall guard him from every species of heresy. In spite of all this clamour, you do nothing; you do not stir a single step; you educate alike the swineherd and his hog;-and then, when a man of real genius and enterprise rises up, and says, let me dedicate my life to this neglected object...you refuse to do your little; and compel him, by the cry of Infidel and Atheist, to leave you to your antient repose, and not to drive you, by insidious comparison, to any system of active utility. We deny, again and again, that Mr. Lancaster's instruction is any kind of impediment to the propagation of the doctrines of the church; and if Mr. Lancaster was to perish with his system tomorrow, these boys would positively be taught nothing; the doctrines which Mrs. Trimmer considers to be prohibited would not rush in, but there would be an absolute vacuum. We will, however, say this in favour of Mrs. Trimmer, that if every one who has joined in her clamour, had laboured one hundredth part as much as she has done in the cause of national education, the clamour would be much more rational, and much more consistent, than it now is.... But our principal argument is, that Mr. Lancaster's plan is at least better than the <u>nothing</u> which preceded it. The authoress herself seems to be a lady of respectable opinions, and very ordinary talents; defending what is right without judgement, and believing what is holy without charity.[5]

In a second review, published in October, 1807, Sydney, explained the Lancastrian system fully, and gave it his strongest endorsement. He stood by it despite allegations that it would "spoil" the working classes, and he felt that it would make for better servants and greater morality among the poor. He added that:

>...we do most firmly believe, that it may be made the means of rescuing thousands of human beings from vice and misery, of teaching the blessings of rational religion, or improving the character, and increasing the happiness of the lower orders of mankind. And for these reasons, the cause of education shall never want our feeble aid, nor the friends of it our good word, from the poor Quaker whose system we have described, to the King, who had conducted himself towards this deserving man with so much goodness and feeling; and for which thousands of ragged children will pray for him and remember him, long after his Majesty is forgotten by every Lord of the Chamber, and by every Clerk of the Closet.[6]

Despite his endorsement of Lancaster's school system, Sydney was more a friend of education than he was of any particular system, and he concluded his review by commending a school established by the Archbishop of Canterbury under the care of Andrew Bell. "If the thing is done", he said, "at all, -if the education of the poor goes on, -we are content." He also offered a left handed apology to Mrs. Trimmer, describing her as "a lady of real piety and estimable character" who had been honest and conscientious; but he defended his review of her book by stating that he would never have attacked her writing had she confined it to the teaching of children, instead of erring by posing as a "religious accuser".[7]

Such had been his public statement on the subject of Mrs. Trimmer and the Bell system, but privately Sydney believed that the Church was so closely associated with the status quo that it could not be a serious proponent of extended education. In 1812 he was to deride Anglican efforts to educate the poor of Yorkshire as a travesty: "...much as if Sheridan were to take to keeping accounts...."[8] At about the same time he sneered at the proposed establishment of schools by the Church as an attempt to teach nothing other than tithe-paying, and thought it incredible that the Church should favor secular education. He believed that the Anglicans were acting only to keep boys out of Lancaster's schools and that in using the Bell system, they would employ sham spellers and false multiplication tables to prevent real learning.[9] His disillusionment with the Bell system and the Church at that time probably resulted from his "exile" in Yorkshire, and from the pressures of housebuilding, both of which disturbed his equanimity about 1812-1813.

Sydney's opinions on education while in London ended with his article on Mrs. Trimmer's work, but in October, 1809, he wrote a somewhat cautious review of R.L. Edgeworth's Essays on Professional Education. While agreeing with much of what Edgeworth said, he resisted endorsing or condemning it fully, but his general opinion seems to have been favorable. "In a canting age", Sydney said, "he does not cant; -at a period when hypocrisy and fanaticism

> will almost certainly ensure the success of any publication, he has constantly disdained to have recourse to any such arts; -without ever having been accused of disloyalty or irreligion, he is not always

> harping upon Church and King, in order to
> catch at a little popularity, and sell
> his books; -he is manly, independent, li-
> beral -and maintains enlightened opinions
> with discretion and honesty.... With these
> merits, we cannot say that Mr. Edgeworth
> is either very new, very profound, or very
> apt to be right in his opinions. He is
> active, enterprizing, and unprejudiced;
> but we have not been very much instructed
> by what he has written, or always satisfied
> that he has got to the bottom of his sub-
> ject.
> On one subject, however, we cordially
> agree with this gentleman; and return him
> our thanks for the courage with which he
> has combated the excessive abuse of clas-
> sical learning in England. It is a sub-
> ject upon which we have long wished for an
> opportunity of saying something; and one
> which we consider to be of the very high-
> est importance.[10]

Sydney saw real value in classical learning, but he believed that schools, particularly public schools, emphasized classical learning at the expense, or even the exclusion, of all other learning; and that this intensive training gave students entirely too much expertise in dead languages. He believed that the purpose of classical education was mental training and discipline, but that scholars often made the means into the end. Most public school boys, he said, wrote more Latin verses during their school years than were contained in the Aeneid, which he felt was entirely too much training.[11]

Sydney thus defended the classics but attacked their overemphasis, and he extended his comments to Oxford University, an institution on which he was not uninformed. "There is a timid and absurd apprehension", he said,

> "on the part of ecclesiastical tutors, of
> setting out the minds of youth upon dif-
> ficult and important subjects. They fan-
> cy that mental exertion must end in reli-
> gious skepticism; and, to preserve the
> principles of their pupils, they confine
> them to the safe and elegant imbecility
> of classical learning. A genuine Oxford
> tutor would shudder to hear his young men

> disputing upon moral and political truth, forming and pulling down theories, and indulging in all the boldness of youthful discussion. He would augur nothing from it, but impiety to God, and treason to kings. And yet, who vilifies both more than the holy poltroon, who carefully averts them from the searching eye of reason, and who knows no better method of teaching the highest duties, than by extirpating the finest qualities and habits of the mind. If our religion is a fable, the sooner it is exploded the better. If our government is bad, it should be amended. But we have no doubt of the truth of the one, or of the excellence of the other; and are convinced that both will be placed on a firmer basis, in proportion as the minds of men are more trained to the investigation of truth.[12]

The fact that the English educational system had produced a few men of genius did not ally the fact that some men would rise to the top under any system, he said, and he added that the English universities stultified or destroyed "an infinite quantity of talent" because of their ecclesiastical narrowness and their misplaced values. Sydney's liberal views on education led him to assert further:

> There is a delusive sort of splendour in a vast body of men pursuing one object, and thoroughly obtaining it; and yet, though it is very splendid, it is far from being useful. Classical literature is the great object at Oxford. Many minds so employed have produced many works, and much fame in that department; but if all liberal arts and sciences useful to human life had been taught there, -if some had dedicated themselves to chemistry, some to mathematics, some to experimental philosophy,...if every attainment had been honoured in the mixt ratio of its difficulty and utility, -the system of such an University would have been much more valuable, but the splendour of its name something else.
> When an University has been doing

useless things for a long time, it appears at first degrading to them to be useful. A set of lectures upon political economy would be discouraged in Oxford, probably despised, probably not permitted. To discuss the enclosure of commons, and to dwell upon imports and exports, -to come so near to common life, would seem to be undignified and contemptible. In the same manner, the Parr, or the Bentley of his day, would be scandalized in an University to be put on a level with the discoverer of a neutral salt; and yet, what other measure is there of dignity in intellectual labour, but usefulness? And what ought the term University to mean, but a place where every science is taught which is liberal, and at the same time useful to mankind? Nothing would so much tend to bring classical literature within proper bounds, as a steady and invariable appeal to utility in our appreciation of all human knowledge. The puffed up pedant would collapse into his proper size, and the maker of verses, and the rememberer of words, would soon assume that station which is the lot of those who go unbidden to the upper places of the feast.[13]

Sydney's criticism of Oxford, along with other reviews of that institution in the pages of the Edinburgh Review, prompted a reply in the form of a pamphlet entitled A Reply to the Calumnies of the Edinburgh Review against Oxford; containing an Account of Studies pursued in that University. Two Edinburgh Reviewers, R. Payne Knight and John Playfair, along with Sydney responded to it in April, 1810.[14] Knight and Playfair in the first part of the article warmly defended the reviewers' opinions, and skillfully turned the pamphleteer's words against him; while, at the same time, maintaining the original position of the review. Sydney then completed the essay by asserting that the author was dull by nature, but deceitful by intent, and that he had viciously misquoted his review. He reasserted his stand that classical education was good, but added that it was not the only good, and that all other studies should not be sacrificed for it nor should all students be made into classical scholars. He commented on the lilliputian mentality of his opponent, which, he said, derived from his associations with third-rate persons, apparently referring to the Oxford faculty, and from "compelling boys to listen to him". Sydney further described him as a "plain, plodding, everyday personage", who,

> If he would hold his tongue, and carefully avoid all opportunities of making a display, he is just the description of person to enjoy a very great reputation among those whose good opinion is not worth having. Unfortunately, he must pretend to liberality -to wit- to eloquence- and to fine writing. He must show his brother tutors that he is not afraid of Edinburgh Reviewers. If he returns rolled in the mud, broken-headed, and bellowing with pain, who has he but himself to blame?[15]

Sydney denied charges of malice in his criticism of Oxford, and he said that the Edinburgh Review richly approved of recent improvements in that institution, but that the review deplored the low state to which it had fallen in past years for the reasons he had outlined in his article. Oxford, he maintained, had assumed a superior and sneering attitude towards any field of study which was primarily aimed at dealing with man's bodily wants and needs; all of which ignored the application of mathematics to navigation, law to human problems, and so on. He replied to outraged charges of levity in his review by stating:

> The moment an envious pedant sees any thing written with pleasantry, he comforts himself that it must be superficial. Whether the Reviewer is or is not considered as a superficial person by competent judges, he neither knows nor cares; but says what he has to say after his own manner, -always confident, that whatever he may be, he shall be found out, and classed as he deserves. The Oxford tutor may very possibly have given a just account of him; but his reasons for that judgement are certainly wrong: for it is by no means impossible to be entertaining and instructive at the same time; and the readers of this pamphlet (if any) can never doubt, after such a specimen, how

> easy it is to be, in one small production, both very frivolous and very tiresome.
> Certainly we do not wish that sceptical doctrines should be entertained in Oxford, or in any place whatsoever; and we are obliged to the tutor for not imputing to us any such motives. In his charity and liberality, he only makes it a supposition, -not an assertion by any means! This is base enough; but we are thankful to him for not being more base. Would we could thank him for any occasional abatement of dulness, impudence, or pomp! But his fault is to love extremes.[16]

In the previous issue of the Edinburgh Review Sydney had also written on education, and once again he demonstrated the liberality of his thought by defending education for women. "A great deal has been said", he noted,

> of the original difference of capacity between men and women; as if women were more quick, and men more judicious - as if women were more remarkable for delicacy of association, and men for stronger powers of attention. All this, we confess, appears to us very fanciful. That there is a difference in the understandings of the men and the women we every day meet with, every body, we suppose, must perceive; but there is none surely which may not be accounted for by the difference of circumstances in which they have been placed, without referring to any conjectural difference of original conformation of mind. As long as boys and girls run about in the dirt, and trundle hoops together, they are both precisely alike. If you catch up one half of these creatures, and train them to a particular set of actions and opinions, and the other half to a perfectly opposite set, of course their understandings will differ....[17]

He refused to argue the question of female education on the conservative basis that change itself was evil, and that the situation of women had to be kept as it was lest dire effects result. He similarly rejected the argument that educating women would make them conceited and affected. No lady boasts of speaking French, he pointed out, for the very good reason that everyone of her class spoke French. He denied that educated women would neglect the womanly duties of the home, which claim, he said, was based on the assumption "that the care and perpetual solicitude which a mother feels for her children, depends on her ignorance of Greek and Mathematics".[18] All ignorant men, he added, opposed the education of women because their attainments, indeed their very capacity to learn would diminish the awe in which pedantic men were held.

Opponents of the education of women viewed with alarm the prospect of declining virtue and modesty in those women who were exposed to learning, to which Sydney replied that the sexes were disposed to make themselves agreeable to each other, and that knowledge would not necessarily make women the rivals of men. In short he did not believe that female education would spoil women, or that it would destroy morality and happiness. He did believe that the educating of women would be of immeasureable benefit, especially since boys were normally under female control for the first seven or eight years of their lives.[19]

A recurrent theme in Sydney's writings is his distaste for the veneration, and uncritical acceptance, of platitudes and adages, as shown in the following review in which he took issue with some of the platitudes dealing with the role of woman:

> There are a few common phrases in circulation, respecting the duties of women, to which we wish to pay some degree of attention, because they are rather inimical to those opinions which we have advanced on this subject. Indeed, independently of this, there is nothing which requires more vigilance than the current phrases of the day, of which there are always some resorted to in every dispute, and from the sovereign authority of which it is often vain to make an appeal. 'The true theatre for a woman is the sick chamber;' -'Nothing so honourable to a woman as not to be spoken of at all.' These two phrases, the delight of <u>Noodledom</u>, are grown into common-

> places upon the subject; and are not infrequently employed to extinguish that love of knowledge in women, which, in our humble opinion, it is of so much importance to cherish.[20]

His comments on women are interesting, as is his use of the word "noodledom", a word apparently coined by Sydney, for this is, according to The Oxford English Dictionary, its first recorded use.

Sydney's views on the education of women were liberal and enlightened, and they were to be almost his last printed expression of opinion on education. He did not write on that subject again until June, 1826, when he wrote a cautious but still enthusiastic endorsement of the system of learning languages that had been devised by James Hamilton, an educator who was then in vogue. His system was that of interlineal translation, which Hamilton claimed, enabled boys to learn foreign languages better in a matter of weeks or months than they could in years using traditional methods of study. Sydney seems to have endorsed it cautiously because he was not entirely convinced of its efficacy, but with some degree of enthusiasm because it offered an alternative to the tedium of memorizing classical languages. He summed up his review by saying:

> The old system aims at beginning with a depth and accuracy which many men never will want, which disgusts many from arriving even at moderate attainments, and is a less easy, and not more certain road to a profound skill in languages, than if attention to grammer had been deferred to a later period.
> In fine, we are strongly persuaded, that the time being given, this system will make better scholars; and the degree of scholarship being given, a much shorter time will be needed. If there is any truth in this, it will make Mr. Hamilton one of the most useful men of his age; for if there is any thing which fills reflecting men with melancholy and regret, it is the waste of mortal time, parental money, and puerile happiness, in the present method of pursuing Latin and Greek.[21]

Hamiltonian education was controversial in the early nineteenth century and by supporting it Sydney himself once again in the vanguard of liberal thought, but it was not a political issue.

Catholic emancipation, to the contrary, was very much a political issue, and Sydney took a role in that cause which, even if it was exaggerated by both Sydney and his biographers, was a leading one. At least a tenth of his numerous reviews dealt with Catholic emancipation or Ireland, which was much the same thing during this period as well as in Sydney's own mind; and probably a majority of his longer publications pertained directly or indirectly to the Catholic question. Unfortunately for all concerned, Catholic emancipation became the testing ground for the two major parties, and the fortunes of the Whigs and Tories alike came to be associated with its success. It was long overdue in the opinion of the Whigs, or its passage would mark the beginning of the end of the Constitution from the Tory viewpoint. It is not surprising then that Sydney chose this issue on which to concentrate his attention, for he was both a loyal Whig and a fervent defender of religious toleration.

To attribute Sydney's persistent enthusiasm for Catholic emancipation to ambition and hope for further preferment in the Church is tempting, and certainly those aspirations were present in this thought. The coalition government which had rewarded him for his earlier services with the living at Foston-le-Clay went out of office on the issue of Catholic emancipation and the obstinacy of George III. With this event Sydney's hopes for immediate preferment collapsed. The Ministry of All the Talents had been formed in January, 1806, but fell in March, 1807, before Sydney published any of his works in defense of Catholic emancipation. The Whigs in the ministry, perhaps unwisely, had staked their immediate future on Catholic emancipation, and when the aged king refused it on the basis of conscience and his coronation oath, they were consigned to darkness for an additional twenty years. The violence and overstatement of Sydney's beliefs on Catholic emancipation can thus be explained in part by the dashing of his hopes for advancement on the shoals of royal senility which was greatly abetted by Tory prejudices. Nevertheless, he was more than a Whig placeman and if he hoped for preferment in the Church as a reward for holding and publicizing correct opinions, he also held those opinions because he believed in them. He took it for granted that in times of trouble

England's security hinged on the happiness of the Irish, and that their loyalty could be secured by Catholic emancipation. Therefore, he believed in religious toleration in general, and that of the Catholics in particular.

As Sheldon Halpern[22] points out, Sydney's arguments for Catholic emancipation were not numerous, and they were frequently reiterated. He voiced them in various places at various times, but most of them appeared in print in the period from the summer of 1807 to the spring of 1808 in the pages of <u>Letters of Peter Plymley to my Brother Abraham who lives in the Country</u>,[23] often referred to as the <u>Peter Plymley Letters</u>. As early as December, 1806, he had resolved to write a pamphlet,[24] but he had not made up his mind as to what the subject was to be. By the spring of 1807 he had decided to write on the Catholic question. Insofar as Sydney Smith is regarded as a literary figure, and he has been rashly compared with Jonathon Swift,[25] his reputation to a large extent rests on his efforts of the spring and summer of 1807. Opinions on his success still vary, ranging downward from the comparison with Swift, but it certainly was one of the most successful pamphlets up to that time. Osbert Burdett described it as "perhaps the best Whig pamphlet ever written", but one that was most emphatically not up to the level of Swift, and one which went no deeper than political expediency. He believed that the skill with which it was written demonstrated that Sydney could have excelled in anything he attempted, that his efforts was courageous and it were written with great clarity, and that his style was "effective, lively, and practical", without being anything more than that.[26] Another opinion asserts that the <u>Peter Plymley Letters</u> were "excellent and entertaining party propaganda: they were also irrelevant"; and that in them Sydney "sank to irrelevant sneers".[27]

The <u>Peter Plymley Letters</u> are still a very readable and amusing exercise in political satire, with occasional excursions into invective. The letters were addressed nominally to his non-existant brother, who was a rural clergyman, but actually to all good-hearted Englishmen who opposed Catholic emancipation as a result of ignorance:

        DEAR ABRAHAM
        A worthier and better man than yourself

does not exist; but I have always told you, from the time of our boyhood, that you are a bit of a goose. Your parochial affairs are governed with exemplary order and regularity; you are as powerful in the vestry as Mr. Perceval is in the House of Commons, -and I must say, with much more reason; not do I know any church where the faces and smock-frocks of the congregation are so clean, or their eyes so uniformly directed to the preacher. There is another point, upon which I will do you ample justice; and that is, that the eyes so directed towards you are wide open; for the rustic has, in general, good principles, though he cannot control his animal habits; and, however loud he may snore, his face is perpetually turned towards the fountain of orthodoxy.

Having done you this act of justice, I shall proceed, according to our ancient intimacy and familiarity, to explain to you my opinions about the Catholics, and to reply to yours.

In the first place, my sweet Abraham, the Pope is not landed -nor are there any curates sent out after him - nor has he been hid at St. Alban's by the dowager Lady Spencer - nor dined privately at Holland House - nor been seen near Dropmore. If these fears exist (which I do not believe), they exist only in the mind of the Chancellor of the Exchequer; they emanate from his zeal for the Protestant interest; and, though they reflect the highest honour upon the delicate irritability of his faith, must certainly be considered as more ambiguous proofs of the sanity and vigour of his understanding. By this time, however, the best informed clergy in the neighbourhood of the metropolis are convinced that the rumour is without foundation: and, though the Pope is probably hovering about our coast in a fishing-smack, it is most likely he will fall a prey to the vigilance of our cruisers; and it is certain he has not yet polluted the Protestantism of our soil.[28]

Sydney had no patience with the king's delicate conscience, which, the monarch claimed would violate his coronation oath and which prevented him from agreeing to any relaxation of the legal disabilities against the Catholics. Sydney argued that if the king could not violate his oath in the case of the Catholics, how was he able to do so for the Protestant dissenters? "...the spirit of the oath is", he said, "to defend the Church establishment, which the Quaker and the Presbyterian differ from as much or more than the Catholic", yet the king had repealed the Test and Corporation Acts in Ireland, and had done a great deal for the Catholics earlier in his reign. The problem, as Sydney saw it, was not the king, who had done more for the Catholics than any ruler since the Reformation, but his advisors, who were all Tories, like "the well-paid John Bowles, and by Mr. Perceval (who tried to be well paid)", and who hypocritically advised the king against religious toleration in order to preserve their lucrative offices. The real danger was not that of a Catholic uprising, but of a French invasion of Ireland which the discontented Irish might support, and which could be averted only by the reconciliation of the Irish through Catholic emancipation. If the French did invade Ireland, Brother Abraham was assured that nothing more would be heard of the coronation oath or of the ministers who advised its use. To ease his brother's fears Sydney mentioned that religious persecution had been practiced by Protestant as well as Catholic, but that times had changed and neither practiced it any longer, at least not in the sense of "fire, fagot, and bloody Mary". He concluded the first of the Peter Plymley Letters by saying:

> You tell me I am a party man. I hope I shall always be so, when I see my country in the hands of a pert London joker and a second-rate lawyer. Of the first, no other good is known than that he makes pretty Latin verses; the second seems to me to have the head of a country parson, and the tongue of an Old Bailey lawyer.
> If I could see good measures pursued, I care not a farthing who is in power; but I have a passionate love for common justice, and for common sense, and I abhor and despise every man who builds up his political fortune upon their ruin.
> God bless you, reverend Abraham, and defend you from the Pope, and all of us

> from that administration who seek power
> by opposing a measure which Burke, Pitt,
> and Fox all considered as absolutely
> necessary to the existence of the country.[29]

Oaths were still taken seriously in the early nineteenth century, and national concern for the king's conscience with regard to his coronation oath was echoed in a widespread popular suspicion that Catholics could not be trusted to respect an oath. To that apprehension Sydney observed that no law barred Catholics from Parliament or from various offices in the state. Instead all men were required to take an oath repudiating certain doctrines of Catholic belief, and it was that oath which effectively kept Catholics in an inferior position in the state. Sydney added:

> The Catholic asks you to abolish some
> oaths which repress him; your answer is,
> that he does not respect oaths. Then why
> subject him to the test of oaths? The
> oaths keep him out of Parliament; why
> then he respects them. Turn which way
> you will, either your laws are nugatory,
> or the Catholic is bound by religious
> obligations as you are: but no eel in
> the well-sanded fist of a cook-maid, upon
> the eve of being skinned, ever twisted
> and writhes as an orthodox parson does
> when he is compelled by the grip of reason to admit any thing in favour of a
> Dissenter.[30]

He refused to argue the question as to whether "the Pope be or not the Scarlet Lady of Babylon", but he did attempt to allay the fears of many that the Pope would interfere in British temporal affairs by quoting the results of Pitt, who had consulted six of the leading foreign Catholic universities on that question, and who had received a decided negative from all six. Catholics, he said, merely obeyed the Pope as their spiritual leader, just as evangelicals obeyed Wilberforce and Scots obeyed the General Assembly of their church, and all without disturbance to the government. All of this was well known, said Sydney, but whenever the name of Ireland was mentioned the English abandoned all "common feeling, common prudence, and ...common sense", and they acted with "the barbarity of tyrants, and the fatuity of idots."[31] The real issue was French invasion and Irish disloyalty, but

> Mr. Perceval and his parsons forgot all this, in their horror lest twelve or fourteen old women may be converted to holy water, and Catholic nonsense. They never see that, while they are saving these venerable ladies from perdition, Ireland may be lost, England broken down, and the Protestant Church, with all its deans, prebendaries, Percevals and Rennels, be swept into the vortex of oblivion.[32]

The Irish population, Sydney pointed out, was four-fifths Catholic while one-half of the remaining Protestants were dissenters. Nonetheless, the ministry insisted on the maintenance of the Anglican establishment and the exclusion of Catholics from Parliament even though Irish Catholics could make up no more than twenty members of the House of Commons and ten members in the House of Lords if accorded the fullest representation, which would render them totally incapable of accomplishing any of the feared changes. "Do you fear for your tithes", Sydney asked,

> or your doctrines, or your person, or the English Constitution? Every fear, taken separately, is so glaringly absurd, that no man has the folly or boldness to state it. Every one conceals his ignorance or his baseness, in a stupid general panic, which when called upon, he is utterly incapable of explaining. Whatever you think of the Catholics, there they are -you cannot get rid of them; your alternative is, to give them a lawful place for stating their grievances, or an unlawful one: if you do not admit them to the House of Commons, they will hold their parliament in Potatoe-place, Dublin, and be ten times as violent and inflammatory as they would be in Westminster. Nothing would give me such an idea of security, as to see twenty or thirty Catholic gentlemen in Parliament.... What remains to be done is obvious to every human being - but to that man who, instead of being a Methodist preacher is... become a legislator and a politician.[33]

In his latter comments Sydney referred to Spencer Perceval, who was his particular bete noire. In addition to being a Tory, and hence unlikely to do anything for Sydney's career or for his chosen causes, Perceval was an evangelical, or, in Sydney's terminology, a "Methodist" was was incapable of reason, and possibly even of sanity. He had been defended in the House of Commons on the grounds of his unspotted domestic virtue, to which Sydney replied that he would prefer a profligate who would save his country. To persuade Perceval and the waverers of the basic humanity of Catholics, Sydney urged that several Catholics should be dissected after death by surgeons of either religion to determine whether or not they were fully human, and the results published under due authority.[34]

Peter Plymley's third letter began dolorously with predictions of the fall of England, and with the unfurling of the French flag on the hills of Kent while Canning and Perceval brought in bills to "regulate Easter-offerings" or to "adjust the stipend of curates". Peter confidently prognosticated the ravaging of Abraham's wife by love-struck Gauls and the impressment of his son as a drummer in a French regiment. England, he said, had been totally unrealistic about the French threat, and the Tories had reacted to it only with a renewed vigor in corruption:

> If Austria or Prussia armed, doctors of divinity immediately printed those passages out of Habakkuk, in which the destruction of the usurper by General Mack, and the Duke of Brunswick, are so clearly predicted. If Bonaparte halted, there was a mutiny, or a dysentery. If any one of his generals were eaten up by the light troops of Russia, and picked (as their manner is) to the bone, the sanguine spirit of this country displayed itself in all its glory. What scenes of infamy did the Society for the Suppression of Vice lay open to our astonished eyes: tradesmen's daughters dancing; pots of beer carried out between the first and second lesson; and dark and distant rumours of indecent prints. Clouds of Mr. Canning's cousins arrived by the waggon; all the contractors left their cards with Mr. Rose; and every plunderer of the

> public crawled out of his hole, like
> slugs and grubs, and worms, after a
> shower of rain.[35]

Despite the well-intentioned but misplaced optimism regarding Napoleon's defeat, he was still victorious, and he was destined to conquer England as well, unless Catholic emancipation was immediately accomplished. In a fit of Whig frenzy Peter described England as a nation, in the opinion of Europe, of "blockheads, Methodists, and old women." When faced with an imposing problem like that of Napoleonic France, England should have responded with clear-sighted policy. Instead, he said, they retreated into insanity, and as an example he described:

> ...a frigate attacked by a corsair of immense strength and size, rigging out, masts in danger of coming by the board, four foot of water in the hold, men dropping off very fast; in this dreadful situation how do you think the Captain acts (whose name shall be Perceval)? He calls all hands upon the deck; talks to them of King, country, glory, sweethearts, gin, French prison, wooden shoes, Old England, and hearts of oak: they give three cheers, rush to their guns, and, after a tremendous conflict, succeed in beating off the enemy. Not a syllable of all this: this is not the manner in which the honourable Commander goes to work: the first thing he does is to secure 20 or 30 of his prime sailors who happen to be Catholics, to clap them in irons, and set over them a guard of as many Protestants; having taken this admirable method of definding himself against his infidel opponents, he goes upon deck, reminds the sailors, in a very bitter harangue, that they are of different religions; exhorts the Episcopal gunner not to trust to the Presbyterian quarter-master; issues positive orders that the Catholics should be fired at upon the first appearance of discontent; rushes through blood and brains, examining his men in the Catechism and 39 Articles, and postively forbids every one to spunge or ram who has not taken the Sacrament according to the Church of England.[36]

Sydney rejected as illogical the argument that concessions to the Catholics should be refused because to give in to most present Catholic demands would only lead to more extravagant demands later, and he added:

> I wish the Chancellor of the Exchequer, who uses this reasoning to exclude others from their just rights, had tried its efficacy, not by his understanding but by (what are full of much better things) his pockets. Suppose the person to whom he applied for the Meltings had withstood every pleas of wife and fourteen children, no business, and good character, and refused him this paltry little office, because he might hereafter attempt to get hold of the revenues of the Duchy of Lancaster for life; would not Mr. Perceval have contended eagerly against the injustice of refusing moderate requests, because immoderate ones may hereafter be made?[37]

Perceval, as a Tory and a "Methodist" was one of Sydney's favorite targets, and if his abuse of Perceval was not always fair, it was invariably witty. His purpose, though, was not justice to Perceval but publicity to further the Whig party and the cause of Catholic emancipation. Some of the English, he felt, persecuted the Catholics because they were driven to antagonize someone, or to have a whipping-boy; but he believed that oppressing the Catholics created a national peril, and that other groups such as the "Methodists" or the Quakers, could be abused more safely:

> ...this sport, admirable as it is, is become, with respect to the Catholics, a little dangerous; and if we are not extremely careful in taking the amusement, we shall tumble into the holy water, and be drowned. As it seems necessary to your ides of an established Church to have somebody to worry and torment, suppose we were to select for this purpose William Wilberforce, Esq., and the patent Christians of Clapham. We shall by this expedient enjoy the same opportunity for cruelty and injustice, without being exposed to the same risks: we will compel

them to abjure vital clergymen by a public test, to deny that the said William Wilberforce has any power of working miracles, touching for barrenness or any other infirmity, or that he is endowed with any preternatural gift whatever. We will swear them to the doctrine of good works, compel them to preach common sense, and to hear it; to frequent Bishops, Deans, and other high Churchmen; and to appear (once in the quarter at the least) at some melodrama, opera, pantomine, or other light scenical representation; in short, we will gratify the love of insolence and power: we will enjoy the old orthodox sport of witnessing the impotent anger of men compelled to submit to civil degradation, or to sacrifice their notions of truth to ours. And all this we may do without the slightest risk, because their numbers are (as yet) not very considerable. Cruelty and injustice must, of course, exist, but why connect them with danger? Why torture a bull-dog, when you can get a frog or a rabbit? ....Do not be apprehensive of any opposition from ministers. If it is a case of hatred, we are sure that one man will defend it by the Gospel; if it abridges human freedom, we know that another will find precedents for it in the Revolution.[38]

There is an account, possibly apocryphal, that on one occasion Daniel O'Connell, the Irish leader, introduced Sydney to some Irish friends as the "ancient defender of our faith", at which Sydney laughed and retorted: "Of your cause, if you please, not of your faith."[39] He favored justice for Catholics and although he prefered the Catholic faith to the faith of the frenzied evangelicals he was still an Anglican and, in that sense at least, opposed to Catholicism. He could both attack and defend Catholicism in the same sentence, as when he asserted that it might be centuries "before the absurdities of the Catholic religion are laughed at as much as they deserve to be; but surely, in the mean time, the Catholic religion is better than none...."[40] He was to repeat his preference for Catholic Irish over bestial Irish of no religion at all, and this argument may well have been persuasive to some of the English who regarded the Irish as bestial because they were Catholic.

Sydney also observed that times and circumstances had changed and were changing and that laws needed to be changed to meet the new situations; but oponents of Catholic emancipation based much of their opposition to a modification of the laws on the wisdom of their ancestors and on the "unalterable" laws passed at the time of the Glorious Revolution. "When I hear any man talk of an unalterable law", he commented, "the only effect it produces upon me is to convince me that he is an unalterable fool."[41] Much the same thing had been said about Scotland and her religion in a previous century, he added, and

> ...horse, foot, artillery, and armed Prebendaries, were sent out after the Presbyterian parsons and their congregations. The Percevals of those days called for blood: this call is never made in vain, and blood was shed; but to the astonishment and horror of the Percevals of those days, they could not introduce the Book of Common Prayer, nor prevent that metaphysical people from going to heaven their true way, instead of ours. With a little oatmeal for food, and a little sulphur for friction, allaying cutaneous irritation with the one hand, and holding his Calvinistical creed in the other, Sawney ran away to his flinty hills, sung his psalm out of tune his own way, and listened to his sermon of two hours long, amid the rough and imposing melancholy of the tallest thistles. But Sawney brought up his unbreeched offspring in a cordial hatred of his oppressors; and Scotland was as much a part of the weakness of England then, as Ireland is at this moment. The true and only remedy was applied; the Scotch were suffered to worship God after their own tiresome manner, without pain, penalty, and privation. No lighnings descended from heaven; the country was not ruined; the world is not yet come to an end; the dignitaries, who foretold all these consequences, are utterly forgotten; and Scotland has ever since been an increasing source of strength to Great

> Britain. In the six hundredth year of
> our empire over Ireland, we are making
> laws to transport a man, if he is found
> out of his house after eight o'clock at
> night. That this is necessary, I know
> too well; but tell me why it is neces-
> sary? It is not necessary in Greece,
> where the Turks are masters.[42]

England's conduct towards Ireland had been thoroughly hypocritical, Sydney said, like the man who "weeps at charity sermons, carries out broth and blankets to beggars, and then comes home and beats his wife and children." Threats of Napoleonic oppression in Switzerland or Naples brought a quick response from the treasury. British troops had been sent to protect the Pope, and every non-British Catholic clergyman who sought refuge from Napoleon was instantly presented with "lodging, soup, crucifix, missal, chapel-beads, relics, and holy water: if Turks had landed, Turks would have received coffee, opium, korans, and seraglios." Only the Irish, the victims of English oppression, were treated as if they had cloven feet and were fit only for subjection by Orange masters.[43] Anglicans feared that concessions to the Catholics might result in obligatory conformity to repulsive Catholic beliefs, and, in spite of promises to the contrary, Catholic soldiers in the British army were required to attend what were to them equally repulsive Anglican services, with the result that the priests in Ireland were discouraging recruiting. And what was even more important was that:

> ...there must be some relaxation with respect to tithe; this is the cruel and heart-rending price which must be paid for national preservation. I feel how little existence will be worth having, if any alternation, however slight, is made in the property of Irish rectors; I am conscious how such changes must affect the daily and hourly comforts of every Englishman; I shall feel too happy if they leave Europe untouched, and are not ultimately fatal to the destinies of America; but I am madly bent upon keeping foreign enemies out of the British empire, and my limited understanding presents me with no other means of effecting my object.[44]

The enemies of Catholic emancipation urged the country to wait for the accession of the next monarch, who might have a less delicate conscience on that question, but Sydney replied that he wished the present king a long reign, and that the delay of a single session of Parliament might be fatal. He was solicitous of George III's tender conscience, but he believed that it could also be the duty of the most loyal subject to oppose royal scruples when they endangered the state. He admonished such resistence to the royal will to be both constitutional and respectful, but he suggested that such political dissent presented far less danger to the Constitution than did the actual French opponents, and the potential opposition of the alienated Irish.[45]

Every country parson, said Peter Plymley, considered that the Corporation and Test Acts were the bulwark of the Church, and that to repeal or amend them would bring about its instant demise; but actually, the Indemnity Act annually pardoned all violations, so that for the past sixty-four years the penalties of those acts had been suspended. Nonetheless, the cry still went up that any change would spell out disaster, while Napoleon was following the most enlightened policies of religious toleration, even "assembling the very Jews at Paris, and endeavouring to give them stability and importance."[46] Most Englishmen could not imagine England's defeat, and "for no other reason that I can find, but because it seems so very odd it should be ruined and conquered." Both Austria and Prussia had been brave, military nations but they had fallen. England, he felt, was particularly susceptible to panic because of her unfamiliarity with war and her lack of trained and experienced military officers. He envisaged a situation of:

> Old wheat and beans blazing for twenty miles round; cart mares shot; sows of Lord Somerville's breed running wild over the country; the minister of the parish wounded sorely in his hinder parts; Mrs. Plymley in fits; all these scenes of war an Austrian or a Russian has seen three or four times over; but it is now three centuries since an English pig has fallen in a fair battle upon English ground, or a farm-house been rifled, or a clergyman's wife been subjected to any other proposals of love than the connubial endearments of her sleek and orthodox mate....You are

> persuaded that Lord Amherst will defend Kew Bridge like Cocles; that some maid of honour will break away from her captivity and swim over the Thames; that the Duke of York will burn his capitulating hand; and little Sturges Bourne give forty years' purchase of Moulsham Hall, while the French are encamped upon it.[47]

The cause of such a disastrous defeat, Sydney maintained, was the bigoted recalcitrance of fanactics like Spencer Perceval and his sycophants who refused to accept the inevitability of Catholic emancipation and the full toleration of dissent. "When a country squire hears of an ape", he said, "his first feeling is to give it nuts and apples; when he hears of a Dissenter, his immediate impulse is to commit it to the country jail, to shave its head, to alter its customary food, and to have it privately whipped." Catholic gentlemen might carry their legal disabilities with good nature were it not for the contempt that those disabilities engendered in the commonest of the Protestants. The fact that such laws were venerable gave them an unfortunate degree of sanctification, but if they had not existed, "the sepulchral Spencer Perceval would have been hauled through the dirtiest horse-pond in Hampstead, had he ventured to propose them."[48]

The argument that Catholicism was hostile to liberty was rejected with typical Plymleian zeal along with the counter argument that the foundations of English liberty were laid in the Catholic period. Treated with equal zeal was the observation that if Protestantism alone stood for liberty, how was one to account for the liberty of the Swiss in a mixed nation, or for the lack of liberty in Denmark, Sweden, or Prussia? Typically, Sydney added:

> The purest religion in the world, in my humble opinion is the religion of the Church of England: for its preservation (so far as it is exercised without intruding upon the liberties of others), I am ready at this moment to venture my present life, and but through that religion I have no hopes of any other; yet I am not forced to be silly because I am pious; nor will I ever join in eulogiums on my faith, which every man of common

reading and common sense can so easily refute.[49]

It is, perhaps, worth observing that in a life that lasted eighty-four years, the above passage is the only one in which Sydney Smith was described as being pious; and it is probably significant both that he thus described himself, and that he did so in a less than serious manner. However, if his piety was always open to question his reason was not, and he asked why Anglicans should be so horrified at opening the doors of Parliament to Catholics when they were already open to Scottish Presbyterians and to dissenters who were "infinitely more distant from the Church of England than the Catholics are". Even if fully enfranchised and represented the Catholics could not fill half as many seats as the Scots, and the danger to the Church, if there was a danger, came not from the Catholics, but from:

> ...the Methodists, and from that patent Christianity which has been for some time manufacturing at Clapham, to the prejudice of the old and admirable article prepared by the Church. I would counsel my lords the Bishops to keep their eyes upon that holy village, and its hallowed vicinity: they will find there a zeal in making converts far superior to any thing which exists among the Catholics: a contempt for the great mass of English clergy, much more rooted and profound; and a regular fund to purchase livings for those groaning and garrulous gentlemen, whom they denominate (by a standing sarcasm against the regular Church) Gospel preachers, and vital clergymen....I prefer that nonsense which is grown half venerable from time, the force of which I have already tried and baffled, which at least has some excuse in the dark and ignorant ages in which it originated. The religious enthusiasm manufactured by living men before my own eyes disgusts my understanding as much, influences my imagination not at all, and excites my apprehensions much more.[50]

In his sixth letter to Brother Abraham, Sydney took up the issue of the concessions that had been made to the Irish; all of which he said, in a spirit reminiscent of twentieth century American civil rights proponents, had been denied when petitioned for in a humble, respectful manner, but which had been instantly granted in the face of violence. He suggested that the same wisdom which had denied moderate reform to the Americans in 1775 would deny justice to the Irish while they were quiescent, and sarcastically compared the Tory policies of Perceval with those of Charles James Fox:

> We shall live to hear the Hampstead Protestant pronouncing such extravagant panegyrics upon holy water, and paving such fulsome compliments to the thumbs and offals of departed saints, that parties will change sentiments, and Lord Henry Petty and San Whitbread take a spell at No Popery. The Wisdom of Mr. Fox was like employed in teaching his country justice when Ireland was weak, and dignity when Ireland was strong. We are fast pacing round the same circle of ruin and imbecility. Alas! Where is our guide?[51]

England's policy towards Ireland, he contended, was the true cause of what the English chose to call Irish "character", which was brutish, violent, and exaggerated. He said that the English who made those accusations had never felt "the rod of an Orange master upon their back", and that far from being a millstone about the neck of the English, Ireland could be the "stone of Ajax" in her hand. English policy toward the Irish had been bad, and it continued worse.

> Before you refer the turbulence of the Irish to incurable defects in their character, tell me if you have treated them as friends and equals? Have you protected their commerce? Have you respected their religion? Have you been as anxious for their freedom as your own? Nothing of all this. What then? Why you have confiscated the territorial surface of the country twice over: you have massacred and exported her inhabitants: you have deprived four-fifths of them of every civil privilege: you have at every period made her commerce and manufactures slavishly subordinate to your own; and

> yet the hatred which the Irish bear to you is the result of an original turbulence of character, and of a primitive, obdurate wildness, utterly incapable of civilization.[52]

In his defense of the Irish and of Catholic emancipation, Sydney did indeed descend to personal innuendo; and although Perceval was his most vulnerable quarry, George Canning's position as Foreign Secretary did not protect him from Sydney's partisan barbs. "The Foreign Secretary", he said,

> is a gentleman, a respectable as well as an highly agreeable man in private life; but you may as well feed me with decayed potatoes as console me for the miseries of Ireland by the resources of his *sense* and his discretion. It is only the *public* situation which this gentleman holds which entitles me or induces me to say much about him. He is a fly in amber, nobody cares about the fly: the only question is, How the devil did it get there?[53]

The problem of the Orangemen, the Protestant minority in Ulster, Sydney dismissed with equal facility and equal logic. Their privileges would indeed be impaired by Catholic emancipation, they would be placed on an equal basis with their Catholic fellow-countrymen, and they would probably be disillusioned with the British government for a period of time. But, he said:

> ...I confess I should not much object: my love for poetical justice does carry me as far as that; one summer's whipping, only one: the thumb-screw for a short season; a little light easy torturing between Lady-day and Michaelmas; a short specimen of Mr. Perceval's rigour. I have malice enough to ask this slight atonement for the groans and shrieks of the poor Catholics, unheard by any human tribunal, but registered by the Angel of God against their Protestant and enlightened oppressors.
>   Besides, if you who can count ten so often can count five, you must perceive that it is better to have four friends

and one enemy than four enemies and one friend; and the more violent the hatred of the Orangemen, the more certain the reconciliation of the Catholics.[54]

For the benefit of those who insisted that legal disabilities did not really deprive Catholics of anything of importance Sydney covered half a page with positions ranging from Chancellor of the Exchequer to Bailiff which were closed to Catholics. He further observed that all Irish Sheriffs and Deputy Sheriffs were Protestants, a fact which left the lives and well-being of Catholics in their hands, and in those of Protestant juries. In his terminology, "a poor Catholic in Ireland may be tried by twelve Percevals, and destroyed according to the manner of that gentleman in the name of the Lord, and with all the insulting forms of justice." Similarly no Catholic served on a vestry, but the Protestant minority on the vestry levied taxes on Catholics as well as Protestants; and the grand juries of Ireland possessed extensive powers, the exercise of which was forbidden to those of the Roman Church. Discrimination was real enough, Sydney observed, and when that kind of partiality existed, further prejudice would be suspected, and the Catholic blockhead who failed in his law practice could blame British policy.[55]

For those who still feared Catholic power Sydney announced the willingness, which was later denied, of the Catholics to vest the nomination of the Roman Catholic Bishops in the crown. He further proposed that the salaries of the bishops and other clergy should be paid by the crown, and the salaries of Irish Roman Catholic bishops, which were then from three to four hundred pounds a year should be raised to an average of five hundred to a thousand; while the Roman Catholic priests, who were then being paid from thirty to ninety pounds on the average, should be raised to about two hundred pounds -the whole amount coming to approximately §250,000, "about the expense of three days of one of our genuine, good, English, just and necessary wars."

> The clergy should all receive their salaries at the Bank of Ireland, and I would place the whole patronage in the hands of the Crown. Now I appeal to any human being, except Spencer Perceval, Esq., of the parish of Hampstead, what the disaffection of a clergy would amount to, gaping after

> this graduated bounty of the Crown, and
> whether Ignatius Loyola himself, if he
> were a living blockhead instead of a dead
> saint, could withstand the temptation of
> bouncing from 100 a year in Sligo, to 300
> in Tipperary? This is the miserable sum
> of money for which the merchants, and
> land-owners, and nobility of England are
> exposing themselves to the tremendous
> peril of losing Ireland. The sinecure
> places of the Roses and Percevals, and
> the "dear and near relations" put up to
> auction at thirty years' purchase would
> almost amount to the money.[56]

By this policy Sydney hoped to win the loyalty of the Irish Roman Catholic clergy, and through them the loyalty of the country. "In this way", he added the end of his ninth letter,

> Hoche pacified La Vendee - and in this way
> only will Ireland ever be subdued. But
> this, in the eyes of Mr. Perceval, is im-
> becility and meanness: houses are not broke
> open - women are not insulted - the people
> seem to be happy; they are not rode over by
> horses, and cut by whips. Do you call this
> vigour? - Is this government?[57]

Hesketh Pearson said in his book The Smith of Smiths that "...it is all the more to the credit of Sydney Smith that he fought so hard for the rights of a religion that he did not in the least understand",[58] but it is not clear at all that Sydney did not understand Catholicism. His desire for Catholic emancipation makes it clear that he saw the problem of Ireland as one that transcended religion, and if he never called the problem "Irish Nationalism", his attitudes and actions certainly indicate that he did see it in that light. His writings indicate that while he did not fully approve of the Roman Catholic Church, and while he rejected many of its beliefs and practices, he still found it preferable to the evangelical movement. In his view Roman Catholicism came much closer to his ideal of "rational religion" than did the Methodists, and he freely acknowledged Anglicanism's Catholic ancestry. It is obvious that Sydney understood Roman Catholicism adequately, if not perfectly, and that Pearson was led to deny his insight into Catholicism by the unrealistic reforms he proposed for the Roman Catholic

Church. It is equally obvious though, that Sydney was
led to offer such changes not out of ignorance of the
Roman Catholic Church, but as a result of his political
and social philosophy. Liberals believed that if evil
existed it resulted from bad laws, and that if those laws
were repealed or amended the evil would disappear. Similarly, Sydney believed that the structure and policy of
the Church of England had produced a loyal and contented
population that endorsed the social and political system
of England. It seemed to him to be a simple and obvious
desideratum to apply those practices that worked so well
in England to the Roman Church of Ireland. The fact
that such practices might be uncanonical in the Church of
Rome did not disturb him unduly, for they were uncanonical in the Church of England as well; but he hoped that
by having the government establish clerical salaries and
pay the Roman Catholic clergy, as Napoleon had done in
France, it could secure the loyalty of the clergy, and
through them, the loyalty of the Irish people.

In the tenth and last of the Peter Plymley Letters
Sydney continued his proposals to mollify the Irish and
to save England. His first suggestion was that the landowners should buy up the tithes from the Church of Ireland. His purpose in this reform was not to reduce
tithe payment on the part of the Irish laborers, but to
change the name of it to rent, which would be paid to
the landowner rather than to the Church.[59] Sydney placed
a very high value on property rights, and since the farmer then rented only nine-tenths of the produce of the
land he saw no injustice in requiring the Irish to continue to pay ten per cent in a more palatable form. He
also suggested that if the Roman and Irish churches were
put on a par in this way, and if civil emancipation of
the Catholics were carried out, widespread conversion of
Catholics to the Church of England would follow.

> If a rich young Catholic were in Parliament, he would belong to White's and to
> Brooke's, would keep race-horses, would
> walk up and down Pall Mall, be exonerated of his ready money and his constitution, become as totally devoid of morality, honesty, knowledge, and civility,
> as Protestant loungers in Pall Mall,
> and return home with a supreme contempt
> for Father O'Leary and Father O'Callaghan.
> I am astonished at the madness of the
> Catholic clergy, in not perceiving that

> Catholic emancipation is Catholic infidelity; that to entangle their people in the intrigues of a Protestant parliament, and a Protestant court, is to insure the loss of every man of fashion and consequence in their community. The true receipt for preserving their religion is Mr. Perceval's receipt for destroying it....[60]

Sydney felt that loyalty to the king had reached a high peak, and said that he too was loyal. In response to anticipated charges he said: "I detest Jacobinism; and if I am doomed to be a slave at all, I would rather be the slave of a king than a cobbler." He added that the cry, "God save the King," warmed his heart too, but that he feared it meant in too many cases "God save my pension and my place, God give my sisters an allowance out of the privy purse....". In the name of loyalty, he claimed, Perceval and his ministers proposed to convert four million Irish Catholics, and to defeat France by cutting off her supply of laxatives.

> What a sublime thought, that no purge can now be taken between the Weser and the Garonne; that the bustling pestle is still, the canorous mortar mute, and the bowels of mankind locked up for fourteen degrees of latitude! When, I should be curious to know, were all the powers of crudity and flatulence fully explained to his Majesty's Ministers? At what period was this great plan of conquest and constipation fully developed? In whose mind was the idea of destroying the pride, and the plasters of France first engendered? Without castor oil they might, for some months, to be sure, have carried on a lingering war; but can they do without bark? Will the people live under a government where antimonial powders cannot be procured? Will they bear the loss of mercury? "There's the rub." Depend upon it, the absence of the materia medica will soon bring them to their senses, and the cry of <u>Bourbon and bolus</u> burst forth from the Baltic to the Mediterranean.[61]

The oath of supremacy had been dispensed with, he observed, in the case of the French Canadians in 1774, and could as easily be dispensed with for the Irish. Sydney mentioned that religious toleration in Hungary had strengthened and unified that country, without impoverishing its Roman Catholic hierarchy. A Catholic king of England might be inclined to conspire against the Established Church, but Sydney did not think that Catholics in any other position offered any threat at all. Indeed, he said, a Catholic Prime Minister would be infinitely less dangerous to the Church than a "Methodistical chancellor of the true Clapham breed". He also tried to dissuade Brother Abraham from the notion that if all of the cabinet could be Catholic, all would be; and he added an admonition against bigotry:

> I am astonished to see you, and many good and well-meaning clergymen beside you, painting the Catholics in such detestable colours; two-thirds, at least, of Europe are Catholics, -they are Christians, though mistaken Christians; how can I possibly admit that any sect of Christians, and above all, that the oldest and most numerous sect of Christians, are incapable of fulfilling the common duties and relations of life: though I do differ from them in many particulars, God forbid I should give such a handle to infidelity, and subscribe to such blasphemy against our common religion.[62]

In the Peter Plymley Letters, Sydney expressed very clearly his attitudes towards religious toleration as well as most of the arguments for Catholic Emancipation that are to be found his various sermons and reviews. He later added the idea that Irish Catholics were being discriminated against because of persecutions by non-Irish Catholics in remote times, and said that the English feared Catholicism because of Louis XIV's dragonades and the Spanish Inquisition.[63] The English dread of Catholicism, plus his own delight in "secrecy", led him to write under the name of Peter Plymley and to revel in the public notoriety it brought. His identity as the author was known from the first, but he maintained his over-elaborate facade of anonymity for years afterwards. In 1837, only shortly before he publicly acknowledged the Peter Plymley Letters to be his own, he responded to a letter:

> I have read Peter Plymley a long time since, and, as far as I remember thought it a smart production of a young man and liberal person. I did not write it. I have no copy of it. I do not mean to republish it. I do not know who wrote it. I agree entirely with all the opinions it professes, but the work itself was ephemeral and is dead and gone.[64]

Saba Holland claimed,[65] and most of Sydney's biographers echoed her belief, that the government tried assiduously but unsuccessfully to discover the author; but an investigation of Home Office papers of the period reveals no evidence of any such concern or activity, therefore there is no reason to assume that it happened. While the Peter Plymley Letters were scurrilous, they certainly were not seditious, nor were they written in such a manner as to invite libel charges. Disagreeable as the government may have been in the eyes of Sydney and the Whig liberals, it had little or no reason to seek out the author, especially since his identity could probably have been established by asking any London gossip. The Peter Plymley Letters endangered neither the government not its policies vis a vis the Catholics. Catholic Emancipation did come, but it came over twenty years later; and although Sydney and the Peter Plymley Letters deserve some credit for contributing to it, the major effect of the letters was to unify liberal thought on the Catholic question and to keep it alive over the years.[66]

Partially as a result of his sentiments in favor of Catholic emancipation, Sydney has been described as being theistic, or even un-christian, and Ford K. Brown has said that "...after Paley's death in 1805 he was possibly the best exponent in England of a religion of good-hearted common sense in which the 'peculiar doctrines' of Christianity were wholly wanting."[67] In a sense this statement is true, but Sydney, whose common sense observations and practical sermons were based on basic Christian beliefs, showing his interest in Catholic emancipation, was influenced by a real concern for the Anglican establishment which, he believed, would be strengthened by a wider toleration of dissent. Despite the changes that he saw on every side, he still believed that the eighteenth century political, religious, and social system he had grown up in would continue, even though future decades would see necessary but minor liberal amendments. He felt that the Church of England was the main pillar of "rational religion", and that the Anglican establishment performed an essential role in instructing the nation in moral principles. He said that the learned and rational body of Anglican clergymen caused infidelity to "reason well",[68] and he believed that dissenters of wealth and talent would be drawn into the Church, as they had been in the eighteenth century. He considered also that the Church was a more substantial and durable institution than many of the faint-hearted, who offered to defend it with bigotry and persecution of dissenters, believed.

> Does it behove so learned, so opulent, so pious, so moral a body of men, to tremble for this vast, and venerable establishment, as if it were a little sickly heresy, that had sprung up yesterday in the brain of some distempered enthusiast.... The truth is , it is not frail, and not perishable. If "the gates of hell not prevail against it", it will never be dashed to pieces on the rocks of justice.[69]

To that statement he added that if the Church was nothing but a human institution, or one that was barbarous and monastic, penal laws might prop it up, but that it would and should fall. He asserted to the contrary his belief that the Church was of apostolical origin, and that its divine derivation, bolstered by "good sense and public utility", would carry it through changes of condition and fortune without the aid of intolerance.[70]

Sydney was to continue his interest in Catholic emancipation until it became a reality in 1829, and his concern for Ireland and its problems until his death in 1845. With the publication of the last of the Peter Plymley Letters in 1808 until 1829 he published no less than thirteen reviews, sermons, or letters dealing wholly or partly with the Catholics, most of which reiterated his plymleian arguments. In the mid-twenties, with the decline on the fortunes of the Tory party and the rise of Daniel O'Connell and the Catholic Association in Ireland, Catholic emancipation, which had been stalled in 1813 by the recalcitrance of the Roman Church, and in 1821 by the resistence of the Duke of York, became an issue once more; and meetings of the Anglican clergy, which were generally hostile to the emancipation of the Catholics, were held throughout the country. In March, 1825, such a meeting of the clergy of Cleveland took place at the Three Tuns Inn in Thirsk, and to the consternation of most of the clergy, Sydney spoke on behalf of the Catholics. He was supported by only two clerical friends, Francis Wrangham, Archdeacon of Cleveland, and the Rev. William Vernon Harcourt, son of the Archbishop;[71] both of whom signed the following petition:

> We, the undersigned, being clergymen of the Church of England, resident within the Diocese of York, humbly petition your honourable House to take into your consideration the state of those laws which affect the Roman Catholics of Great Britain and Ireland.
> We beg of you to inquire whether all those statutes, however wise and necessary in their origin, may not now (when the Church of England is rooted in the public affection, and the title to the throne undisputed) be wisely and safely repealed.
> We are steadfast friends to that Church of which we are members, and we wish no law repealed which is really essential to its safety; but we submit to the superior wisdom of your honourable House, whether that Church is not sufficiently protected by its antiquity, by its learning, by its piety, and by that moderate tenour which it knows so well how to preserve amidst the opposite excesses of mankind; -the indifference of one age, and the fanaticism of another.
> It is our earnest hope that any indulgence you might otherwise think it expedient to extend to the Catholic subjects of this realm may not be prevented by the intemperate conduct of some few members of that persuasion; that in the great business of framing a lasting religious peace for these kingdoms, the extravagence of overheated minds, or the studied insolence of men who intend mischief, may be equally overlooked.
> If your honourable House should in your wisdom determine that all these laws which are enacted against the Roman Catholics cannot with safety and advantage be repealed, we then venture to express a hope that such disqualifying laws alone will be

> suffered to remain, which you consider to
> be clearly required for the good of the
> Church and State. We feel the blessing
> of our own religious liberty, and we think
> it a serious duty to extend it to others,
> in every degree which sound discretion
> will permit.[72]

On 11 April, 1825, he attended another meeting of the clergy of the East Riding at the Tiger Inn, Beverley, where he again presented a petition, but, persuasive as he may have been, he failed to sway the clergy, and was left in a minority of one. One clergyman, according to Sydney, whispered to him that he was of Sydney's opinion, but that he had nine children; to which Sydney responded by begging that "he would remain a Protestant".[73] In a letter written at the same time, Sydney reported that he had polled the servants at the inn, and found: "The Chambermaid was decidedly for the Church of England. Boots was for the Catholics. The waiter said he had often (God forgive him) wished them both confounded together."[74]

The controversy over the Catholics, fed by O'Connell's success in Ireland, continued, and in the summer of 1825 Sydney commented on the severe drought in the north by saying: "My cows are drinking small Beer, my horses ale-. The price of Water varies from 2d to 3d per pint-. Are they going to turn us into a Tropical Climate? I shall be Philo Catholicus in all temperatures-"[75] In the early part of the following year he published his Letter to the Electors on the Catholic Question,[76] writing at the same time to Lady Grey to inform her of his support of Lord Grey on that question.[77] Two years later, having been appointed to a vacant prebendal stall at Bristol Cathedral, he was expected to preach an anti-Catholic sermon on 5 November, which was Guy Fawkes' Day, and the occasion for anti-Catholic demonstrations; but as early as the preceding August he had determined not to do so.[78] Instead, when the day came, he preached an "honest" sermon to the most Protestant mayor and corporation in England - and he noted in his letters that he had given them "...such a dose of toleration as shall last them many a year."[79] It was this sermon[80] which so offended the mayor and corporation that they absented themselves from the Cathedral for a number of years.

Disappointingly enough Catholic emancipation did not quiet Ireland, nor did it produce all the benefits Sydney had so confidently promised in the Peter Plymley

Letters and elsewhere; but he could still defend his earlier opinions on the grounds that the action of the government was too little and too late. In 1832, for example, he said that payment of the Roman Catholic priests was the only alternative to civil war; and by 1843 he asserted that since timely measures had not been taken, the only alternative was to destroy the Anglican establishment in Ireland.[81] In 1844, not long before his death, he showed that he still had Irish problems on his mind, and suggested a comprehensive plan which included paying the Roman Catholic and Presbyterian clergy, sending a British ambassador to Rome, dividing the Anglican patronage among the Catholics and Presbyterians, and correcting the system of land tenure, while maintaining an adequate army in Ireland and enforcing the law against O'Connell.[82] Sydney's advice had not been followed in 1807 and was not followed in 1844, but it is tempting to contemplate the benefits to Ireland and Great Britain that might have resulted had his suggestions been carried out in a more timely fashion. Sydney's principles of religious toleration were well known and so greatly reflected in his life that he could use mock intolerance very effectively; and on one occasion he gravely stated to a liberal assemblage that his one small failing, his one secret desire, was to roast a Quaker.

> 'Good heavens, Mr. Smith!' said Mr.----, full of horror, 'roast a Quaker?' 'But do you consider, Mr. Smith, the torture?' 'Yes, Sir...I have considered everything; it may be wrong, as you say: the Quaker would undoubtedly suffer acutely, but every one has his tastes, mine would be to roast a Quaker: one would satisfy me, only one; but it is one of those peculiarities I have striven against in vain, and I hope you will pardon my weakness.'[83]

Having been informed, on another occasion, of the refusal of an Anglican clergyman to bury a dissenter, he was asked if he would. "On the contrary", he replied, "I would be only too glad to bury them all." In another conversation he said that if invited to a masquerade he would go disguised as a dissenter.[84]

His sympathies for dissenters and Catholics were well known, and his liberal tendencies led him to support the abolition of slavery, despite the fact that the

Abolition Society must have been a "Methodist" group in his opinion. In a letter to Thomas Creevey in June, 1812, he announced that he had voted for William Wilberforce "...on account of his good conduct in Africa, a place returning no members to parliament, but still, from the extraordinary resemblance its inhabitants bear to human creatures."[85] In 1839, after the abolition of slavery in the British Empire, Smith received a dinner invitation from Daniel Webster, the American statesman then visiting in England. Sydney offered his regrets on the grounds that he had no disengaged time during that month "...except Sundays when in mercy to Slaves I do not dine."[86] While dining with Edward Everett, the famous American orator and statesman, he is reported, in one account, to have said:

> '...why can't you live on better terms with your black population?' "Why to tell you the truth, Mr. Smith, they smell so abominably that we can't bear them near us.' 'Possibly not...but men must not be led by the nose in that way: if you don't like asking them to dinner, it is surely no reason why you should not make citizens of them.[87]

Just as Sydney was unprejudiced toward Negroes, so was he friendly to the Jews, and to their claims to civil liberty. Since the Jewish population of Great Britain was small he was not as concerned about them as he was about the Catholics, and in 1830 he wrote to Lady Holland to say: "I think the Jews should be kept for the private tyranny and intolerance of the Bishops- thirty thousand Jews, it is but a small matter...."[88] That statement was, of course, serious only in the sense that he felt it was wiser policy to persecute thirty thousand Jews than four million Catholics. In reality though, he defended all minorities; and in 1833, again in a letter to Lady Holland, he said: "I was vexed with the defeat of the Jews wishing earnestly to put an end to this last piece of a long series of nonsense - and cruelty & oppresion...."[89] This last statement demonstrates his liberal desire to eliminate all discrimination based on race or religion, while, at the same time, he could defend social and civil distinctions which were rooted in property, family, and ability.

CHAPTER VII

The New Beginning In Yorkshire:
The Beneficed Clergyman   1809-1829

After his success in London, Sydney's move to Yorkshire has often been characterized as a defeat of sorts, but actually it was a new beginning for him in a new role. After his curacy at Netheravon the country was by no means entirely strange to him, and in 1809 he returned not as a humble curate but as a well known writer as well as the possessor of a substantial living--both of which gave him a position of some considerable prominence in the locality. He undoubtedly left London with some regret, and, as a result of his known political views, he received a mixed reception in the country,[1] but he separated himself from elegant society and politics only in the most limited respect. He was to remain in Yorkshire for nearly twenty years, but he stayed in contact and improved his connections with politicians and influential social figures. An examination of his surviving letters shows that he frequently visited his neighbours, particularly those of the Whig persuasion, and that, in addition to an annual visit to London during the season, he also visited his friends in Edinburgh, York, and elsewhere, occasionally for extended periods of time. Visitors, his friends and acquaintances (and those who wished to become such) from Edinburgh and London, came to call at his temporary home in Heslington, and later at the parsonage he built in Foston. In fact, they visited in such numbers that Sydney jokingly suggested that admission should be by ticket only.[2] It is evident, therefore, that his extended sojourn in Yorkshire, far from being an exile or a "rustication" was a phase of his career, during which he continued to write for the <u>Edinburgh Review</u> and to work for Catholic Emancipation along with various other liberal causes. He remained ambitious, and hoped for a mitre, but his fortunes depended on the well-being of the Whigs, and their future hinged to a large extent on the war, which was finally going well for England and the Tories. It is too much to say that Sydney forsaw Napoleon's defeat, but he did choose the right time to "rusticate" himself, for from 1809 onwards the famed luck of Napoleon changed perceptibly, and with it waned the prospects of a Whig administration in the immediate future.

Sydney often expressed pessimism about the possibility

of his promotion in the Church, and frequently denied any real ambition to become a bishop; but in the former instances he was being more realistic than pessimistic at those specific times, and in the latter he was, like modern American presidential hopefuls, merely coy. In 1805 he had written to Jeffrey to say:

> You ask me about my prospects. I think I shall long remain as I am. I have no powerful friends. I belong to no party, I do not cant, I abuse canting everywhere, I am not conciliating, and I have not talents enough to force my way without these laudable and illaudable auxiliaries. This is as true a picture of my situation as I can give you. In the mean time, I lead not an unhappy life, much otherwise, and am thankful for my share of good.[3]

But having been appointed to the living at Foston-le-Clay, and having been forced by Archbishop Harcourt to reside there, he wrote again to Jeffrey in 1808:

> I am by no means grieved at quitting London; sorry to lose the society of my friends, but wishing for more quiet, more liesure, less expence, and more space for my children. I am extremely pleased with what I have seen of York.[4]

Nearly a year later, in September, 1809, in a letter written in the spirit of cheerful resignation, he said to Lady Elizabeth Holland:

> If (as the greater probability is) I am come to the end of my career, I give myself quietly up to horticulture, and the annual augmentation of my family. In short, if my lot be to crawl, I will crawl contentedly; if to fly, I will fly with alacrity; but as long as I can possibly avoid it I will never be unhappy.[5]

Contrary to his letter of 1805 to Jeffrey, he had powerful friends in Lord and Lady Holland, and through them and his Whig connections he still hoped for a Whig administration and preferment in the Church for himself. Evidence that he had not given up his aspirations for advancement is to be found in a letter to John Allen, written the following December, in which he mentioned that he had sent one of his sermons to the Duke of Bedford and that he "should be obliged to him for the living of St. Paul's, Covent Garden, in return."[6]

In short, although Sydney was reconciled to life in the country for the time being, he still hoped for greater things. He did not despair, for if his ambitions were unfulfilled his hopes remained; and he, as the holder of a good benefice, had little reason to be desperate. Had he been able to foresee the future twenty years in Yorkshire, he might indeed have been more desperate than he was; but he was fortunately not blessed with omniscience, and his basic good nature and optimism enabled him to live with a moderately happy acceptance of his fate, and ultimately with contentment.

He arrived in York on Midsummer Day, 1809, and having ascertained that the parsonage at Foston was unsuitable, he hired a house at Heslington, some twelve miles from the church at Foston. He had tried earlier to exchange Foston for a living in the south, and he continued to do so at least until 1812, after which he became reconciled to a permanent residence in York. Although he hesitated until 1812 to make the major investment of building an adequate manse, a project which he had considered as early as June, 1809, he believed that a desirable rectory would make the living more readily exchangeable. But still, he said to Lady Holland:

> ".....if with a pleasant wife, three children, a good house and farm, many books and many friends who wish me well I cannot be happy, I am a very foolish fellow and what becomes of me is of very little consequence."[7]

The outlay for building a proper house on his living was considerable, and Sydney wavered in his decision to build or not to build. In the autumn of 1812, however, he stood for election to the readership of Gray's Inn, a sinecure, but one that might have made good connections for him. He wrote to Lady Holland, saying:

> Nothing more has transpired respecting my Election, I have done all that can be to insure Success-and I sat down in the thorough persuasion that the greatest fool, and the greatest Scoundrel will be

>   the successful man-how far such princi-
>   ples of election may operate in my favor
>   -I must leave to you to determine.[8]

To that statement he added that he had little hope of success, and that if he failed in the election he had promised to build at Foston.[9] His attempt to secure the readership seems to have been his last hope of avoiding permanent residence in Yorkshire; and when he failed, he rather quickly proceeded with his plans to build at Foston. In December, 1812, he wrote to John Allen admitting that he had an added inducement to build in that he might not be able to keep his house in Heslington, or to find another that would be suitable. Although he was extremely dubious about investing so much in building a rectory, he confessed that if he were the Archbishop, he would require it.[10]

According to his daughter Saba's account, Sydney, upon his arrival in Yorkshire, had requested three years' time in which to exchange his living; but finding himself unable to do so, he had decided to build and to farm the glebe. Having found it impossible to effect the exchange, the Archbishop granted him an additional year in which to build. Once he had decided upon construction, he proceeded with typical Smithian determination, and typical muddling. Advised by the local farmers to use horses for his heavy hauling, and by the gentlemen to use oxen, he unhesitatingly followed the advice of the gentlemen and bought four oxen, which he characteristically named "Lug, Tug, Hawl, and Crawl". They proved to be absolutely worthless for his purposes, so he sold them and replaced them with horses. He also was advised to bake his own bricks, which he did, but finding them to be of inferior quality, he discarded the lot and purchased bricks of higher quality. He had hired an architect to design the house, but finding himself at odds with that gentleman, Sydney paid him off and dismissed him, saying, "You build for glory, Sir; I, for use."[11] With his own plan the utilitarian structure progressed rapidly, and in March, 1814, he was able to move his family into the nearly completed house.

Sydney's own plans for his rectory at Foston still exist in the Borthwick Institute, York University, and it is interesting to note that although the memoirs written by his wife and daughter still refer to him as a "poor" man, he built quite an impressive home. The first floor consisted of two drawing rooms, one 28' x 16', and the other 22' x 16', both with recesses; a dressing room, a store room, and a hall and staircase. The outbuildings on the ground level consisted of a wash house, a wood house, a brewhouse, an open shed, a manure shed, a coal shed, three stables for five horses, a harness room and coach house, a granary, and a privy for men and another for women. The upper floor contained five bedrooms, and there were three chambers for servants above the brewhouse and the granary.[12] It was substantial and comfortable, if unattractive in terms of the architecture of the period, and the Smiths lived contentedly in it for a decade and a half. It still stands in excellent condition as a superior country house.

Sydney was dubious about the wisdom of building, but he was able to borrow the necessary capital from "Queen Anne's Bounty", a long-established foundation for the purpose of lending money to clergymen for projects that would better the Church. Among the papers in the Borthwick Institute is a composition book with a marbled cover which is entitled in Sydney's hand: "Account of the Expenditure of §1600 borrowed from the Governors of Queen Anne's Bounty for the Erection of a Parsonage House at Foston Deanery of Bulmer North Riding of Yorkshire in the Years 1813-1814 by William Storye-of Foston". Blank except for the first two pages, it is typical of Sydney's meticulous record-keeping in financial matters. The account listed is undoubtedly his totaling up of numerous small charges, bills for which are also carefully preserved, into a cogent statement. His management of the building project was excellent, for not only did he carefully preserve estimates, bills, and receipts, but he also held the total cost of the house down to §1616/4, which was agreed to by William Storey.[13] The result was an eminently liveable and well built house, and one whose cost of building exceeded Sydney's original estimate by only one per cent.

It is interesting also, that despite his misgivings on the subject of building, Sydney began construction under his own volition, rather than as a result of pressure from the Archbishop. Sydney, having been granted time to exchange the living and time to construct, felt a compulsion as a gentlemen to live up to his agreements; and he did so rather than put the Archbishop in the discourteous position of having to use coercion. Indeed, according to Saba Holland,[14] the Archbishop actually sent his formal permission to delay or avoid building, but Sydney proceeded with the project from a sense of duty to the Archbishop. On 17 January, 1813, shortly before starting on the building, Sydney wryly commented on the action of the Archbishop in a letter to Lady Holland:

> Is it not a little singular, that his Excellence...should never have given me the most distant hint directly, or indirectly that such a process could be in honor dispensed with? Is it not a little singular that he should have reserved this friendly charge of superogation till I had burnt my bricks, bought my timber, and got into a situation in which it was more prudent to advance, than to recede? The Archbishop is a friendly good man; but such is not the manner of laymen. It would be a bad comfort to an Indian widow, who was half-burnt, if the head Bramin were to call out to her, "Remember, it is your <u>own act and deed</u>; I never ordered you to <u>burn yourself</u>, and I must take the liberty of telling you that you are a fool for your pains". "No, good Sr., but he knew that it was a common custom of our religion; that it was expected of me. I conversed with you upon it; you saw me bringing the faggots, and have reserved this opinion of the superfluity of the act till I am half roasted, and till death is better than life."[15]

Despite his complaint, Sydney was most satisfied with his house, and it helped to make him more contented with residence in the country. Saba Holland asserted that he expended all of his capital in building, and that he went deeply into debt, but it dubious that he did either. He undoubtedly had expenses that were not covered by the loan from Queen Anne's Bounty, but it is not typical of Sydney to expend all of his capital in an investment from which it might not be recovered in the future. He certainly borrowed the bulk of his investment, and although the payments to Queen Anne's Bounty were probably high, they were not beyond his means. In his later published letter to Archdeacon Singleton, Sydney said he had "... built a Parsonage-house with farm offices for a large farm, which cost me 4,000". Perhaps he did invest that much in Foston, which would certainly have taken a good deal of capital investment on his part; but it is not clear from his statement whether he invested that much initially, or whether he did so over an extended period of time while realizing some profits from his farming.16

Once ensconced in his comfortable parsonage, Sydney experienced a feeling of contentment after 1814, and seemed to have reconciled himself to the likelihood that he would be there for an indefinite period of time. Although he came to terms with life in Yorkshire, he never fully accepted country living. He possessed three hundred acres of glebe, of which he rented out two hundred and farmed the remaining hundred himself. He was a gentleman farmer in the truest sense, but as Reid has said, his success in farming was neither immediate nor overwhelming. As a gentleman farmer he had time to tinker about the house and farm, and exhibited a penchant for inventions, experiments, and gadgets that would have made him the envy of Mr. Thomas Jefferson of Monticello, Virginia. He was living in an age when experimentation with expedients to relieve poverty and poor rates was quite popular. Sydney even subdivided several acres of his glebe into sixteenths and let them at a low rent to the villagers, who, being thus able to raise potatoes and a pig were greatly benefitted. Like others of his age he encouraged the laboring classes to help themselves, and offered a prize to the gardener whose plot was most productive. He also fed, at different times, rice, gruel, and broth to his farm laborers to test the effects on their appetites, tinkered with lamps fired by mutton fat, and tested an improved fireplace. Of the invention that pleased him most, he said:

> I am all for cheap luxuries, even for animals; now all animals have a passion for scratching their backbones; they break down your gates and palings to effect this. Look! There is my universal scratcher, a sharp-edged pole, resting on a high and low post, adapted to every height, from a horse to a lamb. Even the Edinburgh Reviewer can take his turn; you have no idea how popular it is; I have not had a gate broken since I put it up; I have it in all my fields.17

But even though Sydney applied himself with zest to such projects and adjusted himself good naturedly to the changed conditions of life, he was not entirely happy in the country. "My living in Yorkshire", he said, "was so far out of the way, that it was actually twelve miles from a lemon."[18] His attitudes towards life in rural retreats did not result from his exile in Yorkshire, for as early as 1799 he had written from Edinburgh to Mrs. Hicks Beach, who was then in the country, to say:

> You are not seriously immersed in all these weighty operations which fill up the sum of country life. You are flinging barley out to the pigeons. You are hearing the hideous death of peafowl that have been eat by foxes. You have drawn half a carnation, you have observed several times that the grass is green and the may sweet. You have gap'd several times and pull'd Caesar by the ears --and heard above eight and thirty stories...about Grandpapa and Grandmama.[19]

In an undated letter, but one that appears to have been written not long after he left London for Yorkshire, he said to Lady Holland:

> I do esctremely well in the Country-every now and then I have the blue devils-but less and less-I find however that I am getting much weaker in my understanding & tremble for the Symptoms of imbecility which Wishaw and Brougham will discover nesct Week.[20]

Sydney, when he was later asked if he liked the country, replied, "I like London a great deal better; the study of men and women, better than grass and grees."[21] He was bored when he was in Foston, but he fought boredom with reading, writing, correspondence with friends, and making and receiving visits. He was a frequent visitor at Castle Howard, the nearby residence of Lord Carlisle, and he visited other people in the area as well as receiving many guests at Foston. Although such visits and visitors were undoubtedly a relief from the monotony of country life for him, they did not satisfy his gregarious spirit, and he often went to nearby York during the racing season or for the assizes. In 1810, while still living in Heslington, he invited Lord and Lady Holland to visit, urging them to:

> ...remember that next week from Monday to Saturday is the Race Week in which you will not be able to procure either a bed for a servant or a stall for a horse.... whatever accomodations we have are entirely at your disposal. We have now another bed in which a maid or a philosopher, or a maid with a philosopher, might be put. God grant in this latter event that they might both merit their respective appellations the ensuing morning.[22]

In 1821 he wrote to say: "I have taken lodgings in York for myself and family during the Assizes to enable them to stare out of the Window, there being nothing visible where we live but Crows..."[23] In York the Smiths were able not only to look out of the windows but also to attend the assizes and to see great lawyers like Brougham, Sir John Copley, and James Scarlett plead their cases. In 1831 he wrote to his daughter Emily to describe a visit to a neighbour:

> I called on Mr. Popham this morning, a drizzling day, he yawning in a shooting jacket. Miss Popham the ugliest of unmarried Sisters was instructing the spoilt child in Roman History. Mrs. Popham as cold as if she was in the last state of blue Cholera, and the ecclesiastical Brother was yawning a second to Mr. Popham. The only news I heard was that Mr. Guerin had been bad in his bowels, but be at ease he is better.[24]

"...one advantage of the country", was, he said, "...that a joke once established

> is good for ever; it is like the stuff which is denominated _everlasting_, and used as pantaloons by careful parents for their children. In London you expect a change of pleasantry; but M. and N. laugh more at my six-year-old jokes than they did when the jokes were in their infancy.[25]

Still, later, in 1838, he said:

> I have no relish for the country; it is a kind of healthy grave. I am afraid

> you are not exempt from the delusions
> of flowers, green turf, and birds; they
> all afford slight gratification, but
> not worth an hour of rational conversa-
> tion: and rational conversation in suf-
> ficient quanities is only to be had from
> the congregation of a million people in
> one spot.[26]

If the country was boring and lacking in rational conversation it did have the redeeming feature of cheap living and cheap labor, which Sydney happily used. It would not be fair to his memory to accuse him of exploitation, for his laissez-faire mentality thought not in terms of exploitation, but rather in the context of obtaining needed goods and services at the natural price established by free competition. When he moved into the new parsonage at Foston he said:

> I had little furniture, so I brought a
> cart-load of deals; took a carpenter
> (who came to me for parish relief, cal-
> led Jack Robinson) with a face like a
> full-moon, into my service, established
> him in a barn, and said, 'Jack, furnish
> my house!' You see the result.[27]

Similarly he acquired a young country girl named Rachel Masterman, nicknamed "Bunch", and trained her as a *factor factotum*, often referring to her as his butler. She became a faithful and dedicated servant.[28] Rachel remained with him during his life, later marrying William Kilvington, the coachman, who also served the Smiths for years, and to whom Sydney bequeathed one of the chairs made by Jack Robinson.[29] If he did not overpay his servants, Sydney treated them well, and received devoted service from them.

Sydney was normally on excellent terms with his servants, but that degree of mutual understanding did not extend to horses. Never a good rider, Sydney was thrown repeatedly, but country living required a certain amount of riding, and he accepted his anticipated falls with a degree of resignation. "I have been lame", he said, in a letter to Lady Holland in 1819, "for some time by a

> fall from my horse. He had behaved so
> well - and so quietly that I doubled
> his allowance of Corn - and in return

> he kicked me over his head in the most ignominious, and contemptuous manner. This should be a warning to you against raising Servants Wages...I am recovering fast tho' sorely bruis'd - fifteen Stone Weight - does not fall from Sixteen hand high-with impunity.[30]

He developed various non-fall gadgets for his safety while riding, none of which worked; and he finally reconciled himself to the fact that if he rode he would sooner or later be unseated:

> I used to think a horse dangerous, but much to the contrary. I have had six falls in two years, and just behaved like the three percents when they fall, -I got up again, and am not a bit the worse for it.... somehow or other, my horse and I had a habit of parting company. On one occasion I found myself prostrate in the streets of York, much to the delight of the Dissenters. Another time, my horse Calamity flung me over his head into a neighbouring parish, as if I had been a shuttlecock, and I felt grateful it was not into a neighbouring planet....It is a great proof, too, of the liberality of this country, where everybody can ride as soon as they are born, that they tolerate me at all.[31]

On the other hand, Sydney could get about London rather readily without recourse to riding, a situation which doubtless contributed to his affection for that city. In spite of his so-called "poverty", Saba Holland said that he "went up to stay a short time in his brother's house in town, as he usually did every spring",[32] sending illegible directions back to Foston for the proper direction of parish and domestic matters. His popularity in London had been established, and it even increased during his years at Foston. In the unpublished memoir of her husband, Catherine Smith said that invitations to dine poured in preceding his visits, and that she had known him to be engaged for dinner every night for three weeks.[33] Some invitations were extended because of his literary notoriety, but Sydney's great attraction was his bubbling good nature and his never-failing wit. On 23 May 1811, he wrote whimsically to the negligent Lady Elizabeth Holland:

> How every odd, dear Lady Holl to ask me to dine with you on Sunday, the 9th, when I am coming to stay with you from the 5th to the 12th. It is like giving a gentlemen an assignation for Wednesday when you are going to marry him on the Sunday preceding - an attempt to combine the stimulus of gallantry with the security of connubial relations.[34]

Sydney imparted his intense enjoyment of London to his children, and wrote in 1818:

> I have brought all my children up to town; and they are, as you may suppose, not a little entertained and delighted. It is the first time they have ever seen four people together, except on remarkably fine days at the parish church.[35]

When invited to dinner by an eager host or hostess he proved to be even more eager to accept, often arriving before the lady of the house was dressed, and receiving the remainder of the company for her. His enthusiasm for good company and good conversation exceeded his concern for style and fashion, and his "neck-cloth always looked like a pudding tied round his throat....."[36] His conversation was not always, or even usually, rational, and in 1819 he wrote to Lord Grey and announced:

> I will send Lady Grey the news from London when I get there. I am sure she is too wise a woman not to be fond of gossiping; I am fond of it and have some talent for it.[37]

Sydney was indeed a gossip in a social group which considered gossip an art. Saba Holland recorded the famous account of Sydney's friend, Richard Brinsley Sheridan, confiding to Thomas Creevey that he and his wife had just inherited a fortune:

> 'Mrs. Sheridan and I', said he, 'have made the solemn vow to each other to mention it to no one, and nothing induces me now to

>confide it to you but the absolute conviction that Mrs. Sheridan is at this moment confiding it to Mrs. Creevey upstairs.'38

Although Sydney found the visits and company in London delightful, almost seeming to live for them while residing at Foston, the effort of travelling in his age, especially <u>en famille</u>, was very great indeed. "...you cannot conceive the blunders and agony", he said, in 1818, "the dust and distraction, the roaring and raving with which a family like mine in conveyed through three degrees of latitude...."39 He enjoyed his visits to London and elsewhere, but often found accomodations, even in friends' homes, less than attractive. "What is the use of fish or venison", he said, "when the backbone is 6 degrees below the freezing-point? Of all miserable habitations an English house in very hot or very cold weather is the worst."40 But being English his creature comforts mattered less to him than matters of the mind, and in 1819, in the midst of the currency cirsis he could comment that "he obtained nothing at table but soup and bullion."41

Sydney's reputation as an eminent wit was responsible for his great success as a guest, but his popularity was not entirely universal. Numerous, and sometimes influential, members of English society deplored his lampooning of established values, and many of them felt that as a clergyman he was lacking in propriety. Thomas Creevey wrote in 1824 that he never saw Sydney Smith "without thinking him too much the buffoon"; and he noted in 1828 that Lord Robert Spencer considered Sydney to be a "boisterous mountebank".42

Nonetheless, Sydney remained himself in spite of such criticism, of which he must have been aware, and in 1827 he wrote to his nephew Cecil:

>All London are talking of the Lady who is Mark'd Thomson & Co Londini 1827 a Lady bought a Stove with this inscription upon it in large letters - weather cold & Petticoats up She imprudently backed upon the Stove - and is marked in the largest letters Astley Cooper attended her - and though he never saw her <u>face</u> is quite sure she <u>is</u> a Lady of <u>the</u> highest quality.....43

Presented at court, Sydney was able to turn the rigid protocol into a joke:

> I found my colleague Tate, the other day, in his simplicity consulting the Archdeacon of Newfoundland what he should wear at the levee; - a man who sits bobbing for cod, and pocketing every tenth fish. However, I did worse when I went, by consulting no one; and, through pure ignorance, going to the levee in shoestrings instead of shoe-buckles. I found, to my surprise, people looking down at my feet; I could not think what they were at. At first I thought they had discovered the beauty of my legs, but at last the truth burst on me, by some wag laughing, and thinking I had done it as a joke. I was of course excessively annoyed to have been supposed capable of such a vulger, un-meaning piece of disrespect, and kept my feet as coyly under my petticoats as the veriest prude in the country, till I could make my escape....[44]

In 1829, although his fortunes had changed for the better, he was still the same Sydney, and he said:

> Luttrell came over for the day; he was very agreeable, but spoke too lightly, I thought, of veal soup. I took him aside, and reasoned the matter with him, but in vain; to speak the truth, Luttrell is not steady in his judgements on dishes. Individual failures with him soon degenerate into generic objections, till, by some fortunate accident, he eats himself into better opinions. A person of more calm reflection thinks not only of what he is consuming at that moment, but of the soups of the same kind he has met with in a long course of dining, and which have gradually and justly elevated the species. I am perhaps making too much of this; but the failures of a man of sense are always painful.[45]

Sydney's comments on Henry Luttrell were typical of his effervescent spirit which, if not invariable, was characteristic of him; and it was this side of his nature that he fairly constantly exhibited to his immediate family. He retained a joyous but matter-of-fact attitude towards his beloved wife and his increasing progeny, and confessed a degree of bafflement at the degree of seriousness and effort that the aristocracy expended on reproduction:

> I am happy to hear that there appears now to be a solid foundation laid for a young Petty. Nothing astonishes the country clergy so much as the difficulty which the Nobility experience in making these arrangements.[46]

He was genuinely fond of his brothers, especially Bobus, but had less patience for more distant and less interesting relatives; in a letter to Lady Holland regarding such visitors he commented: "Oh that these first cousins were but once removed".[47] Sydney and Bobus were great friends, in addition to being brothers, but their friendship was hampered by a misunderstanding of unspecified cause in 1811.[48] They were, however, quickly reconciled. In 1813, Sydney left his wife Catherine, who was momentarily expecting the birth of another child, in order to nurse Bobus who had contracted typhus.

Catherine Smith's last pregnancy was normal, but it occasioned some comment from Sydney in his letters. On 28 August, 1813, in a letter to Brougham, he said that his wife was "still in an intergral State- but threatening the production of a Parish- or even a Wapentake".[50] The child, a son, was born in September, and Sydney reported to Lady Holland that:

> Few events are of so little consequence as the fecundity of a clergyman's wife; still your kind disposition towards us justifies me in letting you know that Mrs. Sydney and her new born son are both extremely well. His name will be Grafton, and I shall bring him up as a Methodist and a Tory.[51]

In November, still the proud parent, he said to a friend:

> I long to shew you the splendid addition I have made to my collection of <u>animated nature</u>. My little Boy is that most delicious little creature that ever lived, & has all the novelty ...of a first child as it is now near seven years since I have been so agreeably employed...[52]

Despite his avowed intention to name his newest genius-prodigy Grafton, and to raise him as a Methodist, Sydney chose the name Windham, which he often spelled "Wyndham", and the child was destined to be healthy and vigorous. His birth had been accomplished with little fanfare--much less than if he had been an heir, said Sydney, who occasionally enjoyed pricking the ostentation and absurdity of the aristocracy:

> The usual establishment for an eldest landed baby is, two wet nurses, two ditto dry, two aunts, two physicians, two apothecaries; three female friends of the family, unmarried, advanced in life; and often, in the nursery, one clergyman, six flatterers, and a grandpapa. Less than this would not be decent.[53]

After their move to the new parsonage in Foston the family life of the Smiths continued normally. There were no more children, but the four little Smiths, apart from the usual childhood afflictions, grew to be healthy and happy in an atmosphere filled with affection, love, and concern. Douglas Smith, Sydney's favorite child, appeared to be less than robust, but his occasional illnesses were not major. He did have a minor speech impediment, but it was apparently corrected; and in 1818 he was able to enter Westminster School. Syndey had denounced the public schools in his reviews, but they were, nonetheless, the paths to success. Thus, when the time came, Douglas was sent off to Westminster School in spite of Sydney's reluctance, and at the expense of his brother, Bobus.[54] Douglas won his first fistfight at school, which was probably essential to his survival, but he contracted a fever that was serious enough for Mrs. Sydney to go to London and nurse him back to health. In fact, the whole family went to London to spend Christmas with Douglas. By January, however, he had recovered, and was at the head of the class.

Even though Douglas was his favorite child, Sydney seems to have shown little partiality for him. He was fond of Windham, Emily, and Saba. Saba showed signs of an overweening pride that led Sydney at a later date to comment:

> We are debating how to come up to Town, and how to make a Stage Coach compatible with Saba's aristocracy and dignity. The Coach sets off from Taunton at 4 o'clock, it is then dark. I recommended her hurrying in 3 minutes before the Coach departs with her face covered up, but there is a maiden Lady who knows us, and lives opposite the Coach. I have promised to keep her in conversation while Saba steps in, -and once in all chance of detection is over.[55]

Saba also threatened to become that curse of the clerical profession: the unmarried daughter; but Sydney loved her and her sister Emily, and he enjoyed the featherheaded femininity of the growing girls. He named a gate a short distance from the rectory the "screeching gate" because if he went out with the whole family, one of the girls was certain to give out a shriek at the gate and leap out of the carriage to retrieve something she had forgotten.[56] There are few references in the memoirs concerning Windham, and that lack may be explained by accusing the Smiths of slighting the younger and favoring the elder son. Such an explanation may well be true, for Windham's later unsocial actions might be interpreted as those of an unwanted child seeking attention and love. A more likely explanation, though, is that Saba Holland's and Catherine Smith's memoirs were written much later, after Windham's aberrant conduct, and for that reason they, and most subsequent biographers, spoke of Windham as little as possible. He was, in fact, the "Black Sheep" of the family, but his conduct cannot be attributed to discrimination by his father, for no tangible evidence of such mistreatment exists. After attending private school in Hanwell he entered the Charterhouse, which he left in 1831 in order to enroll in Trinity College, Cambridge. He was thus given all the educational opportunities that had been accorded to his brother; and Sydney urged him to enter the Church, where he could have, by that time, given him preferment from his own patronage.[57] In short, Sydney treated his sons with equal justive, loved his daughters as much as his sons, and granted them every care and consideration.

In 1827 Sydney's children who had lived so happily at Foston began to go their separate ways. His less-than-romatic announcement that "I am going to marry my youngest daughter to the eldest son of George Hibbert of Portland Place"[58] heralded the beginning of their leaving the nest; and though the announcement may seem to be a cold and indifferent statement, it by no means reflected his feelings for Emily. He heartily approved of the match, and on 6 October, 1827, he observed that "...the Young man is very sensible-and clever-and hereafter I hope will be well off - but for many years must depend on his own Exertions...he has got a prize in Emily - She is really a very superior Girl-"[59] Emily was married to Nathaniel Hibbert on 1 January, 1828, by Archbishop Harcourt in Foston Church, and her marriage appears to have been the only "social" wedding in that church during Sydney's incumbency. Four days later he wrote to Lady Grey:

> We were married on New Years day and are gone; I feel as if I had lost a Limb and was walking about with one Leg, and nobody pities this description of invalid. How many amputations you have suffered; ere long I do not think you will have a leg to stand upon.[60]

The marriage was a good one, and in March, 1829, Sydney was able to write that "Mrs. Hibbert's marriage has turned out well: a good sort of young man, comfortable fortune, a family who like her, & a child coming immediately...."[61]

Though Sydney had lost a daughter through marriage, he had gained a son-in-law with whom he was to be on excellent terms for the reminder of his life. Immediately before Emily's wedding, the death of Sydney's father, Robert Smith, had diminished the family further. After their quarrel had been settled, relations between Sydney and his father had improved and they had associated on amicable terms, even though Sydney wrote in 1826, "I should like to see my father though he had never been much of a father to me...."[62] Sydney was informed of his father's death by Cecil Smith on about 15 August, 1827, but he refused to exhibit false grief at the elder Mr. Smith's passing. On 30 August he wrote to Cecil to say that he wanted no keepsake of his father, for such an object would only make him melancholy. "I shall be truely obliged to you," he said, "to pay my §10000 as soon as you can conveniently do so. It may be paid into the Bank of Messrs Call Marten & Co Old Bond Street-and Mr. Moore will give the proper receipt-"[63] Although he felt little grief when Robert Smith died, real tragedy did come to Sydney in 1829. Even though his son Douglas had succeeded admirably at Westminster School, finishing as captain of the school, he quite possibly overtaxed himself in the progress, and was never entirely in the best of health afterwards. From Westminster School Douglas went on to Christ Church, Oxford, to study law. Sydney, beyond a doubt, hoped that he might experience vicariously the legal career that had been denied him in his youth through Douglas; but his son's health was ruined. In early January, 1829, Sydney became deeply concerned about his son's condition but he remained optimistic: "Still no better tidings of Douglas--Gout in both feet--and dimness of Eyes--I have desired Hibbert to go down to him--and to give me an accurate report--In the mean time he is in the hands of kind and excellent friends-"[64] Two days later he reported, with relief that "Douglas is a great deal better and we are at our Ease about him-"[65] Despite their hopes, though, Douglas worsened and Sydney went to London to be with him. On 15 April, 1829, he wrote the heartbroken words: "My poor boy died this morning at an early hour".[66] Douglas' death was, as Sydney himself said, his "first real misfortune", and ironically enough, it came only two days after the passage of Catholic Emancipation.

It would be too much to say that the death of his son cast a pall over the rest of Sydney's days on earth, for he retained his wit, exuberance, and good nature throughout the remainder of his life. Nevertheless, his greatest success in the Church may well have seemed hollow to him after the loss of his beloved and promising son at the age of twenty-four. In August, 1829, he wrote:

> ...I have from time to time bitter visitations of sorrow. I never suspected how children weave themselves about the heart. My son had that quality which is longest remembered by those who remain behind, -a deep and earnest affection and respect for his parents. God save you....from similar distress![67]

Perhaps he practiced what he had preached to Lady

Elizabeth Holland in 1819 when she had suffered the loss of a child:

> The world is full of all sorts of sorrows and miseries-and I think it is better never to have been born-but when evils have happened turn away your mind from them as soon as you can to everything of good which remains. Most people grieve as if grief were a duty or a pleasure, but all who can controul it should controul it-and remember that these renovations of sorrows are almost the charter and condition under which life is held. God Almighty bless you dear Lady Holland. I would have cut off one of my hands to have saved your little Playfellow-but we must submit.[68]

Sydney wrote to Lady Holland as a friend and a priest, and the death of his son came at a time when his priestly career had definitely taken a turn for the better. The repressive and conservative policies of the Tories had brought results in the form of growing Whig popularity, that promised a limited number of positions to the Whig faithful as well as preferment to their clerical allies, and the hope of a Whig government in the future. Sydney had, in a sense, stepped down in 1809 from being a London preacher to the position of a Yorkshire country parson; but he had some compensation in security and dignity. He had accepted his lot in life, albeit with some reluctance or bitterness, and at least in his more morose moments, imagined his career had ended at Foston.

Foston was not the living death that some of his biographers have depicted it to be, even though it was not what Sydney wanted as a permanent place. It was a rural parish in a cold and unfashionable section of the country--so unfashionable indeed that it had not known a resident rector for decades. Of the parish church he said:

> When I began to thump the cushion of my pulpit, on first coming to Foston, as is my wont when I preach, the accumulated dust of a hundred and fifty years made such a cloud, that for some minutes I lost sight of my congregation.[69]

In all probability, since Foston was a good living it had not been vacant long, and the parish records indicate that in the years immediately preceding Sydney's tenure the church had been well served, although quite possibly by curates.[70] As rector of Foston, Sydney proved to be a dutiful priest, even if his parish record keeping shows signs of neglect and sporadic efforts to bring the births, deaths, and marriages up to date. It is interesting to observe, in reading the parish records, that although he performed his duties adequately, and quite possibly with a degree of enthusiasm, his ministry at Foston appears to have made no impression on the parish whatsoever. Established practices did not change, and records of church attendance and communicants which may have indicated an increase or decrease in church-going, do not exist. In spite of their absence, though, registers and the Churchwarden's accounts in Yorkshire fail to reflect the success that Sydney had met with in London. It should be remembered, of course, that Foston was a rural parish with a fixed population, and if Sydney had increased church attendance, he would have done so largely at the expense of the local dissenters rather than by attracting a crowd of stylish worshippers as in London.

Sydney had tasted success in London, and his ambition was boundless. From the time he entered the Church he hoped to become a bishop, and the failures of the Whigs had retarded rather than totally dashed that hope in him. His monetary view of the Church was that of a huge lottery containing a few grand prizes and many blanks. He believed that any man who went into the Church invested his life, and frequently a great deal of his fortune, in hopes of winning one of the prizes; and he defended the astounding disparity of salaries on that grounds. Gentlemen, he said, did not enter the clerical profession in expectation of a comfortable subsistence, but rather in hopes of winning dignities and the really big money. It was, therefore, perfectly reasonable that poor curates should have incomes of twenty or thirty pounds a year while bishops and other hierarchs should have incomes in the thousands. Most commonly, he said, clergymen drew the blank; but if a man were well-born, or well-connected, or talented, or lucky, he might win, and that hope kept gentlemen and their wealth flowing into the Church.[71] He spoke of the "lottery" not infrequently, and in 1813, wrote to a clerical friend to say:

> Those accidental visitations of fortune
> are like prizes in the lottery, which

> may not be put into the year's income
> till they turn up.... I may see as
> many croziers in the clouds as I
> please; but...I must presume myself
> rector of Foston for life. God in
> his mercy grant that this may be
> pure Hypothesis.[72]

Foston was a good living, but not one of the grand prizes in the lottery, and Sydney complained frequently of his limited resources. In 1816, apparently in response to an invitation to visit London, he replied that he had only §900 a year, of which he was bound to pay §130 to Queen Anne's Bounty; and that a trip to London en famille, along with a three months' visit, would cost him §100 which he could not afford. Actually, §900 was a very substantial sum, but Sydney compared it unfavorably with the §8000 Lord Carlisle allowed to his son Lord Morpeth.[73] His statement that he had §900 a year was probably fairly accurate, for he was a good account keeper, and had no real reason to minimize or boast of his income to Lady Holland. The income from his living was theoretically §500, but probably more, and it was later to be increased to §800. He also had some small investments from earlier days, plus his farming at Foston; but he continued to complain of his income, and the cost of travel, and in 1819 he wrote to Francis Jeffrey to say that:

> ...locomotion becomes every year more
> difficult because I get poorer and poorer
> as my family grow up. Think yourself
> fortunate that you have a profession
> where you can put out your strenth.
> In the Church, if you are not well born,
> you must be very base, or very foolish,
> or both. God bless you.[74]

In 1818 the Earl of Ossory died and his estates descended to Lord Holland, who immediately offered Sydney the living of Ampthill in Bedfordshire.[75] Sydney was, of course grateful; but an investigation determined that Ampthill did not have as much income as Foston, and that it was too distant to be held jointly with Foston. He was, therefore, "obliged to relinquish what to him would have been a source of constant enjoyment...."[76] The additional income of Ampthill would have been welcome, even though Sydney already possessed an income large enough to permit him to live in dignity. The few hundred additional pounds per year from Ampthill would have given him leeway to spend less carefully and to travel more extensively. In 1819 he wrote to Jeffrey to apologize for not having visited Edinburgh, and listed five reasons for not having done so: a clergyman could not be absent from his living more than three months, if he were he could be informed against, he most certainly would be informed against if he violated the rule since he knew he was watched, he had little money, and his relatives were in England.[77] In the following year he wrote to J. A. Murray and complained that:

> My income remains the same, my family increases in expense. My constitutional gaiety comes to my aid in all the difficulties of life; and the recollection that, having embraced the character of an honest man and a friend to rational liberty, I have no business to repine at that mediocrity of fortune which I <u>knew</u> to be its consequence.[78]

In 1821, however, his fortunes suddenly improved, for "Aunt Mary" died, leaving him a legacy of §8000 in London property.[79] This property brought him §400 a year, which added to his living, placed him in comfortable straits. Nowell Smith says that "Aunt Mary" was Mary Smith, Sydney's father's sister, and he quotes Saba Holland and Reid as sources. Saba Holland, however, identifies her only as "Aunt Mary", and Reid refers to her as Miss Mary Smith, without quoting his source.[80] Another possibility, however, is a "Mrs. Olier", identified as Sydney's aunt, who had been a neighbour and close friend of the Smiths in London. She lived in Portland Place, where she had conducted a finishing school of sorts for heiresses, the enrollment of which she limited to four girls each of whom paid §1000 per year. She doted on Sydney, and in the absence of any source quoted by Reid it would seem more likely that she was the "Aunt Mary" to whom he referred.[81] In any event, the legacy relieved him of any immediate financial problems, and he was able to release his brother from the payments for Douglas' education.

Thus, after a fairly long period with a fixed income, Sydney's fortunes had begun to improve. They were to improve still more in 1823 when, at the urging of Lord Morpeth, a Yorkshire neighbour from Castle Howard, the Duke of Devonshire conferred the living of Londesborough on

Sydney.[82] The exact date when he received the living is obscure, but a letter quoted by the Earl of Ilchester and dated 1823 said:

> "All Sydney's friends are delighted with Ld Morpeth for asking, and the Duke of Devonshire's kindness in conferring upon him the living of Lonsborough. The distance is only eighteen miles from Foston, and the income more considerable than Foston now is, being equal to six of seven hundred a year...."[83]

Characteristic of the Church in that period, the living was a rich one and one that was essentially the private property of the Duke of Devonshire, to dispose of as he saw fit. He was persuaded to grant it temporarily to Sydney, who was to serve as a "pan-warmer" until the Duke's nephew came of age to hold the living. It was cared for by a curate, and Sydney's only responsibility was to collect the salary, but since it was near Foston, he drove over two or three times a year to take a service.[84] It is amusing to note that in the paragraph immediately preceding her description of Sydney's appointment to Londesborough, Saba Holland still referred to her father as being "poor" and "without family or friends"[85], although he possessed a substantial income as well as numerous and influential friends. It has been assumed that Sydney held Londesborough until 1832 when the Duke's nephew came of age,[86] but in a letter to Lord Carlisle, dated 17 April, 1829, he clearly stated:

> I have this day resigned Londesborough my resignation is gone to Mr. Burden 27 Parliament St who will lay it before the Archbishop-I have written to the Duke of Devonshire-many hearty thanks for that kindness which first suggested the idea of giving it to me...[87]

Sydney believed, or liked to believe, that he was subject to persecution for his political opinions, and because of them he was being held back in the Church; but as the possessor of two good livings he was not doing badly. He advised a clerical friend to publish a narrative he had written on "Peterloo", the riot at St. Peter's Fields, Manchester, in 1819, warning him at the same time that such a publication would "for ever put an end to his chance of preferment."[88] But as the twenties wore on, and Tory strength ebbed, he wrote to Francis Wrangham to say that he was "inclined to think from all I hear from Town that Government are somehow or other softening towards the Catholics-So let the Clergy beware they vote not on the losing or unprofessional Side...."[89] A rather cynical, or even bitter statement, it indicates that Sydney did not oppose the principle of persecution as it applied to politically active clergymen so much as he protested his own personal disappointment. Implicit in the assertion is the assumption that "right-thinking" clergymen should be promoted and their opponents denied preferment.

With the increasing strength of the "right-thinking" Whigs in the House of Commons, the hopes of the Whiggish Clergy brightened, and by 1827 Sydney began to actively seek preferment. His claims were excellent, for in addition to his influential connections and his earlier activities as a party propagandist, he had become an established and responsible parish rector with the reputation of an outstanding preacher. Sydney's materialistic interests gave him reason for concern in 1827, for his family was grown up, Douglas was about to begin his study in law, and he would shortly have to resign Londesborough and with it, one-third of his income.[90] His hopes for preferment, the delay of which he had accepted with surprising good nature over the years, now became urgent demands; and his friends and relatives assumed that he would shortly become a bishop.

"You shall hear of the Shovel the first-", he wrote to his nephew Cecil Smith, on 15 January, 1827, "and if I am Bishop I shall give you preferment immediately after my own children. So you may as well begin to read a Work or two upon Tithes-".[91] By 4 June, 1827, Sydney, although still expecting preferment, felt that it might be postponed:

> You suppose I am to be made a Bishop or something with a Petticoat-but I will lay you a bet of a Sovereign if you please-That I am not made a dignitary of the Church before Xmas 1827-Dignitary means a fellow with Rose Shovel Petticoat knee & Shoe Buckles of Or Moulu.... I have put myself so forward about the Catholic Question-that they will be very reluctant to promote me-I have very serious doubts if it will be done

-So I offer the Elizabeth, or Bett-"[92]

The prospects of the Whigs continued to improve, and in August, 1827, Frederick John Robinson, Viscount Goderich, became Prime Minister. Even though his government was insecure it did have patronage to bestow, for which Sydney promptly applied, asking his powerful friends to use their influence in his behalf. He was, however, a controversial figure, and his appointment to a see might have upset an already delicate political balance; so the brief-lived government hesitated to reward him, and Goderich's failure to do so elicited one of Sydney's few really bad-tempered letters:

> I am much obliged by your polite letter. You appeal to my good-nature to prevent me from considering your letter as a decent method of putting me off: your appeal, I assure you, is not made in vain. I do not think you mean to put me off; because I am the most prominent, and was for a long time the only clerical advocate of that question, by the proper arrangement of which you believe the happiness and safety of the Country would be materially improved. I do not believe you mean to put me off; because in giving me some promotion, you will teach the clergy, from whose timidity you have everything to apprehend, and whose influence upon the people you cannot doubt, that they may, under your Government, obey the dictates of their consciences without sacrificing the emoluments of their profession. I do not think you mean to put me off; because, in the conscientious administration of that patronage with which you are entrusted, I think it will occur to you that something is due to the person who, instead of basely chiming in with the bad passions of the multitude, has dedicated some talent and some activity to soften religious hatreds, and to make men less violent and less foolish than he found them.[93]

His letter used very strong language, especially since it was penned by a country parson and addressed to the Prime

Minister, but it reflected his chagrin at the realization that he could expect nothing from the Whigs. In October he wrote to Cecil Smith, and said that he had "been in Town about Emily's marriage-dining with Cabinet Ministers for ever without being the richer for it or the nearer to preferment-I see plainly that I shall have nothing...."[94]

Sydney was disillusioned with his Whig patrons, and he was impatient for advancement, but his anger towards them, if understandable, was misplaced. He did stand high on their list of deserving clergymen, but preferment in the Church was a matter of what livings fell vacant during the Government's term in office and the political conditions that regulated the type of candidate who might be nominated to fill them. The Goderich ministry stood on shaky grounds as it was, and to have nominated Sydney, who was known for his wit and his intellect rather his piety, might well have aroused the royal ire and endangered the government which was destined to hold office for only six months. Among the Holland House Papers in the British Museum there are two copybooks written by Lord Holland and entitled List of Whig Clergy. They are undated and catalogued as "A" and "B", but "A" appears to be a later copy of "B", which shows every sign of having been written at this time, or in 1830 when the Whigs again came to power. They are obviously lists of deserving Whig clergymen upon whom preferment should be bestowed, and Sydney's name appears prominently in both lists.[95] Thus his failure to become a bishop in 1827 resulted not from ill will on the part of the Whigs, but rather from the peculiar circumstances of the times.

It is ironic that Sydney's first major promotion in the Church, his initial prize in the Church Lottery, was to come from the Tories he had so often maligned rather than from the Whigs he had so often praised. It is interesting also that the accounts of this elevation as recorded in the memoirs of Saba Holland and Catherine Smith both coincide, and that they are generally borne out of other data. John Singleton Copley, Lord Lyndhurst, and Lady Lyndhurst were Sydney's friends even though they were Tories. Sydney was on excellent terms with Lord Lyndhurst, and when a good living had opened up in Kent, near London, Lord Lyndurst had offered it to Sydney, only to find that it was already promised to the protegee of a prominent Tory leader. Somewhat abashed by his faux pas, Lord Lyndhurst then promised to give Sydney the next living that became vacant. When a Prebendal Stall at Bristol Catherdral became vacant it was promptly offered to Sydney by Lord Lyndhurst from reasons of "real friendship".[96] A letter from Lord Lyndhurst to Sir William Knighton in January, 1828, throws a little more light on the appointment, and makes it appear to have been more a matter of political expediency than friendship:

> Were you so good as to mention to the King what I told you about Syndey Smith? You know the promise I was obliged to make him, in conseqse..of the mixed character of the former Administration. The vacant stall at Bristol would acquit me, and it would be desirable that this affair should be disposed of before the new Governmt is formed.[97]

Even if Lord Lyndhurst was motivated less by friendship than politics, he was still Sydney's friend, and undoubtedly that had a bearing on his decision. A famous account by Sydney is associated with a gathering dominated by the Lyndhursts in which Sydney jocularly took up a defense of suttee. He was asked what would happen if Lord Lyndhurst should die, to which he gravely replied:

> '"Lady Lyndhurst...would no doubt, as an affectionate wife consider it her duty to burn herself, but it would be our duty to put her out; and, as the wife of the Lord Chancellor, Lady Lyndhurst should not be put out like an ordinary widow. It should be a State affair. First a procession of the judges, then of the lawyers-"
> "But pray, Mr. Smith, where are the clergy?"
> "All gone to congratulate the new Lord Chancellor...."'[98]

To that distressingly accurate observation one might associate another bon mot, one that might be called "Sydney's first law": "Other rules vary; this is the only one you will find without exception-that in this world the salary or reward is always in the inverse ratio of the duties performed."[99] And indeed, although the Prebendal Stall at Bristol had a handsome salary and a dignified title attached to it, few duties, far less than those of a parish priest or a poverty-stricken curate, were required of the incumbent.

Sydney's appointment as a canon at Bristol Cathedral came five days after Emily's wedding at Foston, and it meant that Sydney would have to exchange Foston for a living in the Bristol area. Although he had found it impossible at an earlier date to exchange Foston for a living in the south, Sydney was now under pressure to exchange; and he had enough income to afford some sacrifice in the move. Foston had an excellent house and an increased income, and Sydney had allies in Lord Lyndurst and Cecil Smith, his nephew, a clergyman living at Bishop's Lydiard, near Taunton, and not distant from Bristol. With their help he was able, after protracted negotiations and several visits, to trade Foston for Combe Florey. Prior to the exchange, while visiting the area, he met a Miss Alcock, who made a lasting impression on him. On 29 November, 1828, in a letter to Cecil Smith he said that he had fallen "...in love desperately with Miss Alcock Colonel Alcock's daughter who came to the Coach window to speak to Chilcot...."; and on 1 December, 1828, he added: "...have you been over to see Miss Alcock?-Let me hear your report. Her Latin name would be Domina Omnis Penis...."[100]

Combe Florey was a living of the type he had sought earlier; rich, beautiful, and in the south where better society congregated. For a matter of months he commuted between Bristol and Foston, living in a rented room in Bristol while serving the Cathedral. It inspired him to write to Lady Carlisle:

> I am living quite alone in a large Gothic room with painted Glass, and waited upon by an old woman with only one Gothic Tooth:-about 6 o clock when it is dark the various Ghosts...come into the room, and converse with me dead Deans the color of Rogers-, Antient Sextons of the Cathedral, Prebendaries now no more, Elderly Ladies who lived near.... I have very little pleasure in their conversation, they seem to be limited foolish people, much the same as people still alive-the deceas'd Clergy are particularly inquisitive about preferment, and the elderly Ladies enquire about Patterns. When I am tird of their company I order Tea, and Candles and they hobble away-."[101]

It was, incidentally, while living in this rented room, that he gave his famous toleration sermon in November, 1828; and it was with a great feeling of relief that he received the presentation to Combe Florey in March, 1829. With even greater relief the Smiths moved to Combe Florey in July of that same year, for not only was Combe Florey a more desirable locale, but it also removed them from painful recollections of Douglas, who had died the preceding April.

CHAPTER VIII

Politics and Intellectual Activities at Foston, 1809-1828

Sydney was relatively contented in Yorkshire, but at Foston, he saw people of quality only when they visited, or when he visited them. Sydney was perfectly capable of associating with the farmers and laborers; but he was no democrat and he never lost sight of their inferiority. Saba Holland says that he learned to talk about cows to those who could talk about nothing else, and he gave an annual dinner for the local farmers, at which even "the ladies of his family appeared" and from which the farmer "went away better pleased with himself and less a grumbler than he came...."[1] Although not a democrat socially, Sydney remained an eighteenth century liberal Whig politically; keeping in touch with politics by means of newspapers, correspondence, and trips to the metropolis. As he aged and became more successful, he also became more conservative. Nevertheless, he still stuck to his old liberal principles; and in 1817, upon the suspension of the right of Habeas Corpus, a result of the political and industrial disturbances, he wrote to Lord Holland:

> I entirely agree to, and sympathize with, your opposition to the suspension. Nothing can be more childish and mischievous. Christianity in danger of being written down by doggrel rhymes-- England about to be divided into little parcels, like a chess-board--The flower and chivalry of the realm flying before one armed apothecary-How can old Mother Fitzwilliam swallow such trash as this?[2]

In the following year, he applauded the acquittal of William Hone, whose doggerel poetry had goaded the Tory government into a charge of blasphemous libel. He believed that the acquittal resulted from the "horror and disgust" that excessive previous punishments had excited. Sydney also felt that the decision of the jury would remind other juries of their power, and that it might influence the judges to become more moderate. He attributed the error in prosecuting Hone to Lord Ellenborough, Lord Chief Justice, who was a symbol of Tory reaction; and added that "Church and King in moderation are very good things, but we have too much of both."[3] Later in the year, however, he had altered his opinions to some extent. He believed that, since Hone had attempted to heap ridicule on religion "with the common people", the government had been right to prosecute; still Hone's exoneration had been a good thing because the penalities were too severe.[4] Similarly, the trial of Dr. Richard Watson, who was accused of High Treason in 1817, as a result of the Spa Fields demonstrations late in 1816, ended when he was acquitted. Sydney approved that decision, even though, his county neighbours were "woefully disappointed".[5]

Sydney remained a reformer while in Yorkshire, as he always had been, even though he grew more cautions and more fearful of disorder as the years passed. He could still become upset at the real or imagined invasion of the traditional rights of free born Englishmen; but he had little sympathy for agitators, and none at all for those who addressed themselves to the populace at large. He regarded William Cobbett, the radical writer, as a "consummate villian", and rejoiced in Cobbett's every setback.[6]

Political agitation and demands for parliamentary reform increased during the period of industrial and economic depression from 1815 to 1820, and by 30 July, 1819, Sydney was moved to express his concern to Francis Jeffrey:

> What do you think will become of all these political agitations? I am strongly inclined to think, whether now or twenty years hence, that Parliament must be reformed. The case that the people have is too strong to be resisted; an answer may be made to it, which will satisfy enlightened people perhaps, but none that the mass will be satisfied with. I am doubtful whether it is not your duty and my duty to become moderate reformers, to keep off worse.[7]

He was proposing, in short, what he had proposed at the time of the founding of the <u>Edinburgh Review</u> - limited and timely reform in order to preserve the old system. His ideas were relatively set, and he stood by his principles. It might be said that Sydney had risen above his age earlier, but as time passed and conditions changed, he continued to maintain the same convictions. Those convictions became more and more generally accepted in the 1820's, but by the mid-1830's, they were becoming outmoded. He was an advanced Whig early in the century, a moderate one in the 'twenties, and a conservative Whig in the 'thirties and 'forties, but it was not Sydney who changed; rather it was the political, social, religious and economic climate around him. Although he may have had a more accurate notion of the change taking place than many of his contemporaries, his knowledge of it was still limited.

On 15 April, 1819, Sydney observed that there were no troubles in the Foston area, the agricultural outlook being generally good, but that the situation in the Yorkshire manufacturing districts was "truely alarming".[8] Five days later, he showed that he was concerned both with the political disturbances taking place, and with the economic conditions which were largely responsible for them:

> We are quiet here but near the disturbed Counties-If we are really to cease to be the great Shop of Europe our situation is not to be envied. But the cessation of Demand is too sudden and universal to proceed from such a cause....[9]

In late September, 1819, in a letter to Francis Jeffrey, he asserted pessimistically, "If trade does not increase there will be a war of the rich against the poor: in that case you and I, I am afraid, shall be on different sides".[10] There can be no doubt as to Sydney's meaning in this statement - Jeffrey might side with the poor in such a struggle, he would unhesitatingly support the rich.

It is interesting that Sydney made this statement regarding war between the rich and the poor after the "Peterloo Massacre" of 16 August, 1819. During that incident, a large and orderly crown protesting the Corn Law and calling for parliamentary reform, had been charged by the yeomanry cavalry, acting under orders from the Manchester magistrates. A great number of people had been killed or injured in the attack; and despite the public outcry against the magistrates for attacking a legal and peaceful assembly, the Tory government had chosen to support the actions of the magistrates. In the same letter quoted above, Sydney had concluded by saying to Jeffrey: "I hope the Manchester riots will appear next no. I am ready for them if nobody else is."[11]

There is an apparent contradiction in siding with the rich against the poor in a possible civil conflict, and in siding with the demonstrators at St. Peter's Fields in Manchester against the established order. The apparent contradiction is easily resolved, though, when one observes that in the first instance Sydney acted as a Whig who was concerned about the maintenance of the social structure in the face of possible lower class attacks, and in the second he acted also as a Whig engaged in defending established rights. In an obsurely dated letter regarding Peterloo, he wrote to Lady Morpeth to say:

> If a very important privilege in a free government appears to have been flagrantly violated-and if such violation is approved of by administration, it is high time that the people should meet together, express their Sense of the apparent wrong - call for enquiry: If I were a politician and found the people remiss in meeting on such occasions - I would be the first to rouse them, if they met of their own accord I should think it the most important of all duties to be amongst them - that I might enlighten their ignorance, repress their presumption - and direct their energy to laudable purposes....[12]

He added that one needed to have a "manly love of reasonable liberty", which he was later to repeat. In the following month, he criticized the further action of the Manchester magistrates in their examination of the leaders of the demonstration.[13]

Sydney also saw political possibilities for the Whigs in the Peterloo Massacre, and felt that they outweighted any real danger of a popular uprising. In a letter to Lady Grey, on 3 November, 1819, he asserted his basic agreement with Lord Grey's position on Peterloo. The violence perpetrated by the magistrates was an "enormity", he said and he agreed that county meetings should be held to protest, and that the Tories should be condemned for approving the action of the magistrates and for dismissing Lord Fitzwilliam, who had sponsored protest meetings. "I guess", he wrote, "there is no more danger at _present_ than what vigilance, and activity without any new and extravagant coercion may guard against."[14] A month later he had thought the situation through more thoroughly, and in a letter to Lord Grey, he suggested a list of reforms that would lessen the popular discontent. He argued, as in Peter Plymley, that it was possible to reduce the numbers of one's enemies by easing the laws on Catholic and Protestant dissenters, revising the game laws, commuting tithes into a more palatable form, selling crown lands, revising the penal code, and by granting seats in the House of Commons to Birmingham and Manchester. He warned Lord Grey that democracy was growing among tradesmen, and that force alone would no longer suffice to prevent change. In addition to demagogues like Cobbett and Watson, he noted, there was four times as much literacy as in 1789, as well as numerous private presses. The latter produced libels which could be damaging, especially if they were true, and critics of parliamentary corruption had become too numerous to hang.[15] To a friend, he confided a more confidential opinion of Peterloo:

> My opinion is the same as yours upon the Peterloo business; I have no doubt but that every thing would have ended at Manchester as it did at Leeds had there been the same forbearance on the part of the Magistrates - either they lost (no great loss) their heads - or the Devils of local spite and malice had enter'd into them: or the Nostrils of the Clerical magistrates Smelt preferment & Court favor....[16]

On the evening of 25 February, 1820, an improbable attempt to assassinate the entire cabinet failed when an ill-assorted group of plotters was seized in a stable on Cato Street in London. Even though the plot was contrived in part by an <u>agent provocateur</u>, and with the knowledge of the Home Office, the "Cato Street Conspiracy" was held up by the government as evidence of the danger of revolution, and of the wisdom of Tory repression. The role of the government in the plot was suspected, but it was not proved until many years later. The effect of the conspiracy was to bring those members of the public who had more fear of revolution than they had for the loss of liberty back into the support of Tory policy. Sydney, without suspecting the government's complicity, nonetheless, took a cynical view of the whole affair. In a letter written shortly afterwards, he said:

> We had a little plot here in a hay-loft. God forbid anybody should be murdered! but, if I were to turn assassin, it should not be of five or six Ministers, who are placed where they are by the folly of the country gentlemen, but of the hundred

> thousand squires to whose stupidity and
> folly such an administration owes its
> existence.[17]

The previous day he had written another letter describing the conspirators:

> Thistlewood is taken. I saw him twice at
> Lord Sidmouth's office, looking mean,
> squalid, and miserable, but I dare say if
> he was dressed, and above all at the head
> of 10,000 men, he would be called a good-
> looking man.... Having had occasion to go
> two or three times to the Home Office, I
> saw three or four more of these wretches,
> they looked so intensely miserable that I
> pitied them...[18]

Five of the Cato Street conspirators were quickly brought to trial, convicted, and hanged. The incident proved, to the great satisfaction of the government, the need for repressive measures and its own efficiency in carrying them out. On the other hand, the government was not invariably successful in its prosecution of radicals; and Sydney exhibited his Whiggish ambivalence in that he abhorred the radicals who were on trial, but was concerned about the issue of the preservation of rights that was being jeopardized by the prosecution. He attended the trial of Henry ("Orator") Hunt in York and was attracted by Hunt's "... boldness, dexterity, and shrewdness. Without any education at all, he is the most powerful barrister this day on the Northern Circuit." But he still considered Hunt a "thorough ruffian" and hoped for a six year sentence for him. Sydney was no doubt disappointed when the judge sentenced Hunt to only two years.[20] Sydney was genuinely concerned about the radicals and about the danger of revolution, but because he was closer to the lower classes than many of the Tory leaders, he knew that the possibility of an uprising was vastly exaggerated by those who had supported the Six Acts.

In 1820, the economic picture began to brighten in England, and by the summer, tensions had eased to the point where Sydney again began to see the situation as the traditional Whig-Tory contest for control of policy rather than a crisis that threatened the whole system. He mentioned ruefully at that time that the grain crop had been half ruined, which would force prices up and bring the country gentlemen back into support of the Tories. By October, commerce was improving, and he wrote:

> You will be sorry to hear the trade and manufactures of these counties are materially mended, and are mending. I would not mention this to you, if you were not a good Whig; but I know you will not mention it to anybody. The secret, I much fear, will get out before the meeting of Parliament. There seems to be a fatality which pursues us. When, oh when, shall we be ruined?[21]

Sydney saw both the likelihood that prosperity would redound to the credit of the Tories who were in office, and that even the modest spreading of literacy and the activities of the popular press might produce democratic sentiments that could threaten the whole fabric of the "present order of things". The situation called for liberal reforms to meet the needs of the time and to preserve as much of that present order as possible. In 1820, he wrote:

> There are 4 or 500,000 readers more than there were 30 years ago - among the lower orders. A market is open to the Democratic Writers by which they gain money and distinction - Government cannot prevent this Commerce - a man if he knows his business as a libeller, can write enough for Mischief-without writing enough for the Attorny General; The attack upon the present order of things will go on - and unfortunately the Gentlemen of the People have the devil of a case against the gentlemen of the house of Commons and the Borough Mongers as they call them. - I think all wise men should begin to turn their faces reformwards. We shall do it better than Mr. Hunt and Mr. Cobbet - done it _must_ and _will_ be....[22]

In the face of these challenges, the Tory leadership seemed bent on defending every aspect of the status quo to the bitter end. If successful Tory policy could end in the destruction of British liberty, and if it failed the result might be a revolution and the bloody destruction of the system.

Politics affected not only the arena of Parliament and the Church, but almost every aspect of British life. When, in 1820, John Wilson, the candidate of Sir Walter Scott and the Tories, was elected to the chair of Moral Philosophy at the University of Edinburgh over Sir William Hamilton, the candidate of the Edinburgh Review, Sydney gloomily predicted: "...there is an end to the University of Edinburgh: your professors then become competitors in the universal race of baseness and obsequiousness to power."[23] But, if he was an opponent of the diehard defenders of the established order, and a consistent advocate of eighteenth century liberalism, he was by no means a radical reformer. "...a Whig club", he reminded a friend in 1824, "is not necessarily a reform Club...."[24] and his concept of the "people" still remained that of the privileged, wealthy, and educated.[25] He still conceived of politics as various economic "interests" vying with each other through the machinery of parliament and government for the control of national policy, and thereby acting as checks and balances on each other. In 1822, referring to the cotton manufactures, he said:

> Their wealth and prosperity know no bounds: I do not mean only the Phillipi, but of all who ply the loom. They talk of raising corps of manufacturers to keep the country gentlemen in order, and to restrain the present Jacobinism of the plough; the Royal Corduroys - the First Regiment of Fustian - the Bonbazine Brigade, etc. etc.[26]

The industrial disturbances of the five years following Waterloo had ended, and with the growing prosperity of the mid-twenties Sydney reported, "the northern world profoundly peaceful, and prosperous and the reverse of everything we have prophesied in the Edinburgh Review for 20 years."[27]

Even if Sydney could admit the errors of the doctrinaire thinking of the Edinburgh Review, he still remained its partisan, and continued, in general, to adhere to the same line of thought. His attitude toward Tory leaders did change, and chance remarks in his letters and writings reveal that change. In 1809, for example, he had said that George Canning was the most "mischievous scoundrel" in the British Empire.[28] In 1820, he had written of Castlereagh:

> ...a large and impetuous river, to which they gave the name of Castlereagh. Why Grandeur and impetuosity should have brought to their recollection this polished Member of the Cabinet, we do not exactly perceive....[29]

Sydney approved of the gradual liberalization of the Tories in the "twenties," and claimed credit for a good deal of it for himself and the Edinburgh Review. In 1826 he wrote to Jeffrey, saying that:

> It must be to you, as it is to me, a real pleasure to see so many improvements taking place, and so many abuses destroyed; - abuses upon which you, with cannon and mortars, and I with sparrow-shot, have been playing for so many years.[30]

Slightly later in the same year he wrote to William Huskisson, the liberal Tory who was then the President of the Board of Trade, applauding his enlightenment and professing amazement at finding men of ability and principle in the Tory government. He admitted that Tory policy was enlightened in foreign policy, law, and possibly even with regard to the Church.[31] In that letter he offered various small services, and in a later letter, written on 26 Sept., 1826, he again addressed Huskisson in a laudatory fashion.[32] Sydney is generally conceded to have been a life-long Whig, and that indeed, he was; but these two letters give the impression that he might have toyed with the idea of switching his political loyalties in 1826. He had not, at that time, received preferment from the Whigs, and the long drought on Whig political power was definitively not ending. On 6 March, 1826, he had written to Robert John Wilmot-Horton, then Under-Secretary for War and Colonies to say:

> I pray for Canning by name in the Litany -& I forgive him all his past Sins-As for Huskisson, if he had lived in Ancient Greece or Rome-he would have been worshipped as the God of Tariffs or Exchanges...& I say all good things of Robinson....[33]

Sydney may have thought about joining the Tories in 1826, but it so, he never did. It is quite possible that he merely supported defensible Tory policies in the hopes of ingratiating himself with powerful individuals of the Tory persuasion, or simply because he agreed with them. Certainly the liberalization of Tory policy during the 1820's made it easier for him to find political activities of which he could approve.

If Sydney had thought about switching loyalties in 1826, he probably did not give it much consideration, for he had committed himself to the Whig cause in a very total way. After his writing on the Catholic Question and his excoriation of the Tories, they could hardly be expected to receive him or to forget his past actions. He had continued to write for the Edinburgh Review after arriving in Yorkshire, and from that time until April, 1814, he published about fifteen reviews. From April, to September, 1818, he was preoccupied with agriculture and parish affairs, and because of Jeffrey's temporary absence he did not write any more articles. In July 1818, however, with Jeffrey back in command of the journal, Sydney wrote to say:

> If you can afford me §40 each for five sheets the quantity I could to with ease to myself in the course of a year, it would attach me to the review, and make me think it worth my while.[34]

Whether from desire for the money or from a wish to see himself back in print Sydney obviously wanted to take up reviewing again. He added that if the above salary schedule was not acceptable to Jeffrey, he would accept the old system. In another letter written to Jeffrey in November, 1818, it appears that Sydney was being paid §45 per sheet for his reviews, but he still was not entirely contented. Jeffrey had evidently offered him either a share as an original proprietor, or a fixed rate for his articles. Sydney accepted the fixed rate and set his salary at §45 per sheet.[35]

His reviewing during his residence at Foston covered many topics of varying importance, but some of his reviews undoubtedly had influence in bringing about needed reforms. As a country parson he was also a Justice of the Peace; but, generally speaking, his letters and the memoirs written about him are largely silent about his role as a magistrate. It may be assumed that he took his position as a magistrate seriously, even though, typically, he poked fun at it. In an 1814 letter to John Allen he said:

> Pray tell Lady Holland that I am a Justice of the Peace, -one of those rural tyrants so deprecated by poor Windham. I am determined to strike into the line of analogous punishments, but what am I to do in cases of bastardy; how can I afflict the father analogously; help me in this difficulty.[36]

As a Justice of the Peace he possessed a great deal of authority, especially over the lower classes, and he did not hesitate to exercise it at his own discretion. Often, however, he chose to employ the threat of punishment or a certain degree of slyness rather than the full severity of the law. His daughter's memoir mentions that when he first came to Yorkshire he was very annoyed by the vicious dogs kept by most farmers, so he planted a false but convincing account in the local newspaper of the trial of a farmer in Northampton who had been charged with keeping loose dogs, and who had been fined §5 and imprisoned for three months. "The effect was wonderful and the reign of Cerberus ceased in the land."[37] Sydney did not care for dogs, which helps to explain his actions, and he is quoted as saying:

> "No, I don't like dogs. I always expect them to go mad. A lady asked me once for a motto for her dog Spot. I proposed, 'Out, damned Spot!' but she did not think it sentimental enough.... I called one day on Mrs.------, and her lap-dog flew at my leg and bit it. After pitying her dog...she did all she could to comfort me, by assuring me the dog was a Dissenter, and hated the Church, and was brought up in a Tory family."[38]

Sydney also used his magisterial authority to reprimand carters for unsafe practices, fining them if necessary; and to terrorize juvenile offenders with severe lectures and by threatening them with: "John, bring me my <u>private gallows</u>!"[39] Much later in life he chided his nephew Cecil about his unnecessary enthusiasm for enforcing the law:

> I leave it entirely to your poor Old
> Irish Woman- should have given her a
> Shilling instead of sending her to
> Jail- you are getting <u>Justice of the
> Peacey</u>. I think an old Irish Woman has
> <u>a right</u> to get drunk- and sleep where
> she pleases- if she chose to sleep with
> Popham himself I don't know how Mrs.
> Popham could prevent it.[40]

Sydney's callous terrorization of village children seems heartless to the twentieth century, but to his daughter it appeared to be a reasonable way to treat the lower classes, and a humane one in that children were spared the demoralization of prison and were given a severe fright that might have made better subjects of them. Prisons of the early nineteenth century were, despite some reforms, dreadful places, and Sydney interested himself in their further modification. As a Justice of the Peace he dealt almost exclusively with lower class violators of the criminal code, and the inmates of the prisons fell chiefly into that same category. As a prison reformer he was a firm advocate of stern punishments, which he based on certain liberal preconceptions. He believed for example that prisons were schools for crime, and that their allegedly pleasant conditions encouraged "profligacy and vice".[41]

He was quite correct in that the jails were schools for criminals, but his assumption that jails were pleasant, comfortable, and desirable, and that the inmates enjoyed higher living standards and greater comfort than the working poor was a liberal assumption rather than a fact. As a Justice he sent convicts to prisons, and he visited prisons as well; so he was not entirely uninformed about prison conditions. Nevertheless, he still allowed his overall view of the prison problem to be shaped by theoretical considerations rather than by his own observations. Despite his desire to make prisons as unpleasant as possible he supported some humanitarian reform, and he attacked the opponents of prison reform, most of whom he presumed to be Tory placeholders, as complacent "'well as we are' people". They, he asserted, opposed humane prison reform not because they were hard-hearted, but rather because they feared that reforms of one kind might engender other unwanted reforms.[42]

But if Sydney Smith was a general supporter of clean and humane prison conditions, his most important preoccupation was to make prison life an experience that would excite only "horror and disgust" in convicts, and which could terrify them to the extent that they would abandon their criminal ways.[43] He demanded that offenders should be separated: the untried from the convicted, the hardened criminal from the youthful offender, the male from the female; as well as those who were held only as witnesses, or lunatics who were confined for their own protection. Had his plan been followed, jails would have had some twenty-six different divisions, each with its own regulations. He felt that prison diet was of the greatest importance, and he suggested four widely varying diets, each to be applied to prisoners in accordance with the severity of their offenses.[44] His purpose was to make prison diet, and every other aspect of prison life less appealing than that enjoyed by honest members of the same class. In that way he hoped that prison and the punishment of prisoners would serve as a deterrent to future crime. His purpose was deterrence first and the reformation of criminals which he hoped to accomplish through terror, second. He stated unequivocally that jails should be horrible, gloomy, uncomfortable, and less desirable in every respect than the living conditions of the poorest self-supporting laborer.[45]

Sydney believed that criminals were lower class people who were largely devoid of reasoning power and who could be dissuaded from criminal actions only by physical pain, disconfort, or inconvenience. Any other situation for convicts, he said, would result in the judge saying in effect:

> 'Prisoner at the Bar, you are fairly convicted, by a jury of your country, of having feloniously stolen two pigs, the property of Stephen Muck, farmer. The Court having taken into consideration the frequency and enormity of this offense, and the necessity of restraining it with the utmost severity of punishment, do order and adjudge that you be confined for six months in a house larger, better, aired, and warmer than your own, in company with 20 or 30 young persons in as good health and spirits as yourself. You need do no work; and may have anything for breakfast, dinner, and supper, you can buy. In passing this sentence, the Court hopes that your example will be a warning to

others; and that evil-disposed persons will perceive, from your suffering, that the laws of their country are not to be broken with impunity.'[46]

He urged that prisoners when sentenced should be sentenced not merely to time in prison, but to detailed sentences involving diet, solitude, labor, visitation, etc. He felt that an air of austerity should be maintained throughout the prison, and that prisoners should be kept in solitary confinement as much as possible without driving them insane. Behind all of this thought, of course, was his suspicion that government action might make incarceration more attractive than honest labor. He felt that sentences should serve primarily as a warning to other potential offenders, and that if a convict were sentenced to a situation more comfortable than that of a laboring man the effect would be to encourage crime rather than to prevent it. He believed that six weeks of severe punishment would be more effective than six months of "jolly company and veal cutlets."[47]

Sydney's fear that life for the poor in prisons might be more attractive than that of free laborers was very real; but his fear was based on the theoretical assumptions of the Classical economists, and to a lesser degree on the pain and pleasure principles of utilitarianism. He assumed that the mental and moral inferiority of the lower classes was such that they would not be moved by reason and morality, and that only physical deprivation and punishment would persuade them of the error of their ways. He was keenly aware of the fact that life for them was difficult at best, and he feared that a prison might remove them from the universal struggle for subsistence and comfort. In addition to cutting production and consuming the wealth of others, prison might destroy any further desire to work. The working classes, he believed, were moved chiefly by such material motives as food, comfort, and avoidance of hard work; therefore, if prisons were not characterized by sparse and unpalatable food, physical discomfort, and harsh and unrewarding labor, they would serve as magnets to encourage crime and to decrease productivity. Rather than concerning themselves with the "quiet and content" of prisoners to keep them from trying to escape, he advised that reformers should make certain that prisons would be unpleasant enough to prevent a conspiracy of the poor to break into them.[48]

The twentieth century, faced with different and more

extensive problems with crime, has employed prisons as centers for the rehabilitation and education of prisoners. But Sydney, despite his advanced opinions in many areas, fell back on doctrinaire liberal platitudes on prisons, and the positions he took were consistent with his other attitudes. In his opinion education was an expensive privilege, which if extended to lawbreakers would make crime attractive to poor children and their parents. Rehabilitation, especially as regarded the teaching of a trade, would make ex-convicts more eligible laborers, and might encourage law-breaking. As he said:

> It is quite obvious that, if men were to appear again, six months after they were hanged, handsomer, richer, and more plump than before execution, the gallows would cease to be an object of terror. But here are men who come out of jail, and say 'Look at us, we can read and write, we can make baskets and shoes, and we went in ignorant of every thing: and have learnt to do without strong liquors, and have no longer any objection to work; and we did work in the jail, and have saved money, and here it is.' What is there of terror and detriment in all this: and how are crimes to be lessened if they are thus rewarded?[49]

Sydney's first review on prisons had been based in part on a publication by the Society for the Improvement of Prisons, and the appearance of a second report by the Society resulted in his second review of prisons in February, 1822. Since he was a liberal Whig who supported political and economic reform, his biographers have frequently characterized him as an humanitarian, but his motivation on prisons and on other topics was most assuredly not that of an humanitarian. He was more concerned with dogmatic liberal social principles than he was with the realities of crime and punishment. His approach to prisons was merely an extension of his liberal economic and social thought, but he paid lip service to the humanitarianism of the Prison Society in the opening paragraphs of his report. That their intentions were good he admitted, and he insisted that his intentions were equally humane; but he adhered to his earlier view that their kindness towards criminals encouraged crime.[50]

Despite improvements in prison conditions, he observed, convictions and commitments had about doubled. This proved to Sydney that imprisonment was not performing its most important role - that of preventing crime. He was aware that depression conditions, new laws, modifications of the game laws, and the increase in population had some bearing on the crime rate; but he felt that even a serious drop in the rate of recommitments was not encouraging if the level of crime continued to rise. He also disparaged the "enthusiasm" occasionally exhibited in the report of the Prison Society, which he believed to be at best optimistic and at worst dishonest. An account of two poachers who had been converted by spiritual ministrations to the extent that they foreswore their evil ways and promised regular church attendance struck him not so much as a miracle of human prison management as a well-intentioned fable.[51]

His ideas were limited in number, and as in his first review, he admonished the Society to consider solitary confinement more seriously, as well as to try to make prisons "stern and Spartan" rather than to favor "indulgence and education". As for labor in the prisons, he reiterated, it should be tedious, irksome, and unrewarding. Minor luxuries like sugar and tea should be rigorously denied, and care should be taken that prisoners should leave "unimpaired indeed in health", but fully persuaded that to return to prison would be "the greatest misfortune of their lives". The deterrent effect of prisons would be lost if convicts could expect lenient treatment, educational opportunities, toothsome food, and a share of their earnings.[52]

These attitudes were based on theoretical social and economic assumptions of dubious merit, but they were fully consistent with Sydney's thought generally. He may, particularly in the light of twentieth century thinking, be accused of having been wrong; but he was consistent and, in terms of his own experience, he was thoroughly realistic. The Prison Society, like most of the other humanitarian societies, was strongly influenced by the Evangelical movement. It was deeply concerned with the moral and spiritual regeneration of prisoners, to whom it presented tracts and pamphlets which were typified more by "enthusiasm" and sentimentality than they were by common sense. Of these, Sydney commented:

> If education is to be continued in jails,
> and tracts are to be dispersed, we cannot

help lamenting that the tracts, though full of good principles, are so intolerably stupid - and all apparently constructed on the supposition, that a thief or a peccant ploughman are inferior in common sense to a boy of five years old. The story generally is, that a labourer with six children has nothing to live upon but mouldy bread and dirty water; yet nothing can exceed his cheerfulness and content - no murmurs - no discontent: of mutton he has scarely heard- of bacon he never dreams: furfious bread and the water of the pool constitute his food, establish his felicity, and excite his warmest gratitude. The squire or the parson of the parish always happens to be walking by, and overhears him praying for the king and the members for the county, and for all in authority; and it generally ends with their offering him a shilling, which this excellent man declares he does not want, and will not accept! These are the pamphlets which Goodies and Noodles are dispensing with unwearied diligence. It would be a great blessing if some genius would arise who had a talent for writing for the poor. He would be of more value than many poets living upon the banks of lakes - or even (though we think highly of ourselves) of greater value than many reviewing men living in the garrets of the north.[53]

In spite of the criticism of English prisons and the humanitarianism of the Prison Society, Sydney still imagined that the humanity of the English prisons was exemplary, and that it was serving to enlighten the continent. Abroad, he said, there was no consideration for the health or even the lives of prisoners, and they were treated as if they were no more important than "rats and black beetles".[54] But despite his endorsement of rudimentary humanitarianism in the prisons Sydney had made up his mind that the Prison Society was essentially wrong from the standpoint of the prevention of crime.

In his doctrinaire attitudes toward prisons Sydney demonstrated a less than humanitarian stance, but on the issue of forced labor from prisoners before trial and conviction, he appeared in a better, but still doctrinaire light. The doctrine was, of couse, that the accused was innocent until proven guilty; therefore to require the same labor from an accused person as from a convicted felon was to punish without trial. "...it is neither legal", he said, "nor expedient to compel prisoners before trial to work at the treadmill...and...those who refuse to work should be supported on a plain healthy diet."[55]

> ...we must remind those advocates for the treadmill, a parte ante (for with the millers a parte post we have no quarrel), that it is one of the oldest maxims of common sense, common humanity, and common law, to consider every man as innocent till he is proved to be guilty; and not only to consider him to be innocent, but to treat him as if he was so; to exercise upon his case not merely a barren speculation, but one which produces practical effects, and which secures to a prisoner the treatment of an honest, unpunished man.[56]

The supporters of compulsory labor for untried poor prisoners claimed to believe that labor of that nature was not really punishment for those prisoners but rather a method of requiring them to help provide for their maintenance. Sydney noted, though, that the prisoners who were being held for trial, or in some cases being held only as witnesses, were not there by choice; and that they might be people who were totally unaccustomed to hard labor.

Sydney spoke generally to the upper classes, and in many of his writings he wrote as if he considered the lower classes to be unfeeling brutes, incapable of any motivation other than the purely physical; yet, he showed that while such may have been his attitude basically, it was tempered by his realization that laborers too, had feelings.

> ...there are gentlemen who suppose that the common people did not consider this an punishment!--that the gayest and most joyous of human beings is a treader, untried by a jury of his countrymen, in the fifth month of lifting up the leg, and striving against the law of gravity, supported by the glorious information which he receives

> from the turnkey, that he has all the
> time been grinding flour on the other
> side of the wall! If this sort of exercise, necessarily painful to sedentary persons, is agreeable to persons
> accustomed to labour, then make it voluntary-give the prisoners their choice-
> give more money and more diet to those
> who can and will labour at the treadmill, if the tread-mill (now so dear to
> magistrates) is a proper punishment for
> untried prisoners.57

Untried, thus innocent, prisoners who refused labor of that kind, he maintained, should not be held to be "incorrigibly idle" because they declined the "privilege" of performing the labor of convicts. His opponents on the issue insisted that:

> ...labour may be a privilege as well as
> a punishment. So may taking a physic
> be a privilege, in cases where it is
> asked for as a charitable relief, but
> not if it is stuffed down a man's
> throat whether he say yea or nay. Certainly labour is not necessarily a punishment: nobody has said it is so; but
> ...labour is a punishment, because it
> is irksome, infamous, unasked for, and
> undeserved. This gentleman however,
> observes, that committed persons have
> offended the laws: and the sentiment
> expressed in these words is the true
> key to his pamphlet and his system- a
> perpetual tendency to confound the convicted and the accused.58

Similarly the advocates of compulsory labor for untried prisoners asserted that the prisoners were not really compelled to work since they always had the alternative of a diet of bread and water. To this peculiar obtuseness Sydney replied:

> You take up a poor man upon suspicion,
> deprive him of all his usual methods of
> getting his livelihood, and then giving
> him the first view of the treadmill, he
> of the Quorum thus addresses him: -'My
> amiable friend, we use no compulsion

> with untried prisoners. You are free
> as air till you are found guilty; only
> it is my duty to inform you, as you
> have no money of your own, that the
> disposition to eat and drink which you
> have allowed you sometimes feel, and
> upon which I do not mean to cast any
> degree of censure, cannot possibly be
> gratified but by constant grinding in
> this machine. It has its inconven-
> iences, I admit; but balance them
> against the total want of meat and
> drink, and decide for yourself. You
> are perfectly at liberty to make your
> choice, and I by no means wish to in-
> fluence your judgement. '...For the
> question between us is not, how sus-
> pected persons are to be treated, and
> whether or not they are to be punished;
> but how suspected poor persons are to
> be treated, who want county support in
> prison. If to be suspected is deserv-
> ing of punishment; then no man ought
> to be let out upon bail, but every one
> should be kept grinding from accusation
> to trial; and so ought all prisoners
> to be treated for offences not bailable,
> and who do not want the county allo-
> wance. And yet no grinding philosopher
> contends, that all suspected persons
> should be put in the mill-but only
> those who are too poor to find bail, or
> buy provisions.[59]

As has been observed, Sydney could be indifferent to the feelings of his social inferiors, but in this case he stood firmly on the side of the poor prisoner and in outraged defiance of the callous denial of the rights and humanity of the lower classes. He denied that imprisonment raised the living standards of the poor laborer, for even if it relieved him from arduous labor, it deprived him of his liberty and of association with family and friends.[60]

The saying in English law that it was better that many guilty men should escape punishment rather than one innocent man should be wrongly punished has been so often repeated that it has become a platitude, but Sydney believed in it; and he held that to require penal labor of all accused of law breaking violated that principle. It was fully possible under the system of compulsory labor for the untried, he said, for an innocent prisoner who was poor to suffer more than a guilty prisoner who was rich enough to afford bail. In the first case the poor man would be held perhaps as long as six months awaiting trial, during which time he would be forced to march on the treadmill. Then, being brought to trial, he would be exonerated after having served six months on the treadmill. The second prisoner, out on bail, might be convicted at the same time and sentenced to three months at hard labor, so that the innocent man would have received twice the punishment of the guilty.[61]

Prison practices of 1824 were vastly different from those of the twentieth century, and prisoners with any means at all were expected to provide for themselves in prison. It was only the destitute who were reluctantly supplied at public expense, and it was the cost of that provision that troubled Sydney's antagonists on this question. They equated a prisoner, who was too poor either to provide bail or to support himself in prison, to a pauper subsisting on a more or less permanent basis at the expense of the public. Not so, said Sydney, for a pauper voluntarily accepted parish relief, while most prisoners were presumably self-supporting until arrested and deprived of their livelihood.[62] This was a simple question of justice and the rights of freeborn Englishmen, and in one of the last paragraphs in his review Sydney offered a simple and direct solution to it. Prisoners who were not self-supporting should be "supported upon a very plain, but still plentiful diet", and they should be permitted to work, if they chose, in return for rewards and better diet.[63]

In December, 1826, in the next to the last article Sydney was to publish in the Edinburgh Review, he turned again to a question of legal reform: the right of counsel to speak for certain categories of prisoners. He had adverted to the subject as early as July, 1821, in his review on prisons, in which he had said:

> In this age of charity and of prison improvement, there is one aid to prisoners which appears to be wholly overlooked; and that is, the means of regulating their defense, and providing them witnesses for their trial. A man is tried for murder, of for house-

> breaking or robbery, without a single
> shilling in his pocket. The nonsensi-
> cal and capricious institutions of the
> English law prevent him from engaging
> counsel to speak in his defense, if he
> had the wealth of Croesus; but he has
> no money to employ even an attorney,
> or to procure a single witness, or to
> take out a subpoena. The Judge, we are
> told, is his counsel;- this is suffi-
> ciently absurd; but it is not pretended
> that the Judge is his witness. He sol-
> emnly declares that he has three or
> four witnesses who could give a com-
> pletely different colour to the trans-
> action; but they are sixty or seventy
> miles distant, working for their daily
> bread, and have no money for such a
> journey, nor for the expense of a resi-
> dence of some days in an Assize Town.
> They do not know even the time of the
> Assize, nor the modes of tendering
> their evidence if they could come. When
> every thing is so well marshalled
> against him on the opposite side, it
> would be singular if an innocent man,
> with such an absence of all means of
> defending himself, should not occasion-
> ally be hanged or transported.... it
> seems to us no bad _finale_ of the pious
> labours of those who guard the poor
> from ill treatment during their impri-
> sonment, to take care that they are not
> unjustly hanged at the expiration of
> the term.[64]

In his next review of prisons Sydney again addressed himself to the topic of counsel for prisoners, on which he wrote at some length. Again he tied it in to his thoughts on the humanity of the Prison Society, but with a greater emphasis on the reform of the law. The practice, he said, that forbade a prisoner's counsel to speak for his client in any capital felony was cruel and absurd, and especially so since it did not limit the number of prosecutors who might try to convict him. They might go to any length to secure his condemnation, but not a word could be spoken by his counsel to prevent him from being hanged. Sydney said that the practice was utterly ridiculous to everyone but lawyers, "...to whom nothing that is customary is ridiculous...."; and the argument that the judge served as the prisoner's counsel he dismissed as an idle rationalization. The judge was supposed to moderate the prosecution, sum up the case for the jury, and instruct the jury as to what points were in the favor of the accused; but his role could hardly be equated with a spirited defense as practiced in civil cases, and certainly not with Scottish criminal practice.[65]

In cases of high treason, oddly enough, counsel could be employed, and could speak, but Sydney feared the role of political passions in cases other than high treason. Could judges who were obligated to the establishment be trusted to be objective when trying Peterloo demonstrators? He did not accuse or condemn all judges, but he suggested that any judge might be unconsciously prejudiced, and that the best bulwark against such prejudgement was the freedom for counsel to enter a real defense.[66]

In December, 1826, Sydney was to write a full-length review on the question of counsel for prisoners. In it he said of Robert Peel, later Sir Robert Peel, then Home Secretary:

> We have now the benefit of discussing these subjects under the government of a Home Secretary of State, whom we may (we believe) fairly call a wise, honest, and high principled man- as he appears to us, without wishing for innovation, or having any itch for it, not to be afraid of innovation, when it is gradual and well considered. He is, indeed, almost the only person we remember in his station, who has not considered sound sense to consist in the rejection of every improvement, and loyalty to be proved by the defense of every accidental, imperfect, or superanuated institution.[67]

He also warned the Tories that if such glaring inequities were not reformed, juries would not convict; and that situation might produce "the disgrace of seeing the lower and middle orders of mankind making laws for themselves, which the Government is at length compelled to adopt as measures of their own."[68] Glimpses of both his philosophy of law and his social attitudes appear in his statement that:

> The Judges and the Parliament would have gone on to this day, hanging, by wholesale, for the forgeries of bank notes, if juries had not become weary of the continual butchery, and resolved to acquit. The proper execution of laws must always depend, in great measure, upon public opinion; and it is undoubtedly most discreditable to any man intrusted with power, when the governed turn round upon their governors, and say, 'Your laws are so cruel, or so foolish, we cannot, and will not act upon them.'[69]

The issue of permitting counsel to speak for prisoners was, like that of punishing prisoners before trial, an issue of justice for Sydney, and he took his stand on it in his best crusading spirit. The practices of these criminal courts violated the laws of reason and the right or every freeborn Englishman to a fair trial, which aroused his righteous indigation and brought forth a fetching appeal on behalf of poor prisoners.

> There are seventy or eighty persons to be tried for various offences at the Assizes, who have lain in prison for some months; and fifty of whom, perhaps, are of the lowest order of the people, without friends in any better condition than themselves, and without one single penny to employ in their defence. How are they to obtain witnesses? No attorney can be employed--no subpoena can be taken out....It is impossible but that a human being, in such a helpless situation, must be found guilty; for as he cannot give evidence for himself, and has not a penny to fetch those who can give it for him, any story told against him must be taken for true (however false); since it is impossible for the poor wretch to contradict it.[70]

Sydney was convinced that most prisoners were charged in good faith, and probably that most were guilty, but his fears was that the rare innocent man might be convicted and hanged. It was said of the existing custom that capital cases were watched carefully, and that in some instances dubious convictions of poor men were appealed to the Home Secretary by the watchers. To this apology Sydney replied that such was probably true of men sentenced to be hanged, but that cases involving lesser sentences excited no such concern.[71]

Sydney regarded the energetic defense of justice as deriving from two main sources: confusing accusation with guilt, and the assumption that "a defence of prisoners accused by the Crown" amounted to "disloyalty and disaffection to the Crown." This naive belief was, he said, nothing other than "folly sanctioned by antiquity."[72] Glaring abuses needed to be abolished, and he produced a list of earlier, equally unjust practices, which had been reformed to the amelioration of the rights of the individual.

> A most absurd argement was advanced in the honourable house, that the practice of employing counsel would be such an expense to the prisoner!- just as if any thing was so expensive as being hanged! What a fine topic for the ordinary! 'You are going' (says that exquisite divine)' to be hanged tomorrow, it is true, but consider what a sum you have saved! Mr. Scarlett or Mr. Brougham might certainly have presented arguments to the jury, which would have insured your acquittal; but do you forget that gentlemen of their eminence must be recompensed by large fees, and that, if your life had been saved, you would actually have been out of pocket above 20§? You will now die with the consciousness of having obeyed the dictates of a wise economy; and with a grateful reverence for the laws of your country, which prevents you from running into such unbounded expense- so let us now go to prayers.'
>
> It is ludicrous enough to recollect, when the employment of counsel is objected to on account of the expense to the prisoner, that the same

> merciful law, which, to save the prisoner's money has <u>denied</u> his counsel, and produced his conviction, seizes upon all his savings the moment he is convicted.[73]

The excellence of English justice was a proud claim, and Sydney's attacks on that claim undoubtedly touched sensitive spots in the English conscience; especially when he said:

> It is a most affecting moment in a court of justice, when the evidence has all been heard, and the Judge asks the prisoner what he has to say in his defence. The prisoner, who has (by great exertions, perhaps of his friends,) saved up money enough to procure counsel, says to the Judge, 'that he leaves his defence to his counsel.' We have often blushed for English humanity to hear the reply. 'Your counsel cannot speak for you, you must speak for yourself;' and this is the reply given to a poor girl of eighteen- to a foreigner-to a deaf man-to a stammerer-to the sick-to the feeble-to the old-to the most abject and igorant of human beings!....it is full of brutal cruelty, and of base inattention of those who make laws, to the happiness of those for whom laws were made. We wonder that any juryman can convict under such a shocking violation of all natural justice. The iron age of Clovis and Clottaire can produce no more atrocious violations of every good feeling, and every good principle.[74]

"....we should like to ask Sir John Singleton Copley", he said, "who seems to dread so much the conflicts of talent in criminal cases...that a method of getting at truth...in civil cases should be so much objected to in criminal cases?"[75] His query is interesting, especially since Sir John Singleton Copley, when elevated to the peerage, took the title of Lord Lyndhurst, and two years later, appointed Sydney to the stall at Bristol Cathedral. From available sources it is not clear whether or not Copley knew that Sydney had written the passage, but since the anonymity of the reviewers was largely illusory, it seems quite possible that he did.

In this review Sydney enunciated a solution to the resistence to reform that he was later to employ in other writings--that the best way to reform an abuse was for an important person, the twentieth century would say a Very Important Person, to fall victim to it. In that way, he believed, and possibly only in that way, could needed change take place. In this instance he suggested:

> Let two gentlemen on the Ministerial side of the House (we only ask for two) commit some crimes, which will render their execution a matter of painful necessity. Let them feel, and report to the House, all the injustice and inconvenience of having neither a copy of the indictment, nor a list of witnesses, nor counsel to defend them. We will venture to say, that the evidence of two such persons would do more for the improvement of the criminal law, than all the orations of Mr. Lamb, or the lucubrations of Beccaria.[76]

In his writings on prison reform and the right of prisoners to counsel Sydney had shown that while he was no humanitarian reformer he defended the legal rights and interests of the lower classes, and in the writings on the Game Laws he took much the same position. He assumed that rural bumpkins did not possess mentality enough to be made to understand that game was as much the property of the landowner as were his sheep or fruit trees; therefore, Sydney regarded excessive severity in the game laws as unjust, unreasonable, and ineffective. As in other causes in which he engaged, the number of ideas he had on the game laws was limited, and they were chiefly produced by applying the principles of laissez-faire economics and Whig liberalism to the problem. He asserted that the "evils" of the game laws had been felt for years and that they were growing worse with the passage of time. Sydney believed that field sports "so congenial to the habits of Englishmen" were good in that they made the rural areas of the country attractive to gentlemen who would otherwise pass their time exclusively in the more exciting cities. He imagined that the gentleman in returning to the country-side "diffuses intelligence, improves manners, communicates pleasure... and makes the middling and lower classes better acquainted with, and more attached to their natural leaders."

While enjoying hunting and shooting in the country the
natural leaders came again into contact with "those interests which they may afterwards be called upon to
protect and arrange." The gentlemen also benefited from
being thrown "among simple, laborious, frugal people"
--an experience which would enable them to "resist the
prodigality of Courts, by viewing with their own eyes the
merits and the wretchedness of the poor."[77]

Sydney totally rejected the argument that wild animals were public rather than private property, and that
laws for the protection of game were, therefore, unjust.
In his opinion it was perfectly just to protect game
from the depredations of poachers because, even if it
was impossible to determine exactly on whose land a particular pheasant had been hatched, certainly all the pheasants of a certain area belonged to all the landowners
of that area. The pheasants fed on their land, and in
that way they became the property of the landowners.
Likewise it can be said that the carp in a large pond
jointly owned by four co-owners belongs to the owners;
and even though it is impossible to say that a specific
carp belongs to a particular owner, it could be said
that no one other than the owners had any claim to them.
Sydney's sense of property, and property rights was
deeply ingrained and very English. He said that "nothing which is worth having, which is accessible, and supplied only in limited quantities, could exist at all, if
it was not the property of some individual." If game
was left free to be killed by anyone, and not protected
in private preserves, it would result not in shooting by
more people, but in the annihilation of all shooting.
The extension of that right would also violate another
and even more important property right in that it would
involve "the privilege of trespassing on landed property
-an intolerable evil which would entirely destroy the
comfort and privacy of a country life."[78]

Thus Sydney did not oppose game laws *per se*, but
took the position that the current game laws were evil
because they were failing in their purpose, and, most
important of all, they were corrupting the morals of
the rural poor. Poor men, he said, who would not dream
of raiding a henhouse saw game flying or running all
around them, and not regarding it as property they appropriated it for themselves. Knowing it to be illegal, the
poacher was forced to kill game at night; and that experience led him "from one infringement of law and property to another, till he becomes a thoroughly bad and

corrupted member of society." Sydney's purpose and program for reforming the game laws, then, may be summed up in his own words:

> ...to preserve, as far as is consistent with justice, the amusements of the rich, and to diminish, as much as possible, the temptations of the poor. And these ends, it seems to us, will be best answered,
>
> 1. By abolishing qualification. 2. By giving to every man a property in the game upon his land. 3. By allowing game to be bought by any body, and sold by its lawful possessors.[79]

The abolition of "qualifications" referred to the law then in existence that forbade any man who did not possess an income of §100 a year in land rent to shoot game. Sydney found the law unreasonable in that it banned shooting by the smaller landowner, the prosperous farmers, and even wealthy individuals whose wealth was in trade or in stocks and bonds. In fact, the proponents of the game laws were chiefly country gentlemen who were dedicated to field sports, and whose limited rural lives often revolved around such sport. Their concern for the protection of game, and of their sport, was therefore exaggerated; but these same gentlemen were over-represented in Parliament and they had secured the passage of laws which were:

> ...so capricious a partiality to one species of property....There might be some apology for such laws at the time they were made; but there can be none for their not being now accommodated to the changes which time has introduced. If you choose to exclude poverty from this species of amusement, and to open it to wealth, why is it not opened to every species of wealth? What amusement can there be morally lawful to an holder of turnip land, and criminal in a possessor of Exchequer bills? What delights ought to be tolerated to Long Annuities, from which wheat and beans should be excluded? What matters whether it is scrip or short-horned cattle?[80]

The purpose of the §100 qualification was to prevent

the more common elements of the population from disturbing the game, but Sydney suggested that is had been passed to protect the game of large landowners at the expense of their less affluent neighbors. A man with small holdings worth less than §100 per year might indeed lure game onto his land from the estates of his richer neighbors. On the other hand, game fattened on the land of the smaller landowner as well as the greater, and Sydney considered it an injustice that the small landowner was forbidden to shoot that game, although it could be shot if it crossed into his neighbor's property. This situation put the larger landowner in the position of saying:

> 'Here is a man who has only a twenty-fourth part of the land, and he expects a twenty-fourth part of the game. He is so captious and litigious, that he will not be contented to supply his share of the food, without requiring his share of what the food produces. I want a neighbour who has talents only for suffering, not one who evinces such a fatal disposition for enjoying.'[81]

The second change Sydney proposed was a legal one: "that game should be made property", and that every landowner should have a full legal right to game found on his property. Further violation of that property right should be punishable as poaching. His purpose in this proposed alteration was actually to strengthen the law, for, as then practiced, a landowner's only recourse against intruders who intended to poach was an action for trespass. Some so-called gentlemen, he said, travelled across the country, freely shooting on other men's properties. Under existing law these men could only be charged with trespassing, but under his proposed change the law would offer the same safeguards to rabbits and pheasants that it already extended to chickens and sheep. This legislation was needed, Sydney maintained, but its enactment should not be left to the country gentlemen.

His final proposal for the reform of the game laws asked that game be permitted to be sold by its legal owners, and to be purchased from them by anyone. The sale of game could not be prevented anyway, he observed, and so long as there was an effective demand by wealthy people for game for their tables, that demand would be supplied, legally or illegally.

> Do the country gentlemen imagine, that
> it is in the power of human laws to de-
> prive the three per cents of pheasants?
> That there is upon earth, air, or sea, a
> single flavour (cost what crime it may
> to procure it), that mercantile
> opulence will not procure? Increase the diffi-
> culty, and you enlist vanity on the side
> of luxury; and make that be sought for
> as a display of wealth, which was before
> valued only for the gratification of ap-
> petite. The law may multiply penalties
> by reams. Squires may fret and Justices
> commit, and gamekeepers and poachers con-
> tinue their nocturnal wars. There will
> be game on Lord Mayor's day, do what you
> will....The experiment was tried of in-
> creased severity; and a law passed to
> punish poachers with transportation who
> were caught poaching in the night time
> with arms. What has the consequence
> been?-Not a cessation of poaching, but
> a succession of village guerillas;-an
> internecive war between the gamekeepers
> and marauders of game;the whole country
> flung into brawls and convulsions, for
> the unjust and exorbitant pleasures of
> country gentlemen.[82]

Sydney's purpose in legalizing the sale of game was to undersell poachers, and by such underselling to end that variety of criminality. Risks to the poachers were high, but so were potential profits; so the temptation to poach was great. If game was sold legally by its owners, Sydney thought, prices would fall and poulterers would hesitate to involve themselves with thieves and the risk of indictment when they could obtain legal game equally as cheaply. To the rational Sydney Smith the game laws were both unjust and absurd, and he insisted that the same kind of absurdity could have been produced had the country gentlemen banned the sale of domestic geese:

> ...if goose-keepers had been appointed,
> and the sale and purchase of this savory
> bird prohibited, the same enjoyments
> would have been procured by the crimes
> and convictions of the poor; and the
> periodical gluttony of Michaelmas have
> been rendered as guilty and criminal,

as it is indigestible and unwholesome.[83]

He also believed that the proposed sale of game would help less affluent gentlemen pay their bills as well as end poaching.

Many country gentlemen held such a strong view of their game and their sport, and they took such an antipathetic view of those who attempted to poach it, that they had taken up the practice of setting "spring-guns", loaded weapons fired by a trip wire, for its protection. This practice Sydney assumed an unequivocal position against, for both humanitarian and legalistic reasons. As he said:

> The law says, that an unqualified man who kills a pheasant, shall pay five pounds, but the Squire says he shall be shot;- and accordingly he places a spring-gun in the path of the poacher, and does all he can to take away his life. The more humane and mitigated Squire mangles him with traps; and the supra-fine country gentleman only detains him in machines, which prevent his escape, but do not lacerate their captive. Of the gross illegality of such proceedings, there can be no reasonable doubt. Their immorality and cruelty are equally clear. If they are not put down by some declaratory law, it will be absolutely necessary that the Judges, in their invaluable circuits of Oyer and Terminer, should leave two or three of his Majesty's Squires to a fate too vulgar and indelicate to be alluded to in this Journal.[84]

Sydney's first article on the game laws had been written in March, 1819, and in March, 1821, he returned to the general subject of the game laws placing the emphasis in the second review on his hostility to the spring guns. He wrote again of their illegality and inhumanity. It is probably safe to assume that he was particularly disturbed because the actions of the country squires were endangering his concept of English society. He definitely believed in class distinctions, but he held also that the privileged classes had obligations to their less privileged inferiors. He had no question about the superiority of the upper class, and believed that the lower classes should be respectful and obedient to their betters. Respect, though, became more and more difficult for the lower classes when their "natural leaders" engaged in murderous and illegal acts against them. As Sydney said, an attempt had been made in the House of Commons to reform the game laws along humanitarian lines, but even though it had been voiced in moderate terms, and in provisions respectful of the interests of the lord of the manor, it had been rejected. To this he added:

> Another method by which it is attempted to defeat the depredations of the poacher, is, by setting spring guns to murder any person who comes within their reach; and it is to this last new feature in the _supposed_ Game Laws, to which on the present occasion, we intend principally to confine our notice.[85]

An objective reader might ask why Sydney urged humanitarian reform in the game laws while rejecting it in prison reform. Although he never answered that question directly, it could be said that in all probability he regarded the latter as far more important than the amusement of gentlemen; but in reality his attitudes on the two subject were contradictory, and presumably he was not bothered by the contradiction. It may be seen from the preceding passage that he supported the principle of the game laws, but that he opposed the operation of the existing game laws in practice and was positively revolted by the use of spring guns to prevent poaching. This latter practice, he said, was nothing less than murder, for it punished a non-felonious offense with death. Powder and ball were impersonal, and they might result in the death of a servant or a child, or of a simple passer-by with no larcenous intent towards the treasured game. It had been decided that it was illegal to kill a dog who pursued game onto private estates, but if spring guns were legal, then it was legal to kill a person doing the same thing. Sydney was outraged by the apparent legal support for such booby traps, of which he said:

> ...could the Lord Chief Justice of the King's Bench intend to say, that the impossibility of putting an end to poaching by other means would justify the infliction of death upon the offender? Is he so ignorant of the philosophy of punishing, as to imagine he

> has nothing to do but to give ten
> stripes instead of two....It is im-
> possible so enlightened a Judge can
> forget, that the sympathies of man-
> kind must be consulted; that it would
> be wrong to break a person upon the
> wheel for stealing a penny loaf....
> that if poaching is punished more
> than mankind in general think it
> ought to be punished, the fault will
> either escape with impunity, or the
> delinquent be driven to desperation;
> that if poaching and murder are pun-
> ished equally, every poacher will be
> an assassin.[86]

Sydney attempted to touch the consciences of the squirearchy, for in response to their argument that spring guns need not go off unless set off by a trespasser, he pointed out that the guns were set to go off, and that the trespasser might not be a poacher. He vigorously maintained that the man who loaded and cocked the gun was responsible for its results, even if he had advertised that such traps were set on his manor. If the placing of the weapon resulted in the death of a totally innocent person, or even in the death of a poacher, for that matter, the responsibility for an unwarranted homocide rested on him who had set the gun.[87] He pointed out the selfishness and biased nature of the game laws, which were passed by one class for the protection of its amusements, totally at the expense of the lower classes. He also mentioned another law which severely punished damages of any kind to landed property, or to the crops on it, but which specifically exempted "<u>all mischief done in hunting, and by shooters who are qualified</u>."[88]

Sydney's concern for the lower classes, and for the injury that might be done to their relations with the upper classes, was very real. As for the pretended efficacy of increased severity, he said that it:

> has always been predicated of every fresh
> operation of severity, that it was to put
> an end to poaching. But if this argument
> is good for one thing, it is good for
> another. Let the first pickpocket who is
> taken be hung alive by the ribs, and let
> him be a fortnight wasting to death. Let

> us seize a little grammar boy, who is robbing orchards, tie his arms and legs, throw over him a delicate puff-paste, and bake him in a bun-pan in an oven. If poaching can be extirpated by intensity of punishment, why not all other crimes? If racks and gibbets and tenter-hooks are the best method of bringing back the golden age, why do we refrain from so easy a receipt for abolishing every species of wickedness? The best way of answering a bad argument is not to stop it, but to let it go on its course till it leaps over the boundaries of common sense. There is a little book called <u>Beccaria on Crimes and Punishments</u>, which we strongly recommend....[89]

In July, 1821, Sydney wrote a third review on spring guns, but it contained few new ideas. The bulk of the review was a defense of the journal against charges of misrepresentation which had been made by Mr. Justice William Draper Best, who Sydney had quoted extensively in his previous review. Sydney rose to the occasion, admitting than an error had been made, but insisting that it had been made in a reputable legal journal, and copied in good faith by himself and the <u>Edinburgh Review</u>. At the same time, while lightly accepting Mr. Justice Best's denial of his imputed statement, he still took issue with his legal reasoning, asserting that the "terror" of spring guns could not justify their use when death rather than fright might result, and that giving notice of intent to commit an illegal act could not legalize it.[90]

In October, 1823, Sydney published his last review on the game laws. In it he reitereated his favorite laissez-faire argument that the sale and purchase of game was a matter of supply and demand, and that the severity of punishment could not alter that fact. He also, however, struck off in a new direction by raising the question of the value of sporting gentlemen to the countryside. Some gentlemen, he said:

> ...come into the country for health, some for quiet, for agriculture, for economy, from attachment to family estates, from

love of retirement, from the necessity of keeping up provincial interests, and from a vast variety of causes. Partridges and pheasants, though they form nine tenths of human motives, still leave a small residue, which may be classed under some other head. Neither are a great proportion of those whom the love of shooting brings into the country of the smallest value or importance to the country. A Colonel of the Guards, the second son just entered at Oxford, three diners out from Piccadilly-Major Rock, Lord John, Lord Charles, the Colonel of the regiment quartered at the neighbouring town, two Irish Peers, and a German Baron;-if all this honourable company proceed with fustian jackets, dog-whistles, and chemical inventions, to a solemn destruction of pheasants, how is the country benefitted by their presence? or how would earth, air, or seas, be injured by their annihilation? There are certainly many valuable men brought into the country by a love of shooting, who, coming there for that purpose, are useful for many better purposes; but a vast multitude of shooters are of no more service to the country than the ramrod which condenses the charge....How absurd it would be to offer to the higher orders the exclusive use of peaches, nectarines, and apricots, as the premium of rustication-to put vast quantities of men into prison as apricot eaters, apricot buyers, and apricot sellers-to appoint a regular day for beginning to eat, and another for leaving off-to have a lord of the manor for green gages-and to rage with a penalty of five pounds against the unqualified eater of the gage!....It is the grossest of all absurdities to say the present state of the law is absurd and unjust; but it must not be altered, because the alteration would drive gentlemen out of the country! If gentlemen cannot breathe fresh air without injustice,

> let them putrefy in Cranborne Alley,
> Make just laws, and let squires live
> and die where they please.[91]

He reprinted his earlier plea for the reform of the game laws by calling for the legalization of the sale of game--an idea which was evidently gaining some support. In one brief but moving paragraph he offered what was probably the best explanation of his attitude on the game laws:

> It is said, 'In spite of all game sold, there is game enough left; let the laws therefore remain as they are;' and so it was said formerly, 'There is sugar enough; let the slave trade remain as it is.' But at what expense of human happiness is this quantity of game or of sugar, and this state of poacher law and slave law, to remain! The first object of a good government is not that rich men should have their pleasures in perfection, but that all orders of men should be good and happy; and if crowded covies and chuckling cock-pheasants are only to be procured by encouraging the common people in vice, and leading them into cruel and disproportionate punishment, it is the duty of the government to restrain the cruelties which the country members, in reward for their assiduous loyalty, have been allowed to introduce into the game laws.[92]

It is interesting to note that while supporting field sports for the gentry, Sydney himself did not engage in shooting. In a letter to Lady Holland in 1809 he announced:

> I have laid down two rules for the country: first, not to smite the partridge; for if I fed the poor, and comforted the sick, and instructed the ignorant, yet I should do nothing worth, if I smote the partridge. If anything ever endangers the Church, it will be the strong propensity to shooting for which the clergy are remarkable. Ten thousand good shots dispersed over the country

> do more harm to the cause of religion
> than the arguments of Voltaire and
> Rousseau. The squire never ready but it
> is not possible he can believe that reli-
> gion to be genuine whose ministers des-
> troy his game.[93]

Saba Holland quoted him as saying that he had resolved not to shoot because:

> ....first..I found, on trying at Lord
> Grey's, that the birds seemed to con-
> sider the muzzle of my gun as their
> safest position; secondly, because I
> never could help shutting my eyes when
> I fired my gun, so was not likely to im-
> prove; and thirdly, because, if you do
> shoot, the squire and the poacher both
> consider you as their natural enemy, and
> I thought it more clerical to be at peace
> with both.[94]

Despite his resolutions against participating in field sports, Sydney considered himself a gourmet, and relished game dishes. In 1821, at the height of his involvement in the controversy on the game laws, he wrote to Lord Carlisle, thanking him for his gift of game "at whatever expenditure of human life obtained."[95] In 1841 he wrote, again in thanks for game:

> Many thanks my dear Sr for your kind pre-
> sent of Game. If there is a pure & ele-
> vated Pleasure in this World it is a roast
> Pheasant with bread sauce. Barn door fowls
> for Dissenters, but for the real Churchman
> the 39 times articl'd Clerk-the Pheasant
> the Pheasant-[96]

Sydney coupled his hostility to the game laws with his opposition to the transportation of convicts, poachers among them, to Australia. In addition to the severity of the punishment for offenses like poaching, he stood against transportation for the same reason he had opposed further humanitarian reforms in prisons: transportation offered a better life to the criminal poor and might encourage crime. He paraphrased the theoretical words of a fictitious judge in passing sentence as:

> Because you have committed this offence -the sentence of the Court is that you shall no longer be burthen'd with the support of your Wife, and family, You shall be immediately remov'd from a very bad climate, and Country overburthened with people-to one of the finest Regions of the Earth where the demand for human Labor is every hour increasing-and where it is highly probable you may ultimately regain your Character, and improve your fortune... your fate will be a warning to others.[97]

Sydney's belief in punishment as a deterrent to crime also led him to endorse capital punishment by hanging for the most serious crimes. In this attitude he was, of course, perfectly typical of his age; and he defended capital punishment on many occasions. As early as 1809 he wrote:

> It is wrong to say in so unexplained a phrase that Hanging is cheap, but it answers the objection to Capital Punishment that the Labor of the Pendulous is lost to Society,-whereas it is notorious that Government lose large sums by the Labor of their convicts.[98]

He believed that the well being of society depended upon the respect for authority, which, in the case of the lowest classes, needed to be supported by a strong fear of punishment. In 1820 he expressed his concern for public order in Scotland when he asked a friend whether the disaffection then present resulted from anything other than unemployment, and whether "full employment, interspersed with a little hanging will not extinguish the bad spirit?"[99] In 1828 he described Bristol as:

> ...a town remarkable for Burglary, and Turtle; Everybody's Stomach is full of green fat, every bodies house is broken open; all this comes of not hanging people. It is seven years since any one was hung here. How can 100,000 people live together in peace upon such terms?[100]

Three years later, in the aftermath of the Bristol Riots, he wrote to Lady Grey to suggest that the government should send down a special commission to hang ten people and to publish a proclamation banning further violence.[101]

Sydney continued to defend hanging, even in his sermons,[102] but unlike many of his contemporaries, he was not an eager onlooker at public executions. Rationally he upheld the necessity of capital punishment to maintain public order, but emotionally he recoiled from the spectacle of the social destruction of human life. In 1813, on the occasion of the executions arising from the Luddite disturbances, he wrote:

> Conceive the horror of 14 men hung yesterday morning; and yet it is difficult to blame the judges for it, tho' it would be some relief to be able to blame them. The murderers of Horsefall were all Methodists; one of them I believe a preacher.[103]

Although little attention has been paid to Sydney's role as a magistrate, and quite possibly little can be known about it, his daughter characterized him in that role as being "popular and gentle".[104] Even though that opinion may be absolutely correct, her judgement was undoubtedly biased and quite possibly conjecture rather than actual evidence. Burdett suggested that Sydeny sided with poachers, but failed to quote a source. While it is tempting to assume that Sydney would have carried his attitudes toward the game laws into his function as a country magistrate, it is also highly possible that Burdett, knowing his antipathy, simply assumed that he did so. Burdett does add, again without quoting a source, that Sydney was deeply concerned about carters who followed unsafe practices in driving un-reined and un-led horses, and that he reprimanded and fined them if they were recalcitrant.[105]

In this period of his life Sydney showed a deep concern for several social issues, of which two, the game laws and prison reform, were the most important. His opinions on them were consistent, with the limitations of his personal attitudes; and his reviews were invariably well written, logical, and amusing. Sydney's biographers have tried to attribute to him a major role in the reform of the laws; and while that is probably not true, he did lend his talents, his pen, and his wit to these laudable causes. When reforms took place in these areas of concern, there can be no doubt but that he contributed to that reform, and that his role was an honorable one.

CHAPTER IX

The Achievement of Reform & Clerical Success, 1828-1832

With his appointment to the stall at Bristol Cathedral Sydney ceased to write for the Edinburgh Review, and his last review in that journal, fittingly enough on Catholic Emancipation, was published in 1827. According to his daughter, he abandoned writing reviews because he considered it unseemly for a dignitary of the Church to write anonymous articles,[1] to which it might be added that his improved financial situation made the remuneration less attractive to him, and that his activities as Canon of Bristol Cathedral and newly appointed Rector of Combe Florey parish probably occupied a great deal of time. He was much taken with the area of southern England to which he had moved, and even more so with the social opportunities afforded there. He had been comfortable at Foston-le-Clay in Yorkshire, and his residence in Combe Florey was almost idyllic, even though his early days there were overshadowed by the death of first son, Douglas.

Combe Florey was located in one of the most beautiful sections of England and possessed an attractive and comfortable rectory, into which Sydney immediately invested nearly two thousand pounds.[2] It was exactly the sort of living he had hoped for at the beginning of his ministry, but which had been denied to him until this time. The attraction of the living at Combe Florey was not dimished by his periodic absences for his duties, which were not very onerous, at Bristol Cathedral. Under such ideal circumstances it might seem that Sydney's literary productivity should have reached a peak, but apart from his numerous letters, he wrote very little during these years. The major reasons for the scarcity of his literary output were his parochial and Cathedral duties, and his preoccupation with the popular issue of reform.

As in so many other instances, Sydney was not inconsistent in being a moderate reformer, or in giving his support to the Great Reform Bill. He had favored political reform for thirty years, and despite the fact that he vigorously supported the general outlines of the political, religious, and social system that existed in Britain, he continued to endorse a limited extension of the franchise to responsible members of the middle classes.

Although he favored a degree of participation by the middle classes in the political processes, his attitude of superiority and his assumption that order and good government required this exclusion of the lower classes from politics remained, but those opinions, as earlier, were tempered with concern. In 1829 he wrote a letter to Lady Carlisle in which his peculiar lack of punctuation made him appear to be less than interested in any suffering on the part of the working classes, but his apparent callousness should be compared with his other comments on the welfare of the poor. He said: "I never ate such fish as in this Country, nothing surprises me so much as the excellence of the fish- the poor people are all starving."[3] What appears to be a greater interest in a good meal rather than in the welfare of the population was a fault of his punctuation and composition rather than his sentiment; for while it would not be correct to call him either a humanitarian or a philanthropist, he was solicitous for the well being of society and had generally benevolent feelings toward the working classes. Burdett mentions that Sydney carried the meager cash surpluses of poor people from Combe Florey to Taunton to deposit them in a savings bank, and that he had been known to take a poor family from London to Combe Florey for a holiday in the country.[4] He continued to express his concern for the well being of his servants, and in 1837 he wrote to Lady Grey to ask her help in assisting his laundry maid to visit friends in Northumberland.[5]

To Sydney and his liberal Whig friends, political reform had nothing to do with the lower classes except indirectly, for they believed that a reformed Parliament would automatically legislate more wisely, and that such legislation would be of general benefit to all subjects. He occasionally professed disillusionment with politics but a brief glance at his disillusionment usually reveals that he was discouraged by the unending continuation of Tory power, or when there was a threat of popular disorder or an excess of reform. In 1827, for example, he wrote:

> Politics, domestic and foreign, are very discouraging; Jesuits abroad-Turks in Greece- No-Poperists in England! A. panting to burn B.; B. fuming to roast C.; C. miserable that he cannot reduce D. to ashes; and D. consigning to eternal perdition the first three letters of the

alphabet.[6]

In 1829, on the occasion of what should have been his greatest triumph, he remarked that "Men are tired to death with the Catholic Question- all upon the eve of getting rid of it- and will take no more trouble about it....".[7]

Despite his commitment to the successful cause of Catholic Emancipation, the great issue of the early 1830's was not Catholic emancipation but political reform, with which he was also identified, but in a less prominent way. Sydney favored political reform, but he was ambivalent on the question, for while he hoped and trusted that reform would bring about needed improvements, he feared that it might result in unwarranted innovations and open floodgates of ill-considered change or even revolution. "I love liberty..." he wrote on 3 January, 1830, "...but hope it can be so managed that I shall have soft beds, good dinners, fine linen, etc., for the rest of my life. I am too old to fight or to suffer."[8] He endorsed moderate and timely reform to head off the revolution he dreaded so much. In one of his sermons, published in 1809, he had written:

> There lies at the bottom of all vast communities, a numerous sect of men, of open, or disguised poverty, who have lost fortune, and fame, in the sink of pleasure, and quenched every particle of God in voluptuous enormities and crimes; base, bad men, who prey upon industry, and hate virtue; who would tear down the decencies, and pollute the innocence of life....Here is the first nucleus of all revolution.... it matters not whether the object be to enslave the people, or to free them; to give them up to another's tyranny, or to the more cruel dominion of their own folly; to establish a despotism, or a democracy. In all revolutions there is plunder, and change; and here are the hordes of assassins, and robbers, the tools of political violence, tutored by their ancient pleasures, and their present distress, to callous inhumanity, and boundless rapine.[9]

The possibility of revolution, especially in the face of the Tory obstruction for moderate reform, was very real, even if it was frequently exaggerated, but it never terrified Sydney to the point where he lost either his wisdom or his wit. On 15, October, 1830, he wrote to Lady Elizabeth Holland to inform her that:

> We shall return home the beginning of November, stay till the end of the year, and then go to Bristol; that is, if the Church of England lasts so long; but there is a strong impression that there will be a rising of Curates. Should anything of this kind occur, they will be committed to hard preaching on the tread-pulpit (a new machine), and rendered incapable of ever hereafter collecting great or small tythes.[10]

Later in the same month he wrote a letter to an Edinburgh friend in which he mentioned that: "The new Beer Bill has begun its operations. Everyone is drunk. Those who are not singing are sprawling. The sovereign people are in a beastly state."[11] The following month he wrote to John Allen and confessed that he was "...frightened at the state of the world; I shall either be burnt, or lose my tithes, or be forced to fight, or some harm will happen to disturb the drowsy slumbers of my useless old-age."[12]

In the autumn of 1830 agricultural disturbances which took the form of rick burning and smashing of agricultural machinery, broke out in southern England reflecting the distressed conditions of rural labor. They were accompanied by strikes in the industrial areas of the north, and by the growing discontent with the Corn Laws, all of which contributed to the demand for political reform. Sydney was very upset by the troubles, but he was not hysterical, and in November, 1830, he wrote:

> What do you think of all these burnings? and have you heard of the new sort of burnings? Ladies' maids taken to set their mistresses on fire. Two dowagers were burnt last week, and large rewards are offered! They are inventing little fire engines for the toilet-table worked with lavender water!.... I go to Bristol

>for a residence of six weeks at the end of the year, or sooner, if my house is set on fire.[13]

Sydney was profoundly concerned about the agricultural troubles in the early 1830's. He saw them as a personal threat, a danger to society and to modern improvements, and as a retrograde expression of violence that might involve otherwise peaceful rural laborers in crime and sedition. In December, 1830, he wrote an open letter to Mr. Swing, sometimes known as Captain Swing, the mythical leader of the machine-breakers, which was chiefly an appeal for peace and order, and a defense of laissez-faire policies:

>To Mr. Swing.

>The wool your coat is made of is spun by machinery, and this machinery makes your coat two or three shillings cheaper, -perhaps six or seven. Your white hat is made by machinery at half price. The coals you burn are pulled out of the pit by machinery, and are sold to you much cheaper than they could be if they were pulled out by hand. You do not complain of <u>these</u> machines, because they do you good, though they throw many artisans out of work. But what right have you to object to farming machines, which make bread cheaper to the artisans, and to avail yourselves of <u>other</u> machines which make manufactures cheaper to you?

>If you begin to object to machinery in farming, you may as well object to a plough, because it employs fewer men than a spade. You may object to a harrow, because it employs fewer men than a rake. You may even object to a spade, because it employs fewer men than fingers and sticks, with which savages scratch the ground in Otaheite. If you expect manufacturers to turn against machinery, look at the consequence. They may succeed, perhaps, in driving machinery out of the town they live in, but they often drive the manufacturer <u>out</u> of the town also. He sets up his trade

> in some distant part of the country, gets new men, and the disciples of Swing are left to starve in the scene of their violence and folly. In this way the lace manufacture travelled in the time of Ludd, Swing's grandfather, from Nottingham to Tiverton. Suppose a free importation to be allowed, as it ought to be, and will be. If you will not allow farmers to grow corn here as cheap as they can, more corn will come from America; for every threshing-machine that is destroyed, more <u>Americans</u> will be employed, <u>not</u> more <u>Englishmen</u>.
>
> Swing! Swing! you are a stout fellow, but you are a bad advisor. The law is up, and the Judge is coming. Fifty persons in Kent are already transported, and will see their wives and children no more. Sixty persons will be hanged in Hampshire. There are two hundred for trial in Wiltshire-all scholars of Swing! I am no farmer: I have not a machine bigger than a pepper-mill. I am a sincere friend to the poor, and I think every man should live by his labour: but it cuts me to the very heart to see honest husbandmen perishing by that worst of all machines, the gallows, -under the guidance of that most fatal of all leaders- Swing![14]

In late 1830 Sydney was becoming more and more persuaded that Britain as well as Europe was on the brink of a new and extensive revolutionary upheaval, from which he recoiled in horror. The fact that no infallible liberal formula seemed to suggest itself as a guaranteed cure for the economic troubles is an indication of the nature of the changes that were taking place; and he fell back lamely on the Malthusian population theory as an explanation. In a letter to an industrialist he expressed his concern:

> I was in hopes to have spent a quiet old age; but all Europe is getting into a blaze, and that light-headed old fool,

> La Fayette, wants, I see, to crusade it
> for Poland. Swing is retiring. He is
> only formidable when he takes you un-
> awares. He was stopped in his way from
> Kent before he reached us. I can give
> you no plan for employing the poor. I
> took great pains about these matters
> when I was a magistrate, but have for-
> gotten all my plans. There are too
> many human beings on the earth: every
> two ought to kill a third.[15]

Sydney Smith was by no means the only English gentleman, or the only Whig, who was perturbed by the turmoil in the country. If anything, he was more calm in this crisis than many of his contemporaries. He had been delighted, of course, with the Whig assumption of power in 1830, and he supported the Whig reform program. He correctly assessed the political climate of opinion when he said that he thought the country was "decided upon Reform; and if the Tories will not permit Lord Grey to carry it into effect, they must turn it over to Hunt and Cobbett." At the same time he expressed his aversion to the direction that the demands for change were taking, and said he was "...tired of liberty and revolution! Where is it to end? Are all political agglutinations to be unglued? Are we prepared for a second Heptarchy....".[16] He lent his support to reform, but he did so with a degree of caution and a very real awareness of the changes that reform might bring in its train. On 25 February, 1831, he said that he had:

> ...a very bad opinion of public affairs;
> I never thought so ill of the world.
> Arbitrary governments are giving way
> everywhere, and will doom us to half a
> century of revolutions and expensive
> wars....Wild beasts must be killed in
> the progress of civilization....[17]

He regarded the current political situation as being potentially explosive, and was aware of the weakness of the Whigs, but he also believed that the Tories did not want to take back the reins of power. "Another week..." he said, "...will decide the fate of parties, perhaps of the kingdom."[18]

The Great Reform Bill was introduced on 1 March,

1831, and between March and October of 1831 Sydney supported it with three speeches, all delivered at Taunton, near Combe Florey. Their effect can probably not be properly appreciated in the twentieth century, but it might be helpful to recall that when Sydney spoke for reform he spoke not only as an Anglican clergyman, but also as a dignitary of the Church. The Church, through its long association with the ruling Tories was heavily Tory in sentiment and usually hostile to reform; so Sydney's advocacy of political reform, while not unique, was striking, and made still more striking by his advancing years and sober clerical appearance. His eloquence and good sense made manifest his unequivocal position on reform, and the speeches reflected his awareness of the situation and the scope of his information on it; while his occasional bits of humor, which gave the English something to laugh about at a time when they found little else amusing, were typically Sydneian in that they employed humor to express a serious purpose.

In his first speech on reform, on 9 March, 1831, he emphasized his clerical profession and the importance of the Reform Bill, which was, he said, the greatest ever to come before Parliament during his lifetime. He averred that being a clergyman he did not generally meddle in politics, a dubious assertion, but one that was true in the sense that he had never spoken publicly on a purely political question, but that he felt the importance of the issue was such that he could not remain silent. Reform, he said, had been needed and attempted for fifty years, and was long overdue, and at the very moment he was speaking, similar meetings were taking place throughout the kingdom. The spirit of the times demanded immediate action. "Some years ago"...he said:

> ...by timely concession, it might have been prevented. If members had been granted to Birmingham, Leeds, and Manchester, and other great towns as opportunities occurred, a spirit of conciliation should have been evinced, and the people might have been satisfied with a Reform, which though remote would have been gradual; but with the customary blindness and insolence of human beings, the day of adversity was forgotten, the rapid improvement of the people was not noticed; the object of a certain class of politicians was to please the

Court and to gratify their own arrogance by treating every attempt to expand the representation, and to increase the popular influence, with every species of contempt and obloquy: the golden opportunity was lost; and now proud lips must swallow bitter potions.

The arguments and the practices...which did very well twenty years ago, will not do now. The people read too much, think too much, see too many newspapers, hear too many speeches, have their eyes too intensely fixed upon political events. But if it was possible to put off Parliamentary Reform a week ago, is it possible now? When a Monarch (whose amiable and popular manners have, I verily believe, saved us from a Revolution) approves the measure- when a Minister of exalted character plans and fashions it- when a Cabinet of such varied talent and disposition protects it- when such a body of the Aristocracy vote for it- when the hundred-horse power of the Press is labouring for it;- who does not know after this... that the measure is virtually carried....

An Honourable Member of the Honourable House, much connected with this town, and once its representative, seems to be amazingly surprised, and equally dissatisfied, at this combination of King, Minister, Nobles, and People, against his opinion: - like the gentlemen who came home from serving on a jury very much disconcerted, and complaining he had met with eleven of the most obstinate people he had ever seen in his life, whom he found it absolutely impossible by the strongest arguments to bring over to his way of thinking.

They tell you, gentlemen, that you have grown rich and powerful with these rotten boroughs, and that it would be madness to part with them, or to alter a constitution which had produced such happy effects. There happens, gentlemen, to live near my parsonage a labouring man, of very superior character and understanding to his fellow labourers; and who has made such good use of that superiority, that he has saved what is (for his station in life) a very considerable sum of money, and if his existence is extended to the common period, he will die rich. It happens, however, that he is... troubled with violent stomachic pains, for which he has hitherto obtained no relief, and which really are the bane and torment of his life. Now, if my excellent labourer were to send for a physician, and to consult him respecting this malady, would it not be singular language if our doctor were to say to him, "My good friend, you surely will not be so rash as to attempt to get rid of these pains in your stomach: have not you risen under them from poverty to prosperity? has not your situation, since you were first attacked, been improving every year? You surely will not be so foolish and so indiscreet as to part with the pains in your stomach?" -Why, what would be the answer of the rustic to this nonsensical monition? "Monster of Rhubarb! (he would say) I am not rich in consequence of the pains in my stomach, but in spite of the pains in my stomach; and I should have been ten times richer, and fifty times happier, if I had never had any pains in my stomach at all". Gentlemen, these rotten boroughs are your pains in the stomach- and you would have been a much richer and greater people if you have never had them at all.[19]

Sydney thus dismissed the Tory argument that England's greatness resulted from such archaic and corrupt practices, and then proceeded to demolish another favorite argument of the Tory defenders of rotten boroughs: that they were good because they enabled the owners to nominate men of ability, like Chatham, who once sat for the infamous Old Sarum, to seats in the House of Commons when they might not have been able otherwise to win an election. Such was true in part, Sydney admitted, "... but nothing is said of those mean and menial men

>who are sent down every day by their aristocratic masters to continue unjust and necessary wars, to prevent inquiring into profligate expenditure, to take money out of your pockets, or to do any other bad or base thing which the Minister of the day may require at their unclean hands. What mischief, it is asked, have these boroughs done? I believe there is not a day of your lives in which you are not suffering in all the taxed commodities of life from the accumulation of bad votes of bad men. But...if this were otherwise, if it really were a great political invention, that cities of 100,000 men should have no representatives, because those representatives were wanted for political ditches, political parks; that the people should be bought and sold like any other commodity; that a retired merchant should be able to go into the market and buy ten shares in the government of twenty millions of his fellow subjects; yet, can such asservations be openly made before the people? ....The moment such a government is looked at by all the people it is lost. It is impossible to explain, defend, and recommend it to the mass of mankind...political Reform is clamoured for by the people- there it stands, and ever will stand, in the apprehension of the multitude- Reform, the cure of every evil- Corruption, the source of every misfortune- famine, defeat, decayed trade, depressed agriculture, will all lapse into the Question of Reform. Till that question is set at rest...all will be disaffection, tumult, and perhaps...destruction.
>
>But democrats and agitators (and democrats and agitators there are in the world) will not be contented with this Reform. Perhaps not, Sir; I never hope

> to content men whose game is never to
> be contented- but if they are not con-
> tented, I am sure their discontent will
> then comparatively be of little impor-
> tance. I am afraid of them now; I have
> no arguments to answer them: but I shall
> not be afraid of them after this Bill
> ...[20]

The opponents of reform, Sydney said, acted as if they thought the bulk of the people were "madmen, robbers, and murderers" who would instantly destroy Church, Crown, and property; but he chose to look upon them as "tranquil, phlegmatic, money-loving, money-getting people" who were chiefly interested in peace and harmony. He similarly rejected the assumption of some that a reformed Parliament would be composed of inferior men, for, he said, "...the free Parliament of a free People is the native soil of eloquence...", and enriched by the new blood of talented men it would continue to flourish. He spoke also of the difference between personal and political fear, as evidenced by the Duke of Wellington, who had disenfranchised 200,000 Irish voters in 1829, but who now hesitated to disenfranchise corporations "containing twenty or thirty persons" which were sold at election time because such disenfranchisement had been called "Corporation robbery".[21] In response to the possibility of claims for compensation for such corporations that had been raised in advance of reform, Sydney suggested the parallel of highwaymen driven out of the practice of robbery by an enclosure, who might have petitioned Parliament in these terms:

> "We your loyal highwaymen of Finchley
> Common and its neighbourhood, having,
> at great expense, laid in a stock of
> blunderbusses, pistols, and other in-
> struments for plundering the public,
> and finding ourselves impeded in the
> exercise of our calling by the said
> enclosure of the said Common of Finch-
> ley, humbly petition your Honourable
> House will be pleased to assign to us
> such compensation as your Honourable
> House in its wisdom and justice may
> think fit."[22]

If members from rotten boroughs who, after having voted against the Bill, should return to their constituents to defend their votes as actions in the interest of the borough, Sydney hoped the voters would reply that they were above bribery by "such a childish and unworthy artifice", and that they had no desire for their representatives to act selfishly at the expense of the general well being of the country. He ended his speech with the hope that reform would be quickly accomplished, an implied warning that violence might result if it did not, and that it should be done constitutionally rather than by the "rude hands of the lowest of the people".[23]

Sydney made another speech in Taunton shortly afterwards which was published, probably because of his position in the Church, as having been given by a "Mr. Dyson", in which he said:

> Stick to the Bill- it is your Magna Charta, and your Runnymede. King John made a present to the Barons. King William has made a similar present to you. Never mind, common qualities good in common times. If a man does not vote for the Bill, he is unclean- the plague-spot is upon him- push him into the Lazaretto of the last century, with Wetherell and Sadler- purify the air before you approach him- bathe your hands in Chloride of Lime, if you have been contaminated by his touch.[24]

He spoke eloquently and effectively on the rotten boroughs, pointing out that many of the best legal minds, many of the most learned clergymen, and numerous gallant military and naval officers went unrecognized and unrewarded in order that the friends and relatives of the boroughmongers might be enriched. What right, he asked, had a member of the aristocracy to buy seats in the House of Commons and to make laws to govern him? He spoke of the reforming Grey ministry in the most laudatory terms, reserving his greatest praise for Lord Althorp, his former Yorkshire neighbour, and for the "gigantic Brougham", the incorruptible patriot who deserved to be placed "amongst your household Gods, and his name to be lisped by your children."[25] He predicted that two thousand years hence the passing of the Reform Bill would be remembered as:

> ....Britannia chained to a mountain- two hundred rotten animals menacing her destruction, till a tall Earl, armed with

Schedule A., and followed by his page Russell, drives them into the deep, and delivers over Britannia in safety to crowds of ten-pound renters, who deafen the air with their acclamations. Forthwith, Latin Verses upon all this- School Exercises- boys whipt, and all the usual absurdities of education. Don't part with an Administration composed of Lord Grey and Lord Brougham; and not only these, but look at them all- the mild wisdom of Lansdowne- the genius and extensive knowledge of Holland, in whose bold and honest life there is no varying nor shadow of change- the unexpected and exemplary activity of Lord Melbourne- and the rising parliamentary talents of Stanley. You are ignorant of your best interests, if every vote you can bestow is not given to such a Ministry as this.[26]

Sydney believed, or said he believed, that the passage of the Bill would also reform the manners of the great and powerful, making them less haughty and more concerned about the opinion of others; and he held that its passage would destroy not the aristocracy, but only their "unfair" power, and that they would continue to lead the people. If Sydney Smith's reasons for being a reformer could be summed up in one sentence, it was when he said:

> The union of the great with the many is the real healthy state of a country; such a country is strong to invincibility- and this strength the Borough System entirely destroys.[27]

He spoke again of the need for timely reform, which had been urged on the Tories, but rejected by them; and he compared the whines of the Tories with those of a man who blames his druggist for his ill health when he, at the same time, has steadfastly refused to take his medicine.

Actually, the Great Reform Bill was more far-reaching than Sydney had anticipated or desired, but he gave it his support, and told his listeners at Taunton that any bill would arouse opposition, and only one as extensive as the Great Reform Bill would attract all reformers.

Unlike his Tory contempories he did not fear the power of the press, and said that reform would exalt the House of Commons and weaken the newspapers. He expressed no concern for the slim Whig majority because, he said, even if it was not borne out of the divisions in the House of Commons, the Tories were so unpopular that:

> ...the Duke of Wellington and Sir Robert Peel...literally would not be able to walk from the Horse Guards to Grosvenor Square, without two or three regiments of foot to screen them from the mob; and in these hollow squares the hero of Waterloo would have to spend his political life. By the whole exercise of his splendid military talents, by strong batteries at Bootle's, and White's, he might, on nights of great Debate, reach the House of Lords; but Sir Robert would probably be cut off, and nothing could save Twiss and Lewis.[28]

Sydney repeated his assertion, which was later proven to be true, that new members in the reformed House would be men of reputation and substance, and not the type who would engage in "mad and revolutionary projects." "The majority..." he said:

> ...of persons returned by the new Boroughs would either be men of high reputation for talents, or persons of fortune known in the neighbourhood; they have property and character to lose. Why are they to plunge into mad and revolutionary projects of pillaging the public creditor?....Is it the interest of such men to create a revolution, by destroying the constitutional power of the House of Lords, or of the King?... The majority of the new Members will be landed gentlemen: their genius is utterly distinct from the revolutionary tribe; they have Molar teeth; they are destitute of the carnivorous and incisive jaws of political adventurers.
>
> There will be mistakes at first, as there are in all changes. All young Ladies will imagine (as soon as this Bill is carried) that they will be instantly married. Schoolboys believe that Gerunds and Supines will be abolished, and that Current Tarts

> must ultimately come down in price;
> the Corporal and Sergeant are sure of
> double pay; bad poets will expect a
> demand for their Epics; Fools will be
> disappointed, as they always are; rea-
> sonable men, who know what to expect,
> will find that a very serious good has
> been obtained.[29]

Obviously not all of these desires could be fulfilled by reform, he admitted, but he insisted that the humblest subject would profit by the economy and wisdom of the reformed Parliament. The reform would benefit many and injure none, and even the poorest subject would benefit from the cessation of unnecessary and unpopular wars and the abolition of "cruel and oppressive" punishments. Poverty could not be abolished, nor wretchedness prevented, but "peace, economy, and justice" would be affected by the proposed changes, and the price of bread and cheese would fall. Sydney added that the unreformed system, contrary to the effusive claims of its defenders, was not working well, and that unless reformed it would cease to work at all. A powerful Tory leader in Edinburgh, had said that there was no eagerness for reform in that city, but crowds of people had unharnessed the horses from the reformers' coaches and had pulled them through Edinburgh in triumph. "Five minutes before Moses struck the rock... Sydney added...this gentleman would have said there was no eagerness for water."[30]

The failure of the Tories to carry out timely reform was one of Sydney's favorite topics, and he pointed to their failures with the American colonists and with Catholic Emancipation. If Tory policy were followed, he said, the effect would be to "O'Connellize" the whole country until reform would be carried out in "hurry and confusion" rather than by calm deliberation. He spoke more prophetically than he knew when he added that if the Great Reform Bill passed, the question of further reform would be put to rest for "thirty or forty years; and this is an eternity in politics."[31]

He told the electors at Tauton that the boroughmongers were not richer than many other wealthy men, but that they had seized strategic positions, like rheumatism, which might be bearable any place other than the joints. He reiterated his trust in the English people, and spoke of his experience with them:

> I live a good deal with all ranks and descriptions of people; I am thoroughly convinced that the party of Democrats and Republicans is very small and contemptible; that the English love their institutions- that they love not only this King, (who would not love him?) but the kingly office- that they have no hatred to the Aristocracy. I am afraid of trusting English happiness to English gentlemen. I believe that the half million of new voters will choose much better for the public, than the twenty or thirty Peers, to whose usurped power they succeed.[32]

Sydney objected to any further delay in the passage of the Bill, his argument being that "the popular spirit may be diverted to other objects." But such a delay could only be temporary, and it would lead to a violent and irresistible demand for more extensive reform. "It is not enough..." he said

> that a political institution works well practically: It must be defensible; it must be such as will bear discussion, and not excite ridicule and contempt. It might work well for ought I know, if, like the savages of Onelashka, we sent out to catch a King: but who could defend a coronation by chase? who can defend the payment of 40,000§. for the three-hundredth part of the power of Parliament, and the resale of this power to Government for places to the Lord Williams, and Lord Charles's, and others of the Anglophagi? Teach a million of the common people to read- and such a government...must perish in twenty years. It is impossible to persuade this mass of mankind, that there are not other and better methods of governing a country. It is so complicated, so wicked, such envy and hatred accumulate against the Gentlemen who have fixed themselves on the joints, that it cannot fail to perish, and to be driven as it _is_ driven from the country, by a general burst of hatred and detestation. I meant,

Gentlemen, to have spoken for another moment; one word before I end. I am old, but....I have lived to see an honest King, in whose word his Ministers can trust....I have lived to see a King with a good heart, who, surrounded by Nobles, thinks of common men; who loves the great mass of English people, and wishes to be loved by them; who know that his real power, as he feels that his happiness, is founded on their affection. I have lived to see a King, who, without pretending to the pomp of superior intellect, has the wisdom to see, that the decayed institutions of human policy require amendment; and who, in spite of clamour, interest, prejudice, and fear, has the manliness to carry these wise changes into immediate execution. Gentlemen, farewell: shout for the King.[33]

As another contribution to the cause of reform, Sydney published a waggish notice in the Taunton *Courier* on 4 May, 1831. In bold type it announced:

GAZETTE EXTRAORDINARY. GLORIOUS VICTORY!

Admiralty, Friday, April 22nd A despatch has been this day received announcing a glorious victory gained by Admirals Grey and Althorp, commanding the Constitutional squadron, over the combined flotilla of the anti-Reformers and Boroughmongers in St. Stephen's Bay.

On board His Majesty's ship *Reform* Anchored off Thorney Island, *April* 22nd I have the honour to communicate (for the information of the friends and supporters of the British Constitution) the details of a splendid victory gained over the combined flotilla of the Boroughmongers, under the command of Admirals Peel and Wharncliffe, in St. Stephen's Bay.

Copious details followed of the frantic but useless maneuvering of the vessels sent out by the rotten boroughs, and of the skillful handling of the reform fleet; and under "Further particulars" were listed some of the defeated craft:

> The Hero of Waterloo.- An excellent troopship; was formerly employed in the war against Bonaparte. Just before the action she sustained great injury by running her head against the rock of Reform, and remained inmovable.
>
> The Cotton Spinner.- Launched from the University Dock, and towed into Tamworth. Veers about like a dogvane in a shift of wind, and cannot keep a straight course. Timbers rotten. It is expected the rats will leave her, as these vermin know by instinct when a ship is not trustworthy.

Numerous other defeated ships, in addition to Wellington and Peel, were listed, and the gazette concluded by saying:

> This brillant victory over the borough-mongers is of the highest advantage to old England. Like the piratical corsairs of Algiers, they not only robbed the people of their property, but of their liberty and constitutional rights. The good ship Britannia has long been kept on the wrong tack, but, with Reform for a pilot, she will put about, steer for free and fair Representation, and sail with a fair breeze into the harbour of Public Prosperity. Our present helmsman knows how to keep her steady by avoiding the rocks and quicksands of Corruption, which obstruct the channel through which the Reformers must navigate.[34]

The enthusiasm for reform was running high by May, 1831, and the reformers met with excited crowds across the country. Sydney met Lord John Russell when he spoke at Exeter, and he later reported to Lady Holland that:

> The people along the road were very much disappointed by his smallness. I told them he was much larger before the Bill

> was thrown out, but was reduced by
> excessive anxiety about the people.
> This brought tears into their eyes.[35]

Russell's Bill had indeed been lost when the Whig government was defeated in April, but a general election gave strength to the Whigs, and they introduced a second bill in June. This bill passed the House of Commons in September, but on October, the House of Lords threw it out. There had been a general assumption that the Bill would pass, and to many its rejection came as a great shock. To Sydney, perhaps because of his knowledge of the votes of the Bishops, it was not a surprise, and in a letter written shortly before that time he had said that he was "afraid the Lords will fling out the Bill... in that case, I believe and trust Lord Grey will have recourse to peer-making"[36] When the House of Lords did as he had predicted, he responded by giving his third address on reform, which was his shortest, but also his most famous speech. Far and away his finest effort on behalf of reform, it was delivered at Taunton on 11 October, 1831, printed in the Taunton Courier, and has been reprinted and quoted extensively. It is brief enough to quote in its entirety:

> Mr. Bailiff, I have spoken so often on this subject, that I am sure both you and the gentlemen here present will be obliged to me for saying but little, and that favour I am as willing to confer, as you can be to receive it. I feel most deeply the event which has taken place, because, by putting the two Houses of Parliament in collision with each other, it will impede the public business, and diminish the public prosperity. I feel it as a churchman, because I cannot but blush to see so many dignitaries of the church arrayed against the wishes and happiness of the people. I feel it more than all, because it will sow the seeds of deadly hatred between the aristocracy and the great mass of the people. The loss of the bill I did not feel, and for the best of all possible reasons- because I have not the slightest idea that it is lost. I have no more doubt, before the expiration of the winter, that

this bill will pass, than I have that the annual tax bills will pass, and greater certainty than this no man can have, for Franklin tells us, there are but two things certain in this world- death and taxes. As for the possibility of the House of Lords preventing ere long a reform of Parliament, I hold it to be the most absurd notion that ever entered into human imagination. I do not mean to be disrespectful, but the attempt of the Lords to stop the progress of reform, reminds me very forcibly of the great storm of Sidmouth, and of the conduct of the excellent Mrs. Partington on that occasion. In the winter of 1824, there set in a great flood upon that town- the tide rose to an incredible height- the waves rushed in upon the houses, and everything was threatened with destruction. In the midst of this sublime and terrible storm, Dame Partington, who lived upon the beach, was seen at the door of her house with mop and pattens, trundling her mop, squeezing out the seawater, and vigorously pushing away the Atlantic Ocean. The Atlantic was roused. Mrs. Partington's spirit was up; but I need not to tell you that the contest was unequal. The Atlantic Ocean beat Mrs. Partington. She was excellent at a slop, or a puddle, but she should not have meddled with a tempest. Gentlemen, be at your ease- be quiet and steady. You will beat Mrs. Partington.

They tell you, gentlemen, in the debates by which we have been lately occupied, that the bill is not justified by experience. I do not think this is true, but if it were true, nations are sometimes compelled to act without experience for their guide, and to trust to their own sagacity for the anticipation of consequences. The instances where this country has been compelled thus to act have been so eminently successful, that I see no cause for fear, even if we were acting in the manner imputed to us by our enemies. What precedents and experience were there at the Reformation, when the country, with one unanimous effort, pushed out the Pope, and his grasping and ambitious clergy? -What experience, when at the Revolution we drove away our ancient race of kings, and chose another family more congenial to our free principles? -And yet to those events, contrary to experience, and unguided by precedents, we owe all our domestic happiness, and civil and religious freedom- and having got rid of corrupt priests and despotic kings, by our sense and our courage, are we now to be intimidated by the awful danger of extinguishing Boroughmongers, and shaking from our necks the igominious yoke which their baseness has imposed upon it? Go on, they say, as you have done for these hundred years last past. I answer, it is impossible- five hundred people now write and read, where one hundred wrote and read fifty years ago. The iniquities and enormities of the borough system are now known to the meanest of the people. You have a different sort of men to deal with- you must change because the beings whom you govern are changed. After all, and to be short. I must say that it has always appeared to me to be the most absolute nonsense that we cannot be a great, or a rich and happy nation, without suffering ourselves to be brought and sold every five years like a pack of negro slaves. I hope I am not a very rash man, but I would launch boldly into this experiment without any fear of consequences, and I believe there is not a man here present who would not cheerfully embark with me. As to the enemies of the bill, who pretend to be reformers, I know them, I believe, better than you do, and I earnestly caution you against them. You will have no more of reform than they are compelled to grant- you will have no reform at

all, if they can avoid it- you will be
hurried into a war to turn your attention from reform. They do not understand you- they will not believe in the
improvement you have made- they think
the English of the present day are as
the English of the times of Queen Anne
or George the First. They know no
more of the present state of their own
country, than of the state of the
Esquimaux Indians. Gentlemen, I view
the ignorance of the present state of
the country with the most serious concern, and I believe they will one day
or another waken into conviction with
horror and dismay. I will omit no
means of rousing them to a sense of
their danger;- for this object, I
cheerfully sign the petition proposed
by Dr. Kinglake, which I consider to
be the wisest and most moderate of the
two.[37]

Sydney acted out his description of Mrs. Partington's struggle with the wrath of the Atlantic Ocean, and the comic story became a ludicrous spectacle as the sober-looking, aging, clerical gentlemen, who had undoubtedly never handled a mop in his entire lifetime, stolidly swabbed away before a cheering crowd which laughed so hard tears rolled down the cheeks of "fair women and veteran Reformers" alike.[38] According to Saba Holland, prints of Mrs. Partington and her mop appeared in shop windows throughout the land, and Sydney's speech became common parlance.[39] To imply that his speech "turned the tide" would be absurd, for it was only one effective speech favoring reform among many at this critical moment. It certainly did little to allay the violent resentment in the Bristol area, when in late October popular anger at the apparent failure of the Bill took the form of un-controllable rioting, much of it directed at the Church and at the Cathedral in which Sydney had served.

It might be assumed that Sydney approved of the Bristol riots, for they along with other popular manifes-tations convinced the waverers that the Reform Bill must pass. Sydney though, was both an advocate of law and order, and a sometime resident of Bristol who was shocked by the violence and destruction. In a letter probably written in November to Lady Grey he said:

> pray do not be good-natured about Bristol. I must have ten people hanged, and twenty transported, and thirty imprisoned; it is absolutely necessary to give the multitude a severe blow, for their conduct at Bristol has been atrocious. You will save lives by it in the end. There is no plea of want, as there was in the agricultural riots.[40]

In another letter which appears to have been written earlier in November he had applauded the use of force at Lamb's Conduit Fields to disperse radicals, whose actions he described as "the scratching of Pismires on an heap of Earth-".[41]

The activities of the radicals were, however, taken very seriously. Mass meetings by the radicals, in favor of the Bill, were held throughout the country, and language approaching that of revolution was heard, especially from the Political Unions which had been formed to support the bill. A slightly milder bill was introduced in December, 1831; but when the House of Lords proposed to water it down still further, Grey's government balked. They asked the King to appoint fifty peers, or more if necessary to pass the bill, and when he refused, they resigned on 9 May, 1832. The Duke of Wellington could not command a majority in the House of Commons, so the King recalled Lord Grey and agreed to accede to the needs of the situation. Tory cooperation, however, made the wholesale creation of peers unnecessary, and the Bill passed the House of Lords on 4 June, 1832. Sydney had little more to do with its passage, but he continued to favor it and to be firm in his conviction that it would pass. In December, 1831, he had written that "...the Bill will pass, partly by defalcation of its opponents, partly by the creation of peers"[42] On 7 January, 1832, he had commented to Lady Grey that the delay in the passage of the Bill was good in that it had helped to prepare the country for the creation of peers, and he expressed his confidence in "a favorable issue".[43] Another of his obsurely dated letters to Lady Grey urged firmness, dignity, and honor in handling the Bill. He urged the ministry to resign if the King refused to appoint enough new peers, and to create them if permitted. If the Bill failed after that, the failure would be an honorable one for the Whigs and the country would remember it. He suggested at that crucial moment that the boldest plan was the most prudent one, and the one most likely to succeed.[44]

In another dubiously dated letter, which may have been written in April, 1832, he wrote again to Lady Grey, promising to see her in May, and hoping that she would be well and victorious by that time.[45]

All in all, Sydney was satisfied with the Reform Bill, but its passage marked his last struggle for a great national cause. He would have preferred a more moderate bill earlier, but he accepted the changes with a degree of enthusiasm. Of the effect of reform in Scotland he wrote:

> What oceans of absurdity and nonsense will the new liberties of Scotland disclose! Yet this is better than the old infamous jobbing, and the foolocracy under which it has so long laboured.[46]

In December, 1832, he said that he was:

> ...delighted to find the elections have gone so well. The blackguards and democrats have been defeated almost universally, and I hope Meynell is less alarmed, though I am afraid he will never forgive me Mrs. Partington; in return I have taken no part in the county election, and am behaving quite like a dignitary of the Church; that is, I am confining myself to digestion.[47]

Chevrillon has said that the Great Reform Bill was Sydney's last combat for the liberal cause, and he was, generally speaking, quite right. Such causes as he campaigned for after 1832 were generally personal or even selfish, and they were to amount to a testy defense of the rights, privileges, and property he had acquired during his life. His role in the passage of the Reform Bill of 1832 was an honorable one, and he played it well, but as the author of his obituary was to observe in 1845, his claims, and those of the Edinburgh Review, to have caused reform, were exaggerated- both Sydney and the Edinburgh reviewers were only workers in the field.[48] As for being a dedicated reformer, Sydney was that indeed, but in October, 1834, he regretted Lord Durham's reforming zeal, and said he was "for no more movements, they are not relished by Canons of St. Paul's."[49]

The passage of the Great Reform Bill was the great

triumph of the Whig party in the nineteenth century, and the beginning of the end of the old system of political manipulation that the Tories had managed so well in the late eighteenth century and early nineteenth century.
It also marked that beginning of the so-called "Victorian compromise", in which the old privileged orders shared power with more newly risen elements of the middle class. For the Whigs it meant a full share of political participation and the spoils of office rather than the shreds and crumbs that had been doled out to them earlier in the century. Sydney had been, as usual, a doughty campaigner in the Whig phalanx, and one who was eminently deserving of a suitable and significant reward. Over the years, however, he had become a controversial figure, which made the usual clerical reward, a bishopric, politically difficult to confer. He expected and demanded payment in full, but his experience made him wary of lofty expectations. As he said:

> We naturally lose illusions as we get older, like teeth, but there is no one to fit a new set into our understanding. I have, alas! only one illusion left, and that is the Archbishop of Canterbury.[50]

He still aspired to be a bishop, and under the circumstances he was as near to becoming a bishop as he was ever to be- so close indeed that he could almost savor the honor and dignity of that office. On 24 January, 1831, he wrote that:

> I think Lord Grey will give me some preferment if he stays in long enough- but the Upper Parsons live Vindictively- and evince their aversion to a Whig Ministry by an improv'd health- the Bishop of Ely has the rancor to recover after three paralytic Strokes- and the Dean of Lichfield to be vigorous a5 82- and yet these are the men who are called Christians-[51]

It is obvious from this letter to J. A. Murray, one of Sydney's fellow Edinburgh reviewers, that he was watching the health of the upper clergy in the hope, if not assured expectation, of early preferment. He was listed with the Holland House clergy as one deserving of a reward, and Holland House was looked upon as a sort of clearing house for Whig clerical preferment.[52] He wanted to be a bishop, and since the Whigs were in a position to appoint him he saw no reason why he should not be made one.

From a political standpoint Sydney was too controversial, and by others, since his wit was well known, for being less than serious. The "serious" clergy of the evangelical wing of the party could not forget or forgive his attacks on them as "Methodists", and the High Church party found his Whig affiliation objectionable. With typical Sydneian zest he replied to those who felt that he was not qualified for a mitre by saying: "They now speak of the peculiar restrictions of the Episcopal office. I read in Scripture of two inhibitions- boxing and polygamy."[53] In fact, when he said that he had passed his life like a razor, continually either in hot water or a scrape,[54] he was not far from wrong, and he was an embarassment for his well meaning but cautious political friends. He persisted in his apparent irreverence, even as regarded the episcopal office itself, for he asked: "...how can a bishop marry? How can he flirt? The most he can say is, I will see you in the vestry after service."[55] On another occasion he remarked that he was compelled to believe in the Apostolic Succession, "there being no other way of accounting for the descent of the (then) Bishop of Exeter from Judas Iscariot."[56]

Syndey's witticisms were exuberant rather than blasphemous, but they offered grounds for denying him the high office he aspired to; at the same time, they did not prevent him from hoping for advancement. In one of the sermons he published in 1809 he had warned his congregation against being overly ambitious, pointing out that while every man hoped to rise above his position in life, and most felt that they had the ability to do so, the world recognized but few, and the remainder were left with their own "overrated pretensions". He counselled his flock to struggle and to "follow that spectre of excellence", but if failure resulted to "submit wisely and cheerfully" and not to prefer a "vicious celebrity to obsurity crowned with piety and virtue."[57] It might be said that he had accepted respectable obsurity in Foston, but he never abandoned his ambition, and throughout his Foston incumbency he sought preferment. In 1817 he wrote:

> Lord Holland has told you the danger I was
> exposed to, of becoming rector of Covent
> Garden, of hortiscortical notoriety. I

> think this is placing a clergyman in the van of the battle. Many of my fashionable female hearers in the chapels at the west end of the town were bad, but they were not professional.[58]

In 1820, when there was some talk of changing the ministry, he wrote to his wife from London to tell her that:

> Nothing is more improbable than that I should be made a Bishop; and if I ever had the opportunity (I am now when far removed) decidedly of opinion that it would be the greatest act of folly and absurdity to accept it- to live with foolish people, to do foolish and formal things all day, to hold my tongue or to twist it into conversation unnatural to me!!!![59]

Despite that statement he still wanted to be a bishop, both for the salary and for reasons of prestige, but his appointment as Canon of Bristol Cathedral, while welcome and remunerative, did not fulfill his ambition. He obviously enjoyed his new eminence, and on 18 February, 1828, in a letter to Lady Carlisle, he wrote:

> I march through the Minster proceded by a Silver Rod. the very type of dignified Gravity- they say I am a severe Solemn looking Man- The Water and the Church Music are better than I ever met with- the people very ugly- the country very beautiful- I know not one Soul- and am living in the most profound solitude upon Mutton Chops.[60]

But even Sydney enjoyed the prestige of his new position, it was at Bristol Cathedral that he gave his famous toleration sermon on Guy Fawkes' Day and so offended the mayor and corporation that they absented themselves for forth years.[61]

Such conduct, while brave and principled, was not conducive to preferment under the reigning anti-Catholic Tories; and while it did endear him to a faction of the Whigs, such actions made it more difficult for them to recommend him for high office in the Church. During the scandal involving the Duke of York and Mary Anne Clarke earlier in the century he had chosen to preach on the seventh commandment, an act which was neither wise nor necessary, and one which certainly did not ingratiate the royal family.[62] Nevertheless, Sydney aspired to higher things, and his daughter, who was not unbiased, said that "...never did anybody to my mind look more like a High Churchman, as he walked up the aisle to the alter- there was an air of so much proud dignity in his appearance... ."[63] He did execute his duties with dignity at Bristol, but those duties were not really burdensome, for it appears that he was required to preach once each Sunday for six weeks in each year. He served during October and the first half of November, 1828, and although the Bristol Chapter Minutes are not clear for 1829, he seems to have served a similar stint in 1829. The schedule was altered in 1829, however, so he served during January and half of February, 1830, in 1831, and was scheduled to serve in 1832.[64] Few records remain that would indicate any effect he may have had at Bristol, other than that of his toleration sermon, but one work on that Cathedral refers to:

> ...the political pseudo-gospel outpourings of some popular divine- perhaps that "Mad Wag, Sydney Smith," during whose Prebendal residence, it was with difficulty that standing place for a child could be obtained inside the choir, and which seldom failed to reap for the Subsachrist a plentiful harvest; whom scandal has accused of supplying his pockets generously with sawdust, to render mute the otherwise discordant notes of half-crowns and shillings from interrupting the harmony of the service.[65]

Sydney was richer and happier at Bristol and Combe Florey, but fame and fortune have prices too; and his appointment to the Prebendal Stall was challenged, although apparently no more seriously than in the press and in public gossip. Lord Lyndurst had defended the appointment as evidence of his non-partisanship, but Lady Lyndhurst was assailed because of it, and was accused of corruption. Sydney defended her from charges of selling the patrimony of the Church, and added that she would "...be compelled next to swear that she had not committed Murder- the whole is an Experiment of the press to see what generous good natur'd forgiving people will bear-"[66] It is a fact that Sydney Smith the clergyman did not operate openly as a politician. His reform speeches were exceptional, and his officially sub rosa political maneuvers, especially with regard to his correspondence, were carried out more frequently with political wives rather than with their office holding husbands. As a result the wives were often his stoutest partisans, and the Ladies Grey, Lyndhurst, and Elizabeth Holland played important roles in his perpetual quest for preferment.

He resented the attacks on Lady Lyndhurst as a result of his appointment to which he felt a self-evident right, and in the letter quoted above to Lady Carlisle, he showed some of the charm and wit that made eminent ladies champion his cause.

> ...dont be angry with me for liking Combe Florey, how is any body accountable for likes, and dislikes? It is really extremely beautiful.- and makes me feel romantic- expect Poetry Trees, Bees- Zephyr- heifer- Leaf Beef- &c- Vide Rogers and Luttrell-[66]

His nomination at Bristol had been challenged, but within the context of the practice of that age it was legal and proper. Sydney probably gave limited thought to the challenge, passing little more than the requisite six weeks at Bristol, and spending the majority of his time either at Combe Florey, the "Valley of the Flowers", or on visits to London.

He enjoyed Combe Florey from the beginning, although he would have preferred London, and on 13 July, 1829, he wrote to Lady Grey to say:

> I am extremely pleased with Combe Florey, and pronounce it to be a very pretty place in a very beautiful country. The house I shall make decently convenient. I have 60 acres of good land round it. The habit of the country is to give dinners, and not to sleep out; this I shall avoid. My neighbors look very much like other people's neighbors; their remarks are generally of a meteorological nature.[67]

In the following month he announced that the "only acquaintance I have made here is that of the Clerk of the Parish a very sensible man with great Amen-ity of disposition."[68] Combe Florey was an attractive living, and Sydney, having found it to his liking, had decided to settle there on a permanent basis. His financial situation was greatly improved, so he did not hesitate to put a good deal of money, probably about §2000, into improvements. In two letters, one written in August, 1829, and the other probably shortly thereafter, he said:

> I have very few years to live, and therefore I cannot afford to waste time in building. I have ten carpenters and ten bricklayers at work. Part of my house has tumbled down, the rest is inclined to follow. We sleep upon props; an enemy or a dissenter might saw me down in the night-time.
>
> I am, after my manner, making my place perfect; and have twenty-eight people constantly at work.[69]

Later in the same year, although a little disenchanted by the overabundance of cider, he was still entranced by Combe Florey, for he wrote:

> This is the most beautiful Country in England & nature in imitation of the Sheppard Paris has given it the Apple- an accursed Gift: every body is drunk from the 1st of January to the last of December- in every other respect it is enchanting....[70]

As Rector of Combe Florey Sydney has been described as having been "punctual" in his performance of the services each Sunday, and offering Communion once a month.[71] Such was probably true in the sense that he saw to it that services were held, but more likely Cecil Smith, his nephew and clerical neighbour, officiated at many of them. No record of services or their officiant exists, but a study of baptismal, burial, and marriage registers shows that Sydney was indeed an active clergyman. These documents demonstrate clearly when he was serving the parish, but not when he was absent, and in the years from 1830 to 1833 they show that he was definitely present from four to six months, or parts of those months.[72] A study of the Holland House Dinner Books discloses the fact that in many of the months when the Combe Florey records do not record his administering the sacraments, he was to be found at Holland House. For example, the Combe Florey registers indicate that he was in the parish in 1831 during the months of March, April, June, August, and November; and the Dinner Books reveal that he visited Holland House in April, May, September, November, and December.[73]

Such observations on absenteeism should not, however, be used to condemn Sydney, because much of his time away from the parish was legitimately used for clerical or political visits; and he seems to have been very scrupulous about insuring the presence of a substitute in his absence. He made firm and very businesslike arrangements for Cecil Smith to serve in the event of his being otherwise engaged, specifying even his objection to a particular clergyman who was

> ...really quite a disreputable person-
> and much too bad to be able to say he
> has been noticed by you or me- If you
> should happen to be ill- I had rather
> the Church should be shut up- than owe
> any thing to his assistance....[74]

Sydney's objections to that clergyman appear to have been moral or personal rather than doctrinal, for Sydney was a broad Churchman, inclined towards Low Church, but too legalistic to be uncanonical. He joked frequently about the thirty-nine articles, the hierarchy, vestments, "enthusiasm", and the clerical greed for favor and preferment, but he never made jokes about the Holy Eucharist or the really important aspects of Christianity which he held in genuine veneration. In one of his later sermons he spoke of those who received the sacrament too rarely because of "negligence or fear, a supineness to every institution of religion, or an over-scrupulous dread of the danger of partaking unworthily." As spiritual comfort to his congregation he hastened to add that "partaking unworthily" did not mean taking communion with good intentions, and then lapsing; for such a resolution to do good was an act of piety, the breach of which was a sin, but one that could be atoned for separately. As for worthiness, he said:

> The worst and the lowest wretch that
> lives, if he does but so much as lift
> his eyes to heaven, if he but smite his
> breast,saying, "God be merciful to me a
> sinner", he shall taste a morsel of this
> bread, and drink a drop of this wine.

> But he who comes to mock at the Lord's
> body, it were better for him... that he
> had drunk the waters of Merah and eaten
> the poison of asps.[75]

As an essentially eighteenth century clergyman Sydney did not believe in unnecessary pomp or complication in the services, and he distinguished clearly between superstition and his views of Communion. Just as it has been said that the Christian should love sinners and hate sin, so he loved religion and hated its excesses. In 1827 he had written to a minor publishing house to ask:

> Is it wise to give to your house the
> character of Publishers of <u>Infidel
> Books</u>? The English people are a very
> religious people, and those who are
> not religious hate the active dissemination of irreligion. The zealots of
> irreligion are few and insignificant
> and confined principally to London.
> You have not a chance of eminence and
> success in pursuing such a line, and
> I advise you prudently and quietly to
> back out of it.
>
> I hate the insolence, persucution and
> intolerance which so often pass under
> the name of religion, and (as you know)
> I have fought against them: but I have
> an unaffected horror of irreligion and
> impiety; and every principle of suspicion and fear wd be excited in me by a
> man who professed himself an infidel.[76]

Sydney's religious beliefs were dignified and demanding, but not so much so as to make them accessible only to the elect. He was Catholic in the sense that he venerated traditional beliefs and held out salvation to prince and pauper alike, rather than only to the theologian or puritan. His efforts to ingratiate himself with influential people have been mentioned often enough, but they were frequently marked by references to his very seriously- taken spiritual responsiblities. In 1818 he stated that:

> ...if Lady Grey ...wishes to see a child
> gracefully held, and to receive proper
> compliments upon its beauty, and to

> witness the proper consummation of
> all ecclesiastical observances, she
> will invite me to perform the cere-
> mony.[77]

In 1819, writing to Lady Georgiana Morpeth, he had offered comfort and advice, adding:

> I like in you very much that you are
> a religious Woman, because though I
> have an infinite hatred, and contempt
> for the nonsense which often passes
> under, and disgraces, the name of
> religion, I am very much pleas'd when
> I see any body religious for hope, and
> Comfort, not for insolence, and in-
> terest.[78]

Several years later he wrote to Cecil Smith, informing him in Combe Florey that on Christmas Day "...there is a poor bed ridden Woman to whom I will ...request you to administer the Sacrament".[79] Such passages are totally lacking in irreverence and are not as quotable as his more earthy lines or his pungent comments on some aspects of religion, so they are not as well known; but his well known definition of heaven as "eating foie gras to the sounc of trumpets"[80] is not blasphemous, and it may well indicate a belief in the afterlife, and an aspiration to its achievement.

Sydney's religious duties were not confined solely to Combe Florey and Bristol Cathedral, for in 1828 the vicarage of Halberton, near Tiverton in Devonshire, became vacant, and its presentation fell to him.[81] Its salary of $400 was a welcome addition to his growing income, and out of it he named a curate to perform the services. His wife's memoir states that he occasionally served that church, and that he gave a great deal of attention to the business of the parish; but actually, (apart from quarreling with the vestry over his right to appoint a churchwarden, a right that he investigated and relinquished when he found the facts against him,) he only visited the parish once a year, preaching always on the text: "I die daily".[82]

Sydney was relatively happy at Combe Florey, and between it, Halberton, and Bristol Cathedral he had a most adequate income; but he still aspired to a mitre, and the Whigs certainly owed one to him. A more recent writer has said that since he founded the Edinburth Review and contributed to it and to the Whig cause for so many years, "when the Whigs came into power in 1830, most people expected he would be made a Bishop." (To which he added that Sydney was not unfitted for the administration of a see, and there were "many worse priests...")[83] Sydney himself had preached against political influence in the Church in 1807, saying that such was the "true way to... disgrace a church establishment; and then...to destroy it";[84] but it may be safely assumed, since the sermon was delivered at about the time of the writing of the political Peter Plymley Letters, that by "faction" he meant "Tory", and by "political clergymen" he referred to his enemies in the Church. He had waited since 1806 for preferment from his Whig friends, which was undoubtedly the origin of his comment that (Tory) "ministers have a great deal of patience, but no resignation."[85]

When the Whigs came to power in 1830 Sydney wrote to Lady Grey, expressing his delight for Lord Grey that:

> ...after such long toil, such Labor, privation, and misrepresentation, that a man should be placed where providence intended him to be, that honesty and Virtue should at last meet its reward is a pleasure which rarely occurs in human Life....[86]

He was genuinely pleased for Lord Grey and Great Britain, because his attachment to Whig principles was very real; but his joy for the cause was mixed with a renewed hope, now amounting almost to a certainty, of preferment. To the Whigs, however, Sydney was something of an embarassment, for although they acknowledged their debt to him, his nomination to a bishopric would have been controversial. To an insecure ministry such action was unwise politically, but Lord Grey, acting under pressure, promised him preferment, without pledging himself to a mitre. He had promised Sydney the Prebendal Stall at Westminster in the likely event of the death of Andrew Bell, the educator, in mid-1831,[87] but in a letter from Downing Street on 10 September, 1831, he wrote to say that:

> You are much obliged to Dr. Bell for not dying, as he had promised. By the promotion of the Bishop of Chichester to the See of Worcester, a Canon Residentiary of

>   St. Paul's becomes vacant. A snug thing,
>   let me tell you, being worth full §2000
>   a year. To this the King, upon my re-
>   commendation, has signified his pleasure
>   that you should be appointed, and I do
>   not think it likely that you can be dis-
>   appointed a second time....[88]

Lord Grey's letter was received with joy, and Sydney wrote that he too thought it was a "very good thing, and puts me at my ease for life. I asked for nothing-never did anything shabby to procure preferment."[89] He was exhilarated by the appointment which occurred almost exactly a month before his "Mrs. Partington" speech on reform. For a Canon of St. Paul's to mimic the motions of a charwoman quite obviously heightened both the amusement and the effect of the speech. Though a canon is not as exalted in the Church as a bishop, his appointment to St. Paul's excited some hostility, not the least of which came from the devout William Ewart Gladstone, later one of the great Liberal prime ministers of the nineteenth century, who quite accurately regarded Sydney as a "regular latitudinarian".[90]

To Lord Grey, Sydney's elevation to St. Paul's was probably payment in full for past services, and it was to be his last major promotion; but to Sydney and his friends, it was a most welcome act of preferment pending a more propitious moment for his nomination to a see. He said, in December, 1832, I have "come to the end of my career, and have nothing now to do but to grow old merrily and to die without pain".[91] He had said much the same thing in Foston years earlier, but without giving up any of his ambition. He did, however, remain the same Sydney, exuberant and superficially irreligious. When he was imploringly invited to visit, and was told:

>   'Do, we shall be on our knees to you,
>   if you come.' He replied: 'I'm glad
>   to hear it...I like to see you in that
>   attitude, as it brings me in several
>   hundreds a year.'[92]

During the same period of time Sydney was attacked, along with many other privileged Anlican clergymen, for pluralism. The <u>Extraordinary Black Book</u> quite erroneously listed him as: "Smith, Sidney, preb. of Bristol, and canon res. of St. Paul's. <u>Foston</u>, r. lord chan. <u>Londesboro'</u>, v duke of Devonshire." Actually, of course, he had resigned his positions at both Foston and Bristol Cathedral (and with it, Halberton), and had returned Londesborough some years earlier; but he retained Combe Florey, and despite the criticism, looked forward to still still more preferment.

CHAPTER X

Canon to the Right 1831-1845

Sydney had become a dignitary of the Church by virtue of his appointment at Bristol, but by Lord Grey's nomination of him to a stall at St. Paul's Cathedral he advanced to far greater income and dignity. Sir Christopher Wren's masterpiece was then, as it remains today, one of the most respected churches in the kingdom, and Sydney had become almost as important as he desired to be. His induction into the offices involved was protracted, and the details were recorded in the Dean and Chapter Muniment Book according to the proper and traditional forms. He appeared before the Dean and Chapter on 27 September, 1831, and was inducted into the profession of Prebend of Neasdon. On the following day the Rev. Thomas Hughes, Canon Residentiary at St. Paul's, acting with the consent of the Dean and Chapter, elected him Canon Residentiary in the place of the Bishop of Chichester. This action was followed by the intimation of Edward Bishop of Llandaff and Dean of the Cathedral, who announced his election to Sydney, under the conditions that he was to preach a quarter of the afternoon sermons on Sundays, and that on or before the first of February he should again appear before the Chapter to signify his consent to the election and to read the first protestation of his residence. Sydney read his first protestation that same day, promising:

> <u>In the Name of God Amen</u>. Before you the <u>Reverend Thomas Hughes</u>, Doctor in Divinity, Prebendary of the Prebend of Consumpta per Mare founded in the Cathedral Church of Saint Paul London, and Canon Residentiary of the said Church, and before you the Notary Public here present. I Sydney Smith Clark, Master of Arts, Canon and Prebendary of the Canonry and Prebend of Neasdon founded in the said Cathedral Church do say, allege, propound and protest, in this writing, as follows, to wit; That it is my <u>will</u> and intention upon the first day of February next (with the Divine Assistance) to make and begin, to the Praise, Glory, and Honour of God, my first and personal residence in the said Cathedral Church, according to the Statutes and laudable

> Customs of the same, but so far only as
> the same are not in any thing repugnant
> opposite and contradictory to the present
> Laws and Statutes of this Kingdom and
> Royal Injunctions and others heretofore
> issued, decreed and enjoined by Royal
> Authority, which said laws and Royal In-
> junctions I do not intend to oppose or
> contradict, or in any wise derogate from,
> but do firmly purpose and herein expressly
> profess and protest to adhere to, and obey
> them in all things, and I do further pub-
> lickly protest before you, that I do will
> and intend to begin, and also in due man-
> ner compleat and end such my first and
> personal residence, according to the man-
> ners and form and qualities aforesaid ...
> unless I shall otherwise be dispensed with
> by the Royal Authority or by you to which
> residence so to be begun, I pray you real-
> ly and effectually to admit me, with good
> will and charity, according to the Stat-
> utes and Customs of the said Church .....

On Sunday, 2 October, the Dean and Chapter Muniment Book recorded that:

> ... the Reverend Sydney Smith Clark, Mas-
> ter of Arts, Canon and Prebendary of the
> Canonry and Prebend of Neasdon founded in
> the Cathedral Church of Saint Paul London,
> publickly read Morning and Evening Prayers,
> as set forth in the Book of Common Prayer
> in the Choir of the said Church at the
> time of Divine Service, and publickly
> declared his Assent and consent to every
> thing prescribed and contained in the
> said Book, pursuant to an Act of Parlia-
> ment made in the fourteenth year of
> Charles the Second late King of England
> and so forth-and did also declare, that
> he would conform to the liturgy of the
> United Church of England and Ireland, as
> it is by law established.[1]

Duly installed in the Cathedral, Sydney became, to the surprise of many, an exemplary Canon, carrying out his duties conscientiously and taking an active interest in the affairs of the Cathedral. As meticulous in the business of the Cathedral as in his own financial affairs, he checked into the most minute details of repairs and maintenance with a suspicious eye, demanding the best of materials and workmanship at the lowest competitive price. He quarrelled with Charles Cockerell, superintendant of the Cathedral, on various matters, but once having convinced himself of Cockerell's probity he then lent him his complete support. It was Sydney who first insured the Cathedral, and who first arranged for a supply of water in the event of fire. The library in the Cathedral had become drenched with moisture, and he dehumidified it with an American stove, and secured more funds for the maintenance of the library.[2] He had always been a good parish administrator, and his role at the Cathedral was fitting to his dignity, so it is not surprising that he threw himself into his labors. He still hoped to become a bishop, and that by demonstrating his energy and ability, he could dissuade his political allies from their doubts about his fitness for the episcopal office.

As Canon Residentiary Sydney was delegated to oversee the Cathedral choir, and the music generally. On 14 July, 1834, he reported that the "insufficiency of the choir" resulted from boys being retained in the choir after their voices had changed. Another problem was the Succentor who selected difficult music which was unsuited to the choir, and he did not provide adequate time for its mastery. As a solution he proposed the pensioning off of boys when their voices changed, and that the Succentor pay closer attention to the capabilities of the choir, and that he give "longer notice of the music he selects".[3]

On 6 December, 1834, the Chapter ordered "that the Revd S. Smith have the goodness to enquire of the musical attainments of the Boys of the Choir-to ascertain if that branch of education is properly attended to...."[4] An investigation determined that the choirboys rose at 7:30 in the summer, or 8:00 in the winter, and that they practised psalms before breakfast. (which consisted of bread, butter, and milk) They attended and sang at Matins at 9:45, and the hours from 11:00 to 2:00 were devoted to rehearsal and voice training. The hour from 11:30 to 12:30 on Wednesdays, was given over to the study of Italian. At 2:00 they dined on vegetables and bread, with meat every other day, and half a pint of "good table beer, with more beer available if asked for." They participated in Evensong at 3:15, and the time from evensong, to 5:30 was their recreation period. From 5:30 to 8:00, they attended classes in reading, writing, arithmetic, and the Catechism, except for Wednesday after Evensong, which were unscheduled. The boys were free to return home on Wednesday afternoons, and after Evensong Saturdays, but they were required to return before Matins, and to meet the Sunday service. Supper was at 8:00, consisting of bread, butter, and beer; and, unless doing oratorios, the choristers retired at 9:00, sleeping two to a bed, on which the linen was changed twice a week. They received holidays from school, for three weeks at Christmas, two weeks after Easter, and four weeks in the summer, but were required to attend services.[5]

The investigation revealed that the bedrooms for the boys were clean and comfortable, and that there were enough blankets for them. Fagging of the younger boys was not permitted, but the report admitted that it existed. Corporal punishment for infractions of the rules was administered with a "slight hand whip...less severe than the common cane", and in morals offenses, with a rod applied to the bare back; but this last punishment was employed only rarely, and deprivation of meals was never practised. The report concluded that complaints of poor and insufficient food were unfounded, but added that one boy was "constitutionally subject to the Complaint of body", and despite washing with Larkspur seed and brandy he had infected other boys. The problem was solved by giving him a bed to himself.[6]

The organist at St. Paul's in 1831 was Thomas Attwood, a pupil of Mozart and a friend of Mendelsohn. (The latter of whom visited him at the Cathedral in 1829 and played Bach so long on the Cathedral organ that the vergers, despairing of clearing the Cathedral, "persuaded the blowers to let the wind out of the organ". Mendelsohn, it is reported, took the action in good spirit). Attwood served until 1838, when Sydney secured the services of John Goss, who was to serve until 1872. Goss seemed to have upset Sydney slightly with his demands for the upkeep of the organ. "Mr. Goss", Sydney said:

> what a strange set of creatures you organists are. First you want the bull stop, then you want the tom tit stop; in fact you are like a jaded cab horse, always longing for another stop.[7]

Sydney's attitude toward music was ambivalent, which

makes his delegation to musical matters a little puzzling. In 1823 he had written to Lady Elizabeth Holland that:

> They are making immense preparations in the Minster; the general notion is that the chorus in the Messiah 500 fiddles 3 hundred Voices will fetch down all the delicate Gothic ornaments upon the heads of the delighted and about to be bruised Audience-
>
> Nothing can be more disgusting than an Oratorio. How absurd, to see 500 people fiddling like madmen about Israelites in the Red Sea.[8]

In 1825, again in a letter to Lady Holland, he said, regarding a concert at nearby Castle Howard:

> I did not go once. Music for such a length of time (unless under the sentence of a Jury) I will not submit to. What pleasure is there if quantity is not attended to, as well as quality?[9]

In 1835 he attended a performance of Bellini's *I Puritani*, which, he said, "was dreadfully tiresome and unintelligible in its plan. I hope it is the last opera I shall ever go to."[10] Five years later, in response to an invitation to the opera, he replied:

> Thy servant is threescore-and-ten years old; can he hear the sound of singing-men and singing women? A Canon at the Opera! Where have you lived? In what habitations of the heathen? I thank you, shuddering; and am ever your unseducible friend.[11]

Despite these negative comments, however, in 1844, he said: "...if I were to begin life again, I would dedicate it to music; it is the only cheap and unpunished rapture upon earth-".[12] Burdett mentioned that, while Sydney hated oratorios, most operas, and all minor keys, he did learn to play the piano and to sing Thomas Moore's songs.[13] Under these circumstances it is not surprising that the St. Paul's choir became sloppy and plagued by absenteeism, performing the "Hallelujah Chorus" on one occasion with only one tenor and one bass.[14] His lack of concern was shown by a letter written in 1844, in which he said:

> I think the choir of St. Paul's as good as any in England. We have gone on with it for 200 years, why not be content. You talk of competing with other Cathedrals, but Cathedrals are not to consider themselves rival Opera Houses, we shall come by and by to act Anthems, it is enough if your music is decent, and does not put us to shame. It is a matter of perfect indifference to me whether Westminister bawls louder than St. Paul's. We are there to pray, and the singing is a very subordinate consideration.[15]

If Sydney's work with Cathedral music was not all that might be desired, it should be remembered that as a Canon Residentiary he resided at St. Paul's only three months a year, much of the remainder of his time being spent at his rectory in Combe Florey. In 1832 he apparently spent February, March, and July at St. Paul's, but in 1833 his schedule was changed to March, July, and November, and he kept this schedule during the rest of his life.[16] As Canon residentiary he was given a house at Amen Corner, but he turned it over to a friend, and kept only one room for himself. His London addresses from 1831 to 1835 were those of friends with whom he stayed while serving at the Cathedral. In 1835 he bought a fourteen year lease on a house at 33 Charles Street, Berkeley Square, for §1400 plus §10 ground rent per year. It is only, he said to Lady Carlisle, "about as big as one of your travelling Trunks but I mean to be very happy there".[17] He commented in another letter that "The lawyers discovered some flaw in the title about the time of the Norman Conquest; but, thinking the parties must have disappeared in the quarrels of York and Lancaster, I waived the objection,"[18] In 1839 he moved to larger and more comfortable quarters at 56 Green Street, Grosvenor Square, which residence he kept until his death. His love for London continued, and even though he spent part of the year at Combe Florey, he referred to it as a place where there is "no Influenza, Cold, nor any other Evil but dullness."[19]

Sydney's promotion to St. Paul's certainly increased his dignity, but it did not diminish his wit and good nature. About January, 1837, he wrote a letter to Lady

Grey, saying:

> As long as I live I shall send you a cheese; didn't you know it was a bargain between Ld Grey and me, that if he made me Canon I was to send him a Cheese every year. It is not a cheese but an outward and visible mark of my gratitude and affection.[20]

He regarded a winter visit to St. Paul's as suicide because of the cold, and so advised his friends:

> ...to go to St. Paul's is certain death. The thermometer is several degrees below zero-my sentences are frozen as they come out of my mouth and are thawd in the course of the sermon making strange noises and unexpected assertions in various parts of the Church....[21]

Despite his warnings of the cold, however, St. Paul's was a national monument in addition to being a Cathedral Church, and crowds of visitors thronged it. In 1819 Sydney had described the memorials within the Cathedral as "a disgusting heap of trash",[22] little realizing that some day he would be required to assist in their administration. Between July and November, 1837, a curious correspondence regarding public admission to the Cathedral took place between Lord John Russell, the Home Secretary, and the Cathedral Chapter. Russell requested, on 6 July, that the Cathedral be considered a "National Building", and that admission to see the monuments and works of art be made free to all. He assured the Chapter that order would be maintained, and he said that parts of the Cathedral could be restricted, and shown only by appointed officers.[23] On 11 July, the Chapter responded, essentially rejecting Russell's suggestion on the grounds that although the Cathedral had been built with a parliamentary grant it was a church and not a public building, and hence was not subject to governmental control. The Chapter stood on its "rights and immunities", maintaining that the presence of the monuments did not make any difference. The low fee of 2d admission was charged, they said, to help pay the vergers, and it was not collected during the hours when services were being held. To throw the Cathedral open, they believed, would destroy "decency and quiet and order" and lead to vandalism. The Chapter added that a "Church ought not to be regarded in the light of a gallery of art" and that Russell's request was "derogatory from our legal rights and privileges", and that compliance with it would give the Chapter responsibility without the necessary control.[24]

On 20 July, Sydney, acting in the absence of the Dean of the Cathedral, ordered the vergers to allow all who came in free during the services to remain until closing time.[25] On 20 September, Russell wrote again. Obviously dissatisfied with Sydney's minor concession, he asked if further changes were contemplated, adding that he could supply police to keep order if they were needed. Sydney rather testily replied from Combe Florey on the 22nd of September, stating that the Cathedral was open without charge to the public from 9:45 to 11:00 A.M., and from 2:45 to 4:00 P.M. (Sundays 10:00 to 12:00 A.M., and 3:00 to 5:00 P.M.), the same hours as the British Museum, and that the Chapter was not contemplating any further changes. Any freer access, he felt, would make St. Paul's "a Rendezvous for the worst characters of both sesces in the metropolis"; and he added firmly that the use of police was not legal in the Cathedral. With equal firmness he concluded his letter by saying that while the Chapter was willing to listen to suggestions, it would settle all matters "respecting their own Church".

The Home Office's response to Sydney's letter was written on 29 September, and it urged the Chapter to keep the Cathedral open an extra hour in the week; to which Sydney replied on 15 November that the Chapter entirely agreed with the suggestion and had carried it out. On 19 November, Sydney wrote to Russell that the "...Dean and Chapter have now complied entirely and to the utmost extent with your Lordship's request...."[28] His assertion was not true, but his action in soliciting a suggestion, acting on it because it was trivial, and then presenting that fait accompli as a final solution was enough to frustrate any further action by Russell. Sydney continued on behalf of the Chapter, to claim the right to close or open the Cathedral, and to charge a minor admission fee. Such was the Anglican practice, and he pointed out that the same practice was followed in Roman Catholic countries. He observed that the Statutes of Queen Anne did not give the public an unqualified right to enter the churches, and that the fulltime vergers needed to be paid. The 2d admission fee was sanctified by a hundred year old tradition, and Sydney denied the right of the public to force unwanted expense on the Cathedral. Regarding earlier problems, he said:

> ...the Cathedral is constantly and shamefully polluted with ordure, the pews are some times turned into Cabinets d'aissance, and the Prayer books torn up; the monuments are scribbled all over and often with the grossest indecency.29

The issue was probably not very important, for, apart from the very poorest, the admission fee did not keep anyone out, and it certainly did not protect the Cathedral from desecration, as the antique graffiti, which may still be seen, attest. Sydney was at his Whiggish best in defense of the established rights of his Cathedral from encroachments by the Whigs. The admission fee did bring in a substantial sum, for in 1840, the poorest year for visitors in that period, about 48,000 people visited St. Paul's, and by 1845 this number had increased to 71,000.30 The government tried again in 1842 to abolish the admission fee, and finally succeeded in doing so in 1851.31

Sydney performed his administrative duties at the Cathedral competently, and he carried out his spiritual responsibilities equally well. He was expected to be present at Matins and Evensong each Sunday during his three months' duty, but his main duty was to preach the afternoon sermon each Sunday in those three months. His duties were not overly burdensome, and he could avoid even the afternoon sermon "if he wants Health, or has weighty affairs preventing him".32 He was a good preacher, however, and St. Paul's was a good place to preach, and it appears that his record there was of regular service. Charles Greville, the diarist and gossip, recorded in 1834:

> Went to St. Paul's yesterday evening, to hear Sydney Smith preach. He is very good; manner impressive, voice sonorous and agreeable, rather familiar, but not offensively so, language simple and unadorned, sermon clever and illustrative.33

Greville was not alone in going to St. Paul's to hear Sydney's sermons, for many of his aristocratic friends also went to hear him preach.

His friends visited him at his home, because he was something of an innovation from previous canons who had "no reputation for learning or for social graces".34 His sociability and his hospitality were studied, however, for, like most of the people of his age, Sydney Smith was a respecter of persons, and he refused to waste his time and talents on unimportant people. In a letter to the Chapter Clerk on 9 August, 1841, he said: "I am building an ark-for fear of a flood-there shall be no Minor Canons in it nor Vicars Choral...."[35] He showed by that reference his aversion to the requirement of his office, that he provide entertainment "to dinner" for the minor canons and the vicars-choral on Sunday. He objected strenuously to that obligation, claiming failing eyesight, a need for the extra time to prepare his sermons, and that preaching after dinner gave him headaches. "If I continued my dinners I should be under the necessity of absenting myself from them, an incivility and want of respect for my reverend brethren..."[36] he said; but in reality he did not want to be bothered by the lower clergy and unimportant laymen of the Cathedral. He offered cash remuneration in place of the dinners, but his offer was spurned by the College of Minor Canons. At his insistence the dinners were abolished by the Chapter in 1843, and the minor canons and vicars-choral, who were deprived of their Sunday dinners, were compensated by an increment of §15 per year to be paid by the Cathedral.[37]

Sydney Smith is usually held up as an example of a highly principled man, and he was, but the issue of the dinners for the minor canons is an example of his violation of his own principle of the defense of existing rights. He had done so in his opposition to the rotten boroughs, but in that case it could be argued that the possessors of those rights had abused them; but no such claim can be made against the inoffensive vicars-choral and minor canons. Had Sydney been fully consistent he should have defended the dinners with his usual vigor (and under other circumstances he might well have done so), but in this instance it was a question of the established right of the minor canons and his present convenience, and he proved that he was less than selfless and less uniform in his principles. The issue was not a critical one, but his actions were less than genteel in his handling of it. Generally speaking, however, he adapted himself well to the conditions in the Cathedral Chapter, and although he had some differences of opinion with the Dean and another Canon, they do not appear to have been serious.[38]

Sydney was a controversial person, and it is interesting that William MacDonald Sinclair's <u>Memorials of</u>

St. Paul's Cathedral[39] does not mention him, while later works describe him as " a vigorous reformer, who threw himself into the affairs of the chapter and the improvement of their conduct",[40] or as a man of "character and enterprise" who was active in guiding and governing the Cathedral.[41]

G. L. Prestige in his history of St. Paul's says that Sydney's appointment was:

> ...not excessive recompose for his intellectual honesty, and passion for social justice, his independence of mind, his magnificently lucid prose, his exuberant imagination and antiseptic irony, his... common sense, and his devasting respectful disrespect for persons, not to mention a lifetime of practical service... to the poor.[42]

In most respects his statement is true, but the latter part of it reflects earlier opinions on Sydney Smith. It is demonstrably true that Sydney was a respecter of persons, perhaps even something of a snob, and he most emphatically did not devote his life to the service of the poor. On the other hand, the statement is quite correct in that, considering the rewards meted out for services performed, a stall at St. Paul's was not excessive compensation; and Sydney saw it as an inadequate reward for a lifetime of service in the Whig cause. He still aspired to be a bishop, even if he covered his eagerness with a denial of further ambition and a coy availability. In 1833 he wrote:

> Lord Grey is very well-I see a good deal of him-perhaps he may offer to make me a Bishop-but I doubt very much if I would accept it-My present Parsonage is most beautiful-and I shall never be so well off as I am-but after all the temptation may not come if it does I hope I shall not be such a fool as to yield to it-[43]

In October, 1834, Joseph Allen, then Canon of Westminister, was made Bishop of Bristol by the Whigs. The promotion, while not in itself objectionable to Sydney, who regarded the see of Bristol as "a very lean and ill-fed piece of preferment", aroused his ire, for in it he saw an old and familiar pattern of being passed over in preferment, more particularly because an ill-phrased statement from Lord Holland intimated, probably only too accurately, that he had not been considered for the position. On 17 November, 1834, he wrote to Lord Holland, protesting that:

> You said something the other night which gave me pain, not meaning I am sure to do so. You said I am not pleased with the appointment of Allen: Butler of Shrewsbury should have been the new Bishop. Now you have said to me an hundred times what pleasure it would give you to see me a Bishop, and that you had given my name to Canning for that purpose; have I done anything to forfeit your good opinion? Is there any one occasion where I have shrunk from expressing and defending Liberal opinions in Church and State? Is there any other clergyman who has done it so long, so much, and I think I may add so successfully? Why then do you pass me over now and not think me worthy even to be thought of, when before coming into office you expressed yourself so desirous of my elevation?
>
> I have no other right to put this question but as a friend of 40 years standing, and I should really be obliged to you to tell me whether I am to consider myself as entirely laid upon the shelf, and past over by that party for whom I have all my life hazarded so much abuse and misrepresentation. It is not that I care for being a Bishop. If the See of Bristol had been offered to me nothing would have induced me to take it—there is scarcely any Bishopric <u>I would</u> take; but I think I do not deserve the disgrace from my party of being past over and the dignity never offered to me.
>
> It is of little consequence perhaps to any party whether I adhere to it, or not; but I always shall adhere to my party whoever may be put over my head, because I have an ardent love of truth and

> justice, and they are its best defenders, but adhering to them under all circumstances I cannot but feel whether I am ill, or well treated by them.
>
> I do not write to complain of your change of opinion of me, but to lament it and to beg to know if it proceeds from any fault of mine. I also request you to tell me if I am to consider myself as permanently laid aside by the Whigs and expunged from the list of future Bishops.[44]

It is eminently clear from this letter that Sydney had not ceased to covet a mitre, and since his previous preferment from the Whigs had been bestowed for political reasons he expected further rewards from them. The Diocese of Bristol was not the question, and if it had been offered to him he might, despite the dignity of the title, have declined it; for he said, in a letter to Lord Holland:

> If any chance had remained of my being a Bishop I should probably (that I might not be suspected of interested motives) have said nothing about the matter,-but I cared much more for the <u>slight</u> than the <u>sacrifice</u>. I think your observation (unexplained) might in all fairness have led to the inference I drew from it without supposing in me any extraordinary degree of irritability; and if I <u>did</u> draw the inference you must in fairness admit it would be to any man a very painful one. I was the more easily led into the mistake because it so happens that I am utterly ignorant on what the claims of Dr. Butler consist. I have never heard that Butler had written anything which proved him to be a great Scholar, or a great Theologian, nor did I ever hear that in the worst times of Protestantism he had ever put himself <u>forward</u> as the friend of Catholic Emancipation, and sacrificed himself for his party. I do not <u>deny</u> that he may have done all this, but I can safely say that living with all sorts of people I never heard it, and I therefore imagined that he was one of those men of prudent

and suppressed Liberality who were selected not <u>for what he has done for friends</u>, but that he might <u>not alarm enemies</u>. A Ministry may think <u>it their duty</u> to do this; it <u>may</u> be their duty. I think otherwise, and don't call it mean or base, but <u>wrong</u> and <u>unjust</u>. I care very little what 3/4ths of the late cabinet think of me, but I care a good deal what <u>you</u> think of me. You have often said to me <u>"I would get drunk on the day you were made a Bishop"</u>. You then say that Butler ought to have been the man. I ask kindly and civilly for an explanation, and you say 'I am only one of many. If it had depended on me alone, from joint considerations of regard, and fairness I would have chosen <u>you</u>, from fitness alone, <u>Butler</u>. This is perfectly fair and I am obliged to you for taking the trouble to explain yourself to me, -but I wonder you should wonder at my feeling. And now there being an end of the Mitre for ever, I must say that Lord Grey, and the Cabinet, have chosen a man who instead of staunchly defending those bold Church measures for the destruction of the Irish Protestant Church and the payment of the Catholic Clergy which will become more necessary every day will (if I am rightly informed) be as great a Bigot and as foolish and blind a Churchman as any Bishop of the Bench. It is an appointment in which I'm sure the Ministry are 'wholly wrong'.45

The violence of Sydney's reaction obviously upset the Hollands, but their efforts to placate him, which were apparently something short of a promise of a mitre, seem to have fallen on deaf ears. In another letter, written on 25 November, he said:

Lord Holland (who before coming into Office had expressed so strongly and frequently his wish to see me a Bishop) tells me that he thinks another person ought to have been the man; it is very natural for me to say to myself What have I done?-why am I laid aside? why is Lord Holland's opinion changed? and feeling all this I am sure it was much wiser to express than to suppress it. The Contest was not about a Bishopric but about something of much greater Consequence, a slight and a degradation. Lord Holland has been so kind as to explain to me his views and opinions; I am much obliged to him for having done so, I am satisfied, and silent.

I never asked Lord Holland why he had not made me a Bishop, but why he thought I ought not to be one. I selected Lord Holland because he is the only person who (as far as I know) had ever expressed any wish to make me a Bishop, and the only person who told me that if Allen had not been the man it ought not to have been me. I now know that many others thought so but I did not know it before Lord Holland told me. To such members of the Cabinet I would say that they are a set of political Cowards not worth serving, who desert a bold and honest man who has always turned out in danger and difficulty for a prudent and plausible man who has done nothing for his party; but thank God I never acted from the hope of preferment but from the Love of Justice and truth which was bursting within me. When I began to express my opinions on Church politics what hope could any but a mad man have of gaining preferment by such politics what hope could any but a mad man have of gaining preferment by such a line of conduct?[46]

He deprecated the quality of the men elevated to bishoprics, largely on the basis of their political unreliability in the event of a critical question, and he largely exonerated his friend Lord Holland from the previously implied slight.

Lord Grey had stepped down as Prime Minister in July, 1834, giving way to Lord Melbourne, who occupied the post only until November. The Duke of Wellington held office provisionally until December when Sir Robert Peel formed a Tory government. During this interim, since the Whigs had no preferment to offer, Sydney had little to complain about, but when Peel resigned and was replaced again by Melbourne, he opened a new campaign for the episcopal dignity. On 18 April, 1835, he wrote to Lord Holland:

> I wrote you some time since when you were out of office about being a Bishop. My own opinion of myself is that I should make a very good Bishop, that I should be a firm defender of Liberal opinions, and I hope I am not too much a man of honor to take an office without fashioning my manners and conversation so as not to bring it into discredit.
>
> You have said and written that you wish to see me a Bishop, and I have no doubt would try to carry your wishes into effect. If proper vacancies had occured in the beginning of Lord Grey's administration I believe this would have been done. Other politicians have succeeded who entertain no such notion and Lord Melbourne always thinks _that_ man best qualified for any office whom he had seen and known the least. Liberals of the eleventh hour abound, and there are some of the first hour of whose work in the toil and heat of the day I have no recollection. These are the obstacles to my promotion; but there is a greater obstacle and that is that I have entirely lost all wish to be a Bishop; the thought is erased from my mind, and in the very improbable event of a Bishopric offered to me I would steadily refuse it; in this I am perfectly honest and sincere and I make this communication to you to prevent your friendly exertion in my favor, and perhaps to spare you the regret of making that exertion in vain.[47]

On the face of it, this is a clear enough statement that he no longer aspired to the episcopal dignity; but at the same time he affirmed his fitness for that office, and he left the door of the refusal of promotion not tightly shut, but ajar enough for a dignified refusal of an unattractive diocese. A month later he wrote to Lady Holland, asserting, after Lord John Russell had suffered a hostile public reception, that:

> You always accuse me of grumbling against my party. As a refutation of that calumny, I send you my declaration of faith. I will take good care you shall never make me a bishop; but if all your future Whig bishops would speak out as plainly, Little Johns would not be driven away from large counties. Lord Melbourne always thinks that man best qualified for any office, of whom he has seen and known the least. Liberals of the eleventh hour abound! and there are some of the first hour, of whose works in the toil and heat of the day I have no recollection.[48]

By this time Sydney seems to have reconciled himself to the fact that he was not going to become a bishop. His political activities and friends had carried him near the top, but then, after about 1835, it became evident that his solely political claims to promotion were not enough for the leaders of the Whig party to risk the alienation of important interests by granting him further preferment. His earlier claims that he had been held back in the Church because of his bold and liberal opinions were not particularly valid, for he had received substantial rewards throughout his clerical career. A see was denied to him not because of his liberal principles, but because England was changing while Sydney steadfastly held the same liberal ground he had stood on years before the Age of Reform began. He had been a reformer, but the reforms he desired had largely been accomplished. He was a responsible clergyman, but changes in the Church were taking place that he neither understood nor approved; he still viewed the Church as the archaic institution into which he had been ordained in the eighteenth century. The center of power in the Whig party was shifting, and it was shifting away from those young liberals he had cultivated early in the century, for they too were advancing in years and receding in their enthusiasm for up-to-date ideas. Lord Grey's Administration had indeed been his last, great hope for a mitre, and it had by-passed him in the interest of political expediency. For these reasons it became clear that there would be no offer of a bishopric for Sydney Smith, and he reluctantly accepted it. It is only in this light that his Letters to Archdeacon Singleton can be understood.

Between February, 1837, and February, 1839, Sydney published three open letters to Thomas Singleton, Archdeacon of Northumberland, who suggested the letters as a protest against proposed changes in the Church. The Whigs advocated new sees to be carved out of the old ones in the populous areas, new urban parishes, and a commission to manage episcopal and cathedral endowments, but they were unable to accomplish any of their goals before turning the government over to Peel in 1834. Peel, like most Englishmen of the age, recognised the need for some reform, and he, following the Whig plan, appointed a commission of inquiry to look into various reforms of the Church. It recommended, in 1835, formation of new sees, reorganization of the older dioceses, and the reduction of income among the richest dioceses. The Whigs returned to power under Lord Melbourne in 1835, and passed several acts dealing with tithes, pluralism, and the subdivision of parishes; and they appointed a permanent board of ecclesiastical commissioners to supervise the revenues which were to be appropriated from episcopal and cathedral sources as a result of the earlier recommendations. In 1836 the commission of inquiry recommended that cathedral chapters be restricted to a dean and four canons, and that much of their remaining revenue be used to supplement poor livings, elsewhere in the Church.

It was this latter recommendation that set Sydney into motion once again, and really for the last time, as a controversialist. He had never held bishops in excessive awe, regarding them chiefly as well-paid administrators who were appointed for political reasons; and although there is no evidence that he was less than obedient to his clerical superiors, he was no more than obedient, and he clearly understood his rights in the Church and the extent of the bishops' authority over him. He became more antipathetic towards the bishops after 1834 because they dominated the commissions, and because the commissions did not, he believed, concern themselves with the best interests of the parochial clergy, but rather left them "...to be tormented by Laws and by Bishops, as frogs and rabbits are given up to the experiments of Philosophers."[49] He opposed the Whig bills in 1834, especially that on pluralities, which would, he said, "...make the clergy contemptible in a rich country for their poverty, and vexatious from their fanaticism";[50] and he opposed restrictions on residence requirements which would make it more difficult for the country clergy to introduce their families to London society and manners.[51] During Peel's brief tenure of office Sydney was dismayed by the apparent intention to reform the Church extensively, the Tory bill being, in his own words, "a much more severe bill than the Whiggs could have ventured upon."52 He was discreet enough in his dealing with bishops, but in May, 1834, nearly three years before his major publication on the Ecclesiastical Commission, he showed that he was no more obsequious to Church hierarchs than he was to titled aristocrats. In his position as Canon of St. Paul's Cathedral he had become involved in the administration of the vicarage of Edmonton, Middlesex, which was a populous and rich living, worth nearly $1500 per year.53 Charles James Blomfield, Bishop of London, urged the subdivision of Edmonton in order that it might be better served, and Sydney replied:

> I observe in bishops a great readiness to break in pieces the larger livings of their diocese, but none in those who have the better sees to dedicate any portion of their own superior emoluments to the improvement of smaller Bishoprics....if the Laity are to be conciliated by putting an end to the inequalities of the Church property it is a striking injustice not to begin where that inequality is the greatest and most visible....
>
> There is not...enough of property in the Church to pay to each man a decent competence; they must therefore be paid by a lottery of Preferment, some more, some less. I do not want to lessen the value of your See, and to give it to others... If there is an undissolved Bishop of London there may surely be an integral Vicar of Edmonton.
>
> I see no reason why the Parish may not go on quite as well with a Curate under the Rector as with a small autocratical clergyman in the midst of it, and if a Bishop can exercise a pastoral care over 300 Parishes, a vicar may easily do so over one chapel of ease close to his own residence.54

Bishop Blomfield replied quickly and urbanely to Sydney's letters, granting him his "full and free permission to urge the expediency of dividing the larger Bishoprics, and of abolishing Cathedral sinecures, as earnestly...as I have urged...the propriety of dividing the Vicarage of Edmonton...."55 To the Bishop's reply Sydney wrote a second letter on 10 May, 1834, in which he again rejected the Bishop's request, reasserting his argument that since there was not enough wealth in the endowments "to give a competence to all, therefore it is expedient that Church property should remain as it is, unequally divided." If Church properties were to be divided, he added, the great inequalities, such as existed in bishoprics, should be divided <u>first</u>. He reiterated his lottery argument; that since the Church could not pay every clergyman adequately in money, they had to be paid in hope. He accused the Bishop of "correcting small errors on our side of the hedge and only intending to correct much larger ones on yours." He pointed out that he had been inadequately compensated for a number of years, but that he had remained in the Church in hopes of becoming a Canon of St. Paul's, and that the Bishop had done similar service in the expectation of becoming a bishop. He suspected that the Bishop wanted not only to subdivide the living, but also to attach the patronage to himself, and he restated his assertion that a vicar could oversee a curate better than a bishop could supervise five or six hundred parishes.56

In these two letters Sydney's basic reasons for his hostility to the Ecclesiastical Commission may be seen; his suspicion of the ambitions of the bishops, and his desire to prevent any significant reform in the Church. He had accepted the fact that he was not to be a bishop, which did not endear the episcopal office to him, and he was securely ensconced in a position that was safe from episcopal wrath. He had affection for the Church, but his love was for it was for the Church of his youth. Despite his failure to win a mitre, the Church had not done badly by him. He made every effort to make his opposition appear to be that of an upright individual defying the exercise of arbitrary power, but it was actually the dogged resistance of a disappointed man to change. He was to say over and over again that he was not opposed to reform in the Church, but in every instance he hinged his approval of change on impossible conditions. He began his <u>First Letter to Archdeacon Singleton</u> by saying:

> As you do me the honour to ask my opinion respecting the constitution and proceedings of the Ecclesiastical Commission,

and of their conduct to the Dignitaries of the Church, I shall write to you without any reserve upon this subject.

The first thing which excited my surprise, was the Constitution of the Commission. As the reform was to comprehend every branch of Churchmen, Bishops, Dignitaries, and Parochial Clergyman, I cannot but think it would have been more advisable to have added to the Commission some members of the two lower orders of the Church-they would have supplied that partial knowledge which appears in so many of the proceedings of the Commissioners to have been wanting-they would have attended to those interests (not episcopal) which appear to have been so completely overlooked-and they would have screened the Commission from those charges of injustice and partiality which are now so generally brought against it. There can be no charm in the name of Bishop-the man who was a Curate yesterday is a Bishop today. There are many Prebendaries, many rectors, and many Vicars, who would have come to the Reform of the Church with as much integrity, wisdom, and vigour, as any Bishop on the Bench; and I believe, with a much stronger recollection that all the orders of the Church were not to be sacrificed to the highest; and that to make their work respectable, and lasting, it should, in all (even its minutest provisions), be founded upon justice.[57]

Sydney said that the failure of the Ecclesiastical Commission to include dignitaries and parochial clergymen was an example of "contempt and neglect", which was further proven by the fact that of seven communications sent by the cathedrals to the Commission, the receipt of six was not even acknowledged. He accused the Commission of attempting too much, in that it should only have found out what abuses were causing complaint and corrected them. Instead, he said, the Commission was attempting to perform major surgery on an aged and infirm institution. Any changes it made should agree "as much as possible with institutions already established." The real solution, Sydney maintained, was to combine "wealth and labour", and as aged Prebendaries died off, to annex their stalls to populous parishes. The monies thus appropriated in localities should be expended in those localities, and "All patronage would have been left as it was."[58]

He said that the real object of the reform should not be to equalize all livings or to add a pittance to numerous small livings, but to "remove the causes of hatred" and envy by reducing great incomes, such as those of the bishops. He noted that there were over thirty-five hundred livings ranging in value from §50 to §125, and that to raise them all to §200 would cost more than §371,000, which could not be raised by the confiscations. The most the Commission could hope to raise would be about §130,000 a year, so the situation was hopeless; and it was made more hopeless by the fact that gentlemen did not enter the Church in hopes of a decent living of §200 or §250 a year, but in hopes of a mitre and a substantial salary. Since the country could not or would not pay its priests equitably, and since it demanded gentlemen of culture and learning in the clergy, it could only pay them by lottery.[59]

Sydney realized the objections that might be made to his approach to the Ecclesiastical Commission, and he observed that:

> This it will be said is a Mammonish view of the subject; it is so, but those who make this objection, forget the immense effect which Mammon produces upon religion itself. Shall the Gospel he preached by men paid by the State? shall these men be taken from the lower orders and be meanly paid? shall they be men of learning and education? and shall there be some magnificent endowments to allure such men into the Church? Which of these methods is the best for diffusing the rational doctrines of Christianity? not in the age of the apostles, not in the abstract, timeless, nameless, placeless land of the philosophers, but in the year 1837, in the porterbrewing, cotton-spinning, tallow-melting kingdom of Great Britain, bursting with opulence, and flying from poverty as the greatest of human evils... I must take this people with all their follies, and prejudices, and circumstances,

and carve out an establishment best suited for them, however unfit for early Christianity in barren and conquered Judea.[60]

Sydney accused the Archbishop of Canterbury of violating his oath to protect the rights and privileges of the Church of Canterbury, when "...as Chairman...he siezes the patronage of that Church, takes two thirds of its Revenues, and abolishes two thirds of its Members." He recalled earlier Tory insistence on the sanctity of George III's oath of office, which had prevented him from emancipating the Catholics, and compared it with the actions of some bishops who had then stood by the King's oath, but who now violated their own solemnly-taken oaths to protect and defend the Church.[61]

He attacked the Whig government's overdone veneration of bishops, for, as he said:

> ...I remember the case of a Bishop, dead not six years ago, who was scarcely ever seen in the House of Lords, or in his diocese; and I remember well also the indignation with which the inhabitants of a great Cathedral Town spoke of the conduct of another Bishop (now also deceased) who not only never entered his palace, but turned his horses into the garden.[62]

Sydney realized that he was putting the fat into the fire, and, anticipating charges against himself, he hurried to place the blame for an unseemly clerical brawl on his opponents:

> This squabble about patronage is said to be disgraceful. Those who mean to be idle, and insolent, because they are at peace, may look out of the window and say, "This is a disgraceful squabble between Bishops and Chapters:" But those who mean to be just, should ask, Who begins? the real disgrace of the squabble is in the attack, and not in the defense. If any man puts his hand into my pocket to take my property, am I disgraced if I prevent him?[63]

He did not deny past wrongdoing in the handling of patronage by cathedral chapters, but he asserted that they were not the only malefactors, and that the bishops were at least equally guilty of nepotism. He made note that Deans and Chapters served as safeguards against episcopal rapacity in the instance of concurrent leases, to which he added:

> This view of Chapters if of course overlooked by a Commission of Bishops, just as all mention of bridles would be omitted in a meeting of horses; but in this view Chapters might be made eminently useful. In what profession, too, are there no gradations? Why is the Church of England to be nothing but a collection of Beggars and Bishops-the Right Reverend Dives in the palace, and Lazarus in orders at the gate, doctored by dogs, and comforted with crumbs?[64]

Sydney pointed out that the old Cathedrals had been in the possession of their rights for over seven hundred years, and the newer ones since the reign of Henry VIII, which, in virtually all cases, was longer than the Members of Parliament had owned their properties. Nonetheless, he said, the rights and privileges of the cathedrals were to be torn away "without the least warning, or preparation", and not by low-born rebels, but by the bishops and archbishops themselves.[65]

The Ecclesiastical Commission proposed to strip the patronage from the cathedrals and to bestow it on the bishops, who, despite their past record of nepotism, would presumably administer it most justly, honorably, and equitably, or at least so they promised. Sydney wryly commented that "we are ready to promise as well as the Bishops", and he felt compelled to add that the assumption that the bishops would be held in check by public opinion was erroneous, and that:

> ...five years hence the public eye will no more see what description of men are promoted by Bishops, than it will see what Doctors of Law are promoted by the Turkish Uhlema-and at the end of this period...the <u>public eye</u> turned in every direction may not be able to see any Bishops at all.[66]

Sydney mentioned the fact that bishops too could be biased, and that they had not only used their offices for their own advancement, and that of their families, but that they discriminated against their clergy for reasons of doctrine and politics; and that when aged, their preferment was frequently distributed by sons, daughters, wives, or even butlers and valets. Cathedrals might be venal with their patronage, but at least, he said, they had never sold their patronage openly, as had certain archbishops, for the "options" of an archbishop became his personal property, and in the event of his dying in debt they could be put up for public auction.[67]

In a succeeding paragraph Sydney raised an even more troublesome problem that had been avoided by the Ecclesiastical Commission: lay patronage. Laymen were the patrons of many livings, and they were free to bestow them on friends or relatives, or to sell them, pocketing as much of the income of the living as they chose. The Ecclesiastical Commission did not trouble the lay proprietors, however, he said, because they were powerful, but the cathedrals and the parochial clergy were without friends on the commission.[68]

In response to the plea that if the Church did not acquiesce in these changes it would be swept away by "democratic" reforms, he replied:

> Be it so; I am quite ready to be swept
> away when the time comes. Every body
> has their favorite death; some delight
> in apoplexy, and others prefer marasmus.
> I would infinitely rather be crushed
> by democrats, than, under the plea of
> the public good, be mildly and blandly
> absorbed by Bishops.[69]

He followed up this passage by his famous account of a supposed Dutch chronicle, one of his finest pieces of satire, in which he described a meeting of the Dutch clergy, who met in two bodies, bishops and archbishops in one, and Deans and Canons in another. Despite the local famine a feast had been prepared for the clergy, but no sooner had the archbishop finished saying grace than a mob began to stone the palace, shouting for bread and against bishops. In a panic, the upper clergy immediately cast down their dinner to the rioters, then,

> ...you might have seen my Lords standing,
> with empty plates, and looking wistfully
> at each other, till Simon of Gloucester,

he who disputed with Leoline the Monk, stood up among them and said, 'Good my Lords, is it your pleasure to stand here fasting, and that those who count lower in the Church than you do should feast and fluster? Let us order to us the dinner for the Deans and Canons, which is making ready for them in the chamber below.' And this speech of Simon of Gloucester pleased the Bishops much; and so they sent for the host, one William of Ypres, and told him it was for the public good, and he, much fearing the Bishops, brought them the dinner of the Deans and Cannons; and so the Deans and Cannons went away without dinner, and were pelted by the men of the town, because they had not put any meat out of the window like the Bishops; and when the Count came to hear of it, he said it was a pleasant conceit, and that the Bishops were right cunning men, and had ding'd the Canons well."[70]

Sydney's point was, of course, that the bishops claimed to be making great sacrifices, but that they were spoliating the cathedrals of more revenue and patronage than they were giving up, and yet the general opinion was that the bishops were acting disinterestedly while the cathedrals were being selfish. He accused the Bishop of London of trying to be the most powerful clergyman since Archibishop Laud, and he added that it was most painful to contemplate that the Ecclesiastical Commission had been established by the Whigs, who had delegated such extensive and unchecked authority to him.[71]

The errors of the bill, Sydney said, were a public matter, but the injury done to men like himself was private and personal, and he demanded that existing patronage should be left as it was during the lives of the incumbents. Livings should not be divided during the lives of incumbents without their consent. He deplored the rashness and indescretions of the Ecclesiastical Commission, and their "contempt for existing institutions", and he said that it was ominous that Lord John Russell had stated in the House of Commons that "we showed no disposition to make any sacrifices for the good of the Church." As far as Sydney Smith was concerned, it had not been demonstrated that the proposed alterations were in the best interest of the Church. He rejoined that he was a "sincere advocate for Church reform", but that the odium should be removed from the establishment without injustice, and he credited the lay Commissioners with good intentions but undue and misplaced trust in bishops. He protested that the Commission had been rushed into premature reforms by fear of the mob, and the "impetuosity of one man, who cannot be brought to believe that wisdom often consists in leaving alone, standing still and doing nothing."[72]

Well known for his wealth and pluralism, Sydney defended himself in advance against charges of being a "rich and overgrown Churchman":

> Till thirty years of age I never received a farthing from the Church, then §50 per annum for two years-then nothing for ten years- then §500 per annum, increased for two or three years to §800 till, in my grand climacteric I was made Canon of St. Paul's; and before that period, I had built a Parsonage-house with farm offices for a large farm, which cost me §4000, and had reclaimed another from ruins at the expense of §2000. A lawyer, or a Physician in good practice, would smile at this picture of great Ecclesiastical wealth; and yet I am considered as a perfect monster of Ecclesiastical prosperity.[73]

He concluded his letter, offering an olive branch to the Whigs, who, he said, he did not wish to offend, for he had been one of their number before the birth of many of them, and when still others had been active Tories. Their fights had been his fights, and he reminded them that among clergymen he alone had turned out to support them, and that his liberality then had condemned him "to the grossest obloquy, and the most hopeless poverty." He said that he believed that the Whigs had risked the destruction of national institutions in their domestic reforms. But, he added:

> In the mean time, the old friends of, and the old sufferers for, liberty, do not understand this new meanness, and are not a little astonished to find their leaders prostrate on their knees before the Lords of the Church, and to receive no other answer from them than that, if they are

disturbed in their adulation, they will immediately resign![74]

Sydney's First Letter to Archdeacon Singleton received a mixed reception, but no reaction was more forceful than that of Lord Melbourne, who wrote to Lady Holland:

> Do not dream of making Sydney Smith anything. It would now offend every party in the country. His pamphlet disgusted the High Church, the religious of the Low Church never liked him, and, as a politician, he was never popular with those who go principally by politics.[75]

On the other hand, evidently some clergymen sided with him in his opposition to Church reform, for they, too, approved of the prizes to which they might aspire, and William IV was considering the further enrichment of some dioceses at that same time.[76] Archdeacon Singleton richly approved of his actions, and told him that"... it seems to me that you have a chance of more effectually serving and saving the Church of England than any individual has ever enjoyed."[77] Sydney was far more concerned about the preservation of established privilege than he was with ill-paid curates, who, he felt, should either be independently wealthy or satisfied with their lot, and he was by no means alone in his desire.

He had written the First Letter in a rage, and, as he wrote to Lady Ashburton on 9 January, 1837:

> My attack on the Bishops - or rather I should say my defense of the Prebendaries appears at Longmans-on the 15th.-... I hope you will not think it too severe but the truth is I wrote it to save my Life-I should have died of bile, and rage but for this remedy-[78]

Shortly afterwards a political friend commended the letter. "You have cut it somewhat sharply", he said, "but, I believe not more so than was requisite..."[79] C. K. Murray, Secretary to the Ecclesiastical Commission, spurred by Sydney's publication, had replied on 23 January, 1837, to his charge that of seven chapter memorials addressed to the Commission only one had been acknowledged, asserting that the oversight was his, and extending explanations

and apologies.[80] Sydney retorted skillfully, placing the
blame on the Commissioners for presumably instructing
Murray to ignore their petitions.[81] In a letter to Lady
Ashburton he boasted that he had "broke his head...I
hope in several places".[82] The Bishop of London, obviously
discomposed by the violence of Sydney's public attack,
wrote to ask what harm there was in the Commission's proposals regarding St. Paul's, to which Sydney replied that
the proposals were grossly unjust to the canons, and that
the making of them shook the confidence of the public in
the bishops. He threatened to make further statements
that might "surprise the public not a little", and which,
if they injured the Church, would not be his responsibility but that of the bishops for starting the controversy.
He predicted that the cathedrals would be in ruins within a short time and the Church of England ended, but he
advised the Bishop to be cheerful and to consider emigration, along with the rest of the clergy, to the United
States.[83]

  The attention he received from his First Letter to
Archdeacon Singleton did not inspire any undue humility
in Sydney, who began his second letter with:

> It is a long time since you have heard
> from me, and in the mean time the poor
> Church of England has been trembling,
> from the Bishop who sitteth upon the
> throne, to the Curate who rideth upon
> the hackney horse. I began writing on
> the subject to avoid bursting from indignation; and as it is not my habit to
> recede, I will go on till the Church of
> England is either up or down-semianimous
> on its back, or vigorous on its legs.[84]

Although opposed to reform in the Church generally, he
seemed to have reconciled himself to the necessity for
some change, and he suggested that while resident Prebendaries, like himself, performed important functions,
those who were non-resident performed no function at
all, and could be safely abolished without serious detriment to the Church. He believed that Prebends did no
harm, and in many instances they did a great deal of good
in providing for men of learning or piety. He assumed
that a "parliament of Curates" would prefer "splendid
hope, and the expectation of good fortune in advanced
life" to a miserable equalization of salaries.[85]

Sydney pointed out that great opportunity existed in the Church for the lower classes to improve themselves. A successful baker, for example, might see little chance for his son in the government, but the Church was a different store:

> Young Crumpet is sent to school-takes to his books-spends the best years of his life, as all Englishmen do, in making Latin verses-knows that the crum in crum-pet is long, and pet short-goes on to the University-gets a prize for an Essay on the Dispersion of the Jews-takes orders-becomes a Bishop's chaplain-has a young nobleman for his pupil-publishes an useless classic, and a serious call to the unconverted-and then goes through the Elysian transitions of Prebendary, Dean, Prelate, and the long train of purple, profit, and power.[86]

He also defended the multiplicity of Church offices on the grounds that there needed to be many offices, in order to reward a few deserving men, for the very good reason that aristocrats and bishops would intrude their tutors and sycophants into many of the available places. He said that he had feared for the Church in the period before the reform of Parliament, but that Russell had carried out enough reform, and no further changes were needed. He charged Lord Melbourne with false indifference to the Church, and feigned ignornace of the issues involved. Rather strangely, and very much out of keeping with his previous pronouncements on the monarch, he denounced the sacrifice of a great deal of the patronage of the Crown. "... and when every atom of power and patronage ought to be husbanded for the Crown." His unprecedented support may be explained by his growing conservatism, for he had enough of reform, and he complained that further change was contemplated in copyright laws, church rates, imprisonment for debt, the cathedrals, voting by ballot, the Septennial Act, Corn laws, voting by proxy in the House of Lords, county rates, primogeniture, and in the privileges of the universities. "In a fortnight's time", he said,

> Lord John Russell is to take possession of, and to re-partition all the cathedrals in England; and what a prelude for the young Queen's coronation! what a medal for august ceremony!-the fallen

Gothic buildings on one side of the gold, the young Protestant Queen on the other:-

> And then, when she is fill of noble devices, and of all sorts enchantingly beloved, and amid the solemn swell of music, when her heart beats happily, and her eyes look Majesty, she ...shudders to see she is stalking to the throne of her Protestant ancestors over the broken altars of God. 87

Sydney admitted the right of Parliament to deal with the cathedrals, but he believed such action to be "inexpedient, uncalled for, and mischievous", undesired by the lower clergy, and that it would depress the quality of men entering the Church and accustom the public to confiscations. He returned to his mammonish theme, implying, quite probably with a great deal of justice, that the bishops were as mammonish as he was, for when they had decided to enrich small livings they proposed to do so, not by reducing their own swollen salaries, but by seizing the revenues of the cathedrals. Why, he said, should the Archbishop of Canterbury have two palaces and §15000 a year, and the Bishop of London have a palace at Fulham and a house in St. James' and §10000, when the same functions could be carried on for half the cost?

> Is it necessary that the Archbishop of Canterbury should give feasts to Aristocratic London; and that the domestics of the Prelacy should stand with swords and bag-wigs round pig, and turkey, and venison, to defend as it were, the Orthodox gastronome from the fierce Unitarian, the fell Baptist, and all the famished children of dissent? I don't object to all this; because I am sure that the method of prizes and blanks is the best method of supporting a Church which must be considered as very slenderly endowed, if the whole were equally divided among the parishes....I could not, as a conscientious man, leave the Archbishop of Canterbury with §15,000 a year, and make a fund by annihilating

Residentiaries of Bristol of §1500.[88]

It was plain to Sydney Smith that the confiscations were punitive and partial because only bishops were represented on the Commission, but he warned them, that having protected their interests by despoiling the cathedral, the day would come when the government would demand control of all the property of the Church. This would throw the bishops into hysterics, but their frenzies would not save their salaries, or the Church; and he envisaged a print of the sordid scene that would come to pass:

> "The Bishops's Saturday Night; or, Lord John Russell at the Pay-Table."
>
> The Bishops should be standing before the pay-table, and receiving their weekly allowance; Lord John and Spring Rice counting, ringing, and biting the sovereigns, and the Bishop of Exeter insisting that the Chancellor of the Exchequer has given him one which was not weight. Viscount Melbourne, in high chuckle, should be standing, with his hat on, and his back to the fire, delighted with the contest; and the Deans and Canons should be in the back-ground, waiting till their turn came, and the Bishops were paid; and among them a Canon, of large composition, urging them on not to give way too much to the Bench. Perhaps I should add the President of the Board of Trade, recommending the truck principle to the Bishops, and offering to pay them in hassocks, cassocks, aprons, shovel-hats, sermoncases, and such like ecclesiastical gear.[89]

He felt that the Whig changes were empty-headed, and he proposed the use of a "foolometer, the acquaintance and society of three of four regular British fools" as a guide to the establishment of further policy. Even the fools, he said, would have seen the errors in the proposed bills. He also chose to attack Lord John Russell, of whom he said:

> There is not a better man in England

than Lord John Russell; but his worst
failure is, that he is utterly ignorant
of all moral fear; there is nothing he
would not undertake. I believe he would
perform the operation for the stone-
build St. Peter's -or assume (with or
without ten minutes' notice) the command of the Channel Fleet; and no one
would discover by his manner that the
patient had died-the Church tumbled
down-and the Channel Fleet been knock-
ed to atoms. I believe his motives
are always pure, and his measures often able; but they are endless, and
never done with that pendentous pace
and pedentous mind in which it behoves the
wise and virtuous improver to walk. He
alarms the wise liberals; and it is impossible to sleep soundly while he has the
command of the watch.[90]

Sydney began his third letter by asserting that he was thoroughly tired of the subject, although his opinion was unchanged, and that the third would be his last letter. He said that the impending Plurality and Residence Bill was now a good bill, but only because of the "material alterations for the better since it came out of the hands of the Commission, and all bearing materially upon...the parochial clergy", or, in other words, change which had been brought about by the publication of his earlier let- ters. He continued his defense of the cathedrals, deny- ing the allegation that since they were not parochial they performed little spiritual service in the Church. It was true, he admitted, that the "Vicar of St. Fiddlefrid" did not officiate at Westminster Abbey, but did not the cathe- drals "in the most material points instruct the people precisely in the same manner as the parochial Clergy?". It was quite possible, he insisted, that there could be as much piety in cathedrals as in the most "roadless, post- less, melancholy, sequestered hamlet preached to by the most provincial, sequestered bucolic Clergyman in the Queen's dominions".[91]

He persisted in his attacks on the Whigs for their seizure of cathedral endowments, and their application of them to other purposes, which was, he said, nothing less than robbery. He also said no one was a greater robber than the public, which chose to have an established Church, but without making adequate provision for it, and then it seized properties intended for other purposes to make up the deficiency. The most culpable of the robbers were the prelates of the Ecclesiastical Commission, on whose tombs he proposed to inscribe:..."<u>under their auspices and by their counsels the destruction of the English Church be</u>gan..." To Sydney the concern of the bishops for providing "<u>spiritual food</u>" for the sheep having no shepherd" amounted to no more than "if one affected powerfully by a charity sermon were to put his hand in another man's pocket, and cast, a liberal contribution into the plate ...".92

In this last letter he returned to his claim that the "lottery" system and the hopes of advancement in the Church brought not only men of quality into the Church, but also their capital. "Such men", he said, "intend to do their duty, and they do it; but the duty is, however, not the motive, but the adjunct." The parochial clergy maintained themselves at least as much on their own resources as on the revenues they received from the Church; and he compared the private resources of seven Anglican clergyman who received about a total salary of about §32000, but who brought about §72,000 into the Church, with seven dissenting ministers who he said, were collectively worth no more than §6000. Thus excellent clergy were obtained by the Church of England, but:

> ...to destroy this wise and well-working arrangement, a great number of Bishops, Marquises, and John Russells, are huddled into a chamber, and after proposing a scheme which will turn the English Church into a collection of consecrated beggers, we are informed by the Bishop of London that it is a <u>Holy Innovation</u>.93

Sydney described the plan of the Bishop of London as a "ptochogony-a generation of beggers." The Bishop proposed, he said, to create a thousand new livings, each worth §130; and the result would be a thousand miserable clergymen "unfit for the society of the better classes, and dragging about the English curse of poverty." He suggested that in place of the hope for advancement that then existed in the clergy, the Bishop should substitute an oath to hire the most promising as his butler or gardener. To bring the entire clergy up to a respectable income, and to provide decent housing for each, would require §2,500,000 beyond the present income of the Church; and to divide the cathedral endowments among all the clergy would raise their salaries only by §5/12/6½, so the situation should be left as it was. If the proposed changes were adopted the clergy would become "fanatical and ignorant...their habits would be low and mean, and ...they would be despised." In the place of the learned and pious gentlemen who then made up the Anglican clergy, the average clergyman of the Church of the future would be:

> ...ordinary, uninteresting.,..obese,dumpy, neither ill-natured nor good-natured; neither learned, nor ignorant, striding over the stiles to Church, with a second-rate wife-dusty and deliquescent-and four parochial children, full of catechism and butter; or let him be seen in one of those Shem-Ham-and-Japhet buggies-made on Mount Ararat soon after the subsidence of the waters, driving in the High Street of Edmonton; among all his pecuniary, saponaceous, oleaginous parishioners.[94]

Sydney defended himself from charges by the Bishop of Gloucester of being a scoffer and a jester, language which, he suggested, was "rather too close an imitation of that language which is used in the apostolic occupation of trafficking in fish..." If he were impious, it was because he had struggled against the penal laws and those against Catholics and dissenters, which the bishops had defended, and "if it was impious to struggle for their abrogation, I have indeed led an ungodly life." One bishop speculated on why he had been made Canon of St. Paul's, to which Sydney replied that if such speculation was fair, why not speculate on why each bishop had been elevated? He took pride, he said, in claiming articles in the Edinburgh Review, and he refused to disguise "himself in another's man wit, and to have received a reward to which I was not entitled." He had prepared stern punishment for the Bishop of Gloucester, but he had abandoned it on reading the Bishop's appeal for Divine assistance in his intellect, adding that he wished every Christian might have such an acute awareness of his shortcomings. He concluded that the passage of the bill would be the beginning of the end for the Church of England, but, "Whatever happens, I am not to blame; I have fought my fight.-Farewell."[95]

The value of Sydney's struggle against the Ecclesiastical Commission and the Deans and Chapters Bill is still debatable. On the positive side he won the support of many clergymen and some laymen who favored the continuation of the traditional inequalities; and he did delay the passage of some legislation that was perhaps hasty and ill-considered. On the other hand, he opened a very public breach in the Church with an unseemly controversy, which all too often descended to name-calling and preposterous charges; and his actions neither hastened the reform in the Church that he himself admitted was needed, nor did he put forth any real alternative for the needed expansion and up-dating of the Church. It was a personal triumph in that his pen and his wit were more than equal to the task, but it was a hollow victory in that, apart from giving him the opportunity of venting his spleen and delighting his supporters, he stood to gain little by his actions. Lady Holland believed that:

> ...the <u>mischief is done</u> by his former publication; but he is shutting the door closer to a Bishopric, as the Archbishop would strongly resist any disposition in his favor from the Ministry ....he is woefully deficient in tacte....[96]

It is quite clear, however, that although she may still have hoped for a bishopric for Sydney, he had given up the hope, and quite possibly the aspiration. He was becoming too old, and he was now definitely too controversial, and it would appear that the sin he committed in writing of his letters to Archdeacon Singleton was not one of deficiency of tact, but one of a lack of solicitude for certain proprieties after the avenues of further advancement had been closed. His pronouncements towards the bishops may have been at least partially justified by the existing conditions, but they were extremely indiscreet.

Sydney defended his assults on the bishops on the grounds that he had only reacted against their illegal and unprecedented activities; for, as he said, "A man is not to play the part of a revolutionary desperada, & to consider after that, that his Cassock and Mitre render him invulnerable."[97] His political friends were even more perturbed by his attacks on the Whigs, and Lord Carlisle wrote that he had read Sydney's second letter with sorrow, both because he had ridiculed the bishops, and because he had impugned the motives of his old friends and patrons.[98] Sydney replied to Lord Carlisle in a revealing letter that said:

> I have as a professional man opposed myself to the folly & unjustice of the

> Government, upon the church question a
> Government which has treated me with
> the greatest inattention & Neglect.
> -This last is not a reason why I should
> attack them, but it is a reason why I should
> spare them...[99]

He went on to say that he was indifferent to the continuation of the Whigs in office, and while he had respect and affection for his friends in the Government, he resented the "double injustice done to my profession and myself", and under similar circumstance he would act accordingly. In September, 1838, he wrote to Lord Lansdowne to express his indifference to further legislation on the Church, reserving only his right "in shilling pamphlets to protest that we are the most injured, persecuted, and ill-treated persons on the fact of the Earth."[100] On 25 February, 1839, Lord John Russell proposed certain alterations in the number of Canons of St. Paul's to the Chapter, and that their patronage be shared between a canon appointed by the Bishop and one appointed by the Crown.[101] The Dean and Chapter replied in a firm and dignified negative, defending the status quo but leaving the door open for some future change. The Chapter Minute Book recorded that:

> This Chapter is of opinion that the
> wisest plan would be to leave the Church
> as it is-but if alterations must be made,
> it appears to them that a Bill founded
> upon the following principles would be
> much preferable to the Bill now under
> consideration....
>
> 1st Vested interests to be completely
>   protected, including in that expression-Patronage
> 2nd The various dignified preferments
>   of the Church to be left just as
>   they are at present exist-and not
>   to be either diminished or augmented in point of number.
> 3rd Such preferments after the next
>   avoidance to be put in different
>   schedules of Tascation so as to
>   raise an effective fund for the
>   improvement of small livings.
>
> The dean and Chapter will not offer any
> opposition to a Bill founded on those

principles.[102]

In a letter to the London *Times* on 13 April, 1839, Sydney defended himself against newspaper attacks, claiming that he was not opposed to all reform in the Church, and offering, as evidence, a plan to abolish sinecures in the Church and to limit the salaries of Deans of cathedrals to §2000 and Prebendaries to §1000.[103] It was not a particularly ambitious or imaginative reform plan, but it did reflect his acquiescence in limited reforms that did not affect his privileges, yet it hardly served as a substitute for the pressing demand for change. Matthews and Atkins claimed that Sydney's greatest work was his combat with the Ecclesiastical Commission "concerning the revenues of the Cathedral", but despite his fight, the Cathedrals Act of 1840 passed, and the revenues of St. Paul's were drastically reduced.[104] In that same year, in a letter to his daughter, he deprecated comparisons of himself with the heroic Sir Sidney Smith, pointing out that he had "engaged in no other Combats than against the Enemies of the Church & engaged I am sorry to say in vain ...."[105] On 5 September, 1840, he published an open letter to the Bishop of London in response to a speech on Church reform which the Bishop had published. Sydney resented the Bishop's boasting, and his "down-right impertinence" in referring to him as his "facetious friend."[106] In a letter to the *Times* he retorted that since he had been called facetious, he would refer to the Bishop as his "solemn friend; but you and I must not run into commonplace errors; you must think me necessarily foolish because I am facetious, not will I consider you necessarily wise because you are grave...."[107]

Sydney's purported facetiousness in the cathedrals controversy had concealed the real gravity of his purpose in defending the Church against innovations, and a great part of that defense had been directed towards the patronage of the privileged clergymen. In Sydney's case that defense was not purely altruistic, for he too had patronage, and he had no intention of relinquishing it. He had hoped that his younger son, Wyndham, would enter the Church, in which instance he would very likely have been able to give him a good living, but Wyndham showed no inclination for the Cloth. Still, Sydney had patronage, and it was his right to dispose of it as he saw fit.

The patronage of St. Paul's Cathedral which originally involved Sydney with the Bishop of London, was regulated by the action taken by the Chapter of 27 March,

1832, which established that the Dean should be first in the order of patronage, and that the canons followed on the basis of seniority. In this way, the disposal of the first living belonging to the Cathedral would fall to the Dean, the second to the most senior canon, and so on, with Sydney occupying the third position in a total of four.[108] The system was altered slightly by the amendment proposed on 21 January, 1835, that the rules should be dispensed with "as often as it seems good to the Chapter", which amendment was adopted on 24 January, 1835.[109] Under this amendment the patronage of a living fell vacant, and was disputed between Dean Coplestone and Sydney. The dispute was settled by the Chapter Clerk, who suggested that they draw lots, and Sydney, who won the drawing, bestowed the living on the Rev. W. W. Malet, who had married the daughter of a neighbour at Combe Florey.[110]

Even though he had largely abandoned further clerical ambition, Sydney still valued his patronage for what he could do with it, and in an undated letter he wrote:

> The Chancellors rout prevented me from Coming. A Clergyman always attends first to those who have any preferment to give away-& though I am so full of preferment that I can hold no more the old habit prevails.[111]

The really important living, however, that had originally caused the interest of the Bishop of London was the Vicarage of Edmonton, Middlesex, which was worth nearly §1500 a year, and which had two chapels: Winchmore Hill and Southgate. It was a Cathedral living, and the Bishop's request that part of the income of Edmonton be appropriated" as an endowment for the Chapel of Winchmore Hill" was tabled on 25 March, 1836, and a committee made up of Sydney Smith and the Dean was appointed to deal with the affairs of Edmonton. The Chapter refused action on the Bishop's proposal on the grounds that the price of corn was likely to fall by two-fifths, reducing the income, and because the Ecclesiastical Commission was likely to make "material changes".[112] On 25 February, 1839, the issue was raised again, but the Chapter was deadlocked over it because the Dean claimed a casting vote. The issue of the Dean's vote was submitted to the Attorney-General, who decided on 9 March for the Dean; and on that same day Edmonton was given to Canon James Tate, who gave up another living to get it.[113]

In 1843 Canon Tate died, and Edmonton fell to Sydney, who, having the alternative of keeping it himself or giving it away, presented it to the Rev. Thomas Tate, son of the late Canon and Vicar. His action has been described as humane and generous, and "delicately bestowed"[114] on a needy clerical family, and indeed it was, at least in the sense that he might have pocketed it himself, but a letter to Lady Carlisle shows that he first offered it to a well-established clergyman before turning to the son of his colleague.[115] The parishioners of Edmonton thanked him for his appointment, to which thanks he tendered a dignified reply; but his generosity was not mirrored by the younger Tate, who, having been duly appointed, immediately evicted a poor curate.[116]

Sydney granted his patronage to acceptable friends and acquaintances, and since his position in the Church was a product of his political activities rather than his association with doctrinal factions within the Church, it is predictable that he would have expressed relatively little interest in doctrinal disputes within the Church. He lived, however, during the age of the Oxford Movement which he could hardly avoid commenting on, and which he, being the eighteenth century clergyman that he was, found both baffling and repellant. In 1834 he mentioned that he was not on entirely good terms with Dean Coplestone, the reason for their disagreement being "the question of these foolish antiquarians."[117] He stuck tenaciously to his own view of the Church, and in 1841, he said: "Everybody here is turning Puseyite. Having worn out my black gown, I preach in my surplice; this is all the change I have made, or mean to make."[118] In a dubiously dated letter he complimented Lord Holland on remaining "protestant though you will be out of fashion here as all our protestants are turning Catholic."[119]

By 1842 his bafflement with the Puseyites has solidified into hostility, and he commented that:

> I have not yet discovered of what I am to die, but I rather believe I shall be burnt alive by the Puseyites. Nothing so remarkable in England as the progress of these foolish people. I have no conception what they mean, if it be not to revive every absurd ceremony, and every antiquated folly, which the common sense of mankind has set to sleep. You will find at your return a fanatical Church

of England....[120]

In a sermon at St. Paul's a little later in the same year he said that the Oxford movement:

> ...made the Christian religion a religion of postures and ceremonies, of circumflexions and genuflexions, of garments and vestures, of ostentation and parade; that they took tithe of mint and cummin, and neglected the weightier matters of the law,-justice, mercy, and the duties of life; and so forth.

He said that he opposed the movement because it weakened the aversion of the English to Roman Catholicism, it amounted to a surrender to the bishops, and under it religion became a matter of "trifles, postures, and garments."[121]

What is apparently this same sermon is reprinted in a collection of Sydney's sermons published in 1846, and it throws a little more light on his view of Puseysim, which he considered to be a well-intentioned movement, but one which was creating "lamentable division" in the Church. He believed that by opposing laxity and indifference in the Church their doctrines might produce some good in the long run; but he deplored the fact that by drawing nearer to Roman Catholicism they were diminishing "that rooted aversion to the Catholic faith which is the great bulwark of public safety and public freedom in every Protestant country."[122] He complained that:

> ...this sect preach up a blind obedience and a slavish surrender of opinions from the clergy to their bishops; but this is not, nor ever has been, a tenet of the English Church, though it is a tenet of the Church of Rome.

He added that Anglican clergymen were expected to recognize their ecclesiastical superiors, but they were to acknowledge that God was their greater master; and he hurried to explain that this opinion did not mean that he opposed the civil emancipation of the Catholics.[123] He protested against undue emphasis on forms, which he feared might put ceremony above piety, and he assumed that Puseyism was a passing fancy that would soon fade away.[124]

By 1844 Sydney was failing in health and strength.

He had been referring to himself as aged for two decades, and his letters were filled with accounts of his physical infirmities; and in July of that year, in another sermon delivered at the Cathedral, he bade farewell to the Cathedral and his listeners:

> ...with these I conclude my share of duty for the present, in this Cathedral church, and take my leave of my congregation. I never take leave of any one, for any length of time, without a deep impression on my mind of the uncertainty of human life, and the probability that we may meet no more in this world.[125]

He was not completely inactive, for in November or December of 1844 he wrote to Cecil Smith that he still hoped to spend Christmas at Combe Florey, but that he feared the cold of the trip;[126] and on 26 December, 1844, he wrote to the Chapter at St. Paul's, stating that he was too ill to appear, but asking that he might be allowed to vote on preferment by proxy, or to have the Chapter meet at his home.[127] Thus ended his career in St. Paul's Cathedral, and the Church. It had been extended and honorable, and if he may justly be accused of being less than pious, he had been a doughty campaigner for justice as he saw it, and one who saw the Church at it was.

CHAPTER XI

London 1831-1845: Last Years

After leaving London in 1809 Sydney Smith revisited the city many times, on some occasions for extended periods of time, but his appointment to the Cathedral marked his return to the metropolis on a quasi-permanent basis. After having lived in London for several years early in his career, he was gone for over twenty years, and he did not really return until 1835 when he took the house on Charles Street, and even then he kept both his living and his residence at Combe Florey. Nonetheless he had affection for Combe Florey, and considering his earlier pronouncements, he spent more time at his rural perish than might have been expected. Throughout the years he had hoped for such a return, for he had great affection for London and his loathing for the country was a frequent theme in his letters. He was to spend much of the latter part of his life, and especially the last ten years of it, in the city where he felt so at home. In a letter probably dating from about 1838 he had written:

> Every place out of London looks desolate & forlorn and I am not to be gulld by Green Leaves & the Chirping of Birds. I prefer the green of Rogers face to all the Verdure of the Creation, & Luttrell talks better than the Birds can sing.[1]

He was by nature both selectively gregarious and a skilled social performer, and London provided him with the society he longed for, and the stage from which he could display his wit and repartee to the greatest advantage. The most opulent, the most powerful, and the most attractive members of British society congregated in London, and it was into that social sea that Sydney plunged again, with his zest and humor undiminished by the passing of the years.

A list of his friends and social acquaintances in the 'thirties and 'forties would read like a Who's Who? of the period, but apart from those with whom he had close relations, or who became the victims or beneficiaries of his wit there is little point in barren name-dropping. Let it suffice to say that he lived near the center of the social, religious, and intellectual world which he knew, and he was known by virtually everyone of any importance. His connections with Holland House remained excellent, even during the years when he questioned Lord Holland's loyalty to himself and when he affronted the Whigs with his Letters to Archdeacon Singleton.[2] As one of London's most popular diners out, he might be seen at almost any elegant gathering, and he held breakfasts and dinners at his own home. On 12 March, 1841, he invited Thomas Moore to such a breakfast, saying: "I have a breakfast of philosophers tomorrow at ten punctually; muffins and metaphysics, crumpets and contradiction. Will you come?"[3] In May of the same year he invited Thomas Carlyle to a similar gathering.[4] His hilarity was irrepressible, and while its exhibition at fashionable affairs might have seemed by some to have been forced and insincere, he showed much the same spirit in his letters, in private conversations, in relations with his servants, and even with his own family.

As one of the reigning wits in London society, Sydney undoubtedly prepared or pre-thought, some of his lines, and he had no hesitation in repeating successful ones, but a good portion of his table-talk must be assumed to have been ad libbed, or to have been delivered as quick retorts in conversation not of his origination. He is said to have been considered remarkable in that he never led conversations, but that he could follow any conversation.[5] As he showed in his lectures on moral philosophy, he had considered the nature of wit and humor, but the wit of his table talk may perhaps best be described "in midwife's phrase, a quick conception and an easy delivery."[6] His admonition to an artist painting his portrait: "Whatever you do, preserve the orthodox look",[7] might have been pre-conceived, but it has the ring of spontaneity; as does his thanks to Lord Landsdowne for the loan of two volumes of Henry Hallam's history, "having received from them a good of instruction, clear of every particle of amusement."[8] His observation to Wilmot Horton in 1835 that: "the Complete flute Blower [identified as Henry Gally Knight, traveller, minor poet, and Member of Parliament][9] has return'd from Italy-a greater bore than ever-he bores in Architecture, painting Statuary & Music"[10] was probably not original in its use of that humorous twist, but it was clever, and probably apt.

Henry Gally Knight is largely forgotten in the pages of time, and Sydney's artistic and literary judgement was not infallible, but as early as 1814 he discovered and was entranced by the novels of Walter Scott, whom he had known earlier in Edinburgh. Despite their differing political views, Scott having been one of the prime movers in the formation of the Tory Quarterly Review, Sydney admitted his literary and pseudo-historical ability, even daring to differ with hostile Holland House opinion in 1818 when he wrote to John Allen:

> I cannot at all agree about Walter Scott-
> It is a novel full of power and interest
> he repeats his characters but they will
> bear repetition-who can read the Novel
> without laughing and crying 20 times &
> what other proof is needed?[11]

In the following year he asserted that when he began to read a Scott Novel "turnips, sermons, and justice-business are all forgotten."[12] He regarded a new Scott novel as a holiday for the entire nation,[13] and in 1821, although he regarded The Pirate, Scott's latest novel, as inferior to his best, he still referred his works as "my annual amusement".[14]

Scott died in 1832, the year after Sydney's return to London, and much of the popularity he enjoyed was later to be bestowed on the rising Charles Dickens. On 5 September, 1837, Sydney wrote:

> Read Boz's Sketches if you have not already
> read them. I think them written with great
> power & that the soul of Hogarth has migrat-
> ed into the body of Mr. Dickens. I had
> long heard of them but was deterred by the
> vulgarity of the name.[15]

His love for Dickens' work led him into an acquaintanceship with the author, and they exchanged writings and social visits. On 11 June, 1839, he wrote to Dickens to say that:

> The Miss Berrys, now at Richmond, live
> only to become acquainted with you, and
> have commissioned me to request you to
> dine with them...to meet a Canon of St.
> Paul's, the Rector of Combe Florey, and
> the Vicar of Halberton, -all equally well
> known to you; to say nothing of other and
> better people. The Miss Berrys and Lady
> Charlotte Lindsay have not the slightest
> objection to be put into a Number...and
> Lady Charlotte, in particular, you may
> marry to Newman Noggs.[16]

On 17 April, 1841, he wrote again to Dickens rejecting his dinner invitation with thanks and regrets, mentioning his fondness for Dickens' books and his humor, and in turn inviting him to a series of evening parties he was planning.[17]

Sydney seems to have had an unalloyed affection for Charles Dickens and his books, but in his relations with Thomas Babington Macaulay, the great historian, his admiration was not unmixed with jealousy, for in him Sydney saw a younger reflection of himself. Of undoubted brilliance, Macaulay was a sparkling conversationalist, and like Sydney, he had gained a degree of fame quite early in life by his work in the Edinburgh Review. Sydney recommended him to Lord Grey for the position of Solicitor General in 1830, and though he was not given that post, he was put on the Board of Control in 1832. He became a member of the Supreme Council of India in 1834, and in 1838 when it was rumored that he was to become Judge Advocate-General, Sydney wrote: "Macaulay had resolved to lead a Literary Life, but cannot stand the temptation-like Ladies who resolve upon celibacy if they have no offers..."[18] Such cattiness, however, was not invariable, and in the following year he wrote that Macaulay"...is incomparably the first lion in the Metropolis; that is, he writes, talks, and speaks better than any man in England."[19] In a letter to Lady Holland on 20 December, 1839, Sydney murmured about her poor penmanship, which was, he admitted, "...as if Jack Allen was to complain of disbelief- or Macaulay of Loquacity-"[20] It was equally absurd for the garrulous Sydney Smith to accuse Macaulay of loquacity, but nevertheless he told Rogers that if he had been a poet he would have written "an Inferno and I would put Macaulay among a lot of disputants- and gag him!";[21] and he added that he wished that Macaulay might "see the difference between colloquy and soliloquy,"[22] and that he had lately observed "brilliant flashes of silence" in him.[23] Sydney was fair enough when confronting a lady who had noticed that Macaulay had not spoken as much as usual to admit: "Why, my dear, how could he? Whenever I gave him a chance, you cut in.".[24] Of Macaulay's recognised genius, Sydney said that he "not only overflowed with learning, but stood in the slops."[25] Despite this propensity to mildly backbite Sydney was generally fair about Macaulay, and he asserted that: "To take Macaulay out of literature & society and put him in the House of Commons, is like taking the Chief Physician out of London during a Pestilence."[26]

Others of his contemporaries who were less well known than Macaulay were useful to Sydney, as for example when his nephew Cecil wanted a painting either appraised or sold, and Sydney advised him that "Sir Thomas Lawrence will tell you in a moment what the real value of the picture is ..."27 E. H. Landseer, a rising painter at the time, was similarly invited to dine with the Smiths.28

Mr. & Mrs. George Grote, despite their politics, were also friends of the Smiths, and of them Sydney wrote to a friend: "Nothing has happened to us here but the Gout and the Grote. The first remains, the last left this morning."29 He also gallantly admitted to the very attractive Mrs. Grote that: "Now that you have been seduced, my dear, I may tell you that your virtue was sometimes uncommonly disagreeable."30

Sydney probably admired Grote's literary-historical work, for he despised his politics, and Grote was probably better known for his political Radicalism than his literary accomplishments; but such was not true of all literary figures, and Sydney's evaluations of them were not invariably unbiased or keen. Much earlier in life he had endorsed the Edinburgh Review's opinion on William Wordsworth, asserting that "he did not see much in him, nor greatly admire his poems";31 and in 1841, he commented even further:

> I have not read the review of Wordsworth, because the subject is to me so very uninteresting; but may I ask was it worth while to take any more notice of a man respecting whom the public opinion is completely made up? and do not such repeated attacks upon the man wear in some little ways that shape of persecution?32

On the other hand, his admiration for his friends Thomas Moore and Samuel Rogers was unbounded. Both were close friends, and Sydney enjoyed nothing more than gently teasing them about their physical appearance and their politics. Of Moore's talents as a singer he said that he had "one or two notes, and looks when he is singing like a Superannuated cherub."33 In 1826 Moore took Sydney to the studio of Gilbert Stuart Newton to see the portrait of him that Newton was completing. "Couldn't you contrive....to throw into his face somewhat of a stronger expression of hostility to the Church Establishment?"34 Sydney asked. When he heard that the cadaverous Samuel Rogers was to be married he urged that the anile Misses Berry should be bridesmaids, the sexton the best man, and that the Rev. Mr. Coffin should officiate at the Church of St. Sepulchre.35 On another occasion he implored Lady Holland to tell Rogers:

> ...that his Christian name only is a substantive, that his surname is a verb, and that both together form a proposition and assert a fact which makes him the envy of one and the favorite of the other sex.36

Rogers and Moore were, of course, friends of long standing, but Sydney met and associated with many people, among them the great American statesman Daniel Webster, who Sydney fondly described as "a steam-engine in trousers",37 and who he conducted through St. Paul's; George Ticknor, the American scholar, who Sydney helped introduce to the intellectual world of London;38 and Edward Everett, the American Ambassador to St. James's. Among his heterogeneous friends were numbered both Daniel O'Connell, the Irish patriot with whom Sydney had cooperated in the campaign for Catholic Emancipation, and William Wilberforce, the leading Evangelical humanitarian in the kingdom. O'Connell was so able, effective, and successful that Sydney suggested that the only way to deal with him was "to hang him up, and erect a statue to him under the gallows";39 and he described the dimunitive and emaciated Wilberforce in 1827 as "a little Spirit running about without a body, or in a kind of undress with only half a body."40

As mentioned earlier, Sydney was popular with women, and the Ladies Grey, Holland, and Carlisle were among his special admirers. No hint of scandal attached to his relations with those ladies, or with any others, and no evidence of amatory escapades exists. His success with women is no great secret, for it consisted chiefly of the grossest flattery, coupled with overattention, and protestations of undying devotion; all done with tongue in cheek, which added a pixieish quality to the proceedings, which were reinforced by the fact that he was a clergyman, and this made him safe. It was an almost irresistible package, and it was made even more so by his facetiousness, and he was only saying what the ladies wanted to hear. He could be stern and pastoral with them, but when they were handled properly he did not need to be. To Miss Berry he wrote in 1837 that "It gives me great comfort that that you are recovered. I would not have survived you. To precipitate myself from the pulpit of Paul was the peculiar mode of destruction on which I had resolved."41 To Mrs. Elizabeth Gaskell, later a well known writer, he stated, in response to the complaint of aging, that "You and your Sisters who have neither age nor infirmities-but Genelogy Grace & beauty-"[42] To another woman he confided that "I always find that Compassion of Ladies does me good it makes pain more endurable Remedies more efficacious & Life more agreeable."[43] With regard to flattery, while at a garden party a lovely girl exclaimed to him: '"Oh, Mr. Sydney! this pea will never come to perfection." Permit me, then", said he, gently taking her hand and walking towards the plant, "to lead perfection to the pea."' On another occasion he claimed that the girls "were all so beautiful, that Paris could not have decided between them, but would have cut his apple in slices."[44]

With his fulsome compliments Sydney cut a gallant, if portly, figure with the ladies, but his attentions to them were courteous and social rather than romantic, for beneath his flattery Sydney was as rational in his attitude towards love and women as he was towards life more generally. In 1837 he spoke of romantic love as:

> ...that terrible disorder, than which none destroys more completely the happiness of common existence, and substitutes for the activity which Life demands a long and sickly dream with moments of pleasure and days of intolerable pain. The Poets are full of false views: they make mankind believe that happiness consists in falling in love with nobody."[45]

Two years earlier he had advised a young lady not to marry for love, and to settle only for a man with a "tolerable understanding and a thousand a year."[46] He had a deep sense of the sanctity of marriage, and of the duties and responsibilities it entailed, and he preached that it was "...the duty of us all, to make our hearts perfect within our houses, and to convert a family life into a school of religious duty."[47] Thus, even though he did flirt, his flirting was largely persiflage, as in 1818, when he wrote to John Allen:

> Do you think Lady Holland will be persuaded to send by the mail in a box the French chambermaid? I will return her safe sound and clean, when I have done with her in about a fortnight or 3 weeks from the time of her arrival.[48]

In a still earlier sermon he had preached on seduction, which evil, he maintained, menaced the morals of the nation, and he did not hesitate to excoriate the wealthier men of the community for their corruption of poor girls. He told his congregations that seducers of that description were base and dishonorable, especially in that they corrupted innocence by falsehood, and then abandoned their victims, leaving them to become wretched and damned prostitutes.[49] He did not have any romantic notions about prostitution, and very early in his career he had panned Mme de Stael's Delphine because he believed that her romantic moral precepts were weak, and that young ladies who emulated Delphine were likely to have an unfortunate end. There were in London, he said, "...above 40,000 heroines of this species, most of whom, we dare to say, have at one time or another reasoned like the sentimental Delphine...." [50]

With all his rationality about women, however, Sydney was fully masculine, and typical of men in general in admiring and enjoying the company of pretty women. Relatively early in life, but after his marriage, he had written:

> I am not a great psysiognomist nor have I much confidence in a science which pretends to discover the inside from the out; but where I have seen fine eyes, a beautiful complexion, grace, and symetry, in women, I have generally thought them amazingly well-informed and extremely philosophical. In contrary instances, seldom or never. Is there any accounting for this? [51]

In 1835 he complained that:

> Our rout generally consists of half a dozen highly respectable old women, and the same number of greasy philosophers.... There are also half a dozen young ladies, unquestionably the plainest in Europe, and indeed, I might extend my geographical limits for the purpose of this comparison.[52]

He had a genuine fondness for women and girls, and when his daughter gave birth to a girl he said: "I am glad it is a Girl. All little boys ought to be put to death."[53] As already mentioned he held advanced views on the education of women, and his concept of their position in the world was enlightened. He believed in educating them so that they might become intelligent companions for men, and so that they might improve their lives, which were too often insipid and barren. He really admired learning and talents in women, attributes which were substitutes for beauty alone.[54] Not given over to sentimentality over motherhood, he richly endorsed the near-sacramental Anglican rite of the Churching of Women after childbirth,[55] and he urged, despite prudish opposition, the extension and application of science in obstetrics. Why, he said, should society "avert from her the patient eye of science, when she gives a joyful increase, and lends to the earth a living, thinking soul?"[56] He viewed women rationally, and he had observed that:

> ...the heroism and courage of men is nothing in comparison with these qualities as they are developed in women. Women cannot face danger accompanied with noise, and smoke and hallooing; but in all kinds of serene peril, and quiet horrors they have infinitely more philosophical endurance than men.-Put a woman in a boat in a boisterous Sea, let 6 or 7 peiple make as much noise as they can, and she is in a state of inconceivable agony; ask the same woman in a serene Summer's Evening, when all nature is at rest to drink a cup of poison for some good which would accrue from it to her husband and children and she will swallow it like green tea.[57]

In 1838 he wrote a paradoxical statement to, of all people, Lady Elizabeth Holland, in which he said:

> We have had a run of blue-stocking ladies to Combe Florey this summer, a race you despise. To me they are agreeable, and less insipid than the general run of women; for you know, my lady, the female mind does not reason.[58]

Sydney's fondness for women extended enthusiastically to his own family. He was devoted to his wife, and he had earlier regretted the loss of his daughter Emily when she had married, even though he rejoiced in her marital happiness. In 1834 he announced laconically to Brougham, in the postscript of a letter that: "I am going to marry Saba to Dr. Holland",[59] which sounds indifferent; but in a letter written five days earlier to Lady Grey he had said:

> ...she is going to be married to Dr. Holland he has propos'd is accepted by us all-and the marriage will take place in the spring....I shall advertise-perhaps as follows-
>
> Wanted for adoption a daughter She must good naturd cheerful Musical & not ill looking-fit for Town or Country fond of Books & not Evangelical-any person who may accord with this description will find all the necessary explanation by applying &c[60]

Saba's marriage to Dr. Henry Holland, was also to be a happy one, and although she was nearly thirty-two years old when she married, she bore two daughters to Dr. Holland. He was an eminent physician, and a widower with three children when he married Saba, and was later made Baronet Holland of Knutsford as a recognition of his services to the court. Sydney was fond, to the point of doting, of their children, and of Emily's as well, and to one grandchild, who had sent him an overweight letter, he wrote in return:

> Oh, you little wretch! your letter cost me fourpence. I will pull all the plums out of your puddings; I will undress your dolls and steal their under petticoats; you shall have no currant-jelly to your rice; I will kiss you till you cannot see out of your eyes; when nobody else whips you, I will do so; I will fill you so full of sugar-plums that they shall run out of your nose and ears; lastly, your frocks shall be so short that they shall not come below your knees.[61]

On another occasion he returned home, where he: "found everybody very well and very hot here, and many grandchildren, all of whom I whipt immediately-never given any reason; it increases their idea of power and makes them more obedient."[62]

Sydney rejoiced in his daughters and their children, but his sons were a source of sorrow to him. Douglas had been his favorite child, and his loss was one from which Sydney never entirely recovered, as evidenced by his sincere sympathy for friends who sustained similar losses. In 1831, when Lord Durham's son had died, he wrote to Lady Grey to say how difficult it was "to make grief hear reason, but it is a blessing to mourners when it is heard and as great a blessing or greater to those who follow in the train of mourners because they love them."[63]

His second son Windham, often spelled Wyndham, proved to be less than a satisfactory surrogate for Douglas, for whereas Sydney had said that Douglas never gave his parents any cause for anxiety, Windham seems to have been a relatively constant source of annoyance, concern, and expense. Modern psychology might attribute his behavior to parental favoritism, for Douglas was the apple of his parents' eye, but it appears that Sydney treated both sons equally, at least as far as education was concerned. Windham was sent to the Charterhouse, one of the better public schools, where, unlike Douglas, he did not excell, and from there he went on to Trinity College, Cambridge, where he seems to have been outstanding only in the accumulation of debt, which Sydney paid after receiving assurances of better conduct in the future.[64]

Windham did, however, seem to have an infinite capacity for getting into trouble. He had an unfortunate predilection for horse racing and betting, and at Cambridge, he was called "the Assassin" after he reputedly killed a bulldog.[65] In July of 1835 his penchant for betting, which was not permitted at Cambridge, and his poor judgement combined to result in his expulsion from Trinity College. He had made an indiscreet but winning bet with a young man, who left school without having paid it. In some indignation Windham wrote to him demanding payment, but his letter was intercepted by the young man's father, who returned it to the authorities at Trinity College. They summoned Windham, who pled the smallness of the amount and the offense, and was excused, presumably with a warning. Windham, however, was outraged by the action taken by the youth's father, and he immediately wrote an unpleasant letter to him, accusing him of reading mail not addressed to him. This letter was also returned to the college authorities, who decided that Windham had to be removed.[66]

While admitting that Windham was in the wrong,

Sydney stood up for him, asserting that the punishment was too severe, and that a reprimand, a letter to himself, or a years' rustication would have been sufficient.[67] He appealed to Lord Carlisle to intervene, believing, wrongly, as it turned out, that Lord Carlisle was a relative of Windham's classmate.[68] He also appealed to the Rev. Dr. Christopher Wordsworth, Master of Trinity and younger brother of the poet, on the grounds that the complainant would not have been so hard on Windham had he known he was the son of Sydney Smith.[69] Less than a week later he wrote again to Wordsworth, describing Windham's punishment as "one of the most cruel and disproportionate punishments ever inflicted", and asking that his sentence be reduced either to a transfer to another college, or a years' rustication.[70] In his earlier letter he had genuinely begged for mercy for Windham, claiming that: "I lost my other Son by death a year or [less?] since- and this is my only Son- the only Child remaining in my house. I earnestly beg of the College that he may not be damned to ruin and disgrace- for such an act of mere peurile indiscretion."[71]

Sydney was not able to keep Windham in Trinity College, but he was allowed to migrate to Caius College, from which he graduated without distinction in 1836. His future after taking his degree was dubious, and Sydney attempted to secure a lucrative position for him. On 25 March, 1836, Sydney wrote to Lord Melbourne to ask that Windham be appointed to a position in a public office. His son possessed, he said, "some natural shrewdness", but "only a moderate attachment to Greek and Roman learning", and he asked for a post anywhere except the Treasury, which had a qualifying examination, for he believed that Windham was not "incompetent but nervous, and might fail from agitation".[72] Sydney also wrote to Lord Palmerston, stating that:

> I had intended my son for the Church- but he thinks the Church is falling and will not go into it- I had for the purpose of giving him a good Living kept myself at the head of the Preferment List at St. Pauls- and the good things I had in store for him- must now go to some one else.

He added that he wanted a position for him in a public office, and that the salary did not matter.[73] It is interesting to see from this letter that Sydney was unwilling to emulate his father and force Windham into orders, and that he was offering his preferment to Lord Palmerston as a quid pro quo for an appointment for his son. Windham did receive an appointment as an audit clerk as §90 a year, and 3 April, 1837, Sydney attempted to solicit a better position for him from Lord John Russell.[74] In June of that year he was still trying to secure a more attractive situation for Windham, for he sarcastically remarked that Lord Melbourne's patronage was more limited than he had been led to believe.[75]

Windham was a sore disappointment to Sydney, but he was wonderfully consistent in that his conduct never changed: he was a thorough blackguard and he never improved. Thackeray lampooned him as "Spavin the Turfite" in his Book of Snobs, and Sydney commented on: "How regularly packets of misery and misfortune are made up for everybody. I have a son who brings me in §4000 of debt besides Turf debts."[76] Still, he seems somehow to have gotten along with Windham, and as late as 11 December, 1842, Windham was still living with his parents.[77] A year later, however, Sydney informed Lady Grey that:

> ...I have thought it expedient that my Son and I should have separate Establishments. I allowed him §500 per Annum, and he lives at Southhampton. Our habits are incompatible; he was tired to death of the Solitude of this place and the arrangment was as agreeable to him as to me. He is to visit us here from time to time and we have parted good friends.[78]

The fact that Sydney was able to give Windham §500 a year fairly unflinchingly, and to pay off his debts, is an indication of his improved finances. He had an excellent income from his stall at St. Paul's and his livings at Combe Florey and Halberton, and his wealth had been increasing. As he announced with satisfaction in 1836: "I am in prosperity having 2 good livings one the most beautiful in England.- and a Canonry of St. Pauls succulent & productive-"[79] His wealth enabled him to live at ease, and without the financial worries that had nagged him throughout much of his life. Since he preferred to live in London, and since his duties at St. Paul's kept him away from his parish at Combe Florey for at least twelve weeks a year, he arranged to pay his nephew Cecil §50 a year to serve the Church in his absence, with an additional §2 for each Sunday over twenty-five that he served.[80] His wealth was a source of comfort to him both because of the ease it gave him, and the status which it lent to him. In one of his reviews he had mentioned a traveller in Arabia who affected poverty to avoid robbers, and who, he added, received "as much respect, therefore, as a man would do who was to rub down his own horse in England...."[81]

If Sydney Smith's desire for wealth and respect was a fault, it was a fault shared by virtually all of his contemporaries, and there was very little criticism of his materialism during his time. Wealth was spoken of with respect and interest, rather than disdain, and even the fabulously wealthy Lady Holland wrote:

> Mr. Smith's rich Nabob brother, Mr. Courtenay Smith, is just arrived from India. He left this country when only 17, and returns at 50 with an immense fortune. It will be an occupation to amuse & keep him from forming any matrimonial engagement which our good aunt will try, & Sydney, who arrives today, will by overdoing mar.[82]

Courtenay returned wealthy, but he became something of a recluse, and he had little to do with Sydney and Bobus, his surviving brothers. When he died intestate in 1842, his vast estate was divided between Sydney and Bobus, and Cecil, their nephew, each receiving about §33,000. Sydney commented that "in my grand climacteric I became unexpectedly a rich man",[83] and that the wealth arrived "just in time to gild the nails of my Coffin".[84] A few months later he added that the inheritance "puts me at my ease for my few remaining years. After buying into the Consols and the Reduced, I read Seneca 'On the Contempt of Wealth!' What intolerable nonsense."[85]

Dying intestate Courtenay's estate presented problems, but Sydney and Bobus jointly and successfully administered it, disposing of the legal technicalities in a fortnight.[86] From a series of cryptic letters it would seem that Courtenay had borne Sydney some ill-will for unspecified reasons, which animosity he had communicated to Cecil, but no positive information appears to explain his attitude.[87] Since his actions were erratic after his return from India, it is not unlikely that his antipathy for his clerical brother was largely a creation of his own imagination. Less imaginary might have been his reaction to the settlement of his estate, for while it has been stated that Courtenay died intestate, he actually left two wills, neither of which proved to be legal. In the first of these he left §16,000 to a Miss Lee, who was evidently his mistress, and in the second §6000.[88] These intended bequests presented a problem to the executors, and Bobus seems to have inclined towards giving her one figure or the other; but Bobus had been rich for a long time unlike the penny-pinching Sydney who proposed §2000 as a suitable sum. With delight he was able to report to Cecil:

> Miss L accepts on her knees-deprecates all possible idea of opposition.... It is too late to lift up the petticoats of Miss Lee-but we have nothing to do with her virtue...there will be a cry if something is not done for her....You may depend upon my ravishing her if she does not prevent me by a timely compliance.[89]

Sydney was often thought of by his detractors as a clown or a buffoon,[90] but his businesslike handling of Courtenay's estate illustrates both his potential for serious work, and another aspect of his many-faceted career. A meticulous record-keeper, it is not surprising that he was an effective executor, especially since he was working with Bobus, who undoubtedly handled the legal aspects of the estate. He appears to have had decided views on investments, which were conservative rather than speculative, but they were generally sound. Any astonishment that might be expressed over these exhibitions of ability would need to be based on the view of Sydney Smith as an ecdentric cleric, while in reality he was a liberally educated English gentleman who happened to be a competent and effective clergyman. As a gentleman he could be expected to be on speaking terms with business, investments, and the broader aspects of the law, and as a priest his duties required him to be a pastor and a parish administrator.

Although his pastoral responsibilities did not require it, Sydney practised medicine fairly extensively both at Foston and at Combe Florey. In this respect he was different from most of his clerical contemporaries, and he performed the service without expense to his poor parishioners. His qualifications were dubious, in the sense that their extent is not fully known, but while he certainly was not a fully qualified physician, he probably had more training and interest in medicine than might be suspected. It is known that he dabbled with medicine at Oxford, and that he continued his interest in Edinburgh. His widow wrote of his medical training:

> ...Afterwards at Edinburgh, he continued this pursuit;-attending all the medical lectures, & what are called Clinical lectures which Dr. Gregory (then Professor) gave...He continued to read many of the most interesting publications on this science as long as he lived.[91]

He certainly never considered practising medicine in the fullest sense of the word, but he did offer his limited services to his family, his servants, and to the poor of the parish, to whom medical care was probably otherwise totally lacking. He was fascinated with gadgets rather than medical science, and he bosted of having saved his footman's life with a stomach pump after he had accidentally eaten arsenic-laced rat bait.[92] While at Foston he reported that he was "uneasy about Mrs Sydney she has a chronic inflamation of the wind pipe, which she is attacking-and hitherto without much success-by-Leeches,-and Mercury-"[93] When his son Douglas was suffering from an attack of the "croup", perhaps bronchial asthma, Sydney:

> ...darted into him all the mineral, and vegetable resources of the shops, cravatted his throat with blisters, and fringed it with leeches, excited now the Peristaltic, now the antiperistaltic motion like the Strophe and the antistrophe of the Tragedies, and set him in 5 or 6 hours to play at marbles, breathing gently and inaudibly....[94]

Despite his rather serious medical efforts, Sydney brought the same joyousness and gaiety to medicine that he used in so many other fields, and he seemingly deprecated his own skills, and even medical science itself. He had a prescription book, and at Combe Florey he fitted out a crude pharmacy. Of his talents and his concoctions he said:

> I am a great doctor; would you like to hear some of my medicines?.... There is the Gentlejog, a pleasure to take it, -the Bull-dog, for more serious cases, -Peter's puke,-Heart's delight, the

> comfort of all the old women in the village,-Rub-a-dub, a capital embrocation, -Dead-stop settles the matter at once, -Up-with-it-then needs no explanation ....[95]

He was apparently considered to be competent enough to write one review of a medical work on vaccination for the *Edinburgh Review*, but his doubts about vaccination and his apparent belief that small pox was an acute form of chicken pox mark him as less than a medical genius.[96] What he lacked in medical training, however, he made up in wit and style, and he wrote that:

> Much has been written upon Pus and Pimples;-many volumes have been employed upon Eruptions; there are folios on Scabs. If any man has a breaking out on his nose, he may be sure to find it in a book....No phlegmonous variety is unpainted, unprinted, or past over in silence by the doctors.[97]

Despite his jocularity he took medicine seriously, and he ministered to the sick during village epidemics.[98] Perhaps his presence and his bedside manner were more effective cures than his medicines, but he offered both, and they seem to have been received with gratitude. On the other hand, Sydney recognised his medical limitations, and in 1833 he wrote from Combe Florey:

> Our Evils here been want of Rain, and Scarlet fever in our Village where in 3/4 of a Year we have buried 15 instead of one per annum. You will naturally suppose I killed all these people by doctoring them, but Scarlet fever awes me, and is above my aim. I leave it to the professional, and graduated Homicides.[99]

In an undated letter to a London physician he said: "May I beg the favor of your medical advice any time to day-for Mrs Smiths maid-who is again troubld by Varicose Veins."[100]

Sydney also treated his own minor ailments, his most common complaint in his later years being gout, from which he suffered chronically. "I observe", he said, "that gout loves ancestors and geneology. It needs five or six generations of gentlemen or noblemen to give it its full vigor."[101] In 1836 he philosophised on gout, and its control, stating that he had cured himself of it by eating sparingly and drinking only water. In retrospect, he said, most of his discomforts in life had resulted from indigestion, and he advised that "Young people in early life should be thoroughly taught the moral, intellectual, and physical evils of indigestion."[102] (To a friend he confided: "Beware Gout which next to Heresy & Schism is the great misfortune which can happen to an human being-"[103]) He experimented with various gout remedies, finding relief in some, even in his distinctly unscientific use of the Autumn Crocus:

> ...who would guess the virtue of that little plant? But I find the power of colchicum so great, that if I feel a little gout coming on, I go into the garden, and hold out my toe to that plant, and it gets well directly....when I have the gout, I feel as if I was walking on my eyeballs.[104]

In addition to gout, Sydney suffered sporadically, especially in his later years, from what he called Catarrh, asthma, or hay fever; conditions which prevented him from "hearing, seeing, smelling, or speaking for weeks together..."[105] This was undoubtedly a vast exaggeration of his actual condition, but late in life he cheerfully reported that "I have gout, asthma, and seven other maladies, but am otherwise very well."[106] He was also overweight during most of his life, a fact which did not bother him, but one of his letters sounds not unlike that of a twentieth century dieter. "I am writing to you at two o'clock in the morning," he said, "having heard of a clergyman who brought himself down from twenty-six to sixteen stone in six months by lessening his sleep... I shall be so thin when you see me, that you may trundle me about like a mop."[107] He also suffered from mundane afflictions of a temporary nature, of one of which he wrote:

> Of all cu [r] ses in the Earth what is called a Looseness is the Worst. Travelling which binds up other people dissolves me. I left a fourteenth part of myself in Oxford- divided myself into portions- at Birmingham & Sheffield-and brought home about 4/14 of myself

> to Foston- and am now a Composition of pain, wind, and distressed fluid humanity.[108]

He had also a tendency to facetiously associate disease and dissent, and when a Unitarian physician complained of the cold, Sydney said: "I can cure you...Cover yourself with the thirty-nine Articles, and you will soon have a delicious glow all over you."[109]

In a similar vein he commented on Lady Holland's health and John Allen's disbelief, of the former he said that she had an "excellent and plebian constitution," and that she would outlive the Church," and so would Allen if life could be made tolerable to him after the Church had perished."[110] Lady Holland was something of a hypochondriac who was fully persuaded that she was dying of heart disease, and Sydney could not help snickering when one of the most eminent physicians of the period assured her, greatly to her dismay, that she was as healthy as a horse.[111]

Sydney often prescribed pseudo-medical regimens to ailing friends, and one of his most common prescriptions was moderation in the consumption of alcoholic beverages. No prude on the subject, he believed that most gentlemen ate and drank too much for their own good, and that their general health could improved by temperance. He advised Lady Holland on one occasion to avoid all "fermented liquors," which would result in better sleep, a tendency to exercise more without tiring, better sight, and a better understanding, especially of political economy. The only drawback he could see to abstinence was an unfortunate predilection towards overenthusiasm in religion.[112] He himself occasionally abstained, and on one occasion he reported, as a result, that:

> I liked London better than ever I liked it before, and simply I believe from water-drinking. Without this London is stupefaction, and inflammation. It is not the love of wine, but thoughtlessness and unconscious imitation: other men poke out their hands for the revolving wine, and one does the same without thinking of it.[113]

To his poorest parishioners he counselled abstention, clearly stating that while he had no objection to the consumption of ale in moderation, if they could afford it, because every penny they spent in the ale house "comes out of the stomachs of the poor children, and strips off the clothes of the wife."[114]

Such was Sydney's advice to the poor, and he did follow it himself from time to time, but generally speaking he enjoyed the social drinking of alcholic beverages of various descriptions. In an age in which, as he himself said, one third of the gentlemen were drunk all the time,[115] no single mention has yet appeared of him overindulging. In 1805 he had asked Jeffrey: "When are we to drink copiously of warm rum and water to a late hour of the morning?"[116] To another friend he counselled against abstention, for "the wretchedness of human life is only to be encountered upon the basis of meat and wine."[117] When he moved his Yorkshire servants to Somerset they immediately overindulged in cider, even though they imagined that "making a drink out of apples was a tempting of Providence, who had intended barley to be the only natural material of intoxication."[118] About the same time he reported that "The Cyder is such an enormous Crop that it is sold at 10s pr Hogshead; so that an human Creature may lose his reason for an halfpenny."[119] He claimed also to have been:

> ...since my travels, very much gallicized in my character, I ordered a pint of claret; I found it incomparably the best wine I ever tasted; it disappeared with a rapidity which surprises me even at this distance of time. The next morning, in the coach by eight, with a handsome valetudenarian lady, upon whom the coach produced the same effect as a steampacket would do. I proposed weak warm brandy and water; she thought, at first, it would produce inflammation of the stomach, but presently requested to have it warm and _not_ weak, and she took it to the last drop, as I did the claret.[120]

In short he countenanced drinking but abhorred drunkenness, and as Rector of Foston, he permitted the traditional expenditure of parish funds for ale for certain holidays.[121]

The conditions depicted so graphically by Hogarth raised the questions of the licensing of drinking establishments and the controlling of the consumption of alcohol, and Sydney participated in the controvery by means of articles in the Edinburgh Review and by letters to politicians. His solution to the problems was typical of laissez-faire thought believing that they could be solved best by free and open competition. He opposed the existing licensing system because it violated free competition, and because the magistrates who attempted to regulate ale drinking did not drink ale. He believed that legislation should not deny simple pleasures and amusements to the poor, especially by magistrates who he suspected of being corrupt and indifferent to the public interest.[122] In a letter to Lord Lansdowne on 22 December, 1827, he said that the best policy was to "fling the trade open," but since that was politically unfeasible he proposed a complicated system to insure the probity of the justices in granting or refusing licenses.[123] On 18 February, 1828, in a letter to Peel, he suggested much the same system, urging a free trade in ale, to be achieved by degrees.[124] The licensing of ale houses was not a particularly important political issue of the period, but his interest in it was typical of his more general interest in political questions throughout his life.

He had acted prominently in earlier controversies, and he continued to take an interest in politics, even serving as a sort of unofficial clearing house for Whig appointments in the Church. In March or April of 1831 he reported to Lady Grey on the Rev. Charles Dyson, who was under consideration for promotion, and he said:

> I am a better man than Dyson- he attends to friends in power I hate to forget those who are out of power- I beg it as a favor you will make Lord Grey and Lord Howick and Lord Durham read this narrative- and then lock it up...merely make them read it...[125]

Sydney was obviously trying to remind them of his own availability for promotion, and his superior claims to preferment; but Dyson was an excellent parish priest and a fine Anglo-Saxon scholar, and Sydney's hostile recommendation was waspish.

Earlier Sydney supported the Great Reform Bill, but he would have preferred a more moderate measure, and he feared the opening of the floodgates to unwanted change. In 1833 he wrote to Sir Robert Wilmot-Horton, advising him to do nothing "...The turbulence proceeding from the Reform is I think subsiding- at the same time I will not say we are free from danger...."[126] The accession to power by the Tories did not reassure him, and in 1835 he asserted to Wilmot-Horton that "It is impossible to say what the results of all these changes will be... the remaining reforms (rule who will) must go on- The Trojans must put on the Armour of the Greeks...."[127]

Sydney approved of the specific great reforms of the Whigs, especially the working of the New Poor Law, passed in 1834. which punished both the impotent and unemployed poor by granting relief only in workhouses. He was thoroughly progressive, which was to say Malthusian, in his view of the problems of poverty and public welfare, and his comments on Thomas Frankland Lewis, Chairman of the Poor Law Commission under the new law, were typical:

> Lewis is filling his situation of King of the Paupers extremely well- they have already worked Wonders but of all occupation it must be the most disagreeable What is it but to starve to death with decency- and propriety and under false names and pretences a million Wretches whom the folly and carelessness of our Ancestors have tempted into Existence? I don't blame the objects but I dislike the occupation-the object is justified because it prevents a much greater destruction of human beings hereafter.[128]

In reality, the New Poor Law, although considered enlightened and necessary by liberals like Sydney who believed that otherwise the paupers would overpopulate the British Isles and destroy productivity and property, was a harsh, punitive, and inhumane act; but he was typical of the liberals who approved it, and he described it as "one of the best and boldest measures which have ever emanated from any Government."[129] A month later he expressed his approval of the Whigs, who, he said, would be immortalized by that act alone, and that it, (The New Poor Law would have more to do with the causation of Chartism than any other single issue)[130] was working very well.

Sydney also, approved of the Municipal Corporations Act of 1835 which ended the monopolies of privileged and Anglican minorities in the town and city governments, even though he hesitated a little at the extent of the bill.[131] A few months later, however, he had decided that the act was a good one, and that the destruction of municipal monopolies would bring about "important improvements."[132]

His judgment on the Municipal Corporations Act was sound, as were most of his political opinions. For the most part he was generally right in his positions on political questions, or at least "right" from the standpoint of the dogmatic liberal-economic point of view. If he was "wrong" in upholding the harsh and punitive New Poor Law, he was "right" in that the most progressive minds of the age agreed that it was the only way to end runaway population growth and spiralling welfare costs. He was concerned about reforms that might lead to hasty and poorly thought-out changes, but he did not panic or retreat into obscurantism. In 1835 he said: "The battle goes on between Democracy and Aristocracy-I think it will end in a Compromise.-and that there will be nothing of a revolutionary Nature."[133]

Despite his quarrel with the Whigs over the cathedrals, Sydney continued to support them, for as far as he could see they had only committed two faults: foreign intervention and Russell's "unnatural passion for Bishops."[134] In 1837 he viewed the decline of Whig popularity with alarm, and analyzed its causes as the popular reaction against Whig support of O'Connell and Irish agitation, the ill-framed legislation on the Church, and, surprisingly enough, the New Poor Law.[135] By the time of the Bedchamber Question he had regained his earlier aloofness vis a vis the Crown, and he said that: "There was no reason for resigning & still less for coming back, because a young Lady could not abide Sir Robert Peel-"[136]

The popular phenomenon of Chartism was extremely upsetting to Sydney, whose aristocratic proclivities were outraged by the movement. Chartism was at its peak in the late thirties, but few of Sydney's letters of this period have survived. In 1840 he thought it "more probable we shall all be ruind that Church, King, Funds-and-Land will all be carried away in a popular Whirlwind-"[137] For Chartism itself, he offered his earlier solution for dealing with popular demonstrations: "They ought to execute 3 or 4 Chartists, I think they will hardly be so ill advised as not to do so."[138] As late as 1842, when the real danger of Chartism had passed, although Sydney and his contemporaries could hardly have known it, he wrote:

> After the heat come the riots, the only
> difference I see between these and for-
> mer manufacturing riots is that the mob
> have got hold under the name of Chartism
> of some plan for political Innovation but
> that plan is so foolish, that I do not
> think it will be very longlived.[139]

Sydney modified his view of the Tories enough to approve of Sir Robert Peel, who, he believed, "knew how to disguise liberal ideas, and to make them less terrible to the Foolery of a country."[140] Perhaps not much of a commendation of a great political leader, but it is better than his riddle: "Why are old Tories like last year's walnuts? Because they are so troublesome to *Peel*."[141]

Sydney's eleventh hour approval of Peel was only another indication of his increasingly conservative attitudes, and probably in no field did he demonstrate that conservatism better than in his writing on the proposed secret ballot. It is perhaps unkind to say that the pamphlet he wrote on the ballot was a long rationalization of his basic opposition to further change, and he denied that interpretation throughout it, but there is no possible alternative interpretation. As he said:

> There is no end to these eternal changes;
> we have made an enormous revolution with-
> in the last ten years,-let us stop a lit-
> tle and secure it, and prevent it from
> being turned into ruin; I do not say the
> Reform Bill is final, but I want a little
> time for breathing; and if there are to
> be any more changes, let them be carried
> into execution hereafter by those little
> legislators who are now receiving every
> day after dinner a cake or a plum....
> I long for the quiet times of *Log*, when
> all the English common people are making
> calico, and all the English gentlemen
> are making long and short verses....Are
> there to be two distinct methods of as-
> certaining the opinions of the people, and
> these completely opposed to each other?
> A member is chosen this week by a large
> majority of voters who vote in the dark,
> and the next week, when men vote in the
> light of day, some petition is carried
> totally opposite to all those principles

> ....How, under such a system, can Parliament ever ascertain what the wishes of the people really are?[142]

Sydney was both suspicious of the lower orders, and dubious of their ability to vote independently. He also held that the sanctity of property included the right of a landlord to direct his tenants' votes, and while he claimed to deplore that practice, he believed that landlords possessed the right if they chose to exercise it. "...every man", he said,

> has a right to do what he pleases with his own. I cannot, by law, prevent any one man from discharging his tenants and changing his tradesmen for political reasons; but I may judge whether that man exercises his right to the public detriment, or the public advantage....All these practices are bad; but the facts and the consequences are exaggerated.
>
> In the first place, the plough is not a political machine....nineteen tenants out of twenty care nothing about their votes, and pull off their opinions as easily to their landlords as they do their hats.[143]

Ill-behaved or inefficient farmers who had been dismissed were only too quick, he said, to attribute their dismissal to political differences with their landlords. In open voting the lower classes had been excluded not from "want of intellect" but "for want of independence". It had been suggested that the middle classes, having once secured the vote for themselves, would not want to extend it to others, but Sydney believed they would find that "wealth and education" were too powerful to overcome, and they would call on the mass of the population for support. The belief that they could "curb their inferiors and conquer their superiors", by means of the ballot was an illusion, "but universl suffrage is not an illusion. The common people will get nothing by the one, but they gain everything, and ruin everything, by the last."[144] The ballot would, he said, encourage deceit and lying in those who owed their votes to landlords or patrons, and would punish honest men who did not deign to conceal their political opinions. Admittedly, he said, there were faults in the system of open voting, and it was wrong to vote for a man you believed to be less worthy than another,

> ...but if the tenant votes against his landlord under the ballot, he is practising every day some fraud to conceal his first deviation from truth. The present method may produce a vicious act, but the ballot establishes a vicious habit....In the open voting, the law leaves you fairly to choose between the dangers of giving an honest, or the convenience of giving a dishonest vote; but the ballot law opens a booth and asylum for fraud, calling upon all men to lie...forbidding open honesty, promising impunity for the most scandalous deceit, and encouraging men to take no other view of virtue than whether it pays or does not pay.... [145]

His pamphlet on the ballot won a great deal of approval from the possessing classes, to whom it was a matter of convincing the convinced, but it is hard to believe it convinced anyone else. In Sydney's opinion open voting was working, and it was probably working better than a secret ballot would; and in any case, the preservation of the present was preferable to innovation or experimentation.[146] Violently opposed to democracy, Sydney felt that the interests of the lower classes should be kept in mind, and that their interests could best be handled by their betters, but that the lower orders should not be consulted. As he said:

> If the ballot did succeed in enabling the lower order of voters to conquer their betters, so much the worse. In a town consisting of 700 voters, the 300 most opulent and powerful (and therefore probably the best instructed) would make a much better choice than the remaining 400; and the ballot would, in that case, do more harm than good. In nineteen cases out of twenty, the most numerous party would be in the wrong. If this is the case, why give the franchise at all? why not confine it to the first division? <u>because even with all the abuses which</u>

> occur, and in spite of them, the great mass of the people are much more satisfied with having a vote occasionally controlled, than with having none.[147]

In a footnote in the second edition of his Works he appended the opinion that: "The 400 or 500 voting against the 200 are right about as often as juries are right in differing from judges; and that is very seldom."[148] In summation he concluded:

> The people seem to be hurrying on through all the well known steps to anarchy; they must be stopped at some pass or another: the first is the best and the most easily defended. The people have a right to ballot or to any thing else which will make them happy; and they have a right to nothing which will make them unhappy. They are the best judges of their immediate gratifications, and the worst judges of what would best conduce to their interests for a series of years. Most earnestly and conscienctiously wishing their good, I say, NO BALLOT.[149]

As Russell observed, Sydney foresaw universal suffrage and an ultimate victory of the lower classes over their superiors, and he also predicted universal corruption and systematic lying as a result of the ballot, but there is no reason to believe that the existing political corruption was extended by the secret ballot, or that his dire predictions on lying ever occurred.[150] In a letter written in 1838 he admitted that he was an "anti-ballotist", and he regarded his pamphlet as non-political. In the same letter he glumly confessed that "It will be carried, however, write I never so wisely."[151]

He wrote to Lady Carlisle at about the same time, asserting that he intended to dedicate his work on the ballot to her, "with the most fulsome praise-Virtues-Talents-Grace-Elegance-Illustrious Ancestors-British feelings-Mother of Morpeth-Humble Servant-&c. &c."[152] He wrote also to John Allen, after publishing the pamphlet, for assurance that he had been right about the use of the ballot in America. "My idea is," he said, "that in America nobody troubles themselves how their inferiors vote, and that therefore it is a dead lr."[153] Since he was writing during the period of Jacksonian democracy he was clearly mistaken, and his assumptions were exactly that: assumptions arrived at on the basis of English aristocratic experience. To two other friends he admitted that his article would be thought to be on the "wrong side of the question, but I think we are on the way to the Devil;" and that he had come to the point of writing conservative pamphlets.[154] His opinions on the ballot were conservative, so much so, that he said in 1839 that the Tories had generously refrained from panning his collected works out of gratitude for his phillipic on the ballot.[155] In a sermon in 1844 he summed up his feelings about the ballot, and about popular participation in government more generally.

> We are upon the eve of great changes; it is not *that* I fear, for changes are inevitable in human affairs. As time is the greatest of all innovators, man must change also; and it is better to change intentionally, and upon plan and reflection, than suddenly, hastily, and upon the spur of tumult and pertubation.
> The real subject of dread, is not that temperate changes are contemplated by wise men, but that all men are stepping out of their province, and becoming amenders of the law and institutions under which we live:- that those laws and institutions are capable of improvement by men of superior talents, with leisure for their arrangements, and the confidence of their fellow subjects for their support, I cannot doubt; but what I dread, is the number of improvers, the igorance of improvers, the total want of modesty in improvers; their entire imperception of the difficulty of the task, and the wild and visionary schemes of yesterday, pressed forward with as much certainty as if they were sanctioned by the experience of ages.
> In this way, it is that countries are hurried on, beyond the boundaries of reason, to brink of revolution and political ruin.[156]

It may be seen from this quotation, and from Sydney's opinions in his work on the ballot, that he had come full circle from his fiery liberalism of the early part of the century to a timid conservatism in the 1840's, even adopting those attitudes of his earlier opponents of resisting innovation and keeping things as they were. In a manner of speaking, however, his drift to the right was not as pronounced as might be thought at first glance, for the things he had fought for earlier had become realities, and he defended not the status quo, but a new status quo that he had helped to create. He had used liberalism in his previous campaigns, and time and reform had carried those liberal principles into legislation that was, for him, sufficiently advanced and enlightened. Just as the Tories prior to 1832 had regarded the Constitution as perfect, so Sydney after the major Whig reforms of the 1830's looked upon it as having been updated, or perfected. Most of what his Whig liberalism had aspired to in the period before the Regency had been achieved, and he was content to rest on those solid accomplishments, to bask in the glory of his status of great liberal clergyman, and to deplore visionary schemes. If it might seem incongrous to the twentieth century for a great reformer to end as a conservative, it is perhaps less so if one thinks in terms of an aging man enjoying his renown and the well-earned fruits of his labor in his declining years.

Sydney's sally into the breach of the ballot was his last political effort of any significance, and it has been said that he devoted his remaining years to projects that were usually crotchetty, and often querulous. On 12 May, 1842, he wrote a letter to the Editor of the Morning Chronicle complaining of the practice of locking the doors on the passengers cars of the Great Western Railway, a line on which he often travelled. The reason given for the incarceration was the protection of "rash or drunken" passengers who might fall or step out of the moving cars; but Sydney was more concerned about the danger to the whole body of passengers in the event of a wreck. He was particularly concerned because of the terrible trainwreck in Meudon, in France, in which more than fifty passengers, including an eminent admiral, were trapped and burned beyond recognition. He feared, that people in a minor wreck might panic and be killed or injured precisely because they were locked in. He referred to the directors of the Great Western as "monopolists," and he claimed passengers had every right to enjoy free competition. Because passengers were not free to leave the cars at certain stops he was led to say that: "Man is universally the master of his own body, except he chooses to go from Paddington to Bridgewater:

there only the Habeas Corpus is refused." If this kind of concern for passengers was good, he said, "Why are not strait-wristcoats used? Why is not the accidental traveller strapped down?" Outside riders on horse drawn coaches had not been strapped down, nor had travellers in Channel packets been locked in their staterooms to keep them from falling overboard. It was only the Great Western Railway, which having destroyed all competing means of transportation by means of a monopoly, that required the locking in. The directors, he asserted, had a duty to, at least, inform the public of the danger. "Fools there will be," he said, "on roads of iron and on roads of gravel, and they must suffer for their folly; but why are Socrates, Solon, and Solomon to be locked up?" The railroads did possess a form of monopoly, and he concluded his letter by recommending that since the government had granted the monopoly, the interest of the public required governmental regulation, by law if necessary.[157]

Sydney's first letter elicited a quick response form the Great Western, and in a second letter written on 7 June, 1842, he mentioned meeting with two gentlemen from the railway. They failed to persuade him of the wisdom of their policy, and he evidently failed to convince them of their folly. He maintained that their error was that they:

> ...seem to require that the imagination should be sent by some other conveyance, and that only loads of unimpassioned, unintellectual flesh and blood should be darted along the Western rail; whereas, the female homo is a screaming, parturient, interjectional, hysterical animal, whose delicacy and timidity, monopolists (even much as it may surprise them) must be taught to consult. The female, in all probability, never would jump out; but she thinks she may jump out when she pleases; and this is intensely comfortable.

Two dangers existed, he maintained: one to the foolish or drunken individual who might injure himself, and the other to the whole mass of people in a loaded train; and that it was not the better part of wisdom to subject the whole body of passengers to the dangers of fire in order to protect one foolish individual. He claimed that it was only the monopolistic nature of the business that permitted the Great Western to have such a policy, and he submitted that their responsibility should end with adequate warning of the danger. He objected also to what he called the "hemi-plegian law" under which doors on only one side of the cars were locked. If the car should topple over on the unlocked side, the passengers would be trapped as surely as both were locked. "Leave me to escape in the best way I can," he said, even on the off-side, across the tracks, for "I do not remain in the valley of death between the two trains, but am over to the opposite bank in an instant-only half-roasted or merely browned, certainly not done enough for the Great Western Directors."[158]

He called in his aristocratic friends to assist him in his campaign against the Great Western, as a letter to Lord Harrowby attests;[159] and in another letter, written in June, 1842, he announced his victory over the railroad. They had given in, he boasted, just when he had readied a third letter which would have described the carnage in each successive car of a wrecked train as:

1. Stewed duke
2. Bishops done in their own gravy.
3. Three ladies of quality nicely browned
4. Lawyers "stewed in their own briefs a la Maintenon"
5. Legs out windows like pigeon pie
6. An overdone fat woman
7. "Two Scotchmen dead but raw, sulphuric acid perceptible."[160]

In an incomplete letter to Sir Robert Peel Sydney objected to Peel's cruel:

> attack upon me...to attribute all my interference with the arbitrary proceedings of Rail Roads to personal fear-
>
> Nothing can be more ungrateful and unkind: I thought only of you and for you-as many Whig Gentlemen will bear me testimony who rebuked me for my anxiety-I said to myself & to them "our Lovely and intrepid Minister may be overthrown on the rail. the Lock'd door may be uppermost he will kick and call on the Speaker, and the Serjeant

> at arms in vain- nothing will remain of all his graces, his flexibilities, his fascinating facetious fun, his Social warmth...of his dear heavy pleasantry, of his prevailing skill to impart disorderly Wishes to the purest heart nothing will remain of it all but an heap of ashes for the parish Church of Tamworth. he perishes at the moment that he is becoming as powerful in the drawing room of Court as in the house of Parliament..." I have no doubt of your bravery Sr. Robert though you have of mine but then Consider what different lives we have led & What a school of Corage is that Troop of Yeomanry at Tamworth the Tory fencibles: who can doubt your corage who has seen you at their head Marching up Pitt Street through Dundas Square up to Liverpool Lane & looking all the while like those beautiful medals of <u>Bellona frigida</u> & <u>Mars sine sanguine</u>...161

Actually, Sydney approved of the railroads, as he did of most modern inventions, and he appended to his letter his opinion that:

> Railroad travelling is a delightful improvement of human life. Man is become a bird; he can fly longer and quicker than a Solan Goose. The mama rushes sixty miles in two hours to the aching finger of her conjugating and declining grammar boy. The early Scotchman scratches himself in the morning mists of the North, and has his porridge in Piccadilly before the setting sun. The Puseyite priest, after a rush of 100 miles, appears with his little volume of nonsense at the breakfast of his bookseller.

Returning to a technique employed earlier in his reviews, he suggested that nothing would be done about the abominable practice of locking passengers in until a horrible tragedy occurred, and preferably one involving an eminent figure:

> The first person of rank who is killed

will put everything in order, and produce a code of the most careful rules. I hope it will not be one of the bench of bishops; but should it be so destined, let the burnt bishop- the unwilling Latimer- remember that, however painful gradual concoction by fire may be, his death will produce unspeakable benefit to the public. Even Sodor and Man will be better than nothing. From that moment the bad effects of the monopoly are destroyed; no more fatal deference to the directors; no despotic incarceration, no barbarous inattention to the anatomy and physiology of the human body; no commitment to locomotive prisons with warrant. We shall then find it possible

"Voyager libre sans mourir."162

Apart from his annoyance at being locked in, Sydney's experience with railways was excellent. On 5 December, 1838, he had travelled to Combe Florey by rail for the first time, and he said of the trip: "...I have a great many commonplaces to say about it, but I will be merciful. 163 About February, 1841, he had taken the train back to London, travelling some eighty miles on the Bath Railroad, which delighted him. Before the railroads, he said, man had been deficient in locomotion, being able to walk only about four miles in an hour, while a wild goose could fly eighty, but "...I can run now much faster than a Fox or an Hare and beat a Carrier pigeon or an Eagle for 100 miles."164 Sydney's letters on the railroad were clever, and they showed that he still had his old knack for turning a phrase, even if the issue was not a critical one.

In 1842 the state of Pennsylvania repudiated certain of its bonds, including some that Sydney had invested in, and his annoyance ripened into righteous wrath and a petition to the Congress of the United States in 1843. It was as a result of the petition, and his accompanying letters to the Editor of the Morning Chronicle that Sydney became more generally known in the United States, where, as a result of hostility and misrepresentation in American publications, he was frequently thought of an a sneering and sarcastic critic of the new republic.

In vain, to a large extent, he protested his innocence of the charges, and of his long and continuing friendship toward America, and he pointed to his previous publications as evidence.

Sydney had, defended America in his articles in the *Edinburgh Review* during times when memories of the American Revolution and the War of 1812 were still fresh in the minds of the English reading public. He had written three reviews on America, and although interlaced with criticisms of unnecessary American belligerance, sensitivity, and crudity, they were usually favorable towards the United States. He believed that the Tory government had treated America with arrogance and contempt, which was a luxury which Britain could not afford vis a'vis a rapidly growing and developing nation. He approved richly of the economy in American government where:

> The American king has about 5000*l*. per annum, the vice-king 1000*l*. They hire their Lord Liverpool at about a thousand per annum, and their Lord Sidmouth (a good bargain), at the same sum. Their Mr. Crokers are inexpressibly reasonable, -somewhere about the price of an English doorkeeper, or bearer of a mace. Life, however, seems to go on very well, in spite of these low salaries; and the purposes of government to be very fairly answered.[165]

Taxes in America were low, of which he also approved, and the numerous licenses required of Englishmen were simply non-existent. The relative American reluctance to engage in foreign wars pleased him, and he thought, preserved America from ruinous taxation.[166] He pointed out that under the corrupt Tory borough system the British Ambassador to Washington received a higher salary than the President of the United States, while the Vice president received less than a clerk in the House of Commons.[167]

Just as Sydney never questioned his right, and that of his class, to rule through the House of Commons, so he tacitly accepted (and openly proclaimed) British superiority over all other nations, America included. As he justly observed, most Americans were only recently descended from Britain, and the "Franklins and Washingtons, and all other sages and heroes of their revolution were born and bred subjects of the King...." Since independence they had created little or nothing in the Arts, Sciences, or Literature, for: "In the four quarters of the globe, who reads an American book? or goes to an American play, or looks at an American picture or statue?"[168] It was probably one his most famous lines, and the only one known to many Americans. It was resented by Americans of the period, and it was prejudiced; but Sydney was not entirely uninformed, and his opinion was based on more than national chauvinism. As he had written earlier:

> Literature the Americans have none-no native literature, we mean, It is all imported. They had a Franklin, indeed; and may afford to live for half a century on his fame. There is, or was, a Mr. Dwight, who wrote some poems; and his baptismal name was Timothy. There is also a small account of Virginia by Jefferson, and an Epic by Joel Barlow; and some pieces of pleasantry by Mr. Irving. But why should the Americans write books, when a six weeks passage brings them, in their own tongue, our sense, science, and genius, in bales and hogsheads? Prairies, Steamboats, grist-mills, are their natural objects for centuries to come. Then, when they have got to the Pacific Ocean-epic poems, plays, pleasures of memory, and all the elegant gratifications of an ancient people who have tamed the wild earth, and set down to amuse themselves. -This is the natural march of human affairs.[169]

Sydney applauded the American abandonment of wigs and robes in the courts, for he believed that justice had not been impeded in any way by the change, and he doubted that justice was improved in any way by the "colour, quantity, or configuration of cloth and hair."[170] More important than such trivial modifications of legal costumes, he thought, was the American plan of setting aside one thirty-sixth of the land for the support of public education, a plan that proved to him that Americans were a "wise, reflecting, and a virtuous people."[171]

The virtue of Americans was reflected in their

religious practices, and Sydney described them as a religious people. Since they practiced freedom of religion there was no persecution of sects, no exclusion from office, and no collection of the tithe; but nonetheless churches were well attended, and religion was respected, as was the clergy.[172] He pointed out that the "High Sheriff of New York" was a Jew, while in England it was only after great difficulty that a bill had passed "to allow the first Duke of England to carry a gold stick before the King-because he was a Catholic!" The Dissenters' Marriage Bill, which discriminated against Unitarians, would have excited, he said, "the contempt of a Chictaw or Cherokee." As far as religious freedom was concerned:

> ...the Americans are at the head of all the nations of the world: and at the same time they are, especially in the Eastern and Midland States, so far from being indifferent on subjects of religion, that they may be most justly characterized as a very religious people: but they are devout without being unjust (the great problem in religion); an higher proof of civilization than painted tea-cups, waterproof leather, or broad cloth at two guineas a yard.[173]

The topic of emigration to America was one of great interest to many of the British in the 1820's, and Sydney wrote on it as well. Acknowledging the excellent opportunities for laborers or farmers in the New World, he generally discouraged emigration, especially for those who possessed any property. There were great prospects for prosperity in America, but he noted that since the war had ended taxes in England might be lightened, and that there were rich prospects at home. He expected the division of the United States into several countries, for how could "...the dwellers on the Columbia...have common interest with the navigators of the Hudson and the Delaware."[174] He did not oppose emigration, but he warned all potential emigrants that they might feel differently about England when they were five or six thousand miles away on the banks of the Little Wabash:

> He should be quite sure that he does not go there from ill temper or to be pitied-or to be regretted-or from ignorance of what is to happen to him- or because he is a poet-but because he has not enough

>   to eat here, and is sure of abundance
>   where he is going.[175]

The major blot against America in Sydney's opinion was slavery, on which he commented:

> The great curse of America is the institution of Slavery-of itself far more than the foulest blot upon their national character, and an evil which counterbalances all the excisemen, licensers, and tax-gatherers of England. No virtuous man ought to trust his own character, or the character of his children, to the demoralizing effects produced by commanding slaves. Justice, gentleness, pity, and humility, soon give way before them. Conscience suspends its functions. The love of command-the impatience of restraint, get the better of every other feeling; and cruelty has no other linit than fear.[176]

Feelings such as those created by slavery were the "consummation of wickedness", said Sydney, and he deplored their existence among men who presumably knew the value of liberty; and he felt that it was the duty of every American to "efface this foul stain from its character." If one considered that America tolerated slavery, she could not be compared with the most backward European nation. "What is freedom", he asked, "where all are not free: where the greatest of God's blessings is limited, with impious caprice, to the colour of the body?" No nation that countenanced slavery should dare to reproach the English for their rotten boroughs or their corrupt electoral practices. Sydney wished America well, but he considered slavery to an "atrocious crime...which makes liberty itself distrusted, and the boast of it disgusting."[177]

Sydney was criticized by Americans because his reviews were not entirely laudatory, but in all fairness to him, he could also be critical of his own countrymen. English travellers in the Western Hemisphere often criticized Americans because of their loquacity and inquisitiveness, upon which criticism Sydney noted that the fault was not merely with the Americans, for the English enjoyed sulking and not speaking to anyone. Of Englishmen he said:

> It is not so much that Mr. Bull disdains to talk, as that Mr. Bull has nothing to say. His forefathers have been out of spirits for six or seven hundred years, and seeing nothing but fog and vapour, he is out of spirits too; and when there is no selling or buying, or no business to settle, he prefers being alone and looking at the fire. If any gentleman was in distress, he would willingly lend an helping hand; but he thinks it no part of neighbourhood to talk to a person because he happens to be near him....the English are the most disagreeable of all the nations of Europe,-more surly and morose, with less disposition to please, to exert themselves for the good of society, to make small sacrifices, and to put themselves out of their way. They are content with Magna Charta and Trial by Jury; and think they are not bound to excel the rest of the world in small behaviour, if they are superior to them in great institutions.[178]

He observed with satisfaction, reflecting, no doubt, on his days as a fat public school boy, "the total absence of all games in America. No cricket, foot-ball, nor leap-frog-all seems solid and profitable."[179] It is also of interest to observe that in 1824 neither Sydney nor the editorial staff of the Edinburgh Review knew how to spell the name of the President of the United States.[180]

Sydney's friendly views on America were not confined solely to his reviews, and he spoke favorably of the new nation in 1818 in a letter to Jeffrey, referring to himself as a "Philoyankeeist".[181] To Lord Grey he wrote:

> How can anyone in this Country be dead to the Experiment which So many millions of English are making of living without Church, King, or Noble-three institutions of Society which are kind enough to eat up for us the fruits, the power, and the distinction of the land in which we live; I will except you and Myself from the general denunciation of these favored Classes, sincerely convinced that if all Nobles

379

>had been as upright and honorable as you,
>and all parsons as tolerant as I am,
>America would never have been in existence....[182]

He expected that sectional interests and the lack of leadership, rather than slavery, would ultimately result in the fragmentation of the United States, but he continued to approve of American attitudes on independence and on a "cheap Church and King."[183] Much later, but before his quarrel over the Pennsylvania bonds, he wrote to an American friend, asserting his admiration for America and for the "great Number of Agreeable enlightened Americans" he had met.[184]

Sydney Smith was too big a man not to admit error, and he modified his earlier opinion of Washington Irving in 1836 after reading *Astoria*, which was, he said, "a book to put in your library, as an entertaining, well written,-*very* well written-account of savage life, on a most extensive scale."[185] Such an admission, privately made, did nothing to mollify American feelings, and any good impression he might have on America made was largely dissipated by the issue of the Pennsylvania bonds.

An economic recession in 1842 and 1843 caused several American states to default on interest payments, and as early as 19 September, 1842, Sydney mentioned that he had been done out of §50 by Pennsylvania.[186] After that date Pennsylvania repudiated the bonds, and on 18 May, 1843, Sydney, whose actions reflected an imperfect understanding of American federalism, addressed a petition to the Congress of the United States. He asked that Congress take steps to insure the repayment of honorable debts repudiated by several of the states; asserting at the same time that he had lost a small but important sum by the repudiation, which he attributed to fraud rather than to hardship. He told the Congress that Pennsylvania's refusal to pay her just debts would encourage anti-American sentiment in European aristocratic circles, and that in addition to the immorality of the step taken by Pennsylvania, it could result in a loss of American power.[187]

Sydney's petition stirred up a fierce response in America, most of it hostile to him and his presumptions, but it would appear that he had little hope of regaining the limited capital he had invested, and that he hoped mostly to embarrass the Pennsylvanians.[188] Partly as a reaction to hostile letters and comments from America he wrote two letters to the Editor of the Morning Chronicle which were, even though they borrowed some of the humorous techniques of his earlier writings, among his wittiest efforts. In the face of American abuse he had no intention of retracting any of the statements he had made in his petition. He regarded himself as a friend of America, and felt that the Pennsylvanians had tasted the luxury of dishonesty, and had done so at the expense of investors who had lent their money in good faith. He said that he was tempted to seize every Pennsylvanian he saw in London and appropriate his hat and coat, his handkerchief and watch, and "the London Guide, which he always carries in his pockets." He was truly outraged by the action of Pennsylvania, and he described a Pennsylvanian showing the points of interest in his state to a visitor, which might include:

> ...Larcenous Lake, Swindling Swamp, Crafty Canal, and Rogues' Railway, and other dishonest works. "This swamp we gained (says the patriotic borrower) by the repudiated loan of 1828. Our canal robbery was in 1830; we pocketed your good people's money for the railroad only last year."... if I had the misfortune to be born among such a people...I would fly to Newgate for greater purity of thought, and seek in the prisons of England for better rules of life.[189]

In a second letter dated 22 November, 1843, he responded to the charge that he had a "morbid hatred" of America, stating categorically his longstanding friendship for the U.S., and the fact that he had castigated Pennsylvania only "because she had ruined so many helpless children, so many miserable women, so many aged men." America would need credit in the future, he noted, and Pennsylvania's example was not the way to win it. He envisaged a Pennsylvania army as:

> ...immense corps of insolvent light infantry, regiments of heavy horse debtors, battalions of repudiators, brigades of bankrupts, with Vivre sans payer, ou mourir, on their banners, and aere aliena on their trumpets: all these desperate debtors would fight to the death for their country, and probably drive into the sea their invading

creditors.

Sydney was so convinced that Pennsylvania would never redeem her repudiated obligations that he offered to be tarred and feathered, a tempting prospect, no doubt, to his detractors, when she did.[190]

In a letter dating from the same period he announced his intention to sell his Pennsylvia bonds at a loss,[191] which he ultimately did, and in a later letter he confessed that he had never hoped for repayment, but that he merely desired to shame Pennsylvania as much as possible. On 18 December, 1843, he announced with some satisfaction that:

> My bomb has fallen very successfully in America, and the list of killed and wounded is extensive. I have several quires of paper sent me every day, calling me monster, thief, atheist, deist, etc.[192]

Early in the next year he claimed to have forgotten the whole affair, but said that he continued "to receive letters and papers from the most remote corners of the United States, with every vituperative epithet which human rage has invented."[193]

Sydney's annoyance with the bad faith of the Pennsylvanias increased to rage with his very real, if not too substantial, financial loss in his unlucky investment. As materialistic as the rest of his generation, and more principled than most of it, assaults on his property were the quickest and most certain method of arousing his ire; but his experience with Pennsylvania did not alter his general attitude towards America, from which he also received numerous sympathetic letters, as well as gifts of apples and cheeses. As late as February, 1844, he wrote to Charles Dickens: "Many thanks for the 'Christmas Carol' which I shall immediately proceed upon, in preference to six American pamphlets I found upon my arrival...all promising immediate payment."[194]

His letters on the Pennsylvania bonds marked the last polemical effort of Sydney Smith, who was fully aware that his long career was drawing to a close. His pragmatic view of life and its ultimate end, his religious vocation, and his beliefs prevented him from fearing or dreading death, and he awaited it not with resignation but with hope. In life he was constantly aware of death, but instead of dwelling morbidly on it, he regarded death with his usual cheerful acceptance. As early as 1813 he had written to his brother Bobus:

> Pray take care of yourself. We shall both be a brown infragrant powder in thirty or forty years. Let us contrive to last out for the same, or nearly the same time. Weary will the latter half of my pilgrimage be, if you leave me in the lurch.[195]

His friendship with Lord and Lady Holland had, after the misunderstanding over the mitre in 1834, ripened into an even closer and warmer relationship, and Lord Holland's death in 1840 saddened Sydney deeply. He offered his sympathy to Lady Holland, and offered to come to her if she wished. "I urge no topics of Consolation-" he said, "for I know none."[196] Many, probably most, of his friends of his own age were dead or dying, and Sydney commented that he had learned to live, "as a soldier does in war, expecting that on any one moment the best and dearest may be killed..."[197] In a group of maxims which were written about 1837, and which reflect his common sense more than his wit, he had spoken of:

> <u>Death</u>-it must come some time or other. It has come to all, greater, better, wiser, than I
>
> I have lived sixty-six years.
>
> I have done but very little harm in the world, and I have brought up my family.[198]

Another sure indication to Sydney of his impending end was the decline of his health, and his acknowledgement of aging. He was always very concerned about his health, and that of Mrs. Sydney and his children, and from 1830 or so he filled his letters with complaints of physical ailments. In a letter to his son in law in 1835 he said:

> I am suffering from my old complaint, the Hay-fever(as it is called.) My fear is of perishing by deliquescence.-I melt away in Nasal and Lachymal profluvia. My remedies are warm Pediluvium, Cathartics,

> topical application of a watery solution of Opium to eyes ears, and the interior of the nostrils. The membrane is so irritable, that light, dust, contradiction, an absurd remark, the sight of a dissenter,-anything, sets me a sneezing and if I begin sneezing at 12, I don't leave off till two o'clock-and am heard distinctly in Taunton...at a distance of six miles.[199]

His respiratory difficulties bore the symptoms of a form of asthma that affects persons late in life, and which is most difficult to treat and alleviate.

Sydney apparently did not expect to live as long as he did, and on the basis of the life expectancy of his age he was not being unduly pessimistic, and as early as 8 February, 1836, he announced that he was "going slowly down the Hill of Life-one Evil of old age is that as your time is come you think every little illness is the beginning of the End-When a man expects to be arrested every knock at the door is an alarm-"[200] In 1839 he thanked a friend for giving him a key to the Green Street Gate, where he had bought his last London residence, for "Mrs Smith & I are both getting large & less locomotive".[201] His chief complaints were gout, asthma, and a senile decrepitude that affected his physical functions generally. His mind remained clear, and his wit unaffected by his physical decline; and to the end of his life he joked about his infirmities. In 1840 he professed to be "pretty well, except Gout, Asthma, and pain in all the Bones, and all the flesh of my body"; and when he became ill while visiting friends he decided that he was "getting too old to pay visits, and it will soon become my duty to keep my miseries and infirmities to myself."[202] He described himself as being "improved in lumbago, but still, less upright than Aristides.... life goes on very well, except that I am often reminded I am too near the end of it."[203]

In 1842 he sadly admitted that "...we are antient and and ailing people disglued unscrewed & tumbling to pieces and we are often forced to go to bed when we would rather be Lemonading...."[204] Three months later he said: "Mrs Sydney and I are in fair health considering how old we are but death is not far from us all-come when it will I have had a fair Share of the good things of this Life-"[205] Later in the same year, writing with regret but without despair, he said to Lady Holland:

> It is a bore, I admit, to be past seventy, for you are left for execution, and are daily expecting the death-warrant; but, as you say, it is not anything very capital we quit. We are, at the close of life, only hurried away from stomach-aches, pains in the joints, from sleepless nights and unamusing days, from weakness, ugliness, and nervous tremors; but we shall meet again in another planet, cured of all our defects. Rogers will be less irritable; Macaulay more silent; Hallam will assent, Jeffrey will speak slower; Bobus will be just as he is; I shall be more respectful to the upper clergy ...206

By the end of 1842 he complained that "...I am very old 72-Low in Spirits gaity & the least thing or the smallest alteration of habits makes me ill", but with a flash of his old spirit he added, "Mrs. Sydney is still laid up with a Throat-I remember the time when there were no Throats."207

In 1843 he again complained of the gout, and he also developed bladder trouble that he feared might interfere with his preaching at St. Paul's, as it had done already at Combe Florey.208 In the next month, however, he fairly cheerfully reported that: "My Evils were breathlessness and a tendency to faint. The gout broke out & these Evils disappeared...."209 His physical decline did not prevent him from reiterating his even older complaint about the boredom of the country, and in a letter to Lady Grey he announced:

> Combe Florey Gazette
> Mrs. Smith's large red Cow is expected to calve this week.
> Mr Gibbs has bought Mr Smith's Lame Mare
> it rained yesterday, and a correspondent observes that it is not unlikely to rain today.
> Mr Smith is better
> Mrs. Smith is indisposed
> a nest of black Magpies was found near the Village yesterday 210

His mind remained clear, and his wit unimpaired by his physical debilitation, and on 26 August, 1844, he wrote to Miss Berry:

> The general notion here is that the two Miss Berrys, in conjunction with Lady Charlotte, have been destroyed by fire at Richmond. I am told that the Hand-in-Hand and Phoenix fire-engines played upon them for a considerable time without the smallest effect; that they were so brilliant, and emitted so many sparks, and showed themselves to be composed of materials so combustible, that it was impossible to save them; that the elder Miss Berry(Elder Berry) was heard in her last sufferings, inviting a party to dinner after the fire....[211]

In that autumn of 1844 he visited the shore for his health, but the holiday did not restore his strength, and he lamented that he was so weak "that I verily believe, if the knife were put into my hand, I should not have the strength or energy to stick it into a Dissenter." Put on a meatless diet, he pled vainly for "even the wing of a roasted butterfly."[212] In a letter to Sir Robert Peel he said that his stomach could stand only bread and water, but that Dr. Holland, his son-in-law and physician, had promoted him to "light and innocent puddings."[213] In late 1844 Sydney was clearly declining, and in an undated letter, which would appear to have been written in December, 1844, or early in 1845, Mrs. Sydney reported to Lady Holland that:

> Dear Sydney is a little beaten by a bad & restless night; but his cough is better & he continues to gain strength. The great evil is the extreme delicacy of both Stomach & Liver so very liable to be disarranged by trifles not always (by the ignorant) to be foreseen.[214]

A second similarly undated letter added:

> ...you are most kind dear Lady but Sydney can not eat solids at present or wd be most thankful for your kind offer. He has had a good night & his cough seems gone for the present but he still has an

>oppression on his breathing which makes
>any solid food in the Stomach an evil...
>Dr. Holland says this weather is very
>much against his making progress.[215]

Since he practiced what he preached, Sydney approached old age and death, soothed and sustained as much by his own experience as by Christian precepts and he offered the consolation that:

>...Providence has been bounteous to every
>period of life; ...the pleasures of age
>greater, and the pains less, than we com-
>monly suppose them to be; and ...when old
>age is a state of affliction and des-
>pair, it is not rendered so, by a decay-
>ing body, but by a sinful mind... gratui-
>tous happiness is never conceded to man
>at any period of life; but in youth, in
>manhood, in old age, is alike, and alone
>gained by doing well, and by faith in
>Christ.[216]

He advised his congregation not to pity an old man, for he would probably not exchange his white hairs for youth. No longer in bondage to sin and passion, he lived in tranquility and wanted only those things that were righteous. For the aged, it was "more pleasant to walk with God in old age, than to sin in all the flower, and freshness of youth."[217] Mankind generally accorded respect to people who were aged, and usually acknowledged the wisdom their years had brought them. Deafness, blindness, and apathy were aspects of God's mercy, for they deadened the senses while leading man to immortality; for pain, being the wages of sin, was not necessary, and death, which brought man closer to God, should panic only the sinful.[218]

In late 1845 Sydney continued to decline, and as early as 3 January, 1845, Lady Holland sighed: "Alas! I cannot say anything about dear Sydney the least consolatory Hopes of recovery are very slender. He suffers greatly from breathlessness, which of all sufferings is said to be the most distressing. What a loss!"[219] He was dying, probably more from general debility than anything else, but his mind remained clear; and when a nurse mistakenly administered a bottle of ink to him in place of his medicine, and confessed her error, he quipped: "Then bring me all the blotting paper there is in the house."[220] Although failing rapidly he was still cognisant of his duties and prerogatives, and he bestowed a living on a poor Tory clergyman. Sydney's daughter described the scene when, although Sydney protested that he was too weak to stand a visit, the grateful clergyman "entered, -my father gave him a few words of advice, -the clergyman silently pressed his hand, and blessed his death-bed. Surely such blessings are not given in vain!" "He seemed", she said, "to meet death with that calmness which the memory of a well-spent life, and trust in the mercy of God, can alone give."[221]

Sydney had contracted his final illness at Combe Florey, but he had been brought back to his house on Green Street where he could receive better medical attention, and it was there that he died on 22 February, 1845. The cause of his death was given by his daughter as being hydrothorax, resulting from heart disease. His son Windham, who was present, closed his eyes. Following his wishes he was buried privately, in a funeral attended only by members of his family and close friends, next to his son Douglas in Kensal Green Cemetary.

The life and career of Sydney Smith had ended, but his memory was not so easily erased. His widow may have had her intellectual shortcomings, but her love for him was undying, and in a letter to Lady Elizabeth Holland, who had become an even more intimate friend of the Smiths since the death of her husband, Mrs. Sydney wrote:

> I have much of unavoidable trifles to turn over, & inspect, & when the eyes & hands are occupied the thoughts are compell'd to follow them. I am surrounded with papers that it is necessary I should read destroy & understand- The light of My Life is extinguished! Of what use the residue? How touching & afflicting the death of dear Bobus! Almost at the same time & with such a similarity of complaints. Who can every hope again to look on two such men.[222]

The London <u>Times</u> ran an obituary notice on Sydney on 25 February which covered most of the salient facts of his career, and which was generally laudatory. The <u>Annual Register</u> for 1845 gave him a lengthy obituary, much of which the author obviously cribbed from Sydney's own preface to his collected works of 1839. The <u>Gentleman's</u>

Magazine offered the opinion that:

> ...old as Sydney Smith was, he died too soon....No man can fill his place. He has furnished, however, more materials for literary criticism than for diversified narrative; the events of his life were not so extraordinary as the qualities of his mind were peculiar and characteristic.[223]

But perhaps the finest tribute to Sydney was paid to him by John Wilson Croker, his old antagonist in both the Tory party and in the pages of the Quarterly Review, who reviewed Sydney's posthumously published A Fragment on the Irish Roman Catholic Church along with several other works on Ireland. "...the case is stated", he said, "in the posthumous pamphlet of Sydney Smith-alas, poor Yorick!-with a pleasantry that gives poignancy to good sense, a felicity of illustration that comes home to every understanding, and a truth...which everyone... must acknowledge... Serious Tories may, perhaps, be inclined to receive suspiciously the warnings of the facetious Whig, but they will not disregard the advice of, we will not say a wiser(for Sydney was wise in his generation), but a more serious monitor."[224]

Meticulous about financial matters to the end, Sydney left a carefully drawn up will which he had signed on on 6 June, 1843, and which had been witnessed by Sarah Rawlinson and Thomas Oliver, his cook and footman. A first codicil to the will, signed on 3 January, 1844, raised the §200 allowance to Windham to §500 during the life of Mrs. Sydney. This change is interesting in that it probably represents at least a partial return to grace by Windham, although no evidence of it exists other than his presence at his father's deathbed. Sydney signed a second codicil on 18 October, 1844, removing Cecil Smith and Thomas Philips as his executors, and substituting his sons-in-law in their place. His action may reflect a rift with the previously appointed executors, but if so, no independent evidence of it has been found, and it is more likely that it was a gesture of his growing affection and confidence in Nathaniel Hibbert and Dr. Henry Holland. He drew up and signed a third codicil on 14 December, 1844, only about two months before his death, in which he directed that §30,000 in the three per cents were to go to Windham upon the death of Mrs. Sydney.[225]

The will was probated on 27 March, 1845, and proved with the codicils on 9 April, 1845. It has been stated that Sydney left less than §80,000, which was a very respectable estate; and considering the fact that he inherited less than §50,000 during his lifetime, and that he always lived well, if not luxuriously, it represents both good management and wise investment. His incident with the Pennsylvania bonds seems to have been his only bad speculation, and his losses in it were not significant. He left the bulk of his estate to his widow, even specifying that the dilapidations on all of his ecclesiastical preferment be paid out of property other than that bequeathed to her. He left also a number of small bequests, ranging from §10 to §100 to his servants, and a §30 annuity to one if she outlived Mrs. Sydney. He required also that Windham "settle himself apart from his mother" and made his annuity contingent upon his doing so; specifying also that Windham was not to inherit if he should become incapable, bankrupt, or an insolvent debtor. Upon the death of Mrs. Sydney those properties still remaining were to devolve upon Dr. and Mrs. Holland and Mr. and Mrs. Hibbert.[226]

CHAPTER XII

The Wit In Retrospect

The varying assessments of Sydney Smith in the past have not been wrong, for the most part, but for reasons of political or religious antipathy or incomplete information, they have tended to idealize or denigrate him unduly. When viewed totally, and as objectively as possible, his life and career present a picture that is not entirely new, but one that is made up of aspects of the older opinions seen in a new perspective. Neither a villain nor a saint, and most emphatically neither, he was an English gentleman who rose above his age early in his career, only to fall back to its level late in life. Like many other gentlemen of the time he adhered to the Whig party, for which he performed important services, and from which, according to the practices of the period, he expected suitable rewards. He was a good clergyman, for which no apology need be made, and anything he may have lacked in devotion was probably equally lacking in his clerical detractors. His earnest desire for justice and reason, and his conscientious performance of his duties, made up for his lack of devotion. The fact that he solicited and received clerical advancement as a recompense for his political activities is totally extraneous for, as he reminded his Tory enemies, such practices were universal. He was also a genuine wit, which obscured much of his real merit from the more sober-minded among his contemporaries, and which continues to baffle the stolid down to the present; he would have been witty regardless of his politics or his vocation, but since he was a liberal Whig clergyman, he used his wit for those purposes. He was a liberal in the eighteenth century meaning of the term, which did not interfere with any of the other facets of his career, not even his clerical vocation, for Sydney, while a priest, could be an anti-clerical in opposing excessive episcopal power, superstition, and religious bigotry.

The contradictions of Sydney Smith's politics were chiefly those of the Whig party: the difficulties of reconciling liberty with oligarchic government, and those perplexities were increased by his liberalism. Concerned about carrying the principles of the Glorious Revolution to their logical conclusion, he defended institutions that served that end, but he could be indifferent to practices or customs that were merely old. He was suspicious of power and of those who exercised it, and although he generally expressed that mistrust through his diatribes against the Tories, they suffered from his tirades only because they seemed to offer the greatest threat to individual liberty during most of his active years. He was a monarchist in that he preferred monarchial government to popular government, and he could both energetically denounce any attempts to extend royal authority, and later defend existing royal influence against popular encroachment. He steadily supported Whig policy, even when it created change of a threatening nature, as in the Great Reform Bill, but he opposed the Whigs when they exercised their power in reforming traditional practices in the Church. His concept of a completed system which embodied the principles of 1688 was achieved after the passage of the Whig reforms of the 1830's, and it was made up of a set of checks and balances in which the power of the crown was balanced by that of the aristocracy, which in turn was held in check by the wealthy, educated, and responsible elements of the public. Such a system, he believed, was the best guarantee of the rights of the individual and the traditional liberties of Englishmen.

If Sydney Smith believed in Divine Right in government, it was in the Divine Right of the wealthy and able aristocracy of England to rule. They were rich and the influence they had acquired in the years following the Glorious Revolution made them powerful. While they did not possess a monopoly on talent, if properly motivated, they patronized and rewarded men of ability, and they followed enlightened policies which benefitted the whole nation. It was for this reason that Sydney looked upon "the manufacture of Russells" as "a public and important concern",[1] and why he referred to the doctrine of the equality of all men as "that pernicious cant."[2] He was basically a rationalist, but he was also a believing Christian, and his belief in "rational religion" enabled him to associate spiritual and traditional restraints with his concept of liberty. In a sermon he could preach in favor of that" ...useful love of freedom, which is conscious that men must be restained, and busies itself in providing, that the restraints to which they are subjected shall be the wisest, and the best."[3]

Sydney was ambitious and materialistic, perhaps one might say even grasping, but there were limits to his ambitions, and as early as 1801, in a letter to his father, he had commented that most clergymen made a connection with an important aristocrat and hoped for great things, but:

> As for me I confess my ideas are rather lower & more practical- a few dinners-- my salary well pay'd- the power of applying for a frank- a bow in the public Streets- and a good deal of commendation behind my back- these are the limits of my expectations- & the probable limits of my good fortune.[4]

He was remarkably successful in fulfilling his aspirations and the letter of 1801 described his later successes very well. He hoped to fulfill his ambition through his services to the Whig party, a party which he believed to be in possession of the best political principles. He was rewarded for his role in the facilitation of Whig policy, and he ended his life a wealthy man and in a position of prominence; but he acquired much of his wealth by way of inheritance rather than political reward, and he considered that he had been shabbily treated by the Whigs, who never made him a bishop although they had it in their power to do so. His attacks on the Whigs in the later thirties shocked his friends, but he brushed away their disapproval. "If by old and valued friends, you mean political friends", he said, "I have no act of friendship to thank the Whigs for, since the accession of Lord Melbourne, but much the contrary. As a party, they are no friends of mine-"[5] and indeed, Lord Melbourne himself later lamented that "We shall not be forgiven for not having made Sidney [sic] Smith a bishop."[6]

Whether or not Sydney Smith would have been a good bishop or not is idle conjecture, for while he certainly had the ability, no politician had both the courage and the inclination to elevate him to the episcopacy. Lady Elizabeth Holland would undoubtedly have done so, but even though she was influential, she was not that powerful; and had she advanced him to a mitre, his advancement would have been mainly for political services in the liberal cause.

Andre Chevrillon's book, Sydney Smith et La Renaissance des Idees liberales en Angleterre au XIX Siecle was a significant one, not only becuase it was the first critical work on Sydney, but also because it pinpointed his importance. He was indeed one who stood, not alone, but in a minority, for liberal principles based on reason at a time when they were threatened by Burkean traditionalism.

Those principles, which he maintained in all of his major campaigns were, for good or evil, generally triumphant in the latter period of his life, and his role in their vindication was an honorable one. "neither dazzled by visions of impracticable good, nor alarmed by shadows of imaginary evil...", he used reason to guide him, and the technique of the publicist to accomplish his ends.[7] He and many of his earlier biographers claimed that he acted as boldly as he did in the sure knowledge that his actions would retard his clerical career, but to the contrary his activities were those of a gambler staking his future on the prospects of the Whigs. The fact that he wagered badly during much of his life gave him an aura of martyrdom, but he did not remain behind in the race for wealth and preferment out of a willing spirit of self-sacrifice. At the same time, he was not solely self-seeking, and he believed firmly in the liberal principles he espoused; and while he certainly had it within his power to switch his principles and political allegiance throughout his life, he steadily refused to do so.

Burdett suggested that if an "attempt to make the best of both worlds be tested fairly, then Smith sacrificed- this present one."[8] In fact, however, Sydney sacrificed little, unless one regards him as a totally unprincipled fortune hunter. He was a man of liberal principles who entered the Church, and he sacrificed neither his principles nor his career, for he ended his life still holding to his principles after an eminently successful career in the Church. He did feel that he was being held back in the Church, and indeed he was, and he sometimes regretted having entered the Church rather than law or some other profession in which he might have advanced further and more quickly. Late in life he said:

> I often think what a different man I might have been if, like my friend Lord Holland, and others, I had passed my life with all that is most worth seeing and hearing in Europe, instead of being confined through the greater part of it to the society of the parish-clerk. I always feel it is combating with unequal weapons; I have made a tolerable fight of it, nevertheless.[9]

Sydney had been a steady friend of reform, not from bitterness or disappointemnt, but rather because he saw the need for reform earlier and more clearly than many of his contemporaries. Reforms such as those he worked for undoubtedly modified the social and political fabric that helped to protect England from the kind of revolutions that racked Europe. His reforms were clearly reforms, which could be carried out legally within the social and political establishment; and if Sydney was forward-looking in recognizing the need for reform earlier than many, he was myopic in assuming the eternal continuation of the social and political arrangements of 1688, as modified in detail by progressive thought. Like many thinkers of the late eighteenth and early nineteenth centuries he wrote universally for all mankind, but his thought and his experience were parochial and English. He took it for granted that other peoples responded identically to identical stimuli; that their economic, social, and political responses were predictable, and that they could be guided by the application of liberal principles which seemed to work in England.

For this reason Sydney's <u>Fragment on the Irish Roman Catholic Church</u> is not particularly profound, and it is chiefly an apology for the essential failure of his earlier proposals on Ireland. His assurances that Catholic emancipation would end Irish discontent had been based on rational thought that did not account for Irish nationalism, and he tried to explain away the continuing unrest by blaming the situation on the tardiness and reluctance of the changes.[10] He urged the disestablishment of the Church of Ireland and the economic restructuring of the Irish Roman Catholic Church along Anglican lines, which would, he was confident, gradually produce a body of Irish Roman Catholic clergymen who would closely resemble their counterparts in the Church of England.[11]

Irish nationalism was baffling to Sydney because he was an English nationalist who assumed the rightness and superiority of England, and a liberal rationalist who dealt with all problems reasonably. His assertion that "<u>Erin go bragh</u>" should be" ...Erin go bread and cheese, Erin go cabins that will keep out the rain, Erin go pantaloons without holes in them";[12] was reasonable but inadequate, and he was correct in believing that the creation of Irish nationalism had been assisted by retrograde and repressive British policy.

Just as Sydney's nationalism led him to condemn Tory policy in Ireland, so his reason and his Whig sympathies led him to oppose war generally, and the Napoleonic Wars specifically. War was expensive and unreasonable, and he was pessimistic about the outcome of the conflict with Napoleonic France. His predictions of defeat, confidently made throughout the period of the war, were as wrong as they could be, for they were based, not on an assessment of the situation, but on his belief that the Tories could not manage anything successfully, a sentiment which was not unmixed with thoughts of preferment should a major defeat bring the Whigs to power. In a letter to Jeffrey on 20 February, 1809, he sorrowfully announced that:

> Spain is quite gone. In all probability the English army will be entirely destroyed; and though the struggle will be long, the greater chance surely is that this country will at length be involved in the general ruin.[13]

And in the autumn of the same year he deplored the fact that: "...the European world is, I think, here at an end; there is surely no card left to play."[14]

Sydney was wrong about the Napoleonic Wars, but his error was caused partly by his partisanship, for his liberal thought opposed war generally, and because his demands for individual liberty and governmental economy militated against war. In 1823 he opposed British intervention to protect the "nascent Liberties" of the Spanish on the grounds that action on that basis might involve Britain in wars in Greece, Naples, and South America as well.[15] In an earlier letter to Lady Grey he had protested:

> For God's sake, do not drag me into another war! I am worn down, and worn out, with crusading and defending Europe, and protecting mankind; I must think a little of myself. I am sorry for the Spaniards- I am sorry for the Greeks- I deplore the fate of the Jews; the people of the Sandwich Islands are groaning under the most detestable tyranny; Baghdad is oppressed; I do not like the present state of the Delta; Thibet is not comfortable. Am I to fight for all these people? The world is bursting with sin and sorrow. Am I to be champion of the Decalogue, and to be eternally raising fleets and armies

to make all men good and happy? We have just done saving Europe, and I am afraid the consequence will be, that we shall cut each other's throats. No war, dear Lady Grey!- no eloquence; but apathy, selfishness, common sense, arithmetic! I beseech you, secure Lord Grey's swords and pistols, as the house-keeper did Don Quixote's armour. If there is another war, life will not be worth having. I will go to war with the King of Denmark if he is impertinent to you...but for no other reason.

'May the vengeance of Heaven" overtake all the Legitimates of Verona! but, in the present state of rent and taxes, they must be <u>left</u> to the vengeance of Heaven. I allow fighting in such a cause to be a luxury; but the business of a prudent, sensible man, is to guard against luxury.[16]

Sydney feared a new war with France, although he hoped that the pacific Louis Philippe would prevent a direct confrontation; but, oddly enough, he approved of the Opium War of 1839-1842. He had earlier regarded the Manchu Empire as the most powerful in the world, and he had expressed hostility to the "accustomed Insolence"[17] of British policy in the first part of the war; but by 1841 he was able to report that he was pleased by the reports from China, and that he favored "...bombarding the exclusive Asiatics who shut up the Earth, and will not let me walk civilly and quietly through it, doing no harm, and paying for all I want-".[18] By December, 1842, he even suggested that since there was a British army in China, Japan might as well be conquered too. "I utterly deny the right", he asserted righteously, "of those exclusive Orientals to shut up the earth in the way they are doing, and I think it is one of the most legitimate causes of war."[19] It is interesting to observe that his general opposition to war, and he had earlier denied the possibility of a just war, evaporated in the face of a conflict fought to establish rational principles like free trade.

China was, of course, a long way from London, and Sydney was never to travel east of the Rhine, which may possibly have helped him to rationalize British aggression in China. "Four miles from the Tartar Wall"[20] meant outermost Thule to him, for apart from his fairly extensive journeys within Britain, Sydney was not very much of a traveller. He wrote learnedly of Ireland and the Irish, but he had never set foot on the Emerald Isle, and although he had visited France three times during his lifetime, with brief excursions to the Netherlands and Germany, his expertise on foreign lands resulted largely from his reading.

For that reason, perhaps, Sydney enjoyed reading travel books, and he wrote several reviews of them. He found much to commend in some of them, but of the genre itself he said:

> When gentlemen return from distant countries, after long absences, their friends and parents, in the first moments of joy and affection, should tenderly commit to the flames any notes or records that the beloved stranger may have made of his travels- together with any maps or drawings he may have brought with him, or any thing else which may induce him to venture on the perils of authorship:- Because, though it is highly probable that the newly arrived person is eminent in his vocation- that he can wheel Sepoys to the right and left, if belligerent- that he is powerful at an invoice, if mercantile- that he has many tedious things to say about Budha [sic], if a Sanscrit scholar- it may yet be very doubtful if he possess any, or many of those qualities which qualify a man to tell his story to the public, and to write a good book.[21]

In another, a review of Fievee's <u>Lettres sur L'Angleterre</u>, he confided that: "The height of knowledge no man has yet scanned; but we have now [in Fievee's book] pretty well fathomed the gulf of ignorance."[22]

Persuaded by his increasing affluence Sydney went to Paris in 1826, where he was agreeably impressed by French cooking and French manners, but the great Cathedral of Notre Dame did not impress him, nor did the government of Charles X, whose downfall he accurately predicted.[23] In 1835 he took Mrs. Sydney and his daughter and son-in-law, Mr. and Mrs. Hibbert, to Paris for a short visit, and although he claimed that he had no desire to see that great city again, he thought that "every wife has a right to insist on seeing Paris."[24] Sydney claimed to be a gourmet, but deriving from an island renowned for the total absence of culinary skill his claims must be received with reservations. He did, however, enthusiastically acknowledge the quality of French cuisine, and his applause is a comforting redemption for his claims. "I shall not", he said movingly, "easily forget a Matelotte at the Rochers de Concailles, an almond tart at Montreuil, or a Foulet a la Tartare at Grignon's."[25] The trip was apparently uneventful except that he "...vomited as usual into the Channel....Rivers are said to run blood after an Engagement.-the Channel is discolored I am sure in a less elegant and less pernicious Way by English Tourists ..."[26]

In 1837 the Smiths again visited the continent, this time traveling chiefly in the Netherlands and Germany. Sydney did not regard the Netherlands as being fit for human existence, for although they were "historically wonderful-morally grand", they were also "physically odious-I have seen between 7 and 800 large Women without clothes painted by Rubens- till I positively refuse Mrs. Smith to see any more...."[27] The people were uglier than Macaulay, he said, and only about a quarter of the sights were worth seeing, which only confirmed his faith in the "immense superiority of England over the rest of mankind ..."[28] In another passage, written from Brusseis, however, he admitted that Britain was surpassed in baked goods, cooking, architecture, and good manners. Sydney enjoyed the novelty of foreign travel, but since he preferred people to places and society to landscapes he was less than entranced by his jaunts abroad. Writing from Bingen in the Rhineland, he said:

> Mrs. Sydney and I make a good contrast in traveling, she reads a number of books about Castles on the Rhine and plagues me to see the place where Sigbert the fat slew Fiddlefud the Bold, and where Frauerbong the great Robber compelled the Barons to allow him to rob in the Rheingau, but the aujourdhui of Life is enough for me.[29]

Such playful banter and good natured wit obscured and continues to obscure the real Sydney Smith to many, who assume that if he were amusing he could not have been a sincere clergyman. The obligatory concomitant to such thinking, then, is that the "true" clergyman is "serious and earnest", which was probably both impressive and appealing in a John Knox or a Ignatius Loyola, but which may be little more than a bore in more typical clergymen. Sydney was not a totally typical Anglican clergyman, but it should be remembered that they were usually men who, generally speaking, emulated neither the dour and stern Calvinist pastor nor the more pious and celibate of the Roman Catholic clergy. Both the Calvinists and the Roman Catholic clergy rejected some parts of the world, and tried to insulate themselves from it, but the Anglican clergy accepted the world and lived in it as husbands and fathers, playing important social, economic, and political roles in addition to their church duties.

For these reasons, Charles Curran, in his review of W. H. Auden's edition of selected writing of Sydney Smith in 1956, described the Anglican Church as the key to an understanding of Sydney Smith. Curran believed that Sydney was much like his church in understanding the thought and feelings of Englishmen with "intuitive clarity"; and that this perception made it possible for him to succeed in using his wit and his progressive ideas to make men change their minds. Curran added that Sydney was "...cast in the mold of a typical Church of England clergyman, few of whom (past or present) could conceivably be fishermen or tentmakers."[30]

Curran's view of Sydney and the Church of England is sober, reflective, and arrived at distantly enough in point of time to be more objective than opinions on Sydney's churchmanship by his contemporaries, who frequently wrote in the midst of doctrinal or political disputes. Macaulay, for example, said: "His misfortune is to have chosen a profession at once above him and below him. Zeal would have made him a prodigy; formality and bigotry would have made him a bishop; but he could neither rise to the duties of his order, not stoop to its degradation."[31] Macaulay was a great historian, and as recently as 1968 Gertrude Himmelfarb echoed his opinions, asserting that Sydney was too good a liberal to have been a good divine;[32] and while it is usually a good idea to be guided by a great historian like Macaulay, he was as capable of fallibility in his judgements of his contemporaries, as Sydney was in his opinions on Macaulay. Chevrillon, who took a more balanced view of Sydney, saw him as a good example of a man influenced by hereditary prejudices and modern ideas, and one in whom those prejudices were expressed more coherently and completely than in ordinary Englishmen of his class. He saw him also as being generally characteristic of the Anglicanism of the period, even if his attitudes, conduct, and churchmanship were repugnant to factions of Anglican opinion.[33]

Sydney Smith cannot be comfortably categorized as either a Low Churchman, a Middle Churchman, or a High Churchman, but it must be conceded that he was both a believing Christian and a dutiful clergyman of his age. In his concept of "rational religion", professed in a sermon significantly entitled "On True Religion" which was published in 1809, he outlined a system of belief that was both Christian and Anglican, which gave no satisfaction to the evangelicals of that age or to those of the present. On the topics of belief in heaven, the necessity for Christianity, and the sins of bigotry and religious persecution, he wrote:

> Our happiness in this life, as well as in a life to come, depends so entirely upon the cultivation of rational religion, that the efforts to excite a just sense of its importance, in the minds of every Christian congregation, cannot be too frequently, or too warmly repeated. Ever since the revelation of Jesus Christ, man has too often worshiped his God by idolatry, by childish disputes, by the tears of chained heretics, by wasted provinces, by the burnt incense of human bodies; every vice, and every error have been shrined in the name of religion, and the merciless inquisitor, while he blasted his most beautiful creations, did it for the praise, and glory of his God.[34]

By religion he meant "Faith, Devotion, and Practice; a belief in the existence of God, and Jesus Christ, our blessed Lord; prayer, public and private, and obedience to ...the law of God..." Sydney was humble before God, believing that men should adore Him" ...not to make ourselves good, but to make him glorious; not to set before that which is frail a model of purity, but to brighten that which is pure by the breath of frailty."[35] He believed that it was derogatory of God" ...to suppose that religion has any other object than the happiness of mankind; that Jesus Christ dwelt among men for any other purpose but to shew them the rule of mortal life which leads them to life eternal..." "...let us beware", he warned, "that we have something else to offer to our God but sainted words, and holy kneelings, and supplicating hymns..."[36]

Sydney maintained that prayer without good action only increased guilt, that fanaticiam was to be avoided at all costs, and that Christian belief should be simple rather than involved and mysterious. Christianity should, according to Sydney, be approached rationally, but certain beliefs could only be understood and accepted on the basis of faith. He saw a real danger in attempting to reinterpret prophecy, and he never did so in his sermons; and he held that such reinterpretations should be made with humility and received with caution, for they could tax credulity and belief itself.[37] No theologian himself, he believed that lay people could be Christian without studying theology, and that the whole gospel could be understood without theology. As he said:

> ...Almighty God, in revealing to us his gospel, would have defeated his own benevolent purpose, if every thing which that gospel contains, might not be apprehended, without laborious, and critical study. Upon the more important, and practical parts of Christianity there has been little, or no controversy; every body knows that mercy, that charity, that meekness, that obedience to the higher powers, that every fundamental principle of morals, on which the happiness of mankind reposes, are taught in the sacred writings, with a strength...which excludes mistake. It is right that more speculative questions should be agitated by those to whom these matters are properly, and professionally a care...[38]

Far from being the atheist or agnostic he was frequently accused of being by his opponents, Sydney had a deep and very real belief in Christianity, and although he submitted to a great deal of good natured jesting on the subject of his clerical profession from his friends, some of whom were agnostics, he was genuinely offended by attacks on religion. He had earlier reprimanded Jeffery for publishing a review that fell into that category, partly because its publication threatened the future of the journal, and partly because he found it personally offensive; and he is reported, after a splendid dinner, to have asked a foreigner who denied the existence of God whether he also denied the existence of the chef.[39]

Sydney had described any clergyman of his age as being certain to be a bad clergyman, but that description was not so much one of atheism, agnosticism, or free thinking, the charges often flung at him, as it was of obsolescence. The Church was changing, Sydney lived a long time, and by the time of his death he had become a "triangular person who has got into the square hole."[40] His wit offended some people, partly because they expected greater gravity from clergymen, and partly because he made jokes about sensitive political questions and some aspects of religion. George W. E. Russell objected to his occasional "coarseness," by which he meant his earthy and occasionally scatalogical or sexual references;[41] but Russell was a Victorian, judging Sydney by Victorian standards, and while Sydney's wit and conversation was quite probably improper in the eyes of proper Victorians, it was mild and restrained by contrast with the age in which he had matured.

Sydney's daughter Saba Holland expurgated words and passages which were "not convenient" from his letters,[42] but she again was much more of a Victorian, in terms of both years and attitudes, than her father. Lord Melbourne, by contrast, employed the "old-fashioned freedom of speech", which Houghton says, Sydney checked by his suggestion that "they should assume everybody and everything to be damned, and come to the point."[43]

While Sydney expressed himself in his sermons and public statements with great propriety, his letters and private conversation were interlarded with quips, puns, and other expressions of his genial good nature, which were occasionally mildly salacious. Fun-loving rather than wicked, and pixieish rather than diabolical, those expressions are characterized by their wit rather than their pungency, and they were intended to amuse the butt or beneficiary rather than to offend or outrage. "I heard the other day of you", Sydney wrote in 1803, "that you had 3 furnished Lodgings in different Quarters of the Town with 2 impure women in each- if this is the case you must attend my Spring course in moral Philosophy."[44] And to Lady Holland he noted that he had "seen a great number of thrushes hopping before the window this

Evening, but their conduct was by no means innocent or decorous."[45]

Men will be men, and they will talk about attractive women, of whom Sydney said:

> Your critique on Mrs. Apreece is just, but she seems a friendly, good hearted rational woman, and as much under the uterine dominion as is graceful, and pleasing. I hate a woman who seems to be hermetically sealed in the lower regions.[46]

He also described the marriage of William Cavendish, later seventh Duke of Devonshire and who was a mathematician, to the daughter of the Earl of Carlisle, by saying: "The god Hymen favors the Carlisles; Euclid leads Blanche to the altar- a strange choice for him as she has not an angle about her."[47] During the industrial disturbances around York he wrote to Lord Grey about another marriage:

> I hope the Yorkshire district will not be invaded just now; the General of the district is thinking of any thing but War. God send that the ferocious Luddite may not avail himself of his amourous idleness.... I know the lady a little. She is a youthful, buxom Personage who will be active herself, and make him active too. So that I think (whatever other families may be extinct) that of the Greys will remain flourishing and Vigorous in all its Branches.[48]

As a country clergyman and a Justice of the Peace in Yorkshire Sydney had been involved in the moral and legal problems of illegitimate births, and in 1814 he wrote to John Allen to:

> ...tell Lady Holland that I am a Justice of the Peace,-one of those rural tyrants so deprecated by poor Windham. I am determined to strike into the line of analogous punishments, but what am I to do in cases of bastardy; how can I afflict the father analogously; help me in this difficulty.[49]

On still another occasion he remarked to Lady Holland that:

> Agar Ellis looks very ill, he has naturally a bad constitution, is ennuied and blase and vexed that he cannot procure any progeny. I did not say so- but I thought how absurd to discontinue the use of domestic chaplains in cases where landed property is concerned.

Such comments might be taken to be evidence of moral depravity, but in these instances Sydney was corresponding with sophisticated persons in unexceptionable English. His subject matter was similarly legitimate, and while his wit may not have been "convenient" to a Victorian daughter, it is neither vulgar nor primarily prurient. It was merely another expression of his joyousness and of the humor he saw in the world about him; and he intended neither to prove his broadmindedness nor to shock his correspondents, but only to comment on things as he saw them, in his own way.

In 1823 he wrote:

> There are substances in nature called fluxes. The use of which is that they cause true Substances to unite, that if left alone would be perfectly immixable. I am of some use as a flux-as you will see when you find at my house Mrs. Wedgewood the female Potter and her 3 daughters- whom I certainly should not have selected for the Society of so fashionable a Rake as yourself--I need not however point out to a man of your quickness and ingenuity that by paying Court to these people you are sure of Coctile and fictile Vessels for life upon endless Credit- Creampots without End. Washing Basins unnumber'd and other things rather to be fill'd than mentioned-51

Certainly discreet enough, especially in a private letter to a gentlemen, the passage cannot be charged with anything more than high spirits, as in his letter of 1835 in which he announced that "...Peel is grown a little stronger by his (civil) marriage bill. Still I think Ladies married by Civil contract will be at a discount, they are already called Seven Shillings a piece ladies."[52] To another gentleman he complained of his gout in 1843, asserting that on the previous day the pain had been so great that three visiting ladies "might have ravished me with great ease and I could not have defended myself but by a timely compliance..."[53] In the former letter his pun was intentional and unobjectionable in a private letter to a worldly-wise gentleman, and in the latter a great deal of the humor lies in the ludicrous situation he creates in visualizing three superannuated ladies overcome by their physical passion for a fat seventy-two year old clergyman.

After noting the previous quotations, it should be emphasized that all were written privately, and that his more public utterances and publications offended only by their discussion of topics, like Catholic Emancipation, which his opponents would have preferred to have ignored; and that their real offensiveness lay in the reasonable arguments he presented, and in the skill and wit with which he presented them. Although he was occasionally scurrilous, which proves that he was human rather than an atheist or a bad priest, Sydney was very concerned about the feelings of other people. He laughed with rather than at the butts of his jokes, and few seem to have taken deep offense at them. In a fragmentary diary by Lady Saba Holland he is reported to have stated as a maxim: "Remember that every person, however low, has _rights_ and _feelings_. In all contentions, let peace be rather your object than triumph: value triumph only as a means to peace."[54] In a sermon he added:

> Modern manners have adopted a certain language of virtuous sympathy which passes not infrequently...for the excellence itself... Manners are the shadows of virtue; the momentary display of those qualities which our fellow creatures love, and respect.- If we strive to become, then, what we strive to appear, manners may often be rendered useful guides to the performance of our duties.[55]

In his daughter's memoir she described him as having been "more beloved than feared" as a wit, and she said that he had the skill to say the "best thing in the best manner to the right person at the right moment..."[56] Such was the opinion of a doting daughter, and as such it must be discounted to some extent, but it was fairly well borne out by less prejudiced witnesses like Benjamin Disraeli, who, having sat next to Sydney at a dinner party, recorded that he was "...delightful...I don't remember a more agreeable party..."[57] Henry Hart Milman, later Dean of St. Paul's, recalled hearing, as a child when Sydney was visiting, "...the inextinguishable shouts of laughter which were heard proceeding from the dining-room. . . ."[58]

Sydney's wit, although undoubtedly worked over by him for certain occasions, was spontaneous and exuberant, and was intended as much for his own amusement as that of others, and it had that blessed virtue of pleasant surprise. When it was announced that the Bishop of London, not one of Sydney's favorite people, could not attend a dinner because of a dog bite, Sydney blurted out: "I'd like to hear the dog's account of the story."[59] On the occasion of a farewell dinner for a bishop who was going to New Zealand he quipped: "If they eat you, I hope you will disagree with them."[60] Not entirely anti-clerical, he was quoted by Saba Holland as saying:

> The French certainly understand the art of furnishing better than we do; the profusion of glass in their rooms give such gaiety. I remember entering a room with glass all round it, at the French Embassy, and saw myself reflected on every side. I took it for a meeting of the clergy, and was delighted of course.[61]

He had a zest for life, and for its fullest enjoyment, which was really the source of most of his humor, and he poked as much fun at himself as he did at others. "...first", he said, "I am fond of talking nonsense; secondly, I am civil; thirdly, I am brief. I may be flattering myself; but if I am not, it is not easy to get very wrong with these habits."[62] In a letter he commented drolly that: "All my Hay Stacks and Corn Ricks are blown over by this Wind- two of my maids are married- and the pole of my carriage broken. These are the sort of things which render life so difficult".[63] With regard to his clerical dignity he said that "The Miss Codringtons sing delightfully, and much please the Canon of St. Paul's and to please a canon or dignitary of the Church is accounted for as great righteousness as forty acts of charity to other Christians."[64] Sydney also occasionally wrote to people under assumed names, but his nearly illegible scrawl and his typical humor could hardly have fooled anyone. In one such letter, he described himself in the third person as "an odd man, and, I think, a little crazy."[65]

Various attempts have been made to categorize the humor of Sydney Smith, but none have been entirely succussful, for being a genuine wit he saw humor in almost everything, and he expressed it in a bewildering variety of ways. Categories may be established into which much of his wit fits fairly comfortably, but there is always a residue that must almost be entitled "humor beyond description". In 1821, for example, in inquiring after the health of his ailing friend Lord Morpeth he begged of Lady Morpeth: "pray do not vote me a Bore for asking better news of Lord Morpeth. If that cannot be obtained,- send me some better news of Somebody-"[66] Exhibiting his gentle and almost loving prejudice against Gaels, he asked a Scottish friend if his infant son took "his Porridge kindly- does he show any taste for metaphysics...."[67] Still different, however, was his description of a Scottish aristocratic family's progress through France:

> ...on the 2d day we met a long String of Carriages Elephants- Camels- Guards- bands of Music fat Butlers Chaplains- Governesses & Philosophers- It was the Sutherlands- I made my obedience out of the Window-[68]

More readily classified are comments like those to Admiral Sir Sidney Smith, the hero of the Siege of Acre in 1799, for the two were (and sometimes still are) confused one for the other. "I think you and I," said Sydney:

> should set up a Partnership- and accept invitations in common- you shall go as the Clergyman when it suits your convenience, and I will go as the hero. The Physiognomists and Crainologists will discover in you a Love of Tithes- and of conformity to articles- and in me a contempt of death and a Love of Glory[69]

On 4 June, 1827, he wrote to his nephew Cecil Smith:

> All London are talking of the Lady who is Marked Thomson & Co. Londini 1827 a Lady bought a Stove with this inscription

upon it in large Letters- Weather cold and Petticoats up she imprudently backed upon the Stove- and is marked in the largest Letters Astley Cooper attended her- and though he never saw her face is quite sure she is a Lady of the highest quality-[70]

Sydney's ability to entertain was great, and he employed it skillfully, and even systematically, speaking at dinner parties in machine gun-like half-minute bursts, then giving others a chance to speak, and replying by making quips or puns on their remarks.[71] He is reputed to have kept his wife and daughters laughing two or three hours a day,[72] and he so enlivened dinner conversation that from the dullness of dinner parties after his death his widow imagined that the whole guest list was bereaved or otherwise distressed.[73]

It has been averred frequently that Sydney maintained his wit and good spirits despite an unsuccessful career, but the facts indicate that even though he never achieved his goal of a bishopric, he held good livings in the Church throughout most of his life, and he ended it in a position both honorific and remunerative. His personal life was close to idyllic, he married well and happily, and he won the social recognition and acceptance he desired. The loss of his son Douglas has been called the only real tragedy in his life, and it certainly was that, and he suffered disappointment and chagrin in Windham, his second son, who failed to live up to his expectations. On the other hand, his daughters Saba and Emily were exemplary ladies, and his affection and understanding for them was such that no serious disagreements ever appear to have occurred between Sydney and his daughters.

Some misunderstanding exists on the topic of Sydney being a self-made man, but it derives from efforts to equate "self-made" in the case of an eighteenth century gentlemen with "self-made" in the nineteenth or twentieth century sense. Sydney was self-made only in the sense that what fame and recognition he achieved resulted largely from his own efforts rather than from ancestral prominence, but his story is assuredly not one of a struggle from rags to riches. Born in a substantial middle class family, and given the benefits of an excellent upbringing and good education, he used his abilities well to advance from moderate wealth and relative obscurity to a more affluent social position and to intellectual, and literary renown.

His greatest contribution was the founding of the Edinburgh Review, the origination of which was his alone, for it became one of the most influential journals of opinion in the nineteenth century. Its actual influence is undoubted, but difficult to assess, and serving as a sounding board for responsible liberal thought it furthered the reform movement and served as a formative influence for both thought and action. Sydney's most important publication was the Peter Plymley Letters, which appeared at a moment when there was little hope of accomplishing Catholic Emancipation. It helped to bolster and keep the issue alive, and to hasten its ultimate victory. His reviews and speeches on the game laws, parliamentary reform, penal reform, and counsel for prisoners were clever, and they assuredly helped in the shaping of opinion; and his less important reviews contributed to the popularity of the Edinburgh Review and to the creation of a generally more liberal climate of opinion.

Sydney was a reformer, but one of a very moderate nature, and his approach to reform was to attempt piecemeal changes which tended to eliminate glaring injustices and to make the existing system rational. He was neither a revolutionary, a radical, nor an extremist, unless he might have been an extremist for individual liberty, by which he meant freedom for the right-thinking gentleman of independent means to manage his own affairs, and those of his locality, without interference from the government or from what might be called "do-gooders" in the twentieth century. He was thus an arch-Whig who favored government by the Whig oligarchy, which was sanctified by time and its role in the Glorious Revolution, and which would, he believed, rule wisely and well, avoiding the triple pitfalls of tyrannical monarchy, meddling bureaucracy, and egalitarian democracy. He regarded a Whig majority in the elections as a popular plebiscite for the wealthy and independent aristocrats to rule the country, being guided but not directed by public opinion, and following a rational and responsible policy while rewarding men of ability. It was to this concept that Sydney catered, not slavishly, but not in an entirely disinterested manner either; and he seems never to have realized that the realities of the Whig Party varied greatly from his idealization of it. His disappointment with the Whigs for failing to promote him is more understandable from this viewpoint, for whereas the Whigs hesitated to make him a bishop from fear of agitating public opinion against themselves, Sydney felt that they should have done the right and just thing for a good and able man regardless of public opinion. Sydney was ambitious, perhaps even greedy, for wealth and station, and he believed that the Whigs were guilty of nothing less than infidelity for not having made him a bishop when they might have done so; for even if risks of a public reaction were present, he had taken risks for them in his actions and publications.

Sydney loved wealth, power, and social recognition, and he aspired to all of them by means of his pen, but it would be totally erroneous to suppose that those were his only motives. He had a real love of truth and justice, both of which he interpreted in the light of his liberal Whig predilections, and both of which he espoused at indiscreet times, and at some risk to his future. In a sermon published in 1809 he said:

> ...there is an heroic faith,---a courageous love of truth, the truth of the Christian warrior- an unconquerable love of justice, that would burst the heart in twain, if it had not vent, which makes women, men,- and men saints,- and saints angels. ---Often it has published its creed from amid the flames;---often it has reasoned under the axe, and gathered firmness from a mangled body;---often it has rebuked the madness of the people;- often it has burst into the chambers of princes...[74]

Like many other divines Sydney sometimes used what might be called "sermon language", and it could be argued that his statement was little more than that, but the whole sermon has considerable force and the ring of sincerity about it. He added that the "the highest motive, to the cultivation of truth is, that God requires it of us...", even if it resulted in poverty, hatred or exile. Truth was also, to Sydney, the basis of the social order, piety towards God, and justice to man.[75]

It was not a dangerous thing, of course, to stand up for truth in a sermon, but to put such a principle into action, in exposing the hypocrisy and hunger for power in the Tory leadership on an issue like Catholic Emancipation was quite another thing; and Sydney's combination of wit, skill as a publicist, and a passion for truth and justice made him a formidable figure. He demanded results, and his efforts helped to secure change, not, as he said, because he alone had said it, "but because it was no longer possible to avoid doing it."[76]

In such a statement Sydney was more humble about his successes as a reformer than many of his biographers, who have assigned a more important role to him in the accomplishing of reform than he deserves. Saba Holland, for example, mentioned his campaigns of various questions and the successful resolution of those questions, with the implication that her father brought about the changes. Reid said that: "His dreaded powers of ridicule and sarcasm were employed to drive home his arguments, and they never appeared without a purpose, and seldom disappeared before they had accomplished it..."[77] Both Reid and Saba Holland exaggerated his importance, and by overstating it make it questionable; Sydney played a significant role, but not one that was dominant in any major issue. In the theatre of change and liberal reform in nineteenth century England he was not a leading actor, nor even a figure representing the chorus; he was, rather, a public relations figure, responsible for popularizing an <u>avant garde</u> production, and for selling tickets to a dubious public.

Similarly opinions on Sydney Smith's ability have frequently been effulgent rather than accurate, and even the great Macaulay, in a letter to Catherine Amelia Smith in 1847, said that Sydney was a "great reasoner, and the greatest master of ridicule...since Swift".[78] It was a kind and understandable exaggeration in corresponding with the widow of a friend, but even though Sydney was an excellent writer, and one who approached greatness in his writings, and though he used some Swiftian techniques in his writing, he can hardly be put in the same category with Swift. Princess Liechtenstein was more realistic when she said that he blended the beautiful with the ridiculous, which she regarded as the key to his refinement, and that he was "a good writer, a good talker, a good friend, and a good man."[79]

Such an opinion was not shared by all who knew Sydney Smith, and Sir Archibald Alison, a Tory and an eminent historian, said:

> He had no philosophic turn, little poetic fancy, and scarce any eloquence, but a prodigious fund of innate sagacity, vast

> powers of humorous illustration, and a
> clear perception of the practical bear-
> ing of every question....In society he
> was much sought after... but there was
> a constant straining after effect, and
> too little interchange of thought to
> raise his discourse to a very high charm.[80]

Thomas Carlyle, who was not renowned for his good nature, described Sydney as "...a mass of fat and muscularity, with massive Roman nose, huge cheeks, shrewdness and fun, not humor or wit, seemingly without soul altogether."[81] Neither opinion can be entirely discounted, but they are strongly at variance with dozens of more complimentary descriptions by people who, even if they were favorably inclined towards Sydney Smith, knew him far better than either Carlyle or Alison. Baron Pecchio who was not exactly an intimate, but who did spend several days with Sydney, said that he had never been so amused, that every-one laughed like "Homeric Gods" in his presence, and that if England had a dozen more literary figures like Sydney the English would no longer suffer from melancholy.[82] Perhaps the highest compliment ever paid to Sydney Smith was made by Berton Roueche in the New Yorker, when he said that Sydney was "probably the most consistently amusing Englishman that ever lived."[83] If not the most amusing Englishman ever, Sydney was among the most amusing, but he was also an influential clergyman. His stature is overshadowed by his reputation as an entertainer, when in actuality he used humor to further reform.

REFERENCES

CHAPTER I

1. Stuart J. Reid, *The Life and Times of Syndey Smith*, 4th ed., (London, 1896(; (hereafter cited as Reid, *Life*), p. 2.

2. George W. E. Russell, *Sydney Smith*, (London, 1905); (hereafter cited as Russell, *Sydney Smith*), p. 2.

3. Nowell C. Smith, The Letters of Sydney Smith, 2 vols., (Oxford, 1953; hereafter cited as *Letters*, 1. 327.

4. Catherine Amelia Smith, *Narrative for My Grandchildren*, (unpublished and undated MS in the possession of David Holland, hereafter cited as Holland MS I, II & III) MS I, 1-2.

5. Holland, *Memoir*, I, 2.

6. Holland MS I, 23-24; MS III, 300-301.

7. Holland, *Memoir*, I, 2.

8. Holland, *Memoir*, I, 396.

9. Holland, *Memoir*, I, 396.

10. *Letters*, I, 345.

11. *Letters*, I, 258.

12. Osbert Burdett, *The Rev. Smith Sydney* (London, 1934) (hereafter cited as Burdett, Smith) p. 10.

13. SS to Robert Smith, June 26, 1796, Huntington Library Manuscript 185, hereafter cited as Huntington MS.

14. Holland MS I, 9.

15. Russell, Sydney Smith, p. 12.

16. Holland MS I, 15-16.

17. Holland, *Memoir*, I, 10.

18. Reid, *Life*, pp. 20-21.

19. Burdett, *Smith*, p. 287.

414

20. The Rev. Sydney Smith, Sermons at St. Paul's, The Foundling Hospital, and Several Churches (London, 1846, hereafter cited as Sermons, 1846) p. 6.

21. Ibid., p. 27.

22. Holland, Memoir, I, 399.

23. Ibid., p. 368.

24. Holland, MS III, passim.

25. Chevrillon, Sydney Smith, p. 5.

26. The Rev. Sydney Smith, Sermons (London, 1801); hereafter cited as Sermons, 1801, pp. 31-32.

27. Chevrillon, Sydney Smith, p. 5.

28. Burdett, Smith, pp. 12-13.

29. Holland MS II, 10.

30. Holland, Memoir, I, 10.

31. Holland MS II, 16.

32. Holland MS I, p. 26.

33. SS to Robert Smith, n.d., Huntington MS, 19.

34. Holland MS I, 34.

35. SS to Robert Smith, n.d., Huntington MS, 185.

36. Ibid.

37. SS to Robert Smith, 9 July 1796, Huntington MS.

38. SS to Robert Smith, 5 November, 1797, Huntington MS 106.

39. SS to Robert Smith, Huntington MS 206.

40. Ibid.

41. SS to Robert Smith, 29 Dec., 1797, Huntington MS.

42. SS to Robert, [20?] March, 1800, Huntington MS 32. SS to Robert Smith, c.1800, Huntington MS.

43. SS to Robert Smith, n.d., Huntington MS 19.
44. SS to Robert Smith, 24 November, 1801, Huntington MS 28.
45. SS to Robert Smith, 1801, Huntington MS 28.
46. SS to Robert Smith, 28 March, 1803, Huntington MS 63.
47. Holland MS, I, 34:
48. Letters, I 78.
49. SS to Robert Smith, 15 April 1803, Huntington MS 88.
50. Ibid.
51. SS to Robert Smith, n.d., Huntington MS 26.
52. SS to Robert Smith, n.d., Huntington MS 89.
53. Letters I, 103.
54. Ibid., I, 378.

CHAPTER II

1. Holland MS II, 12-13.

2. Burdett, *Smith*, pp. 22-23.

3. Halpern, *Smith*, p. 35.

4. Russell, *Sydney Smith*, pp. 13-14.

5. Sydney engaged in the latter two of these abuses, if not the first, in Londesborough after 1825, where he collected §800 a year for little or no service; and at Halberton where he was paid §400, using only a fraction of that sum to appoint a curate. Holland MS I, 53-54; Holland, *Memoir*, pp. 203-204. Holland MS II, 46-47.

6. Holland MS II, 13.

7. Holland, *Memoir*, p. 10.

8. Reid, *Life*, p. 28.

9. *Letters*, I, 4.

10. *Ibid.*, p. 6.

11. *Ibid.*, pp. 2-3.

12. *Ibid.*, pp. 3-4.

13. *Ibid.*, p. 5.

14. *Ibid.*, pp. 5-6.

15. Burdett, *Smith*, pp. 25-28.

16. Reid, *Life*, p. 29.

17. *Sermons, 1846*, pp. 115-116. *Sermons, 1801*, I, 57-66.

18. *Letters*, I, 186-187.

19. *Ibid.*, p. 391.

20. Sir Lewis Namier, *The Structure of Politics at the Accession of George III*, (London, 1930).

21. George L. Nesbitt, *Benthamite Reviewing: The First Twelve Years of the "Westminster Review," 1824-1836* (New York, 1966; hereafter cited as Nesbitt, *Benthamite Reviewing*) p. 7.

22. The Rev. Sydney Smith, *The Works of the Rev. Sydney Smith*, 2nd. ed. (London, 1840, hereafter cited as *Works*) III, 110.

23. Holland, *Memoir*, II, 233.

24. *Letters*, I, 349.

25. *Ibid.*, pp. 144-145.

26. Holland, *Memoir*, I, 92.

27. *Letters*, I, 111-112.

28. *Ibid.*, I, 169.

29. MS 31.301, *Brougham Papers*, University College Library, University of London, hereafter cited as UCL.

30. Smith, *Letters*, I, 111.

31. SS to Robert Smith, n.d., Huntington MS, 32.

32. *Letters*, II, 456.

33. The Rev. Sydney Smith, *Sermons* (2 vols.), (London, 1809: hereafter cited as *Sermons, 1809*) II, 223-224.

34. *Ibid.*, II, 211.

35. *Ibid.*, II, 208-209.

36. *Ibid.*, II, 224-225.

37. *Ibid.*, II, 220-222.

38. *Ibid.*, II, 223-224.

39. *Ibid.*, II, 224.

40. *Ibid.*, II, 227-229.

41. SS to John George Clarke, 28 September, 1799. B.M. Add. MS. 38650.

42. Ibid., I, 283-421.

43. Ibid., I, 97.

44. Ibid., I, 156-157.

45. Ibid., I, 196.

46. Ibid., I, 452.

47. Ibid., II, 680.

48. Sermons, 1809, II, 164.

49. Foston Parish Marriage Register, 1754-1837. (Foston Parish is presently a part of Flaxton Parish, ne near York and the Foston Baptismal, Marriage and Burial Registers are in the custody of the Vicar of Flaxton.) (Hereafter cited as Foston, Registers).

50. John R. H. Moorman, A History of the Church in England), (London, 1953; hereafter cited as Moorman, Church p. 331.

51. Holland, Memoir, I, 338-339.

52. Ibid., I, 352.

53. Ibid., I, 352-353.

54. Ibid., 352-353

55. Ibid., I, 381.

56. Sermons, 1809, II, 165-175.

57. Holland, Memoir, I, 186.

58. Ibid., I, 120-125.

59. Letters, II, 552.

60. Ibid., I, 379.

61. Holland, Memoirs, I, 226.

62. Letters, I, 5.

63. Register of Baptisms in the Parish of Combe Florey in the County of Somerset, 1813-1904, Somerset

Record Office. (hereafter cited as Combe Florey, Registers) pp. 19-35.

64. Holland MS I, 65: Reid. Life. p. 173.

65. Burdett, Smith, p. 192.

66. Letters, II, 512-513.

CHAPTER III

1. Walter Jerrold, ed., <u>Bon-Mots of Sydney Smith and R. Brinsley Sheridan</u>...With Grotesques by Aubrey Beardsley (London, 1893; hereafter cited as <u>Bon Mots</u>), p. 17.

2. British Museum, Holland House Papers, Dinner Books, MS 799F. No pagination. An insert on blue letter paper.

3. Holland, <u>Memoir</u> I, 100.

4. SS to Robert Smith, 8 April, 1797, Huntington MS 70.

5. SS to Robert Smith, 5 Nov., 1797, Huntington MS 106.

6. SS to Robert Smith, 31 Dec., 1797, Huntington MS 78.

7. SS to Robert Smith, Huntington MS, 31 V 1798.

8. SS to Robert Smith, 29 Dec., 1797, Huntington MS.

9. <u>Letters</u>, I, 17.

10. <u>Ibid</u>., I, 18-20.

11. <u>Ibid</u>., I, 67.

12. <u>London Times</u>, 25 February, 1845.

13. SS to Robert Smith, 31 May, 1798, Huntington MS.

14. B.M. Add. MS. 38650, ff. 93-94.

15. <u>Letters</u>, I, 63-64.

16. <u>Ibid</u>., I, 167.

17. <u>Ibid</u>., I, 143.

18. W. R. Sorley, <u>History of British Philosophy</u> to 1900, (Cambridge, 1965, hereafter cited as Sorley, <u>British Philosophy</u>, pp. 203-210.

19. The Rev. Sydney Smith, <u>Elementary Sketches of Moral Philosophy</u>, (london, 1850).

20. <u>Letters</u>, I, p. 1.

21. Sorley, *British Philosophy*, p. 201.

22. *Sermons, 1809*, I, 40.

23. *Letters*, I, 239.

24. *Sermons, 1809*, II, 331-332.

25. B.M. Add. MS. 38650, ff. 99-100.

26. *Sermons*, 1809, II, 333-334.

27. B.M. Add. MS. 51645.

28. *Letters*, I, 257.

29. *Ibid.*, I, 180.

30. *Bon Mots*, p. 29.

31. Holland, *Memoir*, I, 17.

32. B.M. MS. 51645. Sydney coined many phrases, and when he hit upon a good one he had no hesitation about repeating it, or modifying it to meet a new situation. Lady Holland quotes him on Frency explication: "...they never give you credit for knowing the commonest facts. C'est toujours, 'Commencons au deluge.' My heart sinks when a Frenchman begins, 'Mon ami, je vais vous expliquer tout cela'. A fellow-traveller once explained to me how to cut a sandwich, all the way from Amiens to Paris." Holland, *Memoir*, I, 349.

33. *Letters*, I, 245-246.

34. *Ibid.*, II, 723.

35. *Ibid.*, II, 694.

36. B.M. MS. 51645.

37. Princess Marie Liechtenstein, *Holland House*, 2 Vols. (London, 1874; hereafter cited as *Holland House*) I, 273.

38. *Letters*, I, 370.

39. *Ibid.*, I, 21.

40. B.M. Add. MS. 38650, ff. 93-94.

41. National Library of Wales. MS. 11, 981 E.
42. Letters, I, 79.
43. Ibid., I, 453
44. Ibid., I, 20.
45. B.M. Add. MS. 38650, ff. 93-94.
46. Bon Mots, p. 51.
47. B.M. MS. 51645
48. B.M. Add. MS. 38650, ff. 95-96.
49. National Library of Scotland, Adv. MS. 2.1.15, ff. 73-74.
50. Letters, I, 247-248.
51. B.M. Add. MS. 38650, ff. 99-100.
52. Letters, I, 60.
53. SS to Robert Smith, 1798, Huntington MS.
54. Ibid.
55. Holland MS II, 15.
56. B.M. Add. MS. 38650, ff 97-100.
57. SS to Robert Smith, n.d., Huntington MS 32.
58. Mrs. William Hicks-Beach, A Cotswold Family: Hicks and Hicks-Beach (London, 1909) pp. 307-313.
59. SS to Robert Smith, 28 March, 1803, Huntington MS 63.
60. Holland, Memoir, I, 19.
61. Langham Pamphlets: Wit and Wisdom of Sydney Smith (London, n.d.; hereafter cited as Langham), p. 88.
62. Letters, II, 719.
63. Ibid., I, 21.
64. Ibid., I, 22-23.

65. *Bon Mots*, p. 99.

66. Holland, *Memoir*, I, 262.

67. Andre Chevrillon, *Sydney Smith et la renaissance des idees liberales en angleterre* (Paris, 1894; hereafter cited as Chevrillon, *Sydney Smith*) p. 122.

68. John R. H. Moorman, *A History of the Church in England* (London, 1953; hereafter cited as Moorman), p. 331.

69. SS to Robert Smith, 1798, Huntington MS.

70. Holland, *Memoir*, I, 45-46.

71. Leonard Horner, *Memoirs and Correspondence of Francis Horner, M.P.*, 2 Vols. (Boston, 1853; hereafter cited as Horner, *Memoris*) I, 157.

72. SS to Robert Smith, 20 March, 1800, Huntington MS 32.

73. B.M. Add. MS 38650, ff. 95-96.

74. *Bon Mots*, pp. 29, 39.

75. *Works*, III, 355.

76. Burdett, *Smith*, pp. 56-57.

77. *Sermons, 1846*, II, 14.

78. Holland, *Memoir*, I, 43-44.

79. *Sermons*, 1846, pp. iii-iv.

80. Holland, *Memoir*, I, 42-43.

81. *Letters*, I, 443.

82. *Ibid.*, I, 295.

83. *Sermons*, 1809, I, 231-232.

84. *Ibid.*, I, 238.

85. *Letters*, I, 38.

86. *Ibid.*, I, 38.

87. Hesketh Pearson, *The Smith of Smiths* (London, 1934; hereafter cited as Pearson, *Smith*) p. 117.

88. Holland, Memoir, I, 48-49.

89. Francis Warre-Cornish, The English Church in the Nineteenth Century (London, 1910; hereafter cited as Warre-Cornish, English Church), II, 3.

90. Marion Lochhead, John Gibson Lockhart (London, 1954) p. 291. Quoted from John Clive, Scotch Reviewers: The "Edinburgh Review," 1802-1815 (Cambridge, 1957; hereafter cited as Clive, Scotch Reviewers), p. 149.

91. Edinburgh Review, XXIV (November, 1814; hereafter cited as E. R.) p. 1.

92. Bon Mots, p. 112.

93. Holland, Memoir, I, 333.

94. Letters, I, 67.

CHAPTER IV

1. *Letters*, I, 409.

2. *Ibid.*, I, 254.

3. Col. Harold Malt, "Receipt for Salad," *Notes and Queries*, 25 January, 1890.

4. *Letters*, I, 29.

5. John Rylands Library, Bromley-Davenport Muniments, Letters of Sydney Smith (hereafter cited as JRL), no. 10.

6. B.M. MS. 51645, p. 83.

7. *Sermons*, 1809, II, 37-38.

8. *Ibid.*, I, 277.

9. *Letters*, II, 602.

10. *Ibid.*, II, 502.

11. *Ibid.*, II, 536.

12. B.M. Add. MS. 51645.

13. *Sermons*, 1809, II, 338-342.

14. *Sermons*, 1846, 355-356.

15. *Catalogue of the Collection of Autograph Letters and Historical Documents formed between 1865 and 1882 by Alfred Morrison* (London, 1892; hereafter cited as Morrison, *Catalogue*) VI, 144-145.

16. *Letters*, I, 330.

17. *Ibid.*, II, 828.

18. *Ibid.*, II, 830.

19. Holland, *Memoir*, I, 334.

20. *Sermons*, 1809, I, 268-280.

21. Holland, *Memoir*, I, 20-21.

22. *Letters*, I, 273.

23. Holland, *Memoir*, I, 261.

24. *Bon Mots*, p. 59.

25. Clive, *Scotch Reviewers*, pp. 186-197.

26. Wedgwood Museum, MS 31795.

27. Clive, *Scotch Reviewers*, p. 194.

28. *Ibid.*, p. 26 Frances Hawes, *Henry Brougham* (New York, 1956). p. 36.

29. "Advertisement," *The Edinburgh Review, or Critical Journal*, (hereafter cited as *E. R.*), I.

30. Thomas Constable, *Archibald Constable and His Literary Correspondents*: A Memorial By His Son Thomas Constable) I, 51.

31. Walter E. Houghton, *The Wellesley Index to Victorian Periodicals 1824-1900* (Toronto, 1966; hereafter cited as *Wellesley Index*) I, 416-418.

32. Clive, *Scotch Reviers*, p. 31.

33. George L. Nesbitt, *Benthamite Reviewing: The First Twelve Years of the Westminster Review 1824-1836* (New York, 1966; hereafter cited as Nesbitt, *Benthamite Reviewing*), p. 5.

34. Smith, *Works*, I-III, passim.

35. *Wellesley Index*, I, 423.

36. Holland, *Memoir*, no pagination (p. 426.).

37. *Wellesley Index*, I, 430-469.

38. *Letters*, I, 153.

39. *Ibid.*, I, 331-332.

40. *Ibid.*, I, 332.

41. *Ibid.*, I, 408.

42. "Dr. Parr's *Spital Sermons*". E.R., I, Oct., 1802, pp. 18-24.

43. Ibid.

44. Ibid.

45. "Godwin's Reply to Parr", E. R., I, Oct., 1802, pp. 24-26.

46. "Rennel's Sermons", E. R., I, Oct. 1802, pp. 83-90.

47. Ibid.

48. "Dr. Langford's Sermons", E. R., I, Oct., 1802, p. 113.

49. "Nares's Sermons", E. R. I, Oct., 1802, pp. 128-130.

50. Public Characters, E. R., I, 1802, p. 122.

51. "Bowles' on the Peace", E. R., I, Oct., 1802, pp. 94-98.

52. Ibid.

53. Letters, I, 332.

54. "Sonnini's Travels in Greece and Turkey", E. R., I, Jan., 1803, pp. 281-287.

55. "Mad. Necker, Reflexions sur le Divorce", E. R., I, Jan., 1803, pp. 486-495.

56. "Lewis's Alfonso", E. R., I, Jan., 1803, pp. 314-317.

57. "Neckar's Last Views", E. R., I, Jan. 1803, pp. 382-395.

58. Ibid.

59. Ibid.

60. Letters, I, 75.

61. SS to Robert Smith, 28 March, 1803, Huntington MS.

62. Letters, I, 79.

63. Holland, Memoir, I, 64-65.

64. National Library of Scotland, Adv. MS 2.1.15, ff. 73-74. (Hereafter cited as N.L.S.)

65. Letters, I, 79-80.

66. "Collin's Account of New South Wales", E. R., II, April, 1803, pp. 30-42.

67. "Fievee, Lettres sur l'Angleterre", E. R., II, April, 1803, pp. 86-90.

68. Ibid.

69. "Percival's Account of the Island of Ceylon", E. R., II, pp. 136-147.

70. Ibid.

71. "Catteau, Tableau des Etats Danois", E. R., II, July, 1803, pp. 287-308.

72. "Pallas's Travels in the Russian Empire", E. R., III, Oct., 1803, pp. 146-154.

73. "Wittman's Travels", E. R., II, July, 1803, pp. 330-337.

74. "Accounts of the Egyptian Expedition", E. R., II, April, 1803, pp. 53-64.

75. Ibid.

76. "Mad. de Stael's Delphine", E. R., II, April, 1803, pp. 172-177.

77. "Dr. Craven's Discourses", E. R., II, July, 1803, pp. 437-443. "Necker, Cours de Morale Religieuse", E. R., III, Oct., 1803, pp. 90-99.

78. "Sturges on the Residence of the Clergy", E. R., II, April, 1803, pp. 202-205.

79. "Edgeworth's Essay on Irish Bulls", E. R., II, July, 1803, pp. 398-402.

CHAPTER V

1. Holland MS II, 23-24.

2. Holland, *Memoir*, I, 202.

3. Chevrillon, *Sydney Smith*, pp. 26-27.

4. New River Company, Disbursement Book, Archives of the Metropolitan Water Board (Hereafter cited as New River Records). 29 September, 1803. Huntington MS, 26, SS to Robert Smith, undated.

5. Thomas Wicksteed, *Observations on the Past and Present Supply of Water* (London, 1835) pp. 7-9.

6. H. W. Dickinson, *Water Supply of Greater London* (Leamington Spa and London, 1954) p. 35.

7. J. Kennard, "Sanitary Engineering: Water Supply", *A History of Technology*, 4 vols. (Oxford, 1958), IV, 492-494.

8. Holland MS II, 24.

9. Letters of the New River Water Company, Archives of the Metropolitan Water Board (Hereafter cited as New River Letters) 202/5.

10. New River Records, 2 July, 1807; 3 March, 1808; 24 March, 1808; 19 Jan. 1809; 2 March, 1809.

11. *Letters*, I, 121-122.

12. New River Records, 4 May, 1809.

13. *Letters*, I, 87.

14. David Churchill Somervell, *English Thought in the Nineteenth Century* (New York, 1929) p. 58.

15. *Letters*, I, 109.

16. Holland House Papers, Dinner Books, B.M.MS 51950 (1799-1806) 799, pp. 5, 35, 63, 99.

17. Huntington MS, SS to Robert Smith, 9 July, 1796.

18. Russell, *Sydney Smith*, pp. 29-30.

19. Derek Hudson, *Holland House in Kensington* (London, 1967; hereafter cited as Hudson, *Holland House*) p. 50.

20. David Cecil, *Melbourne* (New York, 1954) p. 52.

21. Princess Marie Liechtenstein, *Holland House*, 2 vols. (London, 1874; hereafter cited as Liechtenstein, *Holland House*) I, 157.

22. Clive, *Scotch Reviewers*, pp. 60-61, 45.

23. *Letters*, I, 101.

24. U.C.L., Brougham MS. 31.299.

25. U.C.L., *Ibid.*, 31,2989.

26. Richard Edgecumbe, ed., The Diary of Frances Lady Shelley 2 vols. (London, 1912); hereafter cited as Shelley, *Diary*) I, 15.

27. Holland, *Memoir*, I, 191.

28. *Ibid.*, p. 261.

29. *Letters*, I, 92.

30. *Ibid.*, I, 101.

31. Holland, *Memoir*, I, 65-66.

32. Duyckinck, *Wit and Wisdom*, p. 38.

33. Holland, *Memoir*, I, 223.

34. *Ibid.*, I, 88-90.

35. *Ibid.*, I, 359.

36. *Letters*, I, 119.

37. Bodleian Library Manuscripts (Hereafter cited as Bod. MS) Eng. Lett. d. 215, ff. 163-164.

38. Holland, *Memoir*, I, 380-381.

39. John Brownlow, *Memoranda; or, Chronicles of the Foundling Hospital, including Memoris of Captain Coram* (London, 1847) p. 175.

40. Bernard Baker, ed., <u>Pleasure and Pain (1780-1818)</u> (London, 1930) pp. 56-57.

41. General Committee Minutes, Foundling Hospital (Hereafter cited as GCM) 26, p. 325.

42. <u>Ibid.</u>, p. 329.

43. <u>Ibid.</u>, 27, p. 110.

44. <u>Ibid.</u>, 27, p. 118.

45. <u>Ibid.</u>, 27, p. 133.

46. <u>Ibid.</u>, 27, pp. 133.

47. <u>Ibid.</u>, 27, pp. 138-139.

48. <u>Ibid.</u>, p. 168.

49. <u>Ibid.</u>, 27, p. 193.

50. <u>Ibid.</u>, 28, p. 12.

51. <u>Ibid.</u>, 28, p. 115.

52. Foundling Estate Protective Association, <u>The Foundling Hospital and its Neighbourhood: with an Introduction by W.R. Lethaby</u> (London, 1926) p. 23.

53. GCM 27, p. 216; p. 28, 163; 29, pp. 47-48, 244-245.

54. <u>Ibid.</u>, 27, pp. 173-174, 179.

55. <u>Ibid.</u>, 29, p. 186.

56. <u>Ibid.</u>, 29, pp.

57. <u>Ibid.</u>, 29, pp. 36, 104.

58. Baptismal Register, Foundling Hospital, Public Record Office, RG4-II-4238, p. 142.

59. J.R. Howard Roberts, & Walter H. Godfrey, eds., <u>London County Council: Survey of London</u> (London, 1949; Hereafter cited as <u>Survey</u>) XXI, 48.

60. Ralph Nevill, <u>Mayfair and Montmartre</u> (London, 1921) p. 92.

61. <u>Letters</u>, I, 114.

62. Wedgwood Museum, MS 16095-89.

63. Survey p. 48.

64. April, 1845, p. 438.

65. Reginald Colby, Mayfair: A Town Within London (London, 1966) p. 74.

66. Holland, Memoir, I, 79-80.

67. Sermons, 1846, 193-194.

68. Survey, XXI, 48.

69. Frederick Miller, Sanit Pancras Past & Present (London, 1874) p. 174.

70. Sermons, 1846, p. 205.

71. Reid, Sydney Smith, pp. 116-117.

72. Holland, Memoir, I, 399-400.

73. 25 February, 1845.

74. Holland MS, II, 24.

75. Holland, Memoir, I, 68.

76. Cherrillou, Sydney Smith, p. 27.

77. Holland, Memoir, I, 182

78. Leonard Horner, ed., Memoirs and Correspondence of Francis Horner, 2 vols. (Boston, 1853; hereafter cited as Horner, Memoir) I, 295-296.

79. Ibid., p. 299.

80. Russell, Sydney Smith, p. 32.

81. Letters, I, 103.

82. Sydney Smith, Elementary sketches of Moral Philosophy (London, 1859; hereafter cited as Moral Philosophy) p. 33. Chevrillon, Sydney Smith, pp. 89-92.

83. Ibid., pp. 187-188.

84. Moral Philosophy, pp. 256-272.

85. Ibid., pp. 388-389.

86. SS to William Whewell, 8 April, 1843. MS. O. 18.
    S195. Trinity College, Cambridge University.

87. Moral Philosophy, p. 60.

88. Ibid., pp. 24-25

89. Ibid., p. 33.

90. Ibid., p. 15.

91. Ibid., pp. 54-55

92. Ibid., p. 59.

93. Ibid., p. 58.

94. Ibid., pp. 97-98.

95. Ibid., p. 126

96. Ibid., pp. 124-125.

97. Ibid., pp. 136-137.

98. "A witty man...can no more exist eithout applause than he can without air; if his audience be small, or if they are inattentive, or if a new wit defrauds him of any portion of his admiration, it is all over with him...The applauses...are so essential to him that he must obtain them at the expense of decency, friendship, and good feeling...." Ibid., p. 144. Sydney certainly did not intend these lines to be self-descriptive, but even though his wit rarely violated decency and never terminated friendship, they do present a very accurate picture of him.

99. Ibid., pp. 158-159.

100. Ibid., pp. 259, 264-265.

101. Letters, I, 113.

102. Wedgwood Museum, MS 16094-89.

103. Letters, I, 115-116.

104. Ibid., I, 117.

105. Holland, MS II, pp. 26-27.

106. "Ingram on Methodism", E.R., XI, Jan., 1808, pp. 361-362.

107. Ibid., pp. 341-342.

108. Letters, I, 269.

109. Sermons, 1809, I, 295-296.

110. Sermons, 1846, pp. 198-202.

111. Ingram, On Methodism, pp. 344, 346.

112. Ibid., pp. 357-358.

113. "Styles on Methodists and Missions, E.R., XIV, April, 1809, pp. 40-41.

114. Ibid., p. 42.

115. Ibid., p. 43.

116. Ibid., p. 44.

117. Ibid., pp. 44-45.

118. Ibid., pp. 50.

119. "Proceedings of the Society for the Suppression of Vice", E.R., XIII, January, 1809, p. 334.

120. Ibid., 339-340.

121. Ibid., p. 343.

122. "Coelebs in Search of a Wife", E.R., XIV, April, 1809, pp. 145-146.

123. Ibid., p. 148-149.

124. Ibid., p. 151.

125. Bodl. MS. Eng. Lett. d. 215, ff. 163-4; Letters, I, 108.

126. Hudson, Holland House, p. 51.

127. Ibid., p. 51.

128. Holland MS I, pp. 40-41.

129. *Letters*, I, 135.

130. *Ibid.*, p. 137.

131. *Ibid.*, pp. 148-149.

132. Ibid., I, p. 145.

133. "Letter on the Curates' Salary Bill", XIII, Oct., 1808, pp. 25-34.

134. *Ibid.*, pp. 125-126.

135. *Ibid.*, p. 29.

136. *Ibid.*, p. 32.

137. *Ibid.*, p. 33.

CHAPTER VI

1. "Mrs. Trimmer <u>on Lancaster's Plan of Education</u>", E.R., IX, Oct., 1806, 177.

2. <u>Ibid.</u>, p. 178.

3. <u>Ibid.</u>, p. 180.

4. <u>Ibid.</u>, p. 182.

5. <u>Ibid.</u>, pp. 183-184.

6. "Lancaster's Improvements in Education", E.R., XI, Oct., 1807, 71.

7. <u>Ibid.</u>, p. 72.

8. <u>Letters</u>, I, 220.

9. <u>Ibid.</u>, I, 219.

10. <u>E.R.</u>, XV, 41.

11. <u>Ibid.</u>, p. 47.

12. <u>Ibid.</u>, p. 50.

13. <u>Ibid.</u>, p. 51.

14. Halpern, <u>Sydney Smith</u>, p. 159.

15. "Calumnies against Oxford", <u>E.R.</u>, XVI, April, 1810, p. 182.

16. <u>Ibid.</u>, p. 186.

17. "Female Education", <u>E.R.</u>, XV, Jan., 1810, p. 299.

18. <u>Ibid.</u>, p. 302.

19. <u>Ibid.</u>, p. 309.

20. <u>Ibid.</u>, p. 305.

21. "Hamilton"s Method of Teaching Languages", <u>E.R.</u>, XLIV, June, 1826, p. 69.

22. Halpern, <u>Sydney Smith</u>, pp. 57-64.

23. (London, 1807-08; and in numerous editions and reprints. The following citations are drawn from Works, 2nd. ed., 1840)

24. Letters, I, 120.

25. Auden, Sydney Smith, p. xii.

26. Burdett, Sydney Smith, pp. 180, 278.

27. Denis Gray, Spencer Perceval (Manchester, 1963) pp. 24, 105.

28. Works, III, 373-374.

29. Ibid., p. 380.

30. Ibid., p. 381.

31. Ibid., p. 382.

32. Ibid., p. 383.

33. Ibid., pp. 384-385.

34. Ibid., p. 386.

35. Ibid., P. 389.

36. Ibid., p. 391-392.

37. Ibid., p. 392.

38. Ibid., pp. 395-396.

39. Bon-Mots, p. 96.

40. Works, III, 397.

41. Ibid., p. 398.

42. Ibid., pp. 399-400.

43. Ibid., p. 402.

44. Ibid., pp. 304.

45. Ibid., pp. 405-406.

46. Ibid., p. 408.

47. Ibid., pp. 409-410.

48. Ibid., p. 411.

49. Ibid., p. 412.

50. Ibid., p. 414-415.

51. Ibid., p. 420.

52. Ibid., pp. 420-421.

53. Ibid., pp. 425-426.

54. Ibid., p. 437.

55. Ibid., pp. 438-441.

56. Ibid., p. 446.

57. Ibid., p. 448 (misprinted as 484 in 2nd edition).

58. Pearson, Smith of Smiths, p. 11.

59. Works, III, p. 449.

60. Ibid., p. 450.

61. Ibid., pp. 452-454.

62. Ibid., pp. 460.

63. A Letter to the Electors, Upon the Catholic Question, Works, III, pp. 232-324.

64. John Green, "Peter Plymley's Letters", Notes and Queries, 6th series, VII, 1883, p. 443.

65. Holland, Memoir, I, 102.

66. Halpern, Sydney Smith, pp. 63-64.

67. Fathers of the Victorians (Cambridge, 1961) p. 363.

68. Bernard Pool, ed., The Croker Papers, 1808-1857 (London, 1967) p. 46. Sermons, 1846, pp. 197-198.

69. Sermons, 1809, II, 102-103.

70. Ibid., p. 108.

71. Burdett, Smith, Sydney, p. 213.

72. Holland, *Memoir*, I, 201-202.

73. Reid, *Sydney Smith*, p. 224.

74. *Letters*, I, 411.

75. Ernest Dillworth, "Letters of Sydney Smith", *Notes and Queries*, CCIX (1964) pp. 419-421.

76. (York, 1826); also in various other editions, including *Works*, III, 315-353.

77. *Letters*, I, 420-421.

78. *Ibid.*, p. 480.

79. *Ibid.*, pp. 481, 483.

80. "A Sermon on Those Rules of Christian Charity....", *Works*, III, 359-370.

81. *Letters*, II, 563-801.

82. *Letters*, II, 854.

83. Holland, *Memoir*, I, 146-147.

84. *Bon Mots*, pp. 66, 70.

85. John Gore, ed., *The Creevey Papers* (New York, 1963) p. 94.

86. D. B. Schneider, "Daniel Webster Visits Sydney Smith", *Notes and Queries*, CCXII (1967) p. 366.

87. Holland, *Memoir*, I, 264-265.

88. *Letters*, II, 516.

89. B. M. Add. MS 51645, f. 82.

CHAPTER VII

1. Chevrillon, *Sydney Smith*, p. 57.

2. "...Luttrell I hear has been Foston and Lady Granville. In future you will observe the House will only be seen with Tickets- and three days a Week- it is absolutely necessary to make some regulations." Castle Howard Photostats, CHI/142(52). Quoted by permission of A.S. Bell, Edinburgh.

3. *Letters*, I, 106.

4. *Ibid.*, p. 146.

5. *Ibid.*, p. 166.

6. *Ibid.*, p. 179.

7. *Ibid.*, p. 158.

8. BMMS, 58645, ff. 65.

9. *Letters*, I, 214. Some differences exist between this letter, and the original in the British Museum, which was quoted in the preceding footnote. Nowell Smith sets the data as 14 Oct., 1811, whereas the original in the British Museum is clearly dated 14 October, 1812. Since the letter says that construction will begin the following spring, and since it did begin in 1813, it appears that Nowell Smith's date was merely a typographical error.

10. *Ibid.*, pp. 228-229.

11. Holland, *Memoir*, I, 157-158.

12. *Foston Vicarage 1813-14*. A large folder of uncatalogued documents dealing with the construction of the parsonage. Borthwick Institute, York University.

13. *Ibid.*

14. Holland, *Memoir*, I, pp. 160-161.

15. *Letters*, I, 231.

16. "First Letter to Archdeacon Singleton", *Works*, III, 204.

17. Holland, *Memoir*, I, 118-119.

18. *Ibid.*, p. 262.

19. Hicks Beach, *A Cotswold Family*, p. 305.

20. BMMS 51645, ff. 46-47.

21. Holland, *Memoir*, I, p. 392.

22. *Letters*, I, 190.

23. John Rylands Library, Bromley-Davenport Muniments, Letters of Sydney Smith, 9.

24. *Letters*, II, 551.

25. *Ibid.*, p. 614.

26. *Ibid.*, p. 668.

27. Holland, *Memoir*, I, 159.

28. Reid, *Sydney Smith*, pp. 174.

29. *Ibid.*, p. 176.

30. BMMS 51645, ff. 75.

31. Holland, *Memoir*, I, 172-174.

32. *Ibid.*, p. 192.

33. Holland, MS III, 282.

34. *Letters*, I, 208.

35. *Ibid.*, p. 308.

36. Holland, *Memoir*, I, 181.

37. *Letters*, I, 307.

38. Holland, Memoir, I, 368-369.

39. *Letters*, I, 308.

40. *Ibid.*, p. 313.

41. Alexander Brady, *William Huskisson and Liberal Reform* (New York, 1967), p. 33.

42. John Gore, ed., The Creevey Papers (New York, 1963) p. 235.

43. New College, Oxford (Bob.), SS to Cecil Smith, 4 June, 1827.

44. Holland, Memoir, I, 222.

45. Letters, II, 505.

46. Ibid., I, 192.

47. BM MS 51645 ff. 62.

48. Ibid., ff. 64.

49. Holland, Memoir, I, 151.

50. UCL, Brougham MS, 10,865

51. Letters, I, 240.

52. SS to Lady Anne Elliot, 13 Nov., 1813. Osborne Collection.

53. Letters, I, 361.

54. Burdett, Sydney Smith, p. 199.

55. Letters, II, 550.

56. Reid, Sydney Smith, p. 164.

57. SS to Lord Palmerston, 7 April, 1836, Osborn Collection.

58. E.U.L., MS. Dc. 4. 101-3.

59. SS to Cecil Smith, New College (Bod.).

60. Letters, I, 477.

61. The Earl of Ilchester, Elizabeth, Lady Holland to Her Son (London, 1946) pp. 99.

62. SS to Cecil Smith, 6 April, New College (Bod.).

63. Ibid., 30 Aug. 1827.

64. CHI/142 (55).

65. CHI/142 (54).

66. Letters, I, 489.

67. Ibid., II, 496.

68. Ibid., I, 192.

69. Holland, Memoir, I, 267.

70. Foston Baptismal Register, 1961-1812; Register of Baptism In the Parish of Foston In the County of York 1813-1892; Register of the Burials In the Parish of Foston In the County of York; Foston Parish Marriage Register 1754-1812; Register of Marriages in the Parish of Foston in the County of York, 1812-1837; Churwarden's Account Book, 1789-1842. All in the custody of the present incumbent of Flaxton Parish.

71. First Letter to Archdeacon Singleton, Works, III, 172-175.

72. Letters, I, 233.

73. Ibid., I, 268.

74. Ibid., I, 326.

75. Reid, Sydney Smith, pp. 185-186.

76. Holland, Memoir, I, 176.

77. Letters, I, 337-338.

78. Ibid., 363.

79. Holland, MS II, 37.

80. Letters, I, 380; Holland, Memoir, I, 191; Reid, Sydney Smith, p. 202.

81. Richard Edgecumbe, Ed., The Diary of Frances Lady Shelley (London, 1912), I, 14-15.

82. The date 1823 here listed is not entirely certain. Holland, Memoir, I, 203-204 lists the date uncertainly around 1825. Nowell C. Smith, in a note in Letters, I, 426, gave the date as 1826. Holland, MS, III, listed it as 1824; and a dubiously dated letter from Sydney Smith to John

Allen in the British Museum is marked 28 April, 1825. MMS 52180, ff. 22.

83. The Earl of Ilchester, Chronicles of Holland House, 1820-1900 (London, 1937) p. 84.

84. Reid repeats an ancedote about Sydney visiting Londesborough and being confronted by a young country boy who stared at him in apparent hostility. '"Where are you going, my boy?"..."To't Sunday-school"...."Who do you think I am?" "I dun noa." "Am I Mr. Mayelstone?" [the curate] "Noa!!" "What do you think I am then?"..."I think you're maist like one of them chaps that gangs aboot wi' knives and razonr!".' Perhaps it was this remark that led Sydney, later in life, to say that "The whole of my life has passed like a razor-in hot water or a scrape." Reid, Sydney Smith, pp. 226-227.

85. Holland, Memoir, I, 202-203.

86. Reid, Sydney Smith, p. 225.

87. SS to Lord Carlisle, Castle Howard Photostats, CHI/142(14).

88. Letters, I, 342.

89. SS to Francis Wrangham, 21 March, 1825. Fondren Library, Rice University.

90. Holland, Memoir, I, 207.

91. New College (Bod.).

92. New College (Bod.).

93. Holland, Memoir, I, 208. It is not entirely certain that this letter was addressed to Goderich, or that it was ever sent.

94. October, 1827. New College (Bod.).

95. Holland House Papers, List of Whig Clergy, BMMS 51922, A & B, 799E.

96. Holland, MS, III, 301-303. Holland MS, I, 62-63.

97. A. Aspinall, ed., The Letters of King George IV, 1812-1830 (Cambridge, 1938) p. 365.

98. <u>Bon Mots</u>, p. 105.

99. The Watergate Booklets, <u>Sayings of Sydney Smith</u> (London, n.d.), pp. 13-14.

100. New College (Bod.).

101. (October?) 1828, Castle Howard Photostats, CHI/142(52).

CHAPTER VIII

1. Holland, Memoir, I, 115-116.
2. Letters, I, 274.
3. Ibid., p. 283.
4. Ibid., p. 296.
5. Ibid., p. 276.
6. Ibid., p. 313.
7. Ibid., p. 330.
8. Ibid., p. 335.
9. SS to Lady Holland, 20 Aug. 1819, Bmms 51645, ff. 77.
10. Letters, I, 338.
11. Ibid., p. 338.
12. SS to Lady Morpeth (Autumn, 1819) CHI/142(26)
13. SS to Lord Carlisle, 1 Sept. 1819. CHI/142(2)
14. Letters, I, 339-340.
15. Ibid., p. 341.
16. SS to Edward Davenport, 3 Jan., 1820. John Rylands Library Bromley-Davenport Muniments, Letters of Sydney Smith, 3.
17. Letters, I, 249.
18. Bernard Pool, ed., The Croker Papers (London, 1967) p. 49.
19. Letters, I, 347.
20. Ibid., p. 352.
21. Ibid., p. 366.
22. SS to Edward Davenport, 3 Jan., 1820. John Rylands Library, Bromley-Davenport Muniments, Letters of Sydney Smith, 3.

23. *Letters*, I, 365.

24. SS to Edward Davenport, 1824, John Ryland Library, Bromley-Davenport Muniments. Letters of Sydney Smith, 14.

25. *Letters*, I, 351.

26. *Ibid.*, p. 392.

27. *Ibid.*, p. 413.

28. *Ibid.*, p. 170.

29. *ER*, XXXIV (Nov. 1820), p. 429.

30. *Letters*, I, 422.

31. 15 March, 1826. BM Add. MS 38747, f. 209.

32. SS to Wm. Huskisson, 26 Sept., 1826. BM Add. MS 38748, f. 169.

33. SS to Wilmot Horton, 6 March, 1826. Catton Papers, Derby Public Library.

34. *Letters*, I, 293.

35. *Ibid.*, p. 305.

36. *Ibid.*, pp. 243-244.

37. Holland, *Memoir*, I, 200-201.

38. *Ibid.*, pp. 379-380.

39. *Ibid.*, p. 165.

40. 14 March, 1842. New College (Bod.)

41. "State of Prisons", *ER*, XXXV (July, 1821). p. 386.

42. *Ibid.*, pp. 287-288.

43. SS to Sir Robert Peel, 27 March, 1826. B.M. Add. MS. 40386, ff. 73-74.

44. "State of Prisons", *op. cit.*, p. 389.

45. *Ibid.*, p. 290.

46. Ibid., p. 291.

47. Ibid., 292.

48. Ibid., p. 295.

49. Ibid., pp. 296-297.

50. "Prisons". ER. XXXVI, pp. 353-354.

51. Ibid., p. 356.

52. Ibid., p. 359.

53. Ibid., pp. 362-363.

54. Ibid., p. 365.

55. "Treadmill-Punishment of Untried Prisoners", ER, XXIX (Jan., 1824). p. 302.

56. Ibid., p. 303.

57. Ibid., p. 304.

58. Ibid., p. 305.

59. Ibid., pp. 306-307.

60. Ibid., p. 308.

61. Ibid., p. 310.

62. Ibid., p. 312.

63. Ibid., p. 313.

64. "State of Prisons", op. cit., pp. 301-302.

65. "Prisons", E.R., XXXVI (Feb., 1822) p. 365.

66. Ibid., p. 369.

67. "Counsel for Prisoners", ER, XLV. Dec., 1826. p. 75.

68. Ibid., p. 75.

69. Ibid., pp. 75-76.

70. Ibid., p. 76.

71. Ibid., p. 78.
72. Ibid., p. 79.
73. Ibid., p. 80.
74. Ibid., p. 85.
75. Ibid., p. 86.
76. Ibid., p. 92.
77. "The Game Laws", ER, XXXI (March, 1819), pp. 295-296.
78. Ibid., p. 296.
79. Ibid., p. 297.
80. Ibid., p. 299
81. Ibid., pp. 299-300.
82. Ibid., pp. 301-302.
83. Ibid., p. 305.
84. Ibid., p. 308.
85. "Spring Guns and Man Traps", ER, XXXV (March, 1821), pp. 123-124.
86. Ibid., pp. 126-127.
87. Ibid., pp. 127-128.
88. Ibid., p. 132.
89. Ibid., pp. 133-134.
90. "Man Traps and Spring Guns", ER, XXXV (July, 1821), pp. 410-415.
91. "Game Laws", ER, XXXIX (October, 1823), pp. 48-49.
92. Ibid., p. 51.
93. Letters, I, 161.
94. Holland, Memoir, I, 143-144.
95. 22 Sept., 1821. CHI/142(5).

96. Ernest Dilworth, "Letters of Sydney Smith", *Notes and Queries*, 209 (Nov., 1964), p. 421.

97. SS to Sir Robert Peel, 13 March, 1826. BM Add, MS. 40386, f. 11.

98. *Letters*, I, 166.

99. *Ibid.*, p. 364.

100. *Ibid.*, p. 484.

101. *Ibid.*, II, 544.

102. *Sermons*, 1846. pp. 367-369.

103. *Letters*, I, 231-232.

104. Holland, *Memoir*, I, 164-165.

105. Burdett, *The Rev. Smith, Sydney*, p. 207.

CHAPTER IX

1. Holland, *Memoir*, I, 229.
2. *Ibid.*, p. 227.
3. 7 July, 1829, Castle Howard Photostats, CHI/142(56).
4. Burdett, *The Rev. Smith, Sydney*, pp. 234, 291.
5. SS to Lady Grey, 20 July. Hickleton (Barrowby) Collection. MS Al. 8.17.6.
6. *Letters*, I, 462.
7. SS to Wilmot Horton, 23 February. Catton Papers, Derby Public Library.
8. *Letters*, II, 515.
9. *Sermons, 1809*, I, 215.
10. *Letters*, II, 521.
11. *Ibid.*, p. 522.
12. 8 November, 1830. BMMS 52180.
13. *Letters*, II, 523.
14. *The Taunton Courier*, 8 December, 1830.
15. *Letters*, II, 525.
16. *Letters*, II, 527.
17. *Ibid.*, II, 527.
18. *Ibid.*, p. 529.
19. "Speech at the Taunton Reform Meeting", *Works*, III, 110-112.
20. *Ibid.*, pp. 112-113.
21. *Ibid.*, pp. 114-116.
22. *Ibid.*, p. 116.
23. *Ibid.*, pp. 116-117.

24. "Speech By the Rev. Sydney Smith", Works, III, 126.
25. Ibid., pp. 126-129.
26. Ibid., p. 130.
27. Ibid., p. 131.
28. Ibid., p. 133.
29. Ibid., pp. 133-134.
30. Ibid., pp. 134-135.
31. Ibid., pp. 135-136.
32. Ibid., p. 136.
33. Ibid., pp. 136-137.
34. The Taunton Courier, 4 May, 1831.
35. Letters, II, 534.
36. Ibid., p. 532.
37. "Speech at Taunton", Works, III, 123-125.
38. Reid, Sydney Smith, p. 278.
39. Holland, Memoir, I, 241.
40. Letters, II, 547.
41. Ibid., pp. 545-546.
42. Ibid., p. 549.
43. Ibid., p. 552.
44. Ibid., pp. 553-554.
45. Ibid., p. 555.
46. Ibid., p. 568.
47. Ibid., p. 569.
48. London Times, 25 February, 1845.
49. Letters, II, 594.

50. Bon Mots, p. 84.

51. New College 572- New College, Oxford. Bundle 4431; John Rylands Library, Eng. MS. 700/78.

52. Letters, II, 546.

53. The Watergate Booklets, Sayings of Sydney Smith (London, n.d.) p. 5.

54. Bon Mots, p. 18.

55. Holland, Memoir, I, 258.

56. Bon Mots, p. 29.

57. Sermons, 1809, I, 216-217.

58. Letters, I, 275.

59. Letters, II, 518.

60. Castle Howard Photostats, CHI/142(51).

61. Ibid., CHI/142(52). Chevrillon, Sydney Smith, p. 325.

62. The Earl of Ilchester, Chronicles of Holland House, 1820-1900 (London, 1937; hereafter cited as Ilchester, Holland House) p. 83.

63. Holland, Memoir, I, 218-219.

64. Chapter Minutes, Bristol Cathedral, 1818-1831. Unpublished. Volumes neither titled nor numbered. Vol. 1831-1841, pp. 119, 130, 151, 170.

65. L. W. G. Bristol [L.W. Gully], Recollections and Reflections During an Occasional Week-day Lounge in Bristol Cathedral (London, 1849) pp. 18-19.

66. SS to Lady Carlisle, 7 July, 1829. CHI/142(56).

67. Letters, II, 494.

68. Dilworth, "Letters", p. 420.

69. Letters, II, 499-500.

70. SS to George Tierney, 23 Nov., 1829. Hampshire Record Office. Tierney Papers, Bundle C.

71. Burdett, <u>The Rev. Smith</u>, Sydney, p. 235.

72. Churchwardens Accounts, D/P/co. Fl., 4/1/1; Register of Baptisms In The Parish of Combe Florey in the County of Somerset, 1813-1904, D/P/co. Fl., 2/1/6; Register of Marriges in the Parish of Combe Florey in the County of Somerset, D/p/co. Fl., 2/1/7. All in Somerset Record Office, Taunton.

73. Dinner Books, BM MS 51954, 799D, pp. 170, 173, 185; BM MS 9155, 799F, pp. 4-5.

74. SS to Cecil Smith, 21 June, 1832. New College(Bod.).

75. <u>Sermons</u>, 1846, pp. 37-42.

76. <u>Letters</u>, I, 466-467.

77. <u>Ibid</u>., I, 305.

78. CHI/142(22).

79. SS to Cecil Smith, 20 Dec., 1843. New College(Bod.).

80. Marjorie Villiers, The Grand Whiggery(London, 1939) pp. 247-248.

81. 1 Dec., 1828. Bristol Chapter Minutes.

82. <u>Letters</u>, II, 515-516. Burdett, <u>The Rev. Smith, Sydney</u>, p. 237.

83. David Churchill Somervell, <u>English Thought in the Nineteenth Century</u>(New York, 1929) p. 20.

84. <u>Sermons</u>, 1809, II, 106.

85. Elizabeth Longford, <u>Queen Victoria, Born to Succeed</u> (New York and Evanston, 1946) p. 164.

86. <u>Letters</u>, II, 523-524.

87. <u>Ibid</u>., p. 539.

88. <u>Ibid</u>., p. 541.

89. <u>Ibid</u>., p. 541.

90. John Morley, <u>The Life of William Ewart Gladstone</u>, 3 vols(London, 1903) I, 56.

91. *Letters*, II, 570.
92. *Bon Mots*, p. 108.

CHAPTER X

1. Dean and Chapter Muniment Book, 1826-1854. In library of St. Paul's (Hereafter cited as: D&C) pp. 63a-65a.

2. W.R. Matthews, and W.M. Atkins, A History of St. Paul's Cathedral and the Men Associated with It (London, 1957; Hereafter cited as: Matthews and Atkins, St. Paul's) p. 257.

3. Chapter Minute Book, 1833-1860. In Library, St. Paul's Cathedral. p. 17.

4. Ibid., p. 18.

5. Ibid., pp. 45-52. Matthews and Atlkins, St. Paul's pp. 255-257.

6. Chapter Minute Book, p. 52.

7. Matthews and Atkins, St. Paul's, p. 255.

8. Letters, I., 400, 401.

9. Ibid., p. 416.

10. Ibid., II, 630.

11. Ibid., p. 702.

12. Ibid., p. 847.

13. Burdett, The Rev. Smith, Sydney, p. 289,

14. Matthews and Atkins, St. Paul's pp. 254-255.

15. SS to W. Hawes, 21 Aug. 1844. B.M. Add. MS 41771 f. 121.

16. Matthews and Atkins, St. Paul's, pp. 252-253.

17. 31 November, 1835. CHI/142(61).

18. Letters, II, 637.

19. University College, London. Brougham MS 31.294.

20. Letters, II, 571.

21. Reid, *Sydney Smith*, p. 643.

22. G.L. Prestige, *St. Paul's in Its Glory: A Candid History of the Cathedral, 1831-1911* (London, 1955; hereafter cited as Prestige, *St. Paul's*), p. 3.

23. Chapter Minute Book, pp. 61-62.

24. *Ibid.*, pp. 62-64.

25. *Ibid.*, pp. 64-65.

26. *Ibid.*, p. 65.

27. *Ibid.*, pp. 65-67.

28. *Ibid.*, pp. 68-69.

29. *Ibid.*, pp. 69-73.

30. Prestige, *St. Paul's*, p. 29.

31. Matthews and Atkins, *St. Paul's*, pp. 257-258.

32. *D & C*, 63-65.

33. Charles C.F. Greville, *The Greville Memoris: A Journal of the Reigns of King George IV and King William IV*, 3 vols., (London, 1874) III, 166.

34. Matthews and Atkins, p. 253.

35. SS to G. Hodgson. Fondren Library, Rice University.

36. Matthews and Atkins, pp. 253-254.

37. Chapter Minute Book, p. 102.

38. Matthews and Atkins, *St. Paul's*, p. xii.

39. (London, 1909).

40. Matthews and Atkins, *St. Paul's*, p. xii.

41. Prestige, *St. Paul's*, pp. xviii-xix.

42. *Ibid.*, p. 1.

43. SS to Sir Robert Wilmot-Horton, 3 Nov. Catton Papers, Derby Papers, Derby Public Library.

44. _Letters_, II, 596-597.
45. _Ibid._, pp. 597-598.
46. _Ibid._, p. 598.
47. _Ibid._, p. 611.
48. _Ibid._, p. 612.
49. _Ibid._, p. 588.
50. _Ibid._, pp. 588-589.
51. _Ibid._, p. 589.
52. _Ibid._, p. 608.
53. Holland, MS, I, 66.
54. _Letters_, II, pp. 585-586.
55. R.A. Soloway, _Prelates and People:Ecclesiastical Social Thought in England, 1783-1852_ (London and Toronto, 1969) p. 344.
56. _Letters_, II, pp. 587-588.
57. _Works_, III, 169.
58. _Ibid._, pp. 170-172.
59. _Ibid._, pp. 172-174.
60. _Ibid._, pp. 174-175.
61. _Ibid._, p. 176.
62. _Ibid._, p. 178.
63. _Ibid._, p. 178.
64. _Ibid._, p. 180-181.
65. _Ibid._, p. 182.
66. _Ibid._, p. 183.
67. _Ibid._, p. 185.
68. _Ibid._, pp.187-188.

69. Ibid., p. 195.

70. Ibid., pp. 195-196.

71. Ibid., p. 197.

72. Ibid., pp. 202-204.

73. Ibid., p. 204.

74. Ibid., pp. 205-207.

75. Ilchester, Holland House, p. 84.

76. Desmond Bowen, The Idea of the Victorian Church (Montreal, 1968) p. 10.

77. Letters, II, 651-652.

78. Harvard MS.

79. Letters, II, 650.

80. Works, III, 224.

81. Ibid., p. 225.

82. E.U.L., MS. Dc.4. 101-3.

83. Morrison Catalogue, VI, 145-146.

84. "Second Letter to Archdeacon Singleton", Works, III, 211.

85. Ibid., pp. 212-214.

86. Ibid., p. 215.

87. Ibid., p. 219.

88. Ibid., pp. 226-227.

89. Ibid., p. 230.

90. Ibid., p. 233.

91. "Third Letter to Archdeacon Singleton", Works, III, 237-240.

92. Ibid., pp. 241-245.

93. Ibid., pp. 246-247.

94. Ibid., pp. 248-250.
95. Ibid., pp. 252-256.
96. Ilchester, Holland House, p. 167.
97. Hickleton(Garrowby)Papers, al.4.22B.2, pp. 5-6.
98. CHI/142(108).
99. CHI/142(109).
100. Letters, II, 669-670.
101. Chapter Minute Book, pp. 78-79.
102. Ibid., pp. 85-86.
103. Letters, II, 685.
104. Matthews and Atkins, St. Paul's, pp. 258-259.
105. SS to Saba Holland, 5 Sept., 1840. Yale MS
106. Hickleton(Garrowby)Papers, A 1.4.22B.2, pp. 15-17.
107. Letters, II, 707.
108. Chapter Minute Book, p. 2.
109. Ibid., pp. 20-23.
110. Col. Harold Malet, Notes and Queries, 25 Jan., p. 69.
111. B.M. Add. MS 37201, f. 457.
112. Chapter Minute Book, pp. 54-55.
113. Ibid., pp. 79-51.
114. Reid, Sydney Smith, p. 363.
115. 17 Sept., 1843. Hickleton(Garrowby)Papers, A 1.4.22B. 2, pp. 9-11.
116. Letters, II, 818.
117. Ibid., p. 583.
118. Ibid., p. 719.

119. Ibid., p. 744. B.M. MS 41045. f. 51.

120. Letters, II, 766.

121. Ibid., pp. 772-773.

122. "Parable of the Sower and the Seed", Sermons, 1846, pp. 148-149.

123. Ibid., p. 150.

124. Ibid., pp. 150-151.

125. "On Keeping the Sabbath", Sermons, 1846, p. 179.

126. New College (Bodleian).

127. Chapter Minute Book, pp. 111-112.

CHAPTER XI

1. SS to Lord Heatherton, (May?, 1838), Heatherton Papers, Staffordshire Record Office.

2. The Holland House Dinner Books show no significant drop in his visits during the middle and later thirties. B.M. MS 91955(1831-38) 799F.

3. Reid, *Sydney Smith*, p. 327.

4. 31 May, 1841. N.L.S., MS. 2883, f. 119.

5. Burdett, *The Rev. Smith, Sydney*, pp. 162-163.

6. *Bon Mots*, p. 11.

7. *Letters*, II, 642.

8. *Ibid.*, p. 643.

9. *Ibid.*, p. 621.

10. 8 August, 1835. Catoon Papers, Derby Public Library.

11. 28 August, 1818. B.M. MS 52180.

12. Letters I, 328. 13.

13. *Ibid.*, p. 342.

14. *Ibid.*, pp. 384-385.

15. Reid, *Sydney Smith*, pp. 305-306.

16. *Letters*, II, 687.

17. SS to Charles Dickens, 17 April, 1841. Huntington MS 133.

18. *Letters*, II, 675.

19. *Ibid.*, p. 686.

20. Harvard MS

21. *Bon Mots*, p. 20.

22. *Ibid.*, p. 52.

23. Ibid., p. 74.

24. Ibid., p. 109.

25. Ibid., p. 71.

26. Holland MS III, p. 306.

27. SS to Cecil Smith, 13 May, 1828. New College (Bod.)

28. SS to Edwin Landseer, 5 May, 1842. RC NN 1-7, Victoria and Albert Museum.

29. Reid, Sydney Smith, pp. 324-325.

30. David Frost and Antony Jay, The English (New York, 1968) pp. 26-28.

31. John Morley, The Life of William Ewart Galdstone, 3 vols. (London, 1903) I, 133.

32. Letters, I, 250.

33. Ibid., II, 796.

34. Duyckinck, Wit and Wisdom, p. 75.

35. Bon Mots, p. 94.

36. Letters, I, 451.

37. Holland, Memoir, I, 267.

38. SS to MacVey Napier, 2 April, 1838. B.M. Add. MS. 36419, f. 4.

39. Bon Mots, p. 1831.

40. Letters, I, 469.

41. Lewis, Journals of Miss Berry, III, 452.

42. SS to Mrs. Gaskell, 8 June, 1843. Fondren Library, Rice University.

43. SS to Mary Ann Milman, 11 November, 1843. Beinecke Collection, Yale University.

44. Ibid., p. 377.

45. Letter, II, 650.

46. Ibid., p. 622.

47. Sermons, 1846, pp. 44-45.

48. Letters, I, 294.

49. Sermons, 1809, II, pp. 411-420.

50. "Mad. de Stael's Delphine", E.R., II(April, 1803) p. 177.

51. Letters, I, 84-84.

52. Ibid., II, 610.

53. Ibid., p. 605.

54. Holland, Memoir, II, xvii

55. Sermons, 1809, II, 337.

56. Ibid., pp. 336-337.

57. Letters, I, 36.

58. Ibid., II, 669.

59. SS to Brougham, 19 Jan. 1834. Brougham Papers, U.C.L. 31.293.

60. 14 January, 1834. Hickleton (Garrowby) MS., A 1. 8.173.

61. Letters, II, 812.

62. Reid, Sydney Smith, p. 293.

63. Letters, II, 542.

64. Ibid., p. 594.

65. Frederick Boase, Modern English Biography(London, 1921) IV.

66. SS to Lord Carlisle, June-July 1835. CHI/142(8)

67. SS to Dr. Wordsworth, 9 July, 1835. Lambeth Palace MS1822, ff. 227-228.

68. SS to Lord Carlisle, 11 July, 1835. CHI/142(17).

69. Lambeth Palace MS 1822, ff. 227-228.

70. SS to Dr. Wordsworth, 13 July, 1835. Lambeth Palace MS 1822, ff. 229-231.

71. Lambeth Palace MS 1822, f. 227.

72. *Letters*, II, 641.

73. 7 April, 1836. Osborn Collection, Yale University.

74. *Letters*, II, 653-654.

75. SS to Wm. Cowper, 7 June, 1837. Melbourne Papers, Box 80, Royal Archives, Windsor.

76. *Letters*, II, 759.

77. *Ibid.*, p. 773.

78. *Ibid.*, p. 814.

79. SS to Sir Robert Wilmot-Horton, 12 September, 1836. Catton Papers, Derby Public Library.

80. SS to Cecil Smith, 18 August, 1832. New College (Bod.)

81. "Burckhardt's Travels in Nubia", *E.R.*, XXXIV (August, 1821) pp. 110-111.

82. Ilchester, *Lady Holland to Her Son*, p. 83.

83. Holland, *Memoir*, I, 280-281.

84. *Letters*, II, 778-779.

85. *Ibid.*, p. 784.

86. SS to Cecil Smith, 15 March, 1843. New College (Bod.)

87. SS to Cecil Smith, 10 Feb., 1843, Feb., 143, Feb., 1843. New College (Bod.)

88. SS to Cecil Smith, 16 March, 1843. New College (Bod.)

89. SS to Cecil Smith, 3 April, 1843. New College (Bod.)

90. "We had a jolly day enough at Whitehall on Saturday, altho' I never see Sydney Smith without thinking him too much of a buffoon." 22 June, 1824. *Creevey Papers*, p. 198.

91. Holland, MS I, 27.

92. Holland, Memoir, I, 357-358.

93. SS to Lady Copley, 26 Dec. 1825. Fondren Library, Rice University.

94. Letters, I, 246.

95. Holland, Memoir, I, 355-356.

96. "Vaccination and Small-pox", E.R., XXXVII(Nov., 1822) pp. 325-337.

97. Ibid., pp. 333-334.

98. Letters, II, 575.

99. Letters, II, 575.

100. SS to Dr. ---, n.d. Fondren Library, Rice University.

101. Letters, I, 267.

102. Letters, II, 649.

103. SS to Edward Lytton Bulwer, 30 June, 1843. Lytton Add. MS, Letters and Papers, III, no. 18. Hertford County Record Office.

104. Holland, Memoir, I, 346.

105. Letters, I, 328.

106. Holland, Memoir, I, 282.

107. Letters, I, 308-309.

108. SS to Cecil Smith, 15 Une, 1827. New College (Bod.)

109. SS to Cecil Smith, 12 June, 1827. New College.

110. Letters, II, 533.

111. Ibid. pp. 600-601.

112. Ibid., I, 486.

113. Ibid., p. 249.

114. Holland, Memoir, I, 342.

115. Auden, *Selected Writings*, p. 317.

116. *Letter*, I, 105.

117. *Ibid.*, p. 277.

118. Holland, *Memoir*, I, 259.

119. *Letters*, II, 500.

120. Ibid., p. 734.

121. Churchwardens' Account Book, Foston Parish, passim.

122. "Licensing of Alehouses," *E.R.*, XLIV(September, 1826) pp. 442-442, 455.

123. Reid, *Sydney Smith*, pp. 240-242.

124. B.M. Add. MS 40395, ff. 250-251.

125. Hickleton(Garrowby) MS A 1. 8.17.2.

126. 3 November, 1833. Catton Papers, Derby Public Library.

127. 15 January, 1835. Catton Papers, Derby Public Library.

128. SS to Sir Robert Wilmot-Horton, 8 August, 1835. Catton Papers, Derby Public Library.

129. *Letters*, II, 635.

130. Ibid., p. 636.

131. Ibid., p. 615.

132. Ibid., p. 636.

133. SS to Sir Robert Wilmot-Horton, 8 August, 1835. Catton Papers, Derby Public Library.

134. *Letters*, II, 645.

135. *Ibid.*, pp. 659-660.

136. SS to Lady Carlisle, September, 1839. Hickleton (Garrowby)Papers. A 1.4.22B. 2, p. 708.

137. SS to Lady Carlisle, 16 January, 1840. CHI/142 (68).

138. *Letters*, II, 699.

139. *Ibid.*, p. 759.

140. *Ibid.*, p. 793.

141. *Bon Mots*, p. 110.

142. "Battot", *Works*, III, 151-152.

143. *Ibid.*, pp. 142-143.

144. *Ibid.*, p. 163.

145. *Ibid.*, p. 157.

146. *Ibid.*, p. 164.

147. *Ibid.*, p. 164.

148. *Ibid.*, p. 165.

149. *Ibid.*, p. 166.

150. Russell, *Sydney Smith*, p. 177.

151. *Letters*, II, 670.

152. Hickleton (Garrowby) Papers. A2.4. 22b, pp. 2-4. N.C.S. 763.

153. *Letters*, II, 679.

154. *Ibid.*, pp. 681. 682.

155. *Ibid.*, p. 698.

156. *Sermons*, 1846, p. 180.

157. *Morning Chronicle*, 21 May, 1842.

158. *Morning Chronicle*, 7 June, 1842.

159. 19 May, 1842. Harrowby Ms.

160. SS to the Hon. Miss Fox, June, 1842. *Miscellanies of the Philobiblon Society*, XV (1877-1884) sec. 7, pp. 17-18.

161. 20 June, 1842. B.M. Add. Ms. 29300, f. 101.

162. *Morning Chronicle*, 7 June, 1842.

163. Reid, *Sydney Smith*, pp. 309-310.

164. *Letters*, II, 721.

165. *Ibid.*, p. 134.

166. "America", *E.R.*, XXXIII (January, 1820; hereafter cited as *America*, II) pp. 77-78.

167. "America", *E.R.*, XL (July, 1824; hereafter cited as *America*, III) p. 427.

168. *America*, II, p. 79.

169. *America*, I, p. 144.

170. *Ibid.*, p. 138.

171. *America*, III, p. 432.

172. *America*, I, pp. 144-145.

173. *America*, III, pp. 429-430.

174. *America*, I, p. 149.

175. *Ibid.*, p. 150.

176. *Ibid.*, p. 146.

177. *Ibid.*, p. 148.

178. *America*, III, pp. 434-435.

179. *Ibid.*, p. 103.

180. *Ibid.*, p. 90.

181. *Letters*, I, 305.

182. *Ibid.*, p. 307.

183. *Ibid.*, pp. 307-308.

184. SS to Charles Sumner, 16 August, 1838. Harvard MS.

185. *Letters*, II, 649.

186. *Ibid.*, p. 765.

187. <u>Letters on American Debts</u>, 2nd Edition (London, 1844; hereafter cited as <u>American Debts</u>) pp. 7-10.

188. <u>Letters</u>, II, 795.

189. <u>American Debts</u>, pp. 15-16.

190. <u>Ibid</u>., pp. 21-23.

191. <u>Letters</u>, II, 808.

192. <u>Ibid</u>., p. 813.

193. <u>Ibid</u>., p. 823.

194. Ibid., p. 823.

195. Holland, Memoir, I, 411.

196. SS to Lady Holland, 26 October, 1840. B.M. Add. MS 51645.

197. Holland, <u>Memoir</u>, I, 282.

198. <u>Ibid</u>., p. 123.

199. <u>Letters</u>, II, 615-616.

200. SS to Sir Robert Wilmot Horton, 8 February, 1836. Catton Papers, Derby Public Library.

201. SS to Lord Duncannon, 29 June, 1839. Athenaeum Club.

202. SS to Lady Carlisle, 5 September, 1840. Hickleton (Garrowby) Papers, A 1.4.22B.2, pp. 15-17. Reid <u>Sydney Smith</u>, pp. 326-327.

203. <u>Letters</u>, II, 715.

204. SS to Charles Babbage, 21 March, 1842. B.M. Add. MS. 37192, f. 66.

205. SS to Francis Wrangham, 17 June, 1842. Fondren Library, Rice University.

206. <u>Letters</u>, II, 763.

207. SS to Col. Tynte, 20 December, 1842. Fondren Library, Rice University.

208. William G. Lane, "Additional Letters of Sydney Smith", *Harvard Library Bulletin*, IX(1955) pp. 397-402.

209. SS to Cecil Smith, 5 November, 1844. New College.

210. *Letters*, II, 856.

211. Lewis, *Miss Berry*, III, 488.

212. Holland, *Memoir*, I, 408-409.

213. 22 November, 1844. B.M. Add. MS 40554, ff. 298-299.

214. B.M. MS 51645, f. 55.

215. B.M. MS 51645, f. 57.

216. *Sermons*, 1809, II, 284-285.

217. *Ibid.*, P. 287.

218. *Ibid.*, pp. 289-295.

219. Ilchester, *Lady Holland to Her Son*, p. 222.

220. Liechtenstein, *Holland House*, I, 152.

221. Holland, *Memoir*, I, 411-413.

222. CAS to Lady Holland, n.d. B.M. MS 51645, ff. 110-111.

223. April, 1845.

224. John Wilson Croker, "Ireland", *Quarterly Review*, CLI (June, 1845) pp. 282-285.

225. A copy of Sydney's will may be found in Somerset House. It is filed in Wills 7-45, and may be located through *Wills and Admons 1845*.

226. *Will*, passim.

CHAPTER XX

1. *Letters*, I, 391.
2. *Ibid.*, pp. 186-187.
3. *Sermons*, 1809, I, 27.
4. 25 October, 1801, New College.
5. SS to Lady Carlisle, Spring, 1838. Hickleton (Garrowby) Papers, A 1. 4.22B. 2, pp. 5-6.
6. David Cecil, *Lord M* (London, 1954) p. 141.
7. Holland, *Memoir*, II, x-xxiv.
8. Burdett, *The Rev. Smith, Sydney*, p. 259.
9. Holland, *Memoir*, I, 390.
10. *Works*, 3rd Edition, 1845. pp. 477-478.
11. *Ibid.*, pp. 468-471
12. *Ibid.*, p. 466.
13. *Letters*, I, 154.
14. *Ibid.*, p. 165.
15. SS to John Allen, 30 March, 1823. B.M. MS 52180, p. 19.
16. *Letters*, I, 396-397.
17. SS to ------ Taylor, 8 April, 1840. Fondren Library.
18. *Letters*, II, 737.
19. *Ibid.*, p. 773.
20. *Ibid.*, I, 83.
21. "Heude's Voyages and Travels", *ER*, XXXII (July, 1819) p. 111. (1809) p. 55.
22. "J. Fievee", *E.R.*, II (April, 1803) p. 88.
23. *Letters*, II, 631.

24. Ibid., p. 625.

25. Ibid., p. 63.

26. SS to Sir Robert Wilmot-Horton, 6 December, 1835. Catton Papers, Derby Public Library.

27. SS to Lady Carlisle, 9 May, 1837. CHI/142(65).

28. Letters, II, 631.

29. Ibid., p. 657.

30. Charles Curran, "How to Convince and Englishman", New Republic, 135, no. 24, 10 December, 1956. p. 17.

31. Russell, Sydney Smith, p. 123.

32. Gertrude Himmelfarb, Victorian Minds (New York, 1968) pp. 226-227.

33. Chevrillon, Sydney Smith, pp. xiii-xvi.

34. Sermons, 1809, pp. 247-248.

35. Ibid., pp. 248-249.

36. Ibid., pp. 250-251.

37. Ibid., pp. 257-258.

38. Ibid., pp. 285-259.

39. Holland, Memoir, I, 328.

40. This bon mot is probably the most frequently repeated quotation, in various forms, of Sydney Smith, In toto it read: "If you choose to represent the various parts in life by holes upon a table, of different shapes,-some circular, some triangular, some square, some oblong,-and the persons acting these parts by bits of wood of similar shapes, we shall generally find that the triangular person has got himself squeezed himself into the round hole." Moral Philosophy, p. 111. Holland, Memoir, p. 259.

41. Russell, Sydney Smith, pp. 197-198.

42. Letters, I, 238, n. 1.

43. Houghton, *Sydney Smith*, p. 261.

44. SS to Richard Heber, ? April, 1803. Bod. MS. Eng. Lett. d. 215, f. 147.

45. *Letters*, I, 124.

46. *Ibid.*, p. 194.

47. *Ibid.*, II, 494-495.

48. *Ibid.*, I, 223.

49. *Ibid.*, pp. 243-244.

50. *Ibid.*, p. 402.

51. SS to Edward Davenport, 17 August, 1823. John Rylands Library, 11.

52. *Letters*, II, 609.

53. SS to Edward Lytton Bulwer, 27 June, 1843. Hartford County Record Office, Lytton Add. MS., Letters and Papers, III, no. 19.

54. Holland, *Memoir*, I, 120.

55. *Sermons*, 1809, I, 190.

56. Holland, *Memoir*, I, 365, 372.

57. William Flavelle Monypenny, and George Earle Buckle, *The Life of Benjamin Diaraeli, Earl of Beaconsfield*, 6 vols. (London, 1910-20) II, 225.

58. *St. Paul's, A Biographical Sketch* (London, 1900) p.164.

59. Desmond Bowen, *The Idea of the Victorian Church* (Montreal, 1968) p. 18.

60. Ilchester, *Holland House*, pp. 116-117.

61. Holland, *Memoir*, I, 378-379.

62. *Ibid.*, p. 382.

63. SS to Lady Morpeth, 1 December, 1821. CHI/142(35).

64. Reid, *Sydney Smith*, pp. 305-306.

65. Ibid., p. 302.

66. 13 January, 1821. CHI/142(29)

67. SS to J.A. Murray, 24 January, 1831. JRL, Eng. MS. 700/87.

68. SS to Lady Carlisle, 25 October, 1835. CHI/142(59).

69. Duane B. Schneider, Notes and Queries, CCXII, 1967, pp. 307-308.

70. New College (Bod.)

71. Reid, Sydney Smith, pp. 150-152.

72. Bon Mots, p. 91.

73. Holland, Memoir, I, 371.

74. Sermons, 1809, I, 45-46.

75. Ibid., pp. 49,51.

76. Bon Mots, p. 63.

77. Reid, Sydney Smith, pp. 74-75.

78. Holland, Memoir, I, 142-143.

79. Holland House, I, 153.

80. Sydney Smith, Essays Social and Political (in Boston's Books for all Time) London, 1877 p. vi.

81. Burdett, Sydney Smith, p. 162.

82. Ilchester, Holland House, p. 84.

83. 9 January, 1954, p. 85.

BIBLIOGRAPHY

I. Published Works

The Ballot, (London, 1839)

Elementary Sketches of Moral Philosophy (London, 1850)

A Fragment on the Irish Roman Catholic Church (London, 1845)

A Letter to the Committee of Magistrates, of the County of York, Appointed to Alter and Enlarge the County Jail (York, 1824)

Letter on American Debts, 2nd. Ed. (London, 1844)

Letters on the Subject of Catholic Emancipation to his Brother by Peter Plymley (London, 1807-1808) Numerous other editions.

Sermons, 2 vols. (London, 1801) An enlarged second edition of Six Sermons....

Sermons by the Rev. Sydney Smith, 2 vols. (London, 1809)

A Sermon Preached at the Temple, May 31, and at Berkley Chapel, Berkley Square, June 28the, Upon the Conduct to be Observed by the Established Church Towards Catholics and Other Dissenters (London, 1807)

A Sermon Preached before his Grace the Archbishop of York, and the Clergy of Malton, at the Visitation, August, 1809 (London, 1809) in Sermons at St. Paul's, The Foundling Hospital, and Several Churches in London (London, 1846)

Six Sermons given at Charlotte Chapel (Edinburgh, 1800)

The Works of the Rev. Sydney Smith, 4 vols. (London, 1839-40). (Second Edition, 1840; Third Edition, 1845; Fourth Edition, 1848; numerous other editions). Most of the above publications, and numerous others, are included in the Works, the most complete edition being the 4th. In this study I have quoted usually from the second edition, which I have in my possession, but in a few instances I have referred to the

1845 edition. The major collections of sermons and Elementary Sketches of Moral Philosophy are not included in the Works.

II. Edinburgh Review Articles

Owing to the practice of publishing reviews anonymously, the number and identity of Sydney Smith's reviews been difficult to establish. In his second edition of his works he listed sixty-four, and sixty-five were mentioned in the fourth edition, in both cases with one error. The difficulty has, however, been largely removed by the work of Walter E. Houghton, ed., The Wellesley Index to Victorian Periodicals, 1824-1900 (Tononto, 1966); and especially of Sheldon Halpern, "Sydney Smith in the Edinburgh Review", Bulletin of the New York Public Library, 66, November, 1962. Mr. Halpern also includes a supplemental bibliography of thirty-seven reviews not listed in the Works in his Sydney Smith (New York, 1966).

III. Letters and Papers

Nowell C. Smith, ed., The Letters of Sydney Smith, 2 vols. (Oxford, 1953) is an improvement over Mrs. Austin's collection in Lady Holland's Memoir and Letters of the Rev. Sydney Smith 2 vols. (London, 1855); but its shortcomings were recognised as early as its publication. A definitive collection of Smith letters is being prepared by A. S. Bell of Edinburgh, and when published it will both expand the number of known letters, and contribute a better transcription and interpretation. I am grateful to Mr. Bell for alerting me to many of the public and private collections listed below. Those enumerated are not a complete collection of sources, but are chiefly those from which I have quoted. Mr. Bell, in his forthcoming collection of Smith letters, will provide a complete listing.

Bodleian Library, Oxford University

The Borthwick Institute of Historical Research, York University

The British Museum

Edinburgh University Library

Enys Autograph Collection, The Royal Institution of Cornwall, Truro

The Fondren Library, Rice University

Archives of the Thomas Coram Foundation

General Library, University of California

Greater London Record Office and Library

Hampshire Record Office, Winchester

Hartfordshire County Council, County Record Office, Hartford

Mr. David Holland
The Henry E. Huntington Library, San Marino, California

Miscellanies of the Philobiblon Society, XV (1877-84) sec. 7

Alfred Morrison, Catalogue of the Collection of Autograph Letters and Historical Documents formed between 1865 and 1882 6 vols. 1883-92.

The National Library of Scotland

The National Library of Wales

New River Company, Disbursement Book, Archives of the Metropolitan Water Board

The Carl H. Pforzheimer Library, New York

The Public Records Office

John Rylands Library, Deansgate, Manchester

Staffordshire County Council, County Record Office, Stafford

Sowerset Record Office, Taunton
The Miriam Lutcher Stark Library, University of Texas

Trinity College Library, Cambridge University

The Library, University College, University of London

The Widener Library, Harvard University

Wills and Admons, 1845, Somerset House, London

The Wedgwood Museum, Barlaston

IV. Church Records

Chapter Minute Book, 1831-1841, Bristol Cathedral

Chapter Minute Book: 1833-1860. St. Paul's Cathedral

Chapter Muniment Books, X-XII, 1832-1848. St. Paul's Cathedral John W. Clay, The Registers of St. Paul's Cathedral (London, 1899)

D & C Muniment Book, 1826-1854. St. Paul's Cathedral

Churchwardens Accounts, Combe Florey (Somerset Record Office)

Members of the Society of Geneologists, Parish Register of Combeflorey 1566-1837. (Typescript in Somerset Record Office and British Museum)

Parish Register of Combe Florey, 1566-1837. Somerset Record Office

Register of Baptisms in the Parish of Combe Florey In the County of Somerset (1813-1904) Somerset Record Office

Register of Marriages in the Parish of Combe Florey in the County of Somerset. Somerset Record Office.

Churchwarden's Account book, 1789-1842, Foston Parish. (All Foston parish records are in the hands of the incumbent of Flaxton Parish, York)

Foston Baptismal Register, 1761-1812

Foston Parish Marriage Register, 1954-1812
Foston Vicarage 1813-14. In Borthwick Institute.

Register of Baptisms In The Parish of Foston In The County of York, 1813-1892

Register of Burials In the Parish of Foston In the County of York, from 1813 (to 1965)

Register of Marriages in the Parish of Foston in the County of York, 1812-1837

Foundling Hospital, Baptisms 1741-1838. 2 vols at Somerset House.

General Committee Minutes, Foundling Hospital, 27-30 (1804-1809) at Thomas Coram Foundation

St. Pancras: St. Saviour. Greater London Record Office. (Fitzroy Chapel Records, 1786-1793; register 1815-1827)

V Contemporary newspapers and journals

The Annual Register

The Edinburgh Review
The Gentleman's Magazine
The Morning Chronicle
The Quarterly Review

The Taunton Courier

The Times

The Westminister Review

VI. Biographies

W. H. Auden, ed., Selected Writings of Sydney Smith (New York, 1956)

Gerald Bullett, Sydney Smith: A Biography and a Selection (London, 1951)

Osbert Burdett, The Rev. Smith, Sydney (London, 1934)

Andre Chevrillon, Sydney Smith el La Renaissance des Idees liberales en Angleterre au XIX Siecle (Paris, 1894)

John L. Clive, Scotch Reviewers (Harvard, 1957)

Lady [Saba] Holland, A Memoir of the Reverend Sydney Smith. By His Daughter Lady Holland. With Selections From His Letters, Edited by Mrs. [Sarah] Austin, 2 vols. (London, 1855)

Lord Houghton, Monographs Personal and Social (New York, 1873)

Hesketh Pearson, The Smith of Smiths (London, 1934)

Stuart J. Reid, A Sketch of the Life and Times of the Rev. Sydney Smith (London, 1884). (The 4th edition (London, 1896) contains otherwise unpublished letters).

George W. E. Russell, Sydney Smith (London, 1905).

In English Men of Letters series.

Catherine Amelia Smith, MS Narrative for My Grandchildren. Two MS copybooks and two typescripts in the possession of Mr. David Holland. The first is untitled, but the typescript bears the above title. It is clearly the work of Mrs. Sydney, and is referred to as Holland MSI in my footnotes. The second copybook is entitled: "Memoir of the Life of the Revd Sydney Smith", but the typescript bears the title "Recollections of Mr. S. Smith's Life and of His Family". It appears to be a family effort at a memoir, and is referred to as MSII in my footnotes. Lady Holland probably worked on the latter, and she used the former in preparing her memoir of her father.

Oswald St. Clair, Sydney Smith: A Biographical Sketch (London, 1913)

VII. Other secondary works

Richard D. Altick, The Cowden Clarkes (London, 1948)

A. Aspinall, ed., The Letters of George IV, 1812-1830, 3 vols. (Cambridge, 1938)

A. Aspinall, Three Early Nineteenth Century Diaries (London, 1952)

R. H. M. Buddle Atkinson, and G. A. Jackson, eds., Brougham and His Early Friends (London, 1908)

J. Bernard Baker, ed. Pleasure and Pain (1780-1818) (London, 1930)

E. A. Ball, "Two Unpublished Letters of Sydney Smith", Notes and Queries, IV, 1881.

[Sir Thomas Bernard], An Account of the Foundling Hospital in London, for the Maintenance and Education of Exposed and deserted Young Children (London, 1807)

G. F. A. Best, Temporal Pillars, Queen Anne's Bounty, The Ecclesiastical Commissioners, and the Church of England (Cambridge, 1964)

Frederick Boase, Modern English Biography, 6 vols. (Truro, 1921)

Desmond Bowen, The Idea of the Victorian Church (Montreal, 1968)

Alexander Brady, William Huskisson and Liberal Reform (New York, 1967)

J. Potter Briscoe, Sydney Smith: His Wit and Wisdom (London, 1900)

L. W. Bristol, and L. W. Gully, Recollections and Reflections During an Occasional Week-day Lounge in Bristol Cathedral (London, 1849)

Henry Peter Brougham, The Life and Times of Henry Lord Brougham, 3 vols. (Edinburgh & London, 1871)

Ford K. Brown, Fathers of the Victorians (Cambridge, 1961)

John Brownlow, Memoranda; or, Chronicles of the Foundling Hospital, including Memoirs of Captin Coram (London, 1847)

David Cecil, Lord M (London, 1954)
          Melbourne (New York, 1954)

George Clinch, Marylebone and St. Pancras (London, 1890)
Mayfair and Belgravia: Being An Historical Account of the Parish of St. George, Hanover Square (London, 1892)

The Clerical Guide, or Ecclesiastical Directory: Containing A Complete Register of the Present Prelates and other Dignitaries....(London, 1822)

Gerald Cobb, London City Churches (London, 1962)

Regional Colby, *Mayfair: A Town Within London* (London, 1966)

Thomas Constable, *Archibald Constable and His Literary Correspondents: A Memorial By His Son Thomas Constable*, 3 vols. (Edinburth, 1873)

John Gore, ed., The Creevey Papers (New York, 1963)

Charles Curran, "How to Convince an Englishman", *New Republic*, 10 Dec., 1956

William Dawbarn, *An Hour with Sidney Smith and His Writings* (London, 1861)

H. W. Dickinson, *Water Supply of Greater London* (Leamington Spa and London, 1954)

Ernest Dilworth, "Letters of Sydney Smith", *Notes and Queries*, II, 1964.

Wilfred S. Dowden, *The Letters of Thomas Moore*, 2 vols. (Oxford, 1964)

Evert A. Duyckinck, *Wit and Wisdom of the Rev. Sydney Smith Being Selections From His Writing and Passages of His Letters and Table-Talk* (New York, 1856)

James Elmes, *London and Its Environs in the Nineteenth Century: Illustrated by a Series of Views from Original Drawings by Thomas H. Shepherd with Historical, Topographical & Critical Notices by James Elmes* (London, 1829; reprinted London and New York, 1968)

Foundling Estate Protective Association, *The Foundling Hospital and its Neighbourhood: with an Introduction by W. R. Lethaby* (London, 1926)

Walter Graham, *English Literary Periodicals* (New York, MCMXXX)

Dennis Gray, *Spencer Perceval, The Evangelical Prime Minister*, 1762-1812 (Manchester, 1963)

Henry Reeve, ed., *The Greville Memoirs, A Journal of the Reigns of King George IV and King William IV* (London, 1874)

Sheldon Halpern, "Sydney Smith in the Edinburgh Review", *Bulletin of the New York Public Library*, 66, 1962.

Frances Hawes, Henry Brougham (New York, 1856)

Mrs. William Hicks Beach, A Cotswold Family: Hicks and Hicks Beach (London, 1909)

Gertrude Himmelfarb, Victorian Minds (New York, 1968)

Leonard Horner, ed. Memoirs and Correspondence of Francis Horner, M. P. (Boston, 1853)

Walter E. Houghton, ed., The Wellesley Index to Victorian Periodicals 1824-1900 (Toronto, 1966)

Derek Hudson, Holland House in Kensington (London, 1967)

The Earl of Ilchester, Chronicles of Holland House, 1820-1900 (London, 1937)
Elizabeth, Lady Holland to Her Son, 1821-1845 (London, 1946)

Langham Pamphlets, Wit and Wisdom of Sydney Smith (London, n.d.)

Lady Theresa Lewis, Extracts of the Journals and Correspondence of Miss Berry From the Year 1783 to 1852 (London, 1865)

Princess Marie Liechtenstein, Holland House, 2 vols. (London, 1874)

John Locke, The Works of John Locke. A New Edition, Corrected, 10 vols (London, 1823; reprinted Darmstadt, 1963)

Elizabeth Longford, Queen Victoria, Born to Succeed (New York and Evanston, 1964)

The Very Rev. W. R. Matthews, and the Rev. W. M. Atkins, A History of St. Paul's Cathedral and the Men Associated with it (London, 1957)

William Law Mathieson, English Church Reform (London, 1923)

Frederick Miller, Saint Pancras Past and Present (London, 1874)

Arthur Milman, Henry Hart Milman, D. D., Dean of St. Paul's A Biographical Sketch (London, 1900)

Henry Hart Milman, Annals of St. Paul's Cathedral (London, 1868)

William Flavell Monypenny, and George Earle Buckle The Life of Benjamin Disraeli, Earl of Beaconsfield, 6 vols. (London, 1910-20)

John R. H. Moorman, A History of the Church in England (London, 1953)

Alfred Morrison, Catalogue of the Collection of Autograph Letters and Historical Documents formed between 1865 and 1882 by A. Morrison. 6 vols. 1883-92

George L. Nesbitt, Benthamite Reviewing: The First Twelve Years of the "Westminster Review", 1824-1836 (New York, 1966)

Ralph Nevill, Mayfair and Montmartre (London, 1921)

R. H. Nichols, and F. A. Wray, The History of the Foundling Hospital (London, 1935)

C. H. Philips, The East India Company, 1784-1834 (Manchester, 1961)

Bernard Pool, ed., The Croker Papers, 1808-1857 (London, 1967)

G. L. Prestige, St. Paul's in Its Glory: A Candid History of the Cathedral, 1831-1911 (London, 1955)

Reform Bill Handbills and Broadsides (Edinburgh, 1832)

Stuart J. Reid, Life and Letters of the First Earl of Durham, 1792-1840, 2 vols. (London, 1906)

J. R. Howard Roberts, and Walter H. Godfrey, eds., Survey of London (London, 1949)

Berton Roueche, "Sydney", New Yorker, 29, 1954

William MacDonald Sinclair, Memorials of St. Paul's Cathedral (London, 1909)

Duane B. Schneider, "Sydney Smith in America: Two Check Lists", Bulletin of the New York Public Library, 70, 1966

Richard Edgecumbe, ed. The Diary of Frances Lady Shelley (London, 1912)

R. A. Soloway, Prelates and People: Ecclesiastical Social Thought in England, 1783-1852 (London and Toronto, 1969)

David Churchill Somervell, English Thought in the Nineteenth Century (New York, 1929)

William Sparrow Simpson, The Charter and Statue of the College of the Minor Canons in Saint Paul's Cathedral (London, 1871)
Documents illustrating the history of Saint Paul's Cathedral (London, 1880)

Charles Suger, E. J. Holland, A. R. Hall, Trevor I. Williams, Eds., A History of Technology (Oxford, 1958) "Sanitary Engineering: Water Supply", in Vol. IV.

Horace Twiss, The Public and Private Life of Lord Chancellor Eldon, with Selections from his Correspondence (London, 1844)

Marjorie Villiers, The Grand Whiggery (London, 1939)

[J. Wade] The Extraordinary Black Book: An Exposition of the United Church of England and Ireland; Civil List and Crown Revenues.... (London, 1831)

Sir Spencer Walpole, History of England from the Conclusion of the Great War in 1815 (London, 1890)

Jerrold Walter, ed. Bon-Mots of Sydney Smith and R. Brinsley Sheridan Edited by Walter Jerrold with Grotesques by Aubrey Beardsley (London, 1893)

Watergate Booklets, Sayings of Sydney Smith (London, n. d.)

Thomas Wicksteed, Observations on the Past and Present Supply of Water (London, 1835)

INDEX

Africans, humanity of, 191
Agitators, 223
Agricultural disturbances, 266-269
Alcock, Miss, 220
Alcohol, moderation in, 360-361
Alison, Sir Archibald, 412-413
Allen, John, 50-51, 193-194, 195, 232, 310, 348, 360, 368, 404
Althorp, Lord, 275
America, 374-382; American books, 376; English travellers in, 378; Games, 379; Justice, 376; Slavery in, 378; Religious liberty, 376-78
Ampthill, living of, 213
Annual Register, 388
Andrewes, the Rev. Gerrard, 131-132
Anglican clergyman, qualities of, 333-334
Anti-slavery, SS's refusal to dine on Sundays because of, 191
Aristocracy, 392
Aristotle, 124, 126
"Assassin", the, 352
Atholl, Duchess of, 52
Attwood, Thomas, 303

Bacon, Francis, 124, 126-128
Ballot, the, 365-370; Democracy, 367-368; Landord's right to tenant votes, 365; Tory appreciation of SS on, 369; Universal suffrage, 366
Barlow, Joel, 376
Beach, William, 41
Bedchamber Question, the, 364
Bedford, Duke of, 194
Bell, A.S., 77
Bell, Andrew, 150-156, 297
Bellini, Vincenzo, I Puritani, 304
Bentham, Jeremy, 75
Benthamism, 75-76
Berkeley, Bishop George, 48
Berkeley Chapel, 117-118, 119, 121
Bernard, Sir Thomas, 113-114, 121-122
Berry, Mary and Agnes, 344, 346, 347, 386
Best, Mr. Justice William Draper, 256
Beverley, site of clergy meeting at Tiger Inn, 189
Bishopric, SS's desire for, 28, 192-193, 216-217, 288, 290, 311-316

Bishops, qualifications for, 289; Salaries of, 330
Bishops, Roman Catholic, proposal to vest appointment of in Crown, 181
Blockade of France, cutting off of laxatives, 184
Blomfield, Charles James, Bishop of London, 318-319, 325, 328, 337-338, 407
Bonaparte, Napoleon, religious freedom favored by, 176
Borthwick Institute, 195-196
Bowerbank, Mr., 188-119
Bowles, John, 88-89, 167
Bowood, Estate of Lord Lansdowne, 43
Bristol, 260-261, 285-286
Briston Cathedral, 219-220, 263, 290-291
Bristol Sermon, on Guy Fawkes' Day, 189
British superiority, 375, 379
Bromley, the Rev. Anthony, 120
Brougham, Henry (later 1st Baron Brougham and Vaux), 42, 77, 79, 81, 90, 109-110, 195, 275, 351
Brown, Ford K., 186
Brown, Thomas, 47-48
"Bunch" (Masterman, Rachel), 201
Burdett, Osbert, 4-5, 9, 20, 24, 304, 394

Cathedrals, rights and privileges of, 322-323
Catholic emancipation, 164-186, 190, 225-226; see Peter Plymley, Letters of Guy Fawkes Sermon, 189; Letter to the Electors on the Catholic Question, 189; Thirsk petition for, 188-189
Catholicism, 182, 185
Cambridge University, Caius College, 353; Trinity College, 208, 352-353; see Smith, Windham
Canning, George, 180, 230
Canterbury, Archbishop of, 322
Carlisle, Lady, 220, 264, 390, 292, 305, 339, 368
Carlisle, Lord, 199, 213, 215, 259, 335
Carlyle, Thomas, 342, 413
Castle Howard, 199, 304
Castlereagh, Robert Stewart, 2nd Viscount, 230
Cato Street Conspiracy, 226-227
Capital punishment, 260-261, 286
Cecil, David, 108
Ceylon, 97-99
Charles I, of England, 35
Charles X, of France, 398
Charterhouse, the, 208, 352
Charlotte Chapel, 58-59
Chartism, 363-365
Cheam, Parish Church, 57
Cheap labor, SS's use of, 201

Chevrillon, Andre, biographer of SS, 9, 60, 287, 393, 400
Chichester, Bishop of, 297
Children, 75, 351
Church of England, 6-7; see Smith, The Rev. Sydney, England, Church of; Best expression of the national religion, 186-187; influence on education, 136, 150; Purity of belief and practice, 177; SS, clearninghouse for Whig appointments in, 362
Cider, 293
Clapham sect, 172-173, 178,185
Clarke, Mary Anne, 35, 291
Classical learning, 163-164
Clergy Residence Act of 1806, 146
Clergy, Roman Catholic, proposed government-paid salaries for, 181-183
Clergymen, Anglican, qualities of, 333-334
Clive, John, 77, 79
Cobbett, William, 223, 226, 228
Cockerell, Charles, 302
Colby, Reginald, 119
Combe Florey, living of, 39, 220-221, 263, 292-294, 305, 342, 354, 357
Constable, Archibald, 78-80, 81
Copley, John Singleton, see Lyndhurst, Lord
Copleston, Dean Edward, 338-229
Coram, Thomas, 113
Cotton mill owners, 229
Counsel, legal, right of prisoners to, 242-248
Country life, SS's dislike of, 200-201
Country squires, stupidity of, 226-227
Creevey, Thomas, 191, 203-204
Crocus, autumn, 359
Croker, John Wilson, 389
Curran, 400
Democratic reform, in Church, 324
Democracy, 25
Devonshire, Duke of, 214-215, 404
Dickens, Charles, 344-345; A Christmas Carol, 382
Disraeli, Benjamin, 407
Dissent, religious, effect on health, 360 SS's
Dissenter, proposal to masquerade as a, 190
Dissenters, burial of, 190
Dogs, 232
Drought, 189
Dundas, Henry, Lord Melville, 47, 52
Dublin Foundling Hospital, 113
Durham, Lord, 352
Dwight, Timothy, 376

East India Company, 3, 6
Eastlake, Sir Charles, 120
Ecclesistical Commissioners, board of, 317, 319-336, 333
Economics, 70; see Laissez-faire
Edgeworth, R. L., 156-159
Edinburgh, 17, 44-47, 49-50
Edinburgh Review, 263, 345, 346, 358, 362, 375; Anonymity of authors, 80; Circulation of, 81; Founding of, 77-79; Motto of, 80; Payment of reviewers, 231; SS's contribution to, 410
Edinburgh, University of, 43, 46-47, 50, 77, 229
Edmonton, Vicarage of, 318-319, 338-339
Education, Classical, 157-159; England, Church of, influence on, 6, 7, 13, 136, 150; English system of, 158-159; Monitorial system, 150-156; Oxford University, 157-161; Women's, 161-163
Ellenborough, Lord, 222
Ellis, Agar, 405
Emigration, 377-378
Enthusiasm, in religion, 7, 134, 178, 237
Erskine, Thomas, 145
Evangelical movement, 7, 237-238
Everett, Edward, 191, 347
Everett, Thomas, 115
Exeter, 281
Exeter, Bishop of, 289
<u>Extraordinary Black Book</u>, 298
Factory legislation, 75
Fievee, Jacob, 96-97, 398
Finchley Common, Petition of Highwaymen of, 274
Fittleton, 21, 41
Fitzroy Chapel, 117-118, 120-121
Forgery, banknote, 245
Foston-le-Clay, 36, 39, 145, 192, 211-212, 263, 357, 361; Decision to build rectory at, 194-195; Investment in, 197-198; Rectory, description of, 195-196
Fox, Caroline, 35
Fox, Charles James, 80, 179
Foundling Hospital, 113-116, 146
Franklin, Benjamin, 376

Game, 249, As property, 251; Legal sale of, 251-252, 258; Laws, 266, 248-260
Gaskell, Mrs. Elizabeth, 347
<u>Gentleman's Magazine</u>, 388-389
George III, 35, 167-168
George IV, (Prince of Wales), 42
Gladstone, William Ewart, 298
Gloucester, Bishop of, 334

Goderich, Viscount, Frederick John Robinson, 217
Godwin, William, 71, 83-85
Gordon, Alexander, 46
Goss, John, 303
gout, 358-359
Governmental regulation, 74; see Laissez-faire
Gray's Inn, 194
Greville, Charles, 308
Great Western Railway, 370-374
Grey, Lady, 50-51, 189, 225, 261, 264, 285, 286-287, 292, 295, 297, 306, 362, 396
Grey, Lord, 30, 146, 189, 225-226, 275, 286, 288, 297-298, 310, 314, 345, 379, 404
Grote, George, 346
Guilt, lack of until proven guilty, 239-241

Habeas Corpus, suspension of, 222
Halberton, vicarage of, 296, 354
Hallam, Henry, 343, 385
Halpern, Sheldon, 20
Hamilton, 163-164
Harcourt, the Rt. Rev. Vernon, Archbishop of York, 146, 188, 193, 196-197, 209
Harrowby, Lord, 372
Haydon, B. R., 120
Heaven, SS's concept of, 296
Heber, Richard, 112
Heslington, 194
Hibbert, Emily, see Smith, Emily
Hibbert, George, 209, 398
Hibbert, Nathaniel, 72, 389
Hicks-Beach, Michael, 20, 23, 41, 43, 53
Hicks-Beach, Mrs. Michael, 22-24, 55, 57, 59-60, 70, 93, 199
Hicks-Beach, Michael (son of above), 43-45, 55, 77
Hicks-Beach, William, 46, 55
Himmelfarb, Gertrude, 400
Hinduism, 140-143
Hogarth, William, 361
Holland House, 44, 107-108, 218, 293-294, 342
Holland, Lady Elizabeth, 107-108, 145-146, 193-194, 199, 203, 210-211, 213, 258, 266, 304, 315, 327, 335, 345, 348, 350, 355, 360, 387, 393, 403
Holland, Dr. Henry (later 1st Baronet Knutsford), 351, 386-387, 389
Holland, Lady Saba, see Smith, Saba, 1-2, 5, 8, 11, 13, 20-22, 28-29, 37-38, 42, 58, 81, 94, 104, 121, 186, 196-197, 202-203, 208, 214-215, 218, 222, 259, 351, 403, 406, 412

Holland, Lord (Henry Richard Fox Vassal, 3rd Baron), 4,
    28, 44, 50, 52, 107-108, 109, 145-146, 199-200, 213,
    289, 311-316, 383, 394
Holy Eucharist, 66, 294-295
Hone, William, 222-223
Horner, 62, 77, 82, 106-107, 122-123
Houghton, Lord, 403
Hughes, The Rev. Thomas, 300
Hume, David, 48
Hungary, religious toleration in, 185
Hunt, Henry, 227-228
Hunter, John, 115
Huskisson, William, 230

Ilchester, Earl of, 215
Industrial disturbances, in 1819, 224
Innocence, principle of, until proven guilty, 239-241
Ireland, 398; see also Smith, the Rev. Sydney, Ireland;
    Catholic disabilities, 181; Curfew laws, 175; Comparison to America in 1775, 179; Danger of French invasion, 167; Economic problems, 74; English treatment of Irish, 175; "Irish character", 179-180;
    Nationalism in, 182, 395; Old women, right to get drunk, 233; Orangemen, 180; Payment of Irish clergy,
    150, 183, 190; Tithe system, need to reform, 175
Irreligious books, 295
Irving, Washington, 376, 380
Iscariot, Judas, 289

Jacobins, 4, 27
James II, 25
Japan, 397
Jeffrey, Francis, 18, 51, 54, 68, 77, 79, 81, 90, 107,
    109, 123, 193, 213-214, 223-224, 230, 361, 379, 385
Jews, civil liberty of, 191
Judge, prisoner's counsel, as, 243-244
Justice, English, excellence of, 247

Kant, Immanuel, 129
Kilvington, William, 201
Kinglake, Dr., 285
King's College, Cambridge University, 5
Knight, Henry Gally, 343
Knight, R. Payne, 159
Knighton, Sir William, 219

Labor, forced, without trial, 238-242
Lafayette, Marquis de, 269
Laissez-faire, 74, 267-269, 362

Lamb's Conduit Fields, riots at, 286
Lancaster, Joseph, 150-56
Landseer, E. H., 346
Langford, W., 86
Languages, teaching of, 163-164
Lansdowne, Lord, 43, 276, 336, 343, 362
Lawrence, Sir Thomas, 346
Lee, Miss, 356
Levity, in writing, 160-161
Lewis, M.G., 91
Lewis, Thomas Frankland, 363
Liberalism, 4, 228-229, 364
Licensing, of public houses, 362
Lindsay, Lady Charlotte, 344
Literacy, 226
Locke, John, 48-49
Lockhart, Hohn Gibson, 67
Londesborough, living of, 214-215
London, 342-390
London, Bishop of, see Blomfield, Charles James
"Lottery", in Church offices, 7, 212, 318-319, 321, 330, 333
Louis Philippe, King of France, 397
Loyola, St. Ignatius, 182
Ludd, "King", 268
Luddite disturbances, 261
Luttrell, 108, 205, 342
Lyndhurst, Lady, 291-292
Lyndhurst, Lord, 218-219, 247, 291

Macaulay, Thomas Babington, 345, 385, 399-400, 412
Machinery, value of, 267-269
MacIntosh, Sir James, 77, 79-80
Magistrate, SS as a, 232
Malet, the Rev. W. W., 338
Malthus, the Rev. Thomas Robert, 71-72
Malthusianism, 269, 363
Marcet, Mrs. Jane, 37
Masterman, Rachel, ("Bunch"), 201
Melbourne, Lord, 314-316, 327, 329, 353, 393, 403
Mendelsohn, Felix, 303
Methodism, 133-134, 136-143, 171, 178
Meudon, railway wreck at, 370
Milman, Henry Hart, 407
Miracles, 134
Mobs, British and French, 91-92
Monarchy, the, 34-35
Mont Villiers, 4
Moore, Thomas 343, 346

Moorman, John R. H., 61
Moral Philosophy, SS's lectures on, 122-131
More, Hannah, 143-145
Morning Chronicle, 370-374, 381
Morpeth, Lady Georgiana, 225, 296
Morpeth, Lord, 213-215, 408
Municipal Corporations Act, 363
Murray, John Archibald, 52-53, 214, 288
Murray, C.K., 327-328

Namier, Sir Lewis B., 26
Nares, Archdeacon Robert, 86-88
National strength, 276
Neasdon, Prebend of, 300-301
Neckar, M., 91
Necker, Mme Suzanne, 90
Negroes, humanity of, 191
Netheravon, 7, 12, 20-24, 41
New College, Oxford University, 4, 9
New Jerusalem, Christians of the, dissenting sect, 131-133
New Poor Law, 363
New River Company, 105-106
New South Wales, 95
Newington, Bilbert Stuart, 346
Newman, Cardinal John Henry, 9
Noel, Col. Gerard, 104-106
Notre Dame, Cathedral of, 398

O'Connell, Daniel, 173, 347, 364
Olier, Maria, see Smith, Marie Olier
Olier, Mary, aunt of SS, 110
Opium War, 397-398
Orangemen, 180
Ossory, Earl of, 213
Oxen, use of in building rectory, 195
Oxford movement, 9, 339-340
Oxford University, 4, 9, 20, 157-161

Paley, William, 48-49
Palmerston, 54, 353-354
Parallelogram, the, 110
Pamphleteers, democratic, 228
Paris, 398-399
Parliamentary reform, 223-226, 228, 263-288
Parr, Samuel, 82-84
Partington, Mrs. 283, 285
Partronage, lay, 324
Pearson, Hesketh, 182

Pecchio, Baron, 413
Peel, Sir Robert, 244, 277, 280-281, 314, 362, 364-365, 372-373, 386, 405
Penal code, 226
Pennsylvania bonds, 380
"People", the, 229
Perceval, Spencer, 146, 147-149, 166-167, 169-170, 172, 174, 177, 179-184
Percival, Robert, 97-99
Peter Plymley Letters, 165-186, 410
Peterloo, 215, 224-226
Philips, Richard, 88
Philips, Thomas, 389
Pitt, William, 93
Playfair, John, 47, 159
Pluralist, SS as a, 326
Plurality and Residence Bill, 332
Paoching, 249-250
Political economy, 70; see Laissez-faire
Political unions, 286
Poor, the, 35-39, 72-73
Poor Law, Old, 74
Poor law, New, 363
Porteus, Bishop, 132
"Poverty", SS's purported, 9-10, 55, 213, 215, 231, 354-355
Prebends, 328
Preferment, 28, 216, 218, 353
Prestige, G. L., 310
Prisons, Diet in, 234-235; Education in, 236; Foreign, 238; Labor in, 237; Pleasant conditions in, 234-235 Reform of, 234-235; Rehabilitation in, 236; Rise in commitments, 237; Schools for crime, 233; Society for the Improvement of, 236; Treadmill, use of, 239-241
Prisoners, Poor, 242
Property, game as, 251
Property qualifications for shooting, 250-251
Prostitution, 249
Punishment, 254-256
Pusey, Edward Bouverie, 67
Puseyites, 339-340

Quakers, 99, 190
Quarterly Review, 342, 389
Queen Anne's Bounty, 196-197, 213
Radicals, prosecution of, 227
Rational religion, 7, 186-187, 392
Recovery, economic, of 1820, 227-228
Reform, parliamentary, 27; Opponents of, 274; Rotten

boroughs, 271-272; Speeches on, 270-280; SS and, 233-234; Success, 370
Reid, Stuart J., 24, 198, 214, 412
Religious persecution, 295
Rennel, Thomas, 84-86, 169
Respecter of persons, 309-310
Revolution, Danger of, 226, 269; French, 4, 27; Glorious, 4; Revolutionary settlement of 1688, 25
Roberts, John, 3
Robinson, Frederick John, see Goderich, Viscount
Robinson, Jack, 201
Rogers, 108, 342, 346-347, 385
Roman Catholic Church, 395
Roman Catholic civil disabilities, 25, 27
Rose, George, 81
Rousseau, Jean Jacques, 85
Royal Institution, the, SS's lectures at, 122-131
Rubens, Peter Paul, 399
Russell, George, W.E., 146, 368, 403
Russell, Lord John, 281, 306-308, 315-316, 325-326, 329, 331-332, 336, 354, 364
Russells, the, 25, 392

St. Paul's Cathedral, 290-298, 354; Cathedrals Act of 1840, 337; Chill in winter, 306; Choir, 302-305; Farewell sermon at, 341; Hours of, 307; Minor Canons, 309; Patronage, 337-339; Organists, 303; Quarell with Lord John Russell, 306-308; Proposed changes in chapter, 336; SS at, 300-310; Visitors to, 308
Salisbury Cathedral, 20
Scotland, 54-55, 59, 174
Scott, Sir Walter, 107, 229, 343-344
Sheridan, Richard Brinsley, 203-204
Sinclair, William MacDonald, 309
Singleton, Archdeacon Thomas, 197, 317, 319-336, 342
Shooting, 250, 258-259
Sinecures, 182
Six Acts, 227
Skiddaw, 45
Slavery, SS's opposition to, 190-191
Smith, Catherine Amelia (Pybus), 1, 9-10, 11-13, 15-17, 55, 57-58, 94, 104-106, 111, 206-207, 218, 357, 386, 388, 398, 412
Smith, Cecil (SS's brother), 3, 15, 18
Smith, Cecil (son of above, nephew of SS), 19, 204, 209, 216, 218, 220, 293-294, 296, 341, 345, 354-355, 389, 408
Smith, Courtenay (SS's brother), 3, 15, 355
Smith, Douglas (son of SS), 4, 110-111, 207, 210, 352,

357, 409
Smith, Emily (daughter of SS), 110, 200, 209, 350, 409
Smith, Noel (son of SS), 94, 110
Smith, Nowell, 214
Smith, Robert (father of SS), 1, 2, 5-6, 10-11, 12-19, 55, 57, 209-210
Smith, Robert Percy (Bobus) SS's brother), 3, 15, 18, 44, 105-106, 206, 355, 383, 385, 388
Smith, Saba (daughter of SS), 114, 409; see Holland, Lady Saba
Smith, Sidney or Sydney (foundling), 117
Smith, Adm. Sir Sidney, 408
Smith, The Rev. Sydney, Accomplishments, 412; Affection for children, 209, 351; Agitators, 223; Aristocracy, 207, 392; Bail, 99; Ballot, 365-370; Beer Bill, 266; Beliefs, religious, 401-423; Berkeley Chapel, 117, 119, 121; Birth of, 3; Bristol Cathedral, 263; Capital Punishment, 260-261, 286; Catholic Emancipation, 164-165, 189, 263, 265; Catholic Question, Letter to the Electors on, 189; Cato Street Conspiracy, 226-227 Charity, 76, see Sermons; Clerical vocation, see England, Church of, Lottery; Ambition, limits of his, 393; Ambition, to become a Bishop, 28, 192-193, 216-217, 288, 290, 311-316; Bishops, 322; Regret at, 394; Sacrifice, self, 394; Coarseness, 403; Combe Florey, 263, 292-294, 342; Constitution, British, 91; Corn Laws, 70; Country, dislike of, 200-201; Country Houses, 204; Death, 387-388; Death of son, 210; Denmark, 99; Dinner Guest, 203; Dissenters, 190; Disturbances; Agricultural, 266-269; Industrial, 224; Dogs, 232; Dyson, 275; Edinburgh Review, see Reviews; Founding of, 77-79, 231, 410; Education, 3-4, 20; Classical, 85-86, 157-159; Public schools, 207; of Women, 161-163; England, Church of; Atheist, 67-68; Absenteeism, 102, 146; Cathedrals Act of 1840, 337; Church officials, need for numerous, 329; Clergymen, 399-400; Eighteenth century, 403; Fertility of, 206; Influence of, 58; Method of selection, 33; Curates' Bill, 1808, 147-149; Decline of, 60; Domestic Chaplains, value of, 405; "Dutch Chronicle", 324-325; End of the, predictions of, 328, 334; Great Watchmaker, 49; Holy Days, 66; Holy Eucharist, 66, 294-295; Irreligion, hostility to, 402-403; Latitudinarianism, 298; "Lottery", the, 7, 212, 318-319, 321, 330, 333; Marriage, 348; Nepotism, 323; Patronage, 321, 324, 337-339; Opportunities for lower classes in, 329; Over-religiosity, 145; Oxford Movement, 339-340; Religious persecution, 295; Personal piety, 177-178; Pluralism, 146, 218, 353; Preferment 216, 218, 353;

498

Ptochogony, 333; Reform of the, 337; Influence of SS on, 334-335; Opposition of SS to, 319-336; Support of SS on, 332; Representation of, 92; Ritual of, 66-67, 294, 401; Saints, 51; Singleton, Archdeacon Thomas, Letters to, 319-336; Skepticism, 66; Sunday schools, 22-24; Vestments, 67; Facetiousness, 337; Flattery, 348; Foston, 191-221; Foundling Hospital, 113-116, 146; Fragment on the Irish Catholic Church, 389, 395; French cooking, 399; Ghosts, 220; Gossip, 203-204; Gourmet, 399; Gray's Inn, nomination as Reader of, 194; Habeas Corpus, Suspension of, 222; Health, 358-360, 383-385; Heaven, SS's concept of, 296; Heslington, 192; Holland House, 44, 107-108, 218, 293-294, 342; Horses and riding, 201-202; Humor of, 408-409; Illegitimacy, rural, 404; Income, 105-106, 111, 121-122, 146, 213, 231; Increasing conservatism, 365, 371; Ireland, SS's opinions on, 164, 398, see Ireland; Catholicism in, 182; Nationalism in, 182; Orangemen, necessity for temporary persecution of, 180-181; Tithes, 183; Justice, 247, 411; Laissez-faire, 87, 96, 267-269; Laws, unalterable, 174; Liberalism, 222, 364, 391-392; Logic, 89; London, 104, 342-390; Affection for, 203; Friends in, 94; Parallelogram, the, 110; Visits to, 202-203; Ludd, King, 268; Luddites, 261; Machinery, value of, 267-269; Magistrate, SS as a, 231-233, 261; Malthusianism, 57, 269; Manners, 112; Marriage, 58; Medicine, 356-358; Methodism, 133-134, 136-143, 145, 150, 153; Miracles, 86; Mobs, British and French, 91-92; More, Hannah, 143-145; Municipal Corporations Act, 363; Napoleon, 100; Netheravon, 20; New Poor Law, 363; New River Company, 105-106; "Noodledom", 162-163; Old Age, 384-385, 387; Paris, 398; Parochialism, 355; Peers, life, 92; Pennsylvania Bonds, 374-382; Personal life, 409; Peter Plymley Letters, 410; Denial of authorship 185-186; Political allegiance, switching of?, 230; Political views; Church and Crown, 222; Democracy, 222; Liberty, 225; Monarchism, 92; National strength, 276; Parliamentary reform, 223-226, 228, 263-288; Patriotism, 100-101; People, the, 229, 266; Political change, 302-364; Republicanism, 92; Revolution, 225-226, 269; Poor, the, 188, 264; "Poverty" of SS, 9-10, 55, 213, 215, 231, 354-355; Preaching, 62, 64-65, 84-88, 119-121; see Sermons; Prisons, 233-236; Property qualifications, for legislators, 92; Protest, 225; Quakers, 99, 190; Railroad travel, 373-374; Rational religion, 7, 186-187, 392; Razor, Comparison of SS's life with, 289; Reformer, 223, 370, 410-411; Respecter of persons, 309-310; Reviews, 68, 81-82, 90, 95, 101-102, 140-143, 248, 260, 374-382; Rich, SS's support of in event of civil war, 224; Roman Catholicism, 86, 173, 185, 189-190, 340; Romantic love, 348; Russells, 392; Russia, 100; St. Paul's Cathedral, 300-310, 341; Scotland, 47-48, 50-59, 93-94; Sermons, 65, 68, 84-88, 349; see Preaching; Charity, 50, 71, 76, 114-115; Guy Fawkes, 64, 290; Publication of, 63; Servants, treatment of, 201; Spring-guns, 253-258; Squires, country, stupidity of, 226-227; Success, 409; Suttee, 197, 219; Transportation, opposition to as punishment, 96, 259-260; Travel, 96-101, 204, 398-395; Tread-pulpit, 266; Truth, 411; War, 395-398; Whig Party, 24-28, 391-394, 410-411; Will, last, 389-390; Wit, 102-103, 129-130, 343, 406-407; Women, 347-351; Education of, 161-163; Yorkshire, 191-221

Smith, Windham (son of ss), 337, 352-355, 389-390, 409; "Assassin", the 352; Audit clerk, 354; Birth of, 206-207; Debts of, 354; Early life, 208; Expulsion from Trinity College, 352-353; "Spavin the Turfite", 354; Southgate Chapel, 338; Spa Fields Riots, 223; "Spavin the Turfite" 354

Southgate Chapel, 338
Spa Fields Riots, 223
"Spavin the Turfite", 354
Speculative Society, 77
Spencer, Lord Robert, 204
Spring-guns, 253-258
Stael, Mme de, 101-102, 349
Stewart, Dugald, 47-48, 77, 127
Storye, William, 196
Styles, the Rev. John, 137-143
Sunday School, 22-24
Sutherlands, the, 408
Suttee, 197, 219
Swift, Jonathon, 185, 412
Swing, Captain, 267-269

Tate, Canon James, 338-339
Tate, the Rev. Thomas, 339
Tauton, 270-280
Taunton *Courier*, 280, 282
Thackeray, William Makepeace, 354
Thirsk, 187
Thistlewood, Arthur, 226
Thompson, the Rev. Archer, 115
Three Tuns Inn, Thirsk, 187
Ticknor, George, 347
Tiger Inn, Beverley, 189

Times, 337, 388
Tithes, 183, 226
Tory Party, 26-27, 230-231
Transportation, 96, 259-260
Travel books, 358
Treadmill, 239-241
Trimmer, Mrs. Sarah, 151-156
Cambridge University, 208, 352-353
Turkey, 175
Tutors, Scots, 50-51
Utility, 158-159
Varvicensis, Philopatris, 81
Very Important People, 248
Vice, Society for the Suppression of, 142-143, 170
Voltaire, 85
Victoria, Queen, 329-330
Victorian Compromise, 288
War, 181
Watson, Dr. Richard, 223, 226
Webster, Daniel, 191, 347
Wedgwood, Josiah, 131
Weimar, University of, 43
Wellesley Index, 81
Wellington, Duke of, 31, 274, 277, 280-281, 286, 314
West, Benjamin, 120
Westminister Abbey, Prebendal Stall in, 297
Westminster School, 4, 207
Whig Party, 211
Whig Principles, SS's, 24-28
White, Blanco, 68
Wilberforce, William, 172-173, 191, 347
Wilkie, Sir David, 120
Williamstrip Park, 41, 43
Wilmot-Horton, Sir Robert J., 343, 362-363
Wilson, John 229
Winchmore Hill Chapel, 338
Whishaw, James, 199
Women, Churching of, 350; Courage of, 350; Education of, 350; Female mind, the, 350; Treatment of, 347-351;
Wordsworth, the Rev. Christopher, 353
Wordsworth, William, 346
Wrangham, Francis, Archdeacon of Cleveland, 188, 216
York Assizes, 200
York, Duke of, 34-35, 291
York Minister, 304
York Street Chapel, 131